An Excess of Quiet

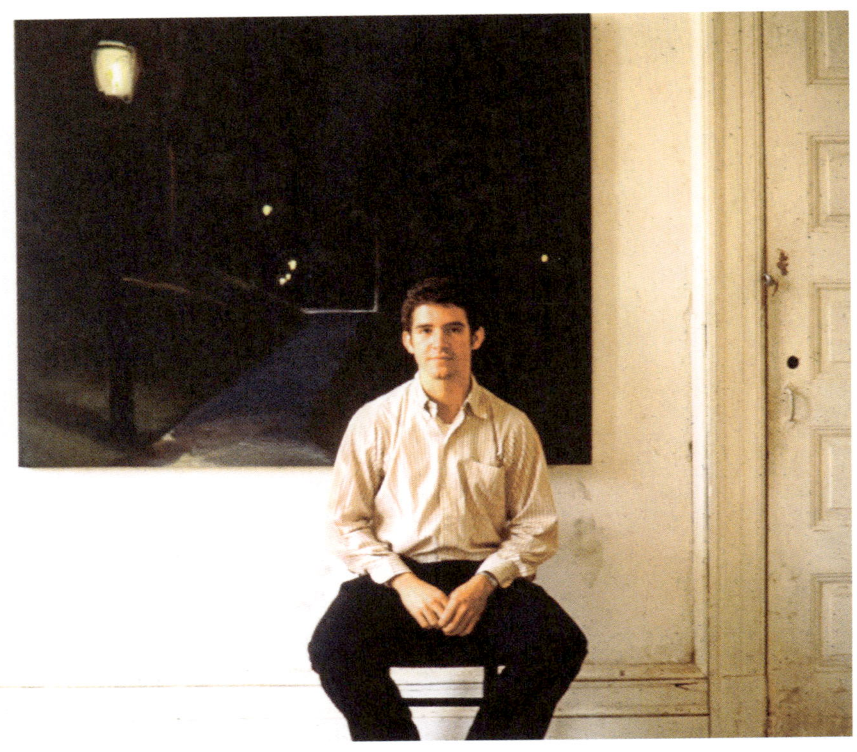

An Excess of Quiet

Selected Sketches by Gustavo Ojeda 1979–1989

EDITED BY
GABRIEL OJEDA-SAGUÉ AND
ERICH KESSEL JR

SOBERSCOVE PRESS
CHICAGO

Soberscove Press
Chicago, Illinois
soberscove.com

Sketches courtesy of Gabriel Ojeda-Sagué and Francisco Ojeda

Library of Congress Cataloging-in-Publication Data

Names: Ojeda, Gustavo, 1958–1989, artist. | Ojeda-Sagué, Gabriel, editor. | Kessel, Erich, Jr, editor.
Title: An excess of quiet : selected sketches by Gustavo Ojeda, 1979–1989 | edited by Gabriel Ojeda-Sagué. Other titles: Drawings. Selections.
Description: Chicago: Soberscove Press, 2020.
Identifiers: LCCN 2020016717 | ISBN 9781940190273 (paperback)
Subjects: LCSH: Ojeda, Gustavo, 1958-1989—Themes, motives.
Classification: LCC NC139.O35 A4 2020 | DDC 741.973—dc23
LC record available at https://lccn.loc.gov/2020016717

ISBN 978-1-940190-27-3
First Printing 2020
Design by Rita Lascaro
Printed in Lithuania

Distributed by
ARTBOOK | D.A.P.
75 Broad Street, Suite 630
New York, NY 10004
artbook.com

Cover: Detail of sketch, page 96
Frontipiece: Gustavo Ojeda in 1982 with *Central Park Evening,* 1982. Oil on canvas, 48 x 60 in.

Contents

Introduction by Gabriel Ojeda-Sagué 7

Sketches, 1979–1989 19

Biography 235

Acknowledgments 237

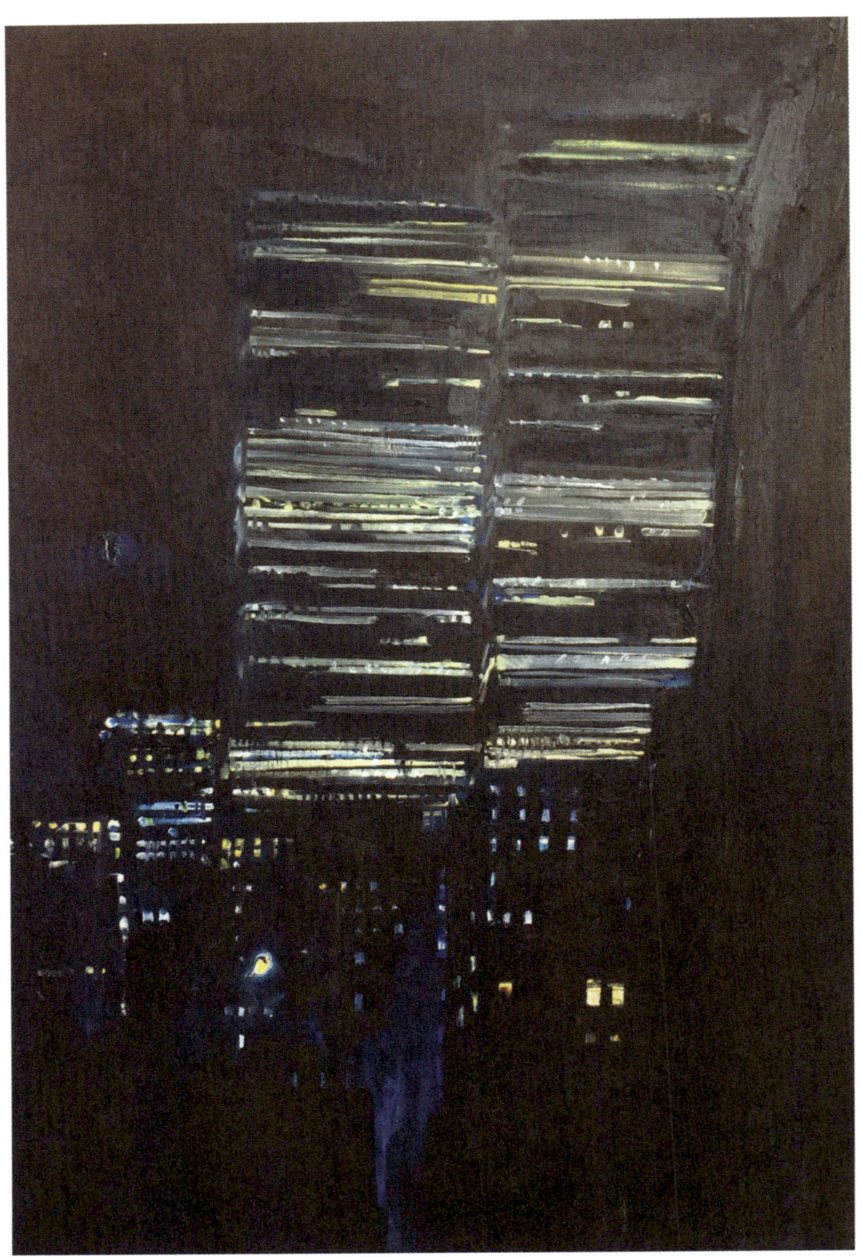

Downtown Manhattan, 1985. Oil on linen, 52 x 36 in.

An Excess of Quiet:
An Introduction to the Sketches of Gustavo Ojeda

by Gabriel Ojeda-Sagué

IN SEVERAL OF HIS SKETCHBOOKS, used variously as journals, accounting papers, organizers, or for reminders, my uncle, Gustavo Ojeda, expressed shame about his productivity as a painter. Even during his most generative period of night paintings and urban landscapes, which brought him notoriety as an artist in 1980s New York, he seemed to be disappointed with the frequency of his output, never able to measure up to his own expectations. The bitter edge of this anxiety is that Gustavo died of HIV/AIDS-related complications in 1989, just two weeks shy of his thirty-first birthday, leaving behind an interrupted body of work. But scrawled into the very same notebooks that contain his self-flagellations are thousands of records of an incredibly rich sketching practice.

Gustavo Ojeda was born on September 8, 1958, in Havana, Cuba. His family exiled from Cuba in 1967, and eventually settled in Fairfax, Virginia. He attended Parsons School of Design, from 1975 to 1979, where he studied with William Clutz and Yvonne Jacquette. Soon after graduating, Gustavo was awarded a Cintas Fellowship, which allowed him to travel to his grandmother's hometown in Madrid, where he spent a year dedicated, in his own words, to getting "school out of [his] system," honing his artistic skills and practice.[1] He began exhibiting his art immediately after, initially in a group show of self-portraiture at the Organization for Independent Artists in New York (1980), which was quickly followed by his first solo show, *Works from Spain, 1980,* at the Seventeenth Street Gallery. The beginning of his career in New York, the city where he would live and work until his death, was further solidified by a two-year studio fellowship at P.S.1 Contemporary Art Center (1981–82).

In personality, Gustavo was known as a charmer, an energetic and handsome young spirit (with just a touch of stubbornness) who quickly befriended strangers. His scant journal entries also imply a softly sad and sentimental person, frequently evaluating the tenors and terms of his life and relationships, often in light of his Catholicism, his commitments to which intensified during the late stages of his illness. As was the case for many people with AIDS in the 80s and 90s, he was initially cared for in sickness by a chosen network of friends, lovers, and his life partner, until his care was taken over by his mother and father, who came to New York from their home in Virginia.

Though his story was, in certain ways, that of the quintessential 1980s gay artist, his artistic style differed significantly from his most famous peers. As part of the "return to painting" and the reemphasis on figuration popularized in the early '80s, his formalist and impressionistic urban landscapes were rarely reminiscent of the more abstract and politicized Neo-Expressionist, Neo-Pop, and graffiti art that proliferated in the New York art scene, under and often against the towering influence of Andy Warhol.[2] Despite this difference, Gustavo is most often associated with the East Village scene. Coverage and praise for his work in *Flash Art*, *ARTnews*, and *Art in America,* accompanied by his participation in major shows like MoMA's *International Survey of Recent Painting and Sculpture* (1984) and Zellermayer Galerie's *East Village Art in Berlin* (1984), smaller exhibitions at East Village spaces like M-13 and the Garet/Kohn Gallery, as well as his inclusion in eclectic projects like the Phyllis Kind Gallery's *Happy Happy: A Coloring Book* (1986), situated Gustavo alongside East Village stars like Jean-Michel Basquiat, Keith Haring, David Wojnarowicz, Brett de Palma, and Stephen Lack.[3] He was also friends with lesser-known artists from the scene like Arch Connelly and Dana Garrett, and the influence of other New York artists, including Mark Innerst and Chema Cobo, is clearly visible in his painting.

Gustavo's American peers took an interest in his work, both despite and because of its formalism and relative stylistic conservativism. Though he found community support in the East Village and the accompanying rise of the SoHo arts scene in the mid-to-late '80s, Gustavo's other artistic milieu was Latin American (especially Latin American exile) art.[4] He gained the support of

Distant Moon, 1985. Oil on canvas, 54 x 26 in.

major Latin American art collectors and critics, like Ricardo Pau-Llosa and Giulio Blanc, and showed work in Latin American–focused exhibitions, including *Six Young Cuban Painters in New York* at the Seventeenth Street Gallery (1981), as well as others in New Jersey, Miami, Los Angeles, Puerto Rico, and Spain. When discussed in the context of Latin American art, his work is compared most often to the architectural paintings of Emilio Sanchez and Humberto Calzada, or the figurative and emotional paintings of Luis Frangella, Luis Cruz Azaceta, and Rafael Ferrer.

Gustavo's work has been called, by turns, "academic," "sentimental," "expressionist," "impressionist," "romantic," and "superficial." Notably unpopulated, his paintings focus on a visual dialogue between urban architecture (skyscrapers, windows, subway tunnels), empty city air, and the light and darkness that moves in between them. His titles reflect a simple labeling of subject matter, such as *Downtown Evening* (1986), *Station* (1983), and *Intersection* (1984–85). There are no tricks up his sleeve, no hidden effects, no obvious conceptual framework, no "deeper" meaning. The Cuban American critic Ricardo Pau-Llosa, an early supporter of Gustavo, wrote that "his work is unsettling because, in some mysterious way, beneath the shell of what seem 'safe' themes and subject matter, lies an instinctive and intuitive sense of art's most necessary function: the placing of craft at the service of altering our sense of the real."[5]

In critical approaches to Gustavo's work, it is easy to see the tension summoned around binaries between the real and the imagined, the ordinary and the supernatural, the quiet and the loud, the formal and the amateurishly sentimental. In 1986, Phyllis Plous called his "silent paintings" "meditative but not ominous" works on a "romantic quest to infinity."[6] Just one year later, Philip Verre described them as "an urban picture of intensity and aggressiveness . . . claustrophobic and unexpected . . . affirming the vertical, and, at times, oppressive quality of urban existence."[7] One could certainly argue that it is the often classed, racialized, and sexualized cultural associations around New York and the urban nighttime that summon these polarized ideas of danger and romantic possibility, but I would also add that Gustavo's practice skillfully controls how those associations are being mediated by his painting, through the use of light and gesture.

Gustavo understood his work to be primarily about his craft, where artistic technique filtered and simulated natural and supernatural experience. "I take a natural response, which is spiritual," he said, "then I take it to a technical means. . . . Then I edit. I take out what I don't need. I try to keep the essence."[8] The natural-spiritual link in his description of the painting process may connote a few things, namely, the presence or feeling of a higher power (in a religious sense) within the ordinary; the capacity of individuals for personal contemplation (in both spiritual and secular senses) within life and within art; and the feeling of one's place within their environment, which could include anything from the sublime to the habituated. Gustavo thought about "medium" through both of its major meanings, as an intervening device that allows one to convey a representation or impression, and as a communion point between the earthly and the supernatural. It is precisely this queer, Catholic, and impressionist framework that causes many of Gustavo's critics to note how streetlamps replace the moon, how in the absence of people buildings become so much more like bodies and faces, and how the darkness of his paintings creates imaginary worlds.[9] Gerritt Henry, in a review published by *Art in America*, described Gustavo's work as capturing an occasional eruption of meaning within the ordinary: "Ojeda's dexterity has an underlying depth that arises out of his search for meaning in the cold metropolis—a meaning that may only reveal itself for an instant, day or night. Ojeda seems to be on the spot whenever such a revelation occurs."[10] At first glance, it may seem perplexing to describe a painting of a dirty street corner in the wee hours as a revelation, but this was an effect Gustavo's work had on his critics. Some feared the vibrations emerging from the quotidian, and stood in awe of them and their "energy."[11] Others took a more neutral view, labeling them, as Michael Kohn did, "solemn and self-reflexive."[12] By and large, what compelled the critics about Gustavo's paintings was an excess of quiet. Not noise, but a volume of quietness that rings in ways that enrapture or disturb.

Though often seen as apolitical, the paintings draw out anxieties about the movement of bodies within urban space, even when his landscapes are unpopulated. Summoning many of the same political tensions as graffiti art, such as the privatization of space, the flow of

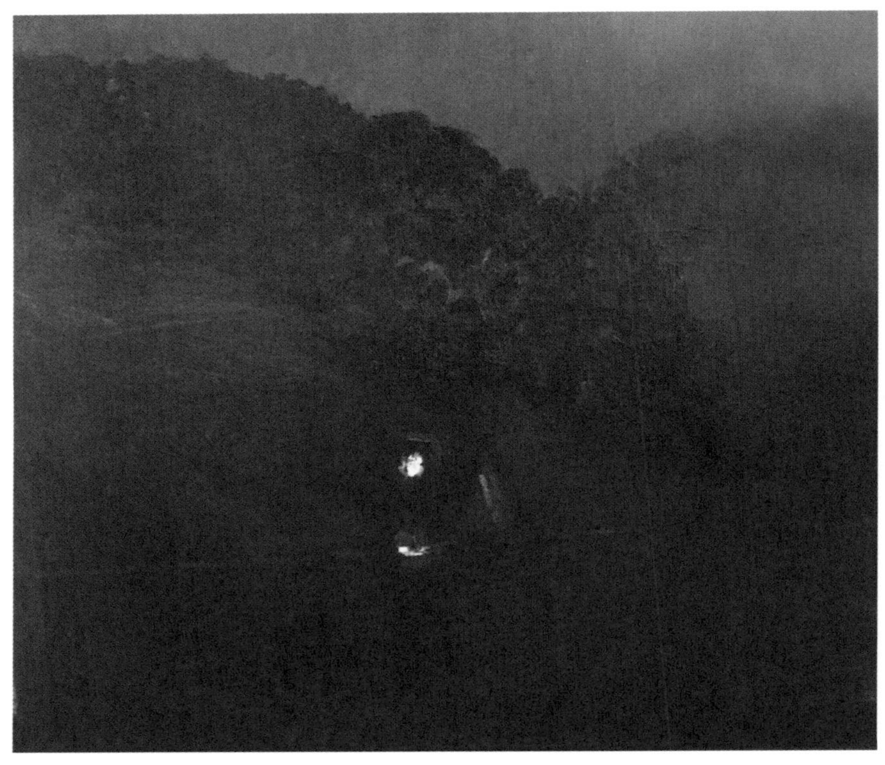

Park Evening, 1983. Oil on canvas, 48 x 60 in.

raced and classed communities in cities, and gay interventions in the relationship between the city and sexuality, Gustavo's work mystifies in large part because of its unclear positions on the tensions it raises and its almost stubborn insistence on returning to form and visual perspective. In the bilingual text of *Outside Cuba: Contemporary Cuban Visual Artists*, Gustavo remarks, "I find that the evening calls out to me; one can really be alone. The lack of light is a perfect situation. I like to capture that mystery, to hint at the things that are there with the slightest dab of color. . . . I see what other people perhaps do not see, and I transform it into a mystical experience."[13] Notably, the phrase, "one can really be alone," is absent in the Spanish version of this text, and not knowing which Gustavo wrote first and which was in translation, the absence or presence of it mirrors what is ultimately described by the other sentences: the urban night brings about an intense and intimate uncertainty with regard to the presence or absence of other people, other things, moving just beside or perhaps underneath.

Growing up near his paintings, mostly his student projects or never-exhibited works that were spread around by my family after his death, I felt that they had something charging beneath them, as if their skyscrapers might at any moment turn volcanic. I used to joke with my grandmother that a specific painting hung in a bedroom looked as if it would eat me. But as I grew into approaching this art with a different set of techniques, I saw my initial intimidation towards Gustavo's work morph, by turns, into vested excitement, solemn sympathy, and confounded frustration. I would attach all of the tension I have laid out above to his ability to reverse the elucidating capacity of light and the obfuscating capacity of the dark. In his work, a streetlight pouring a cone of light onto an otherwise blackened street somehow makes the street feel less, rather than more, real and safe. This suggests why his work might summon so much romantic trouble for his critics and supporters.

When Gustavo died in 1989, his surviving friends and his life partner, Lester Edelstein, took inventory of his work, gathered his belongings, and did what they could to keep his name afloat in the New York art scene, as it was continually brutalized by HIV and AIDS. He received a handful of retrospective exhibitions in the early 1990s, most notably with the David Beitzel Gallery. What was not tucked into galleries and museums, sold at auction, or collected into retrospectives, was housed by Lester, until his death in 2016. When Lester passed away, these materials came into the hands of my brother, Francisco Ojeda, and myself. Included in Lester's collection were hundreds of Gustavo's sketchbooks. On first look, a sketch of a woman caught my eye. Framed from the chest up with her eyes open, staring directly at the viewer, she wears what might be a cross around her neck, though she is otherwise nude. She is drawn with her body parts simply outlined, with little-to-no shading—a style characteristic of most of his sketch work. A collarbone is rendered as a mostly straight line with a small hook at the end, no other detail. But the outlines of the woman's body—her shoulders, her neck, her breasts—have been redrawn several times. Some of these lines are erased almost fully, some reduced, and some left at the same density. It is difficult, in viewing the sketch, to reconcile the simple technique of the drawing with the feeling of the woman's body bursting wildly out of its seams.

Most of Gustavo's sketches follow a pattern. Occasionally, there appears what you might expect from a sketchbook: preparatory drawings of skyscrapers in advance of paintings, still life exercises of furniture, the female nude. But the vast majority of the pages of his sketchbooks are taken up by drawings of sleeping people, most often from the shoulders up. It is safe to assume, from certain sketches that reveal more context, that these are people sleeping on public transportation or in random public spaces in the city. The majority are rendered without shading, often drawn with a single or a handful of lines. Some have no mouth, some no eyes, some no neck, some none of the three, many all of the three. They are neither somber, nor are they joyful. They are, by turns, unsentimental and hopelessly tenderhearted. Much like the paintings, the sketches are deeply invested in silence, but ecstatic in their quietness. They have an underbelly of texture, as when a limb that is "asleep" feels electric. Looking at them collectively, I feel both calmed and disturbed by the volume of sleepers. Their bodies are often expanding with redrawing, or the lines of their faces composed from the same lines of the chairs they sleep in. These sleepers rip out of their environment even as they constitute it.

In their subject matter, the sketches, spanning a decade of production and thousands of images, are a separate but equally rich body of work to Gustavo's painting. Gustavo's exhibited paintings are almost never populated, and in fact, their lack of human bodies emphasizes their complicated spatial reactivity. But in the sketches, people, specifically sleeping people, are the predominant subject. Thematically, however, they share with the paintings a delicately developed relationship between craft and the real, where the real is unbound from its monuments and granted an unstable but potent expressivity as the supernatural, spiritual, or imagined. These sketches also serve as supplement and opponent to the paintings' urban anxieties, in the sense that they finally populate the city space with the people who move within it, though at the same time, rend the city from its inhabitants, decontextualizing them on the blank page. Stylistically, the sketches and the paintings are both related and distinct, sharing a preference for fleeting gestures and blurred boundaries, though the sketches often lack the shading and techniques with light that brought Gustavo's paintings renown.

This selection of sketches, gathered and selected by myself and my coeditor, Erich Kessel, is meant to act as an introduction to Gustavo's aesthetic ideals and techniques as they are situated within this secondary, but integral, artistic mode. In the context of gutting loss, both archival and intimate, which marks the narrative of death from AIDS, this selection is also meant as a recuperation of an artist's position in a lively and often conflicted art scene. In choosing to publish this seemingly minor work instead of his oil paintings, we have set out to argue that such a horizontal approach to an interrupted life and archive produces a new opening for contemporary audiences to interface with artistic work nearly, but never totally, lost to death and archival precarity. In calling these sketches secondary, I mean not to deride them, but to allude to their privateness and their dailiness, since Gustavo's professional career was based almost exclusively on landscape oil paintings and his drawings and sketches were never exhibited, only rarely gifted to friends. From the sheer volume of the sketchbooks and the scant journal entries lodged between images, we can assume that these sketches were Gustavo's record of the ordinary and the everyday, his artistic habit rather than his public presentation.

They vary widely in effort, editing, and completion, but together they signal a young artist with an incredible pace and vested interest in figuration, as well as a knack for interpreting his surroundings. Our goal in publishing them is to reveal Gustavo's artistic practice in a completely new way, by presenting work that was very much part of his life as an artist, despite the fact that he did not exhibit it.

The selection is divided into three sections by subject matter. The first section includes sketches of people, their bodies and faces decontextualized from any location or recognizable space. The second section includes people in localizable, mostly urban contexts, such as park benches, the subway, or the bus. The third section is the most reflective of Gustavo's painting practice; it is composed of images, usually cityscapes, absent of people or human bodies. This organization is meant to emphasize the ostensible differences between his sketching and painting practices but also to find their coalition along the way, as the role of place and its engagement or non-engagement with human forms becomes increasingly tangible through the selection.

"Gustavo Ojeda's work is too well-crafted to be labeled as new," Michael Kohn once wrote, and Gustavo was never interested in the fetish for the new or its Warholian reversal, nor am I now.[14] Nor am I interested in labeling his paintings "timeless," as many once did, as if his sociopolitical situation and his work had nothing to do with one another, and his only intention was to touch upon the truly "human."[15] Instead, I argue that Gustavo's position is an instance of aesthetic ideals held by a person within a sociopolitical context, a gay Cuban exile living in relative health and later with chronic, then terminal, illness in New York's East Village, who found the painting of a street corner or the sketch of a sleeping face a necessary, and perhaps provocative, blend of mundane and otherworldly. By "an instance," I mean that Gustavo is one of many, which is exactly the story his archival precarity tells us; he is, perhaps, one of too many. Yet he is also particular, in the very sense his work portrays a body or edifice that, in its ordinariness, threatens to combust into the extraordinary. It is our hope that this selection of sketches proves exactly that.

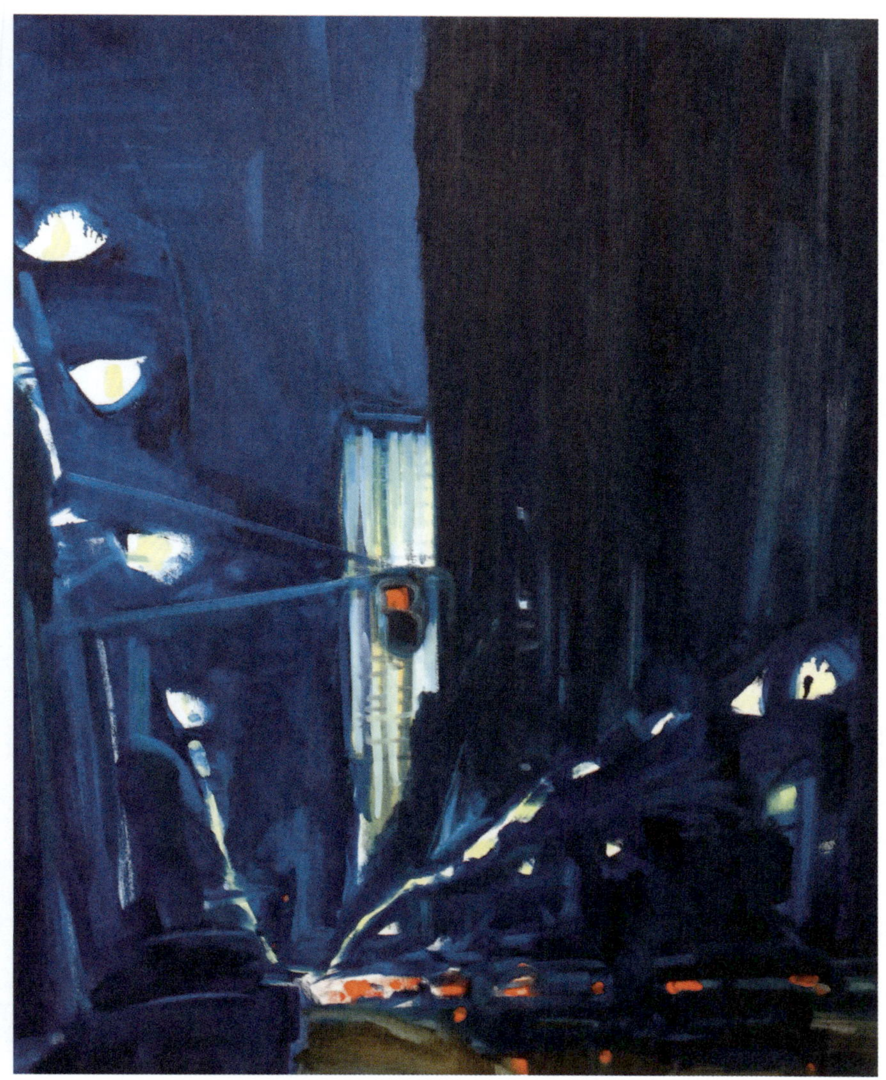

Untitled, 1986. Oil on canvas, 37 x 29½ in.

ENDNOTES

1 "Gustavo Ojeda," in *Outside Cuba: Contemporary Cuban Visual Artists,* eds. Ileana Fuentes-Pérez, Graciella Cruz-Taura, and Ricardo Pau-Llosa (New Brunswick, New Jersey: Transaction Publishers, 1989).

2 Though the phenomenon of the "return to painting" often describes a European change, Gustavo's time in Spain, his exhibitions in both Spain and West Berlin, and the concerns of the *MoMA International Survey* (1984) allude to his connection to that European context. For the US response to the "return to painting," see David Hopkins, *After Modern Art: 1945–2000* (Oxford: Oxford University Press, 2000), 203; Andrew Henry Robert Martindale, et al., "Western Painting: The 'Return to Painting'," in *Encyclopedia Britannica* (2019); and Eric Sutphin, "Introduction," *Rosemarie Beck: Letters to a Young Painter and Other Writings* (Chicago: Soberscove Press, 2018), 8–9.

3 Kynaston McShine, *An International Survey of Recent Painting and Sculpture* (New York: Museum of Modern Art, 1984); *East Village Art in Berlin* (Berlin: Zellermayer Galerie, 1984); *Happy Happy: A Coloring Book,* ed. Roland Hagenberg, published in association with the Phyllis Kind Gallery (New York, 1986). In 1983, the Garet/Kohn Gallery included his work in a group exhibition, *Arch Connelly/Dana Garrett/Gustavo Ojeda/Ricardo Regazzoni,* and hosted a solo show of his work. In 1984, Garet/Kohn also included his work in *Drawings,* and that same year, he participated in *Romantic Painting* and the *Summer Group Show* at the Tracey Garet Gallery. Gustavo participated in *The Liberty Show* at M-13 in 1985.

4 See David Beitzel Gallery, which hosted a one-man show for Gustavo in 1987, and a retrospective show in 1990.

5 Ricardo Pau-Llosa, "Ojeda and the Contours of the Real," in *Gustavo Ojeda: An Intimate Look* (Washington, DC: Pan American Health Organization, 1982).

6 Phyllis Plous, *Scapes* (Santa Barbara: University Art Museum, 1985), 39.

7 Philip Verre, *Curator's Choice III: Contemporary Painting, Photography and Sculpture* (New York City: Bronx Museum of the Arts, 1987), 10.

8 Quoted in Michael Kohn, "Emotionality in Contemporary Art: Recurring Themes and Motifs of Romantic Painting," 1984. Cited from a facsimile sent by Michael Kohn to Gustavo Ojeda, kept in personal collection. Another version of this essay was published in *Flash Art* in 1984.

9 The reminder of the streetlamp standing-in for the moon occurs in several of Michael Kohn's essays on Gustavo Ojeda, including the essay referenced in n8, as well as in his essay for the exhibition catalogue for *Arch Connelly/Dana Garrett/Gustavo Ojeda/Ricardo Regazzoni,* at the Garet/Kohn Gallery (1983).

10 Gerrit Henry, "Gustavo Ojeda at Beitzel," *Art in America,* October 1987.

11 *Seven in the '80s* (Coral Gables, Florida: Center for Latin American Arts and Studies at the Metropolitan Museum and Art Center, 1986).

12 Michael Kohn, *Arch Connelly/Dana Garrett/Gustavo Ojeda/Ricardo Regazzoni* (New York: Garet/Kohn Gallery, 1983), 24–25.

13 "Gustavo Ojeda," in *Outside Cuba: Contemporary Cuban Visual Artists,* eds. Ileana Fuentes-Pérez, Graciella Cruz-Taura, and Ricardo Pau-Llosa (New Brunswick, New Jersey: Transaction Publishers, 1989).

14 Kohn, *Arch Connelly/Dana Garrett/Gustavo Ojeda/Ricardo Regazzoni,* 24–25.

15 See n7 and n12 for two examples.

Sketches, 1979–1989

I.

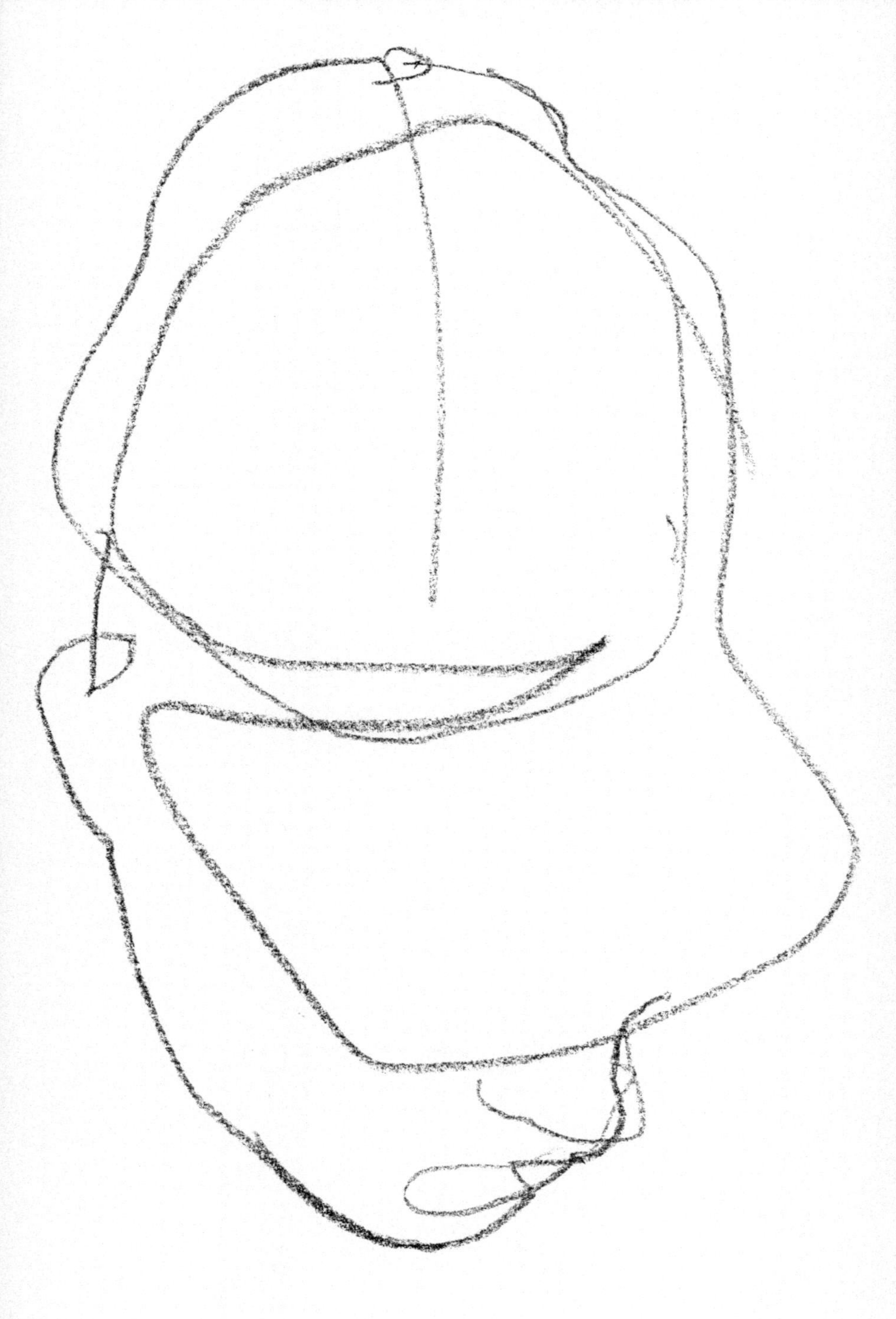

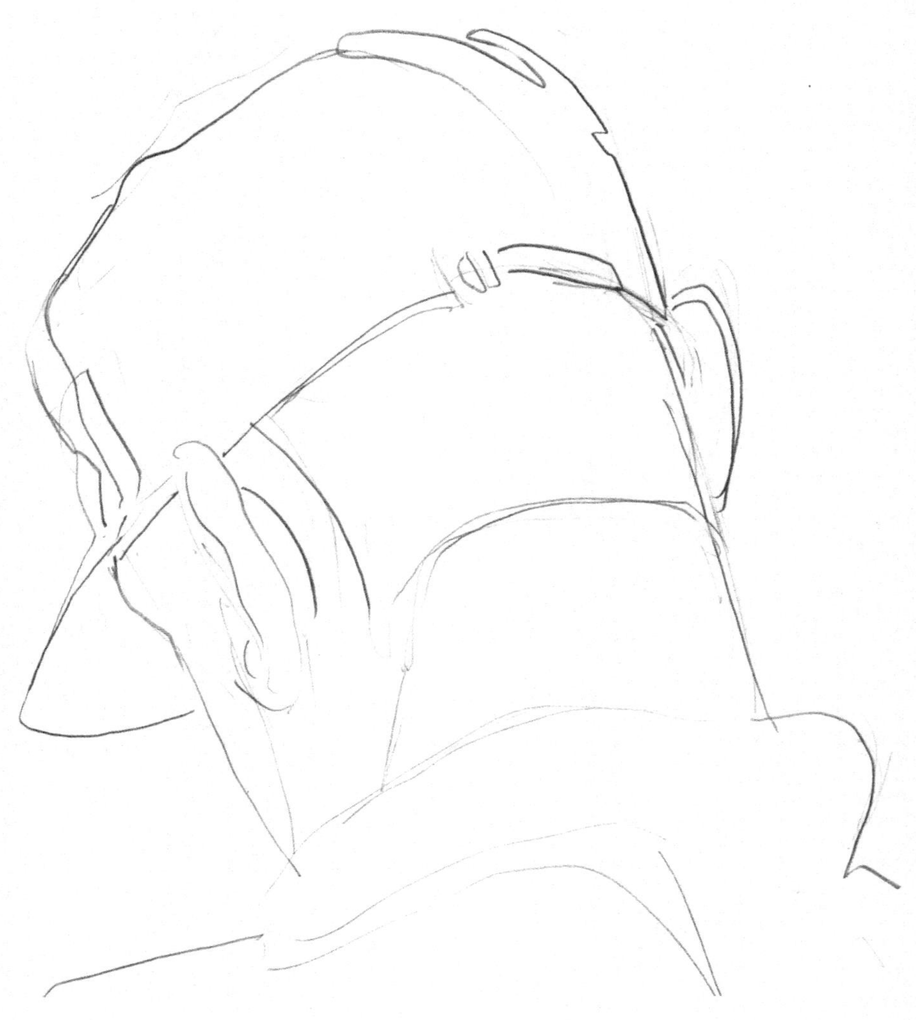

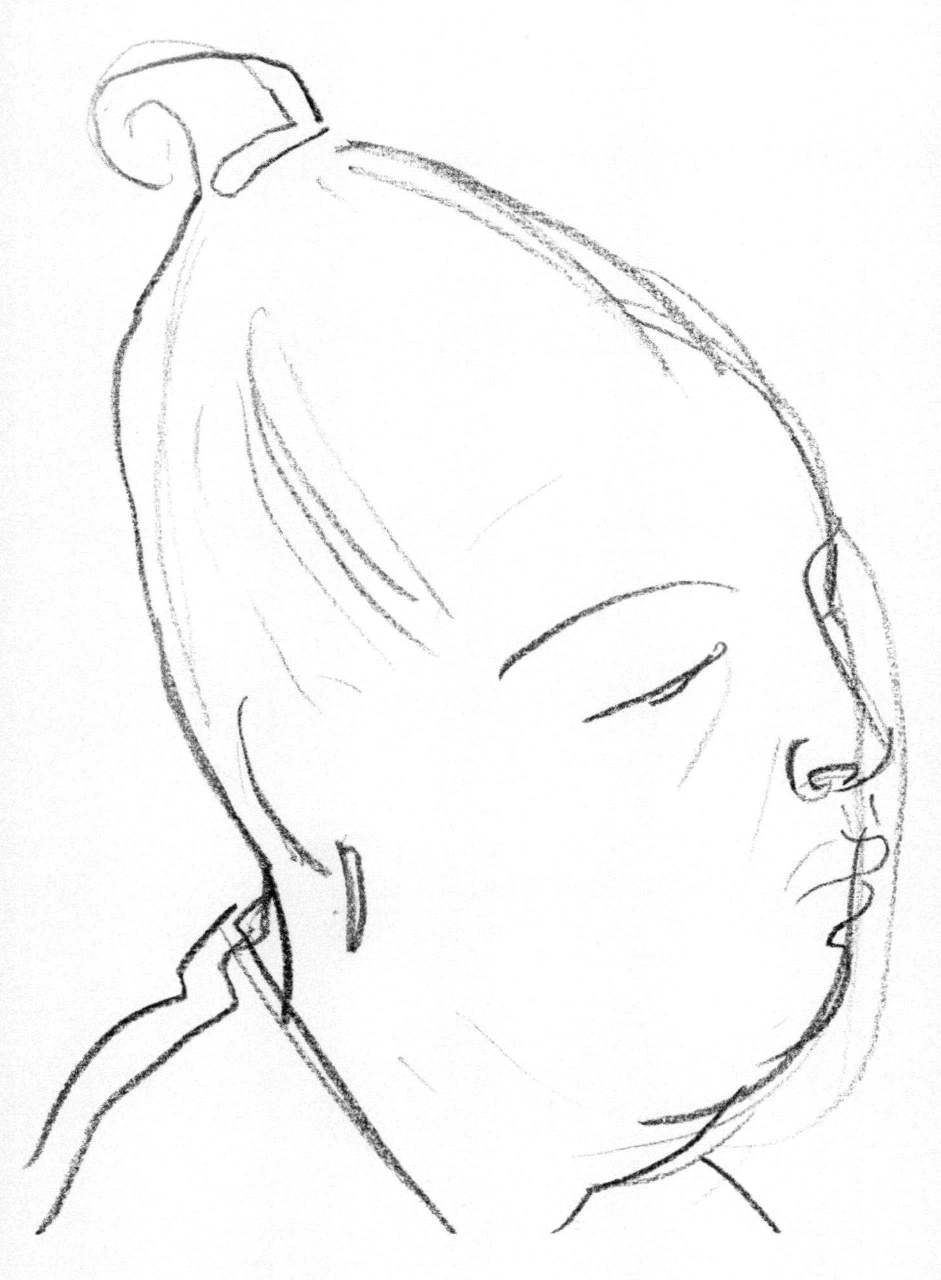

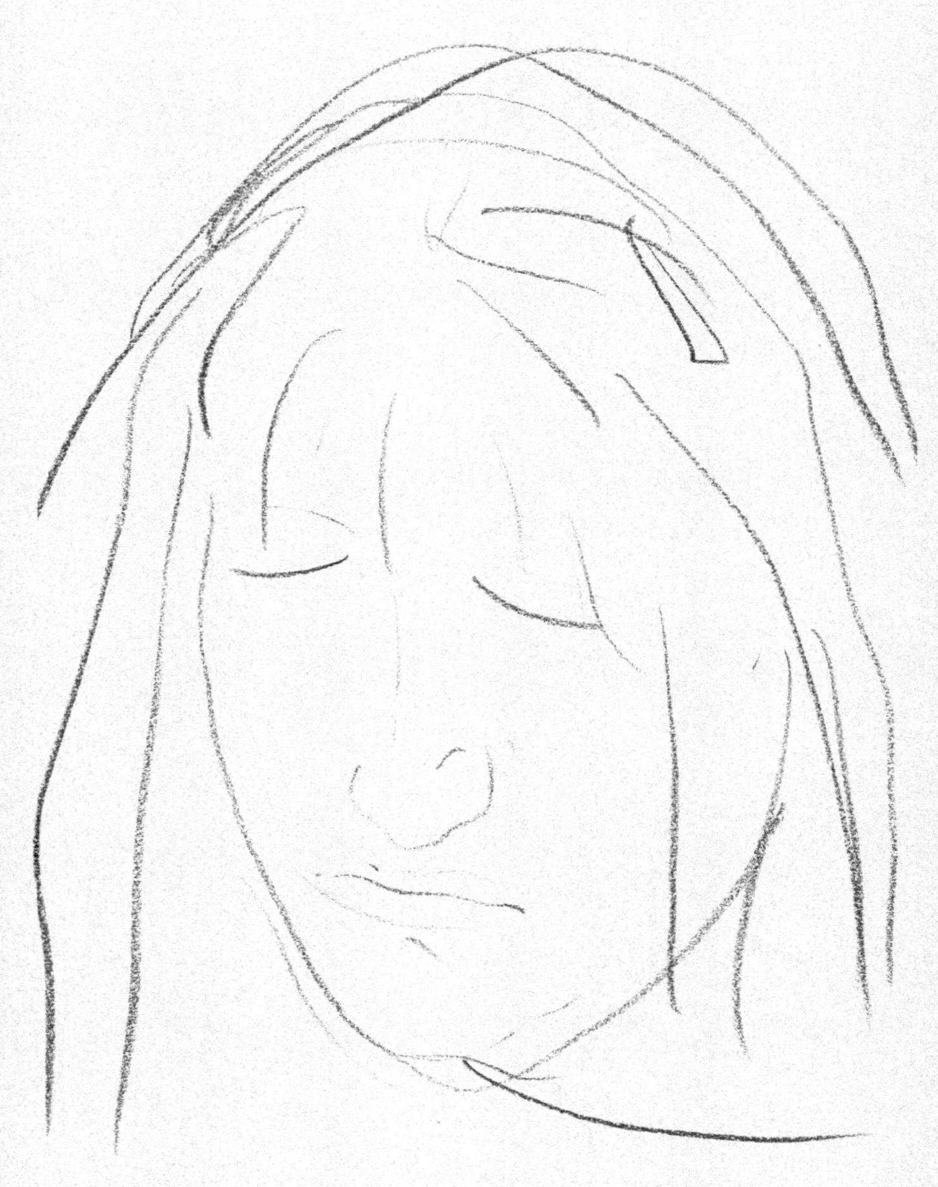

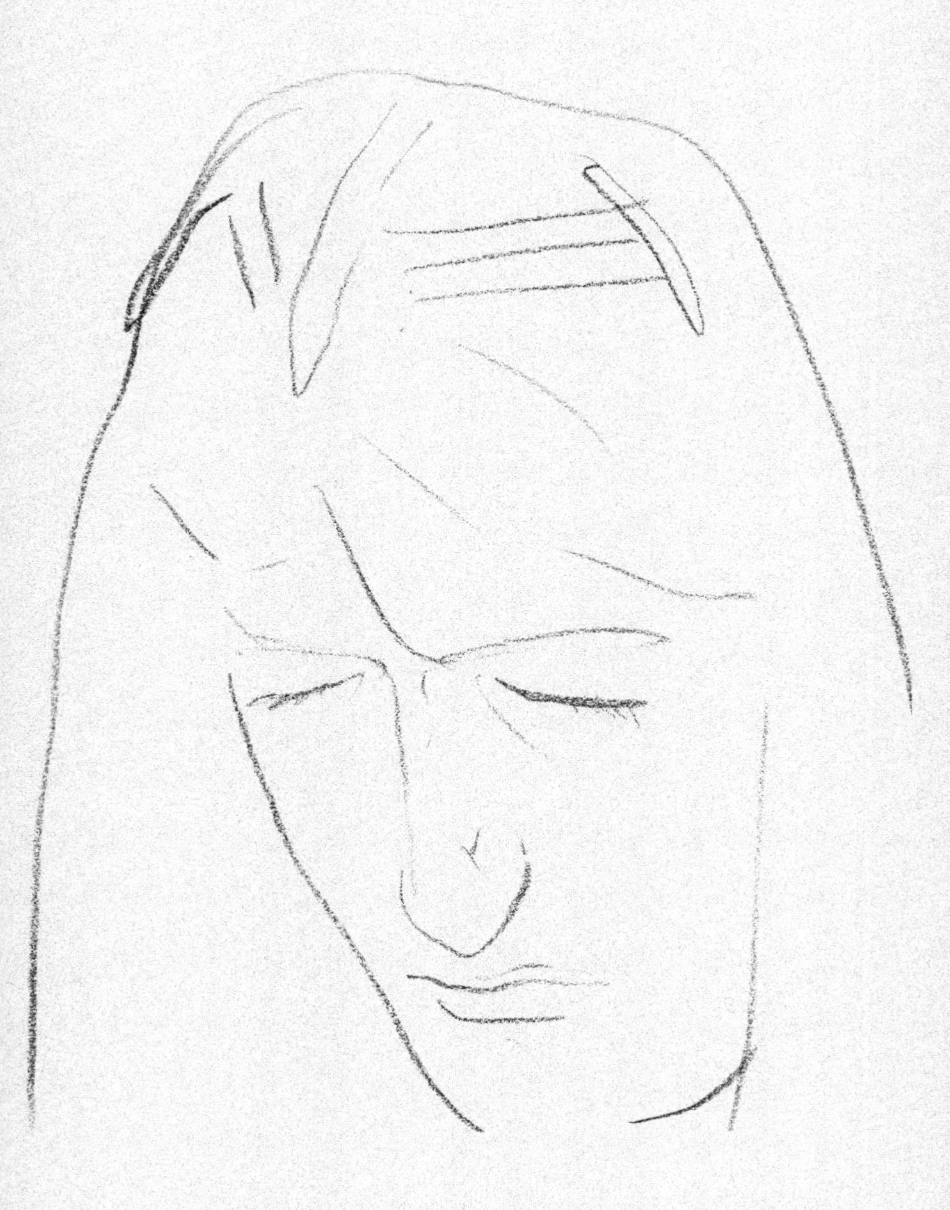

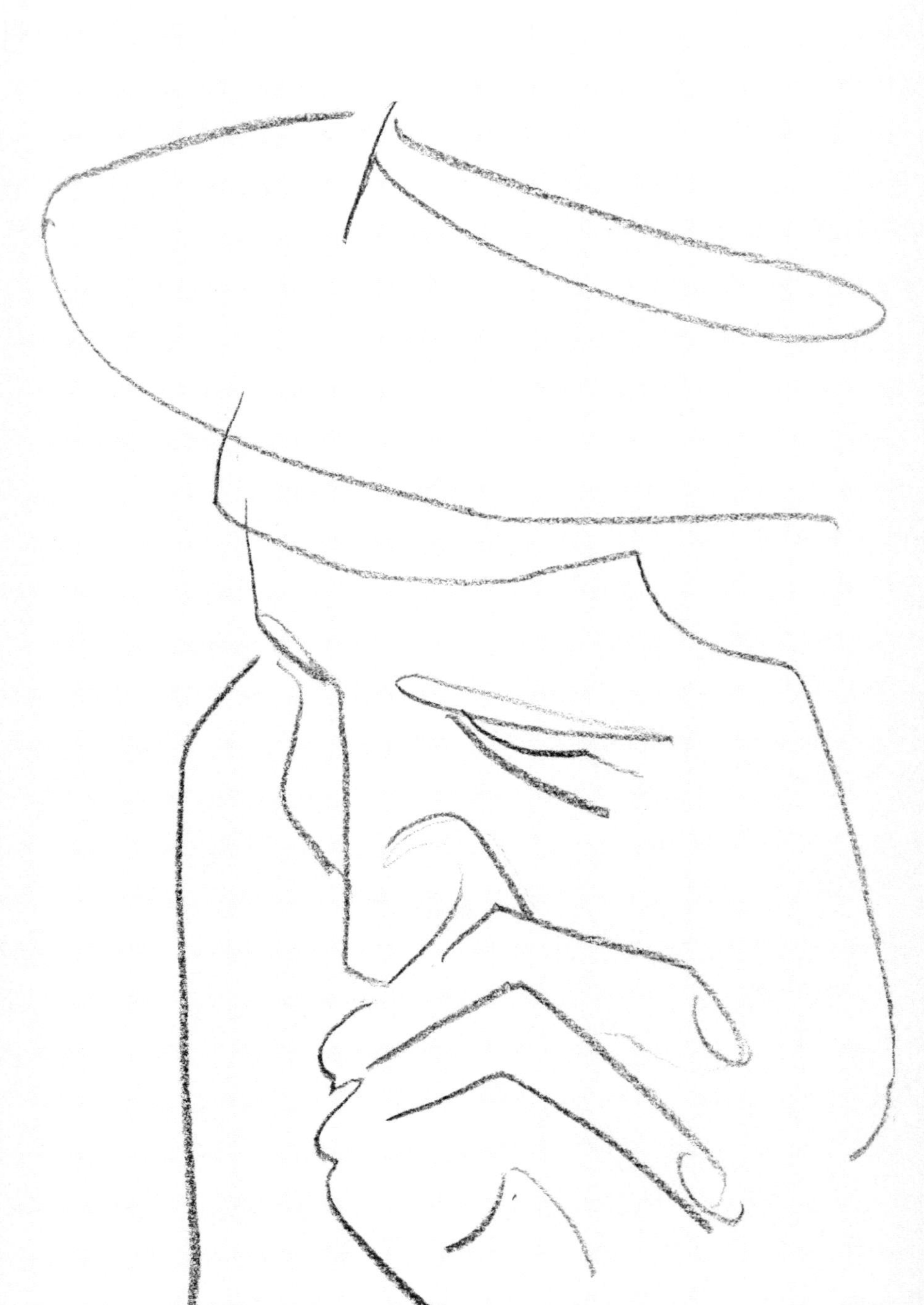

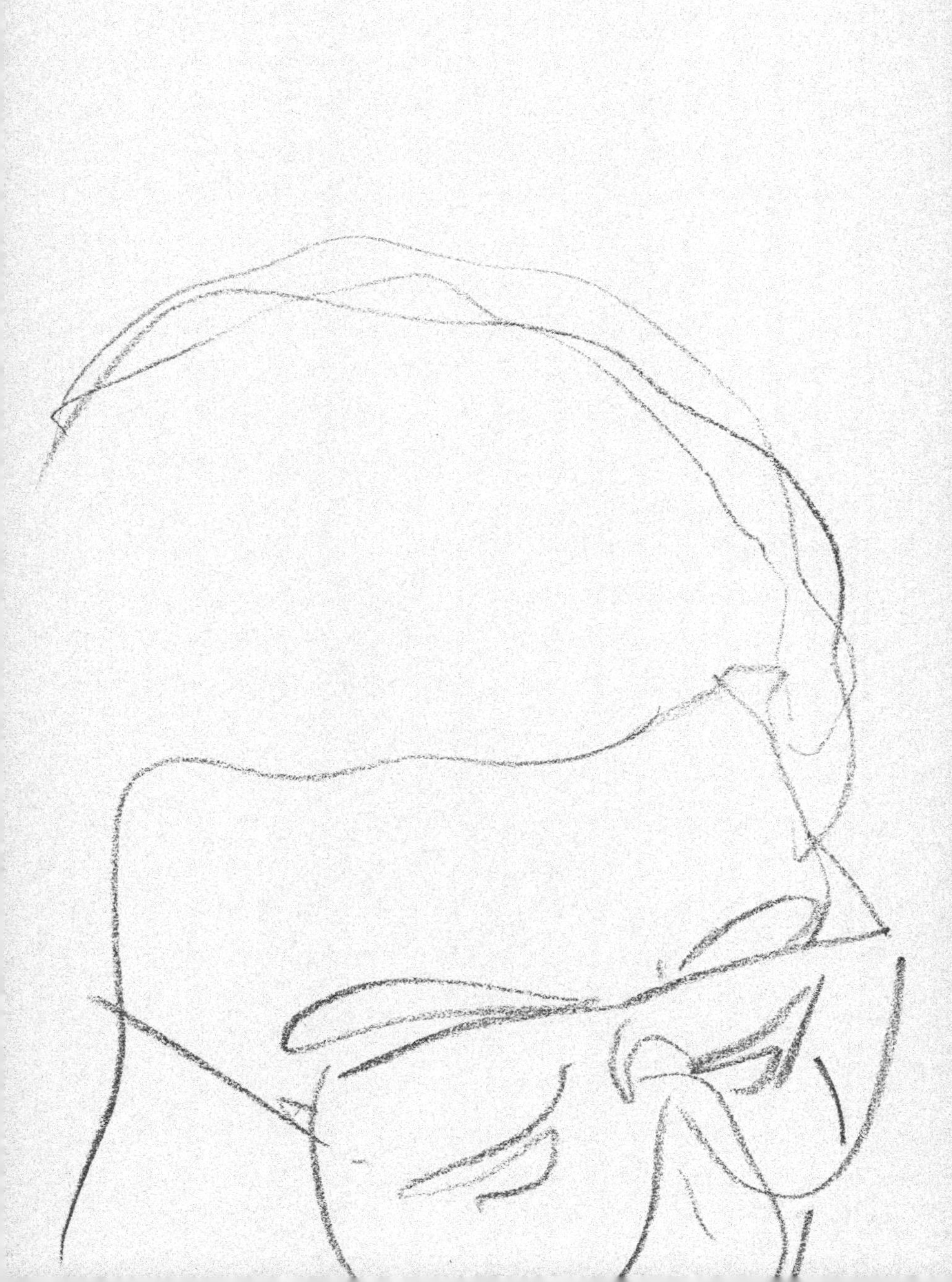

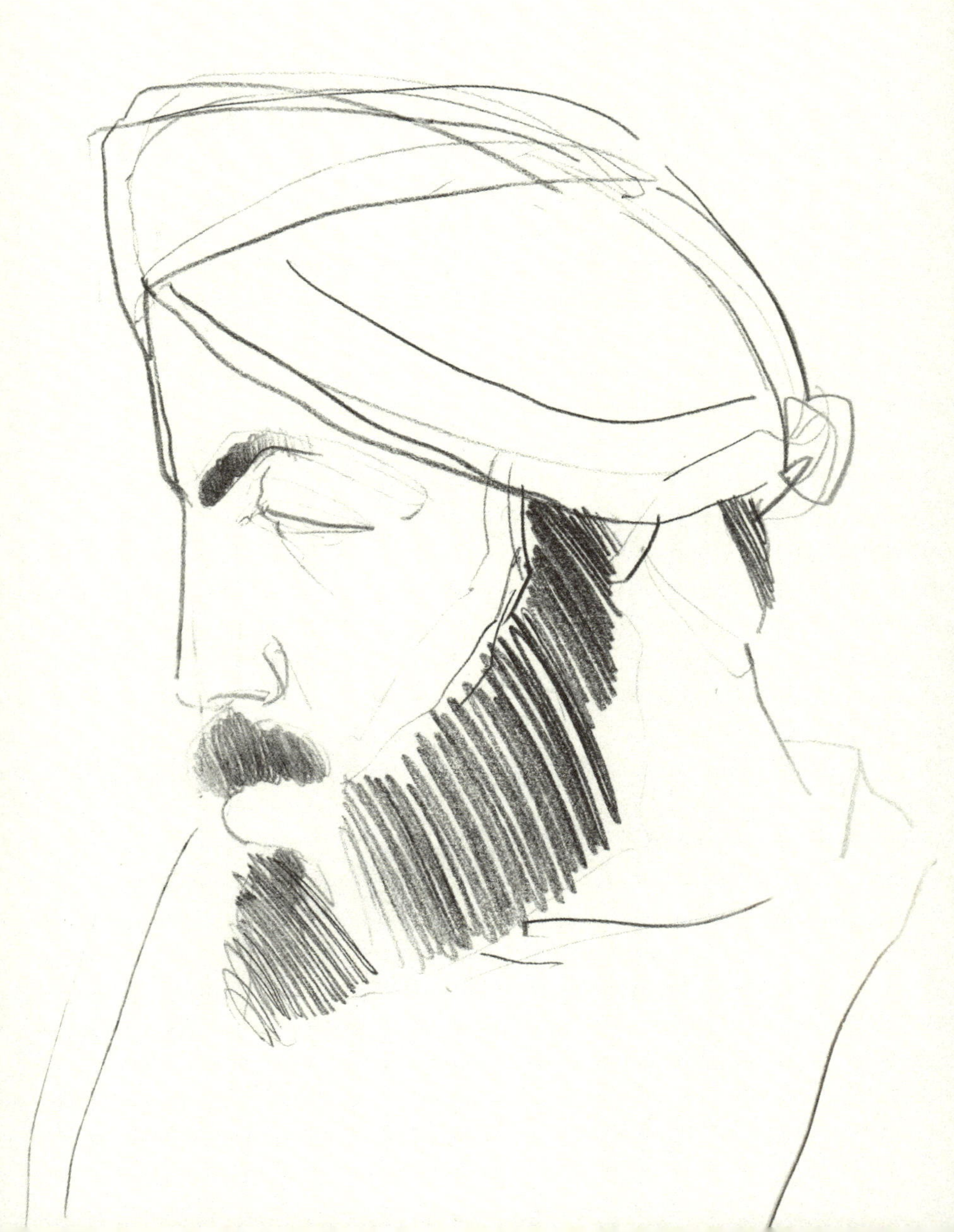

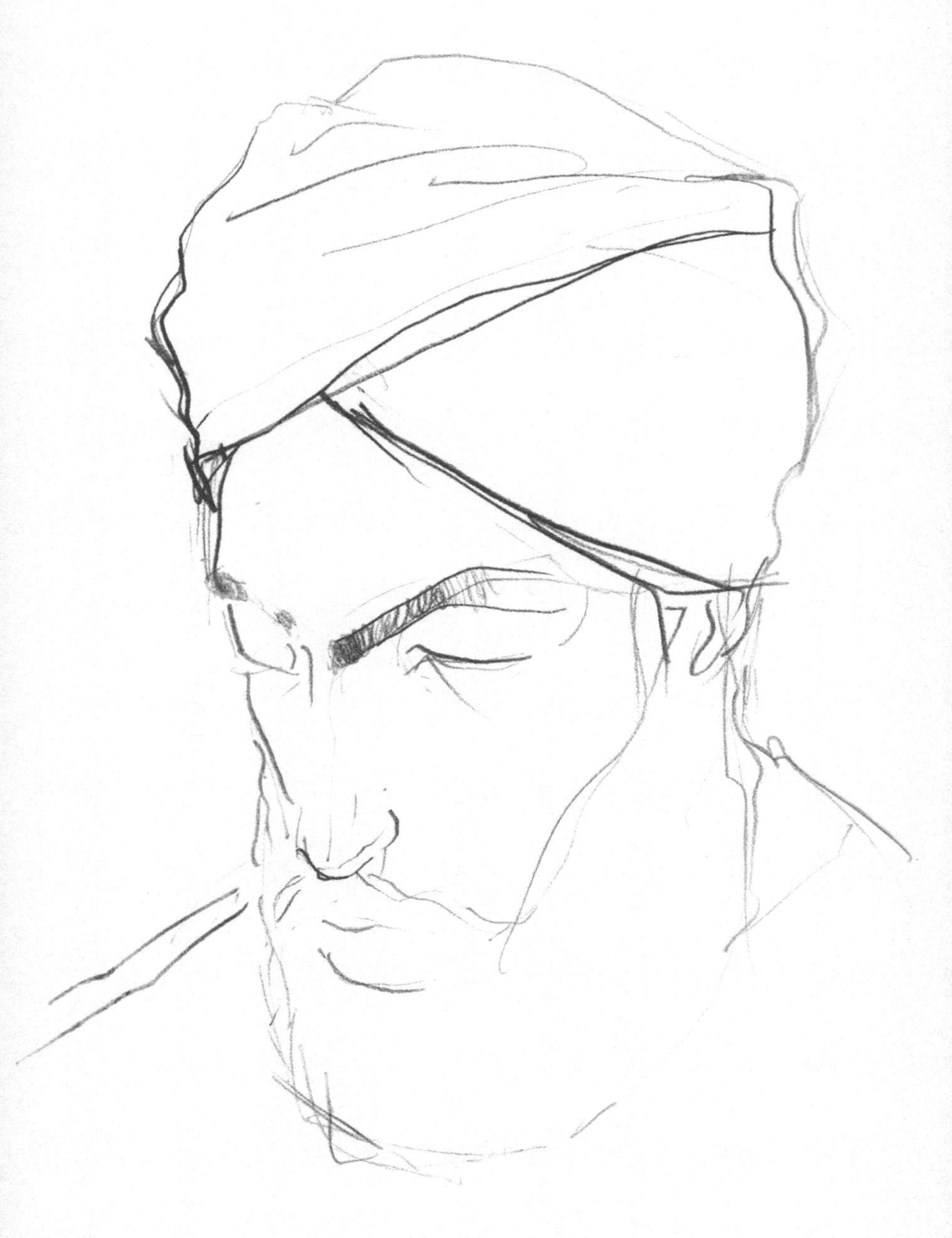

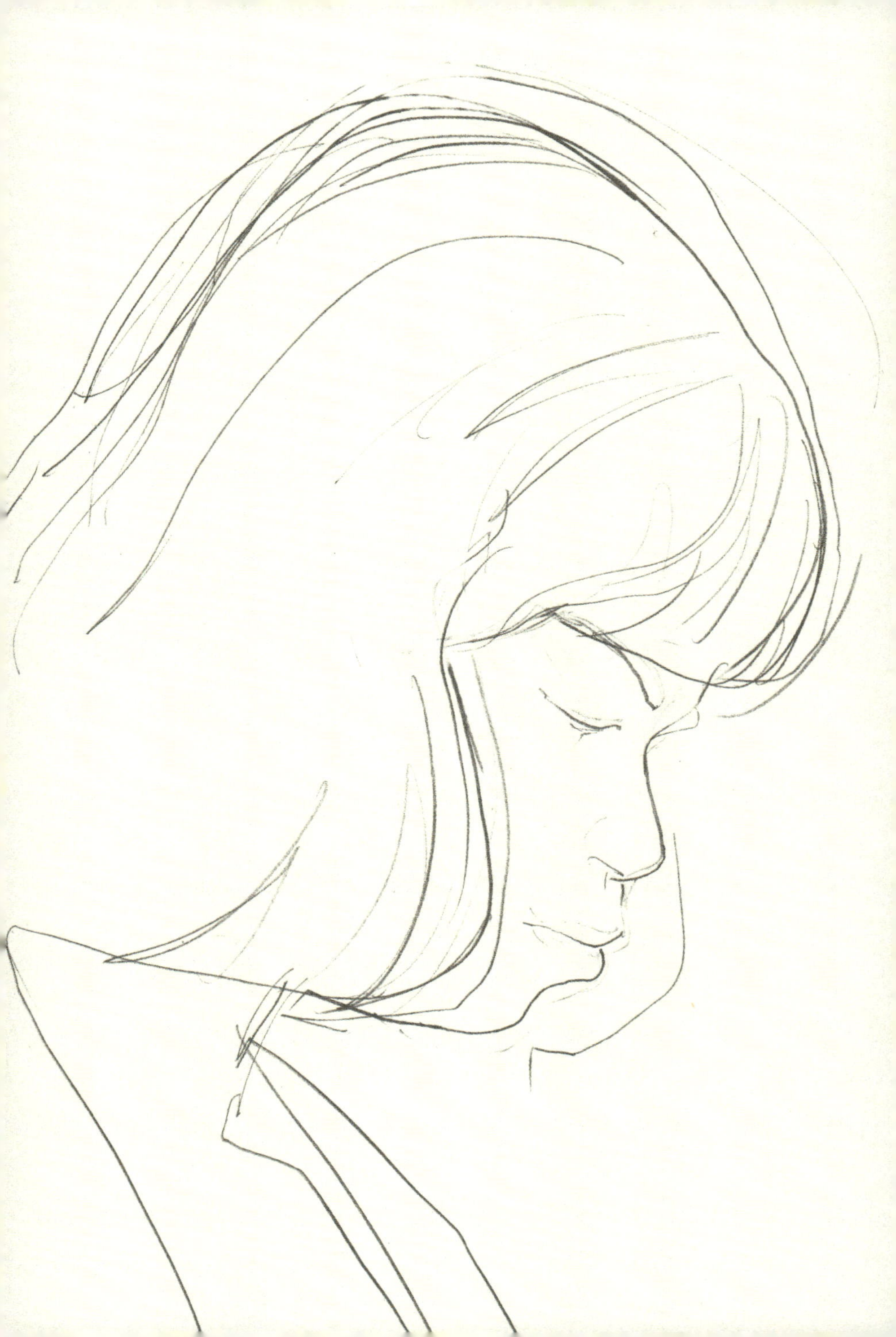

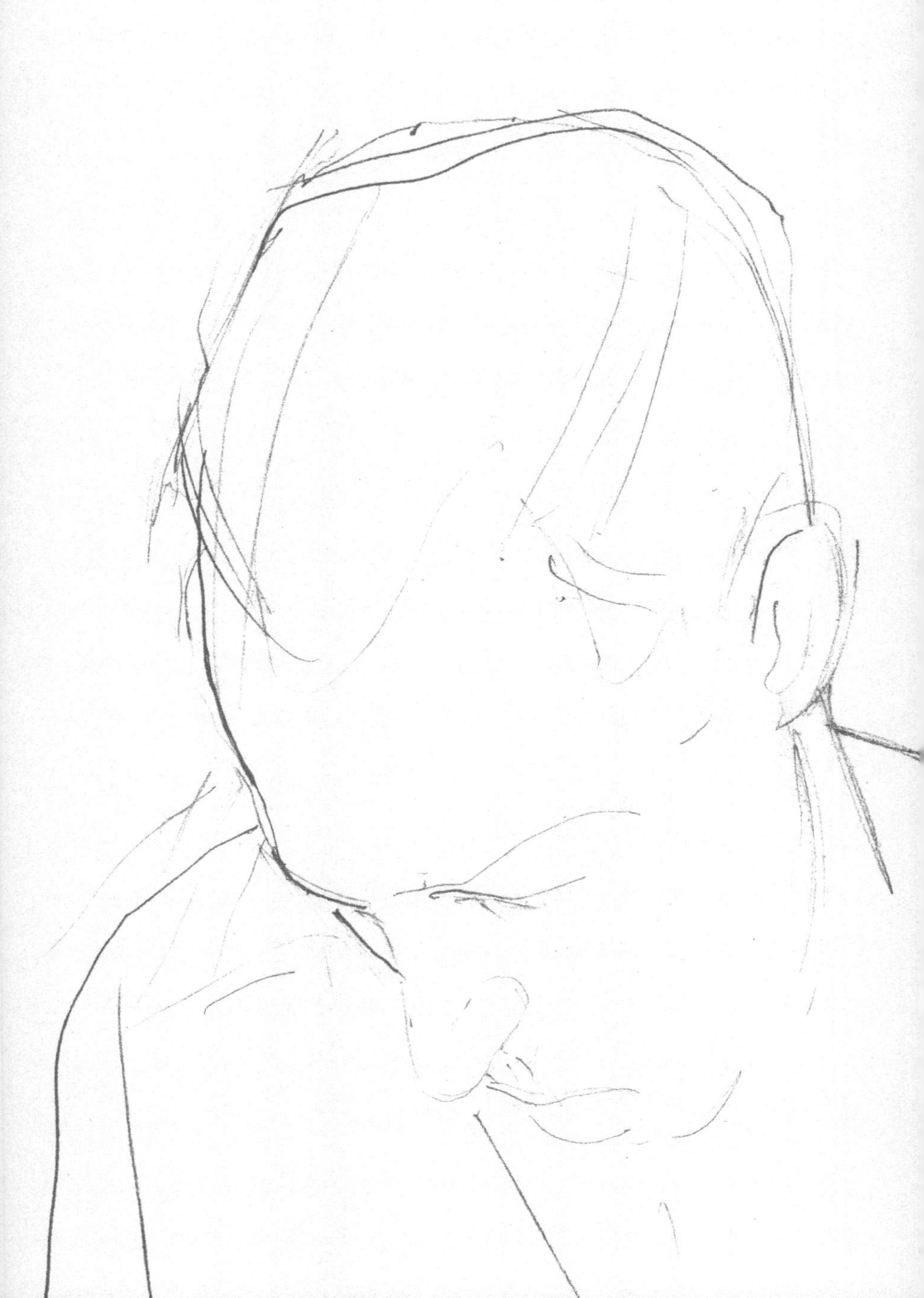

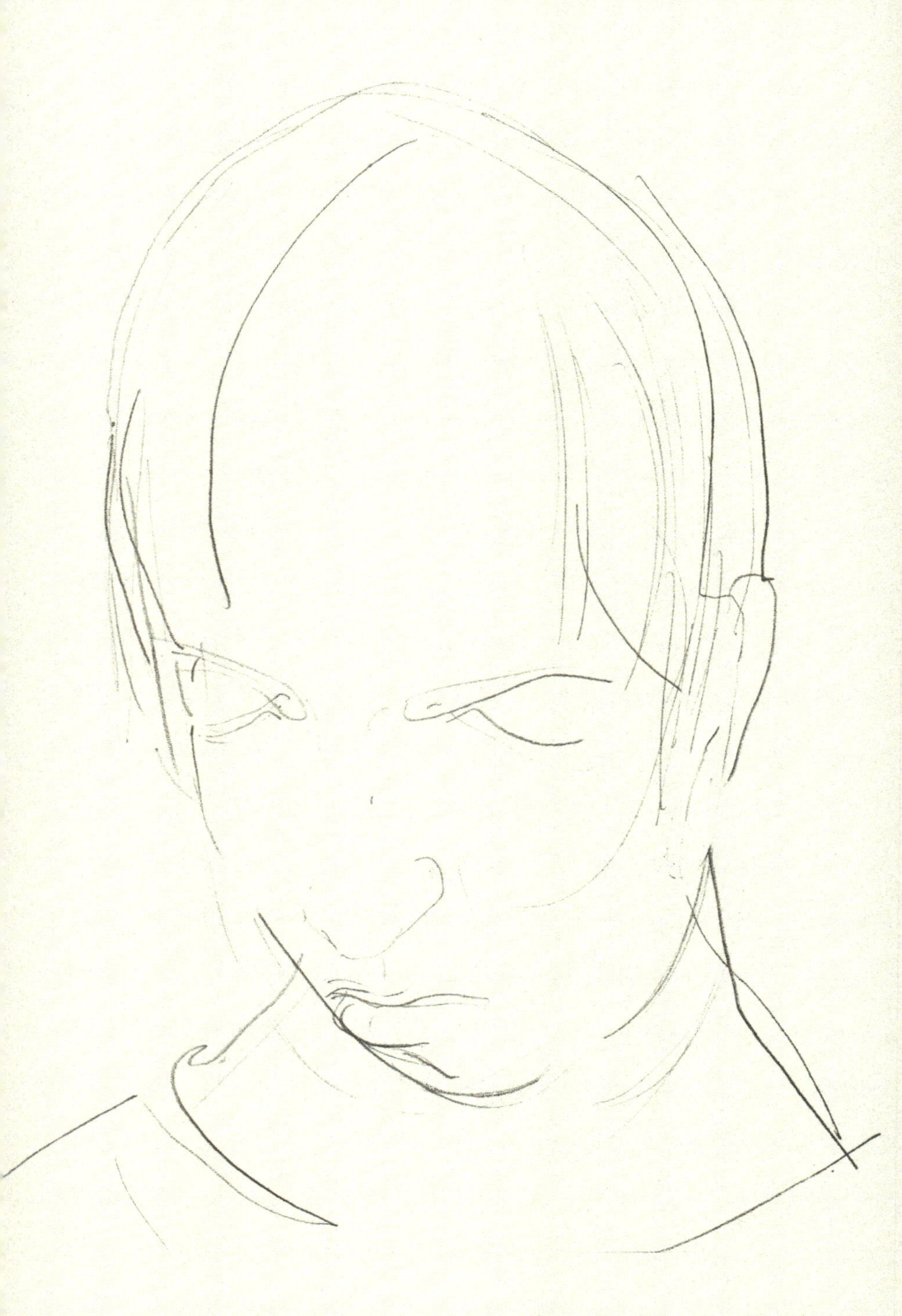

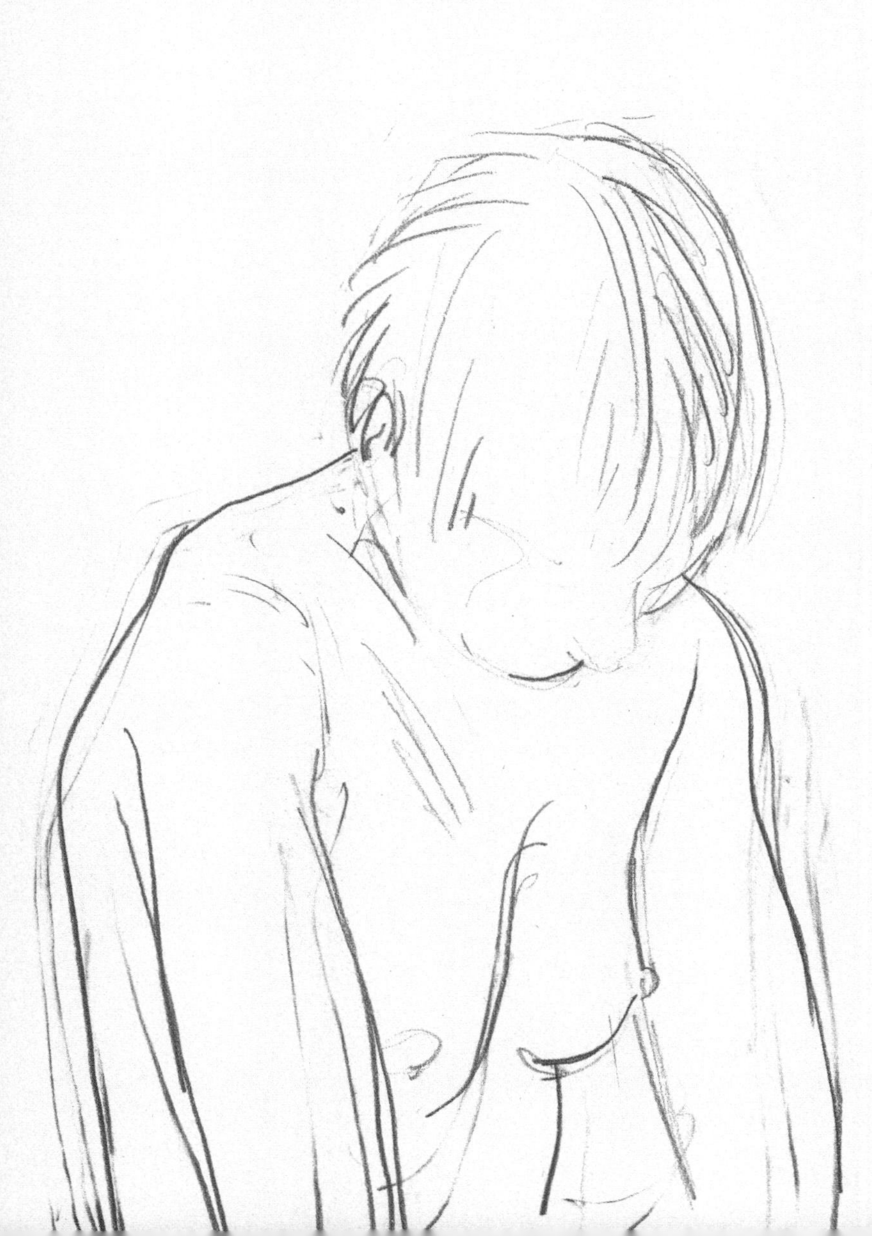

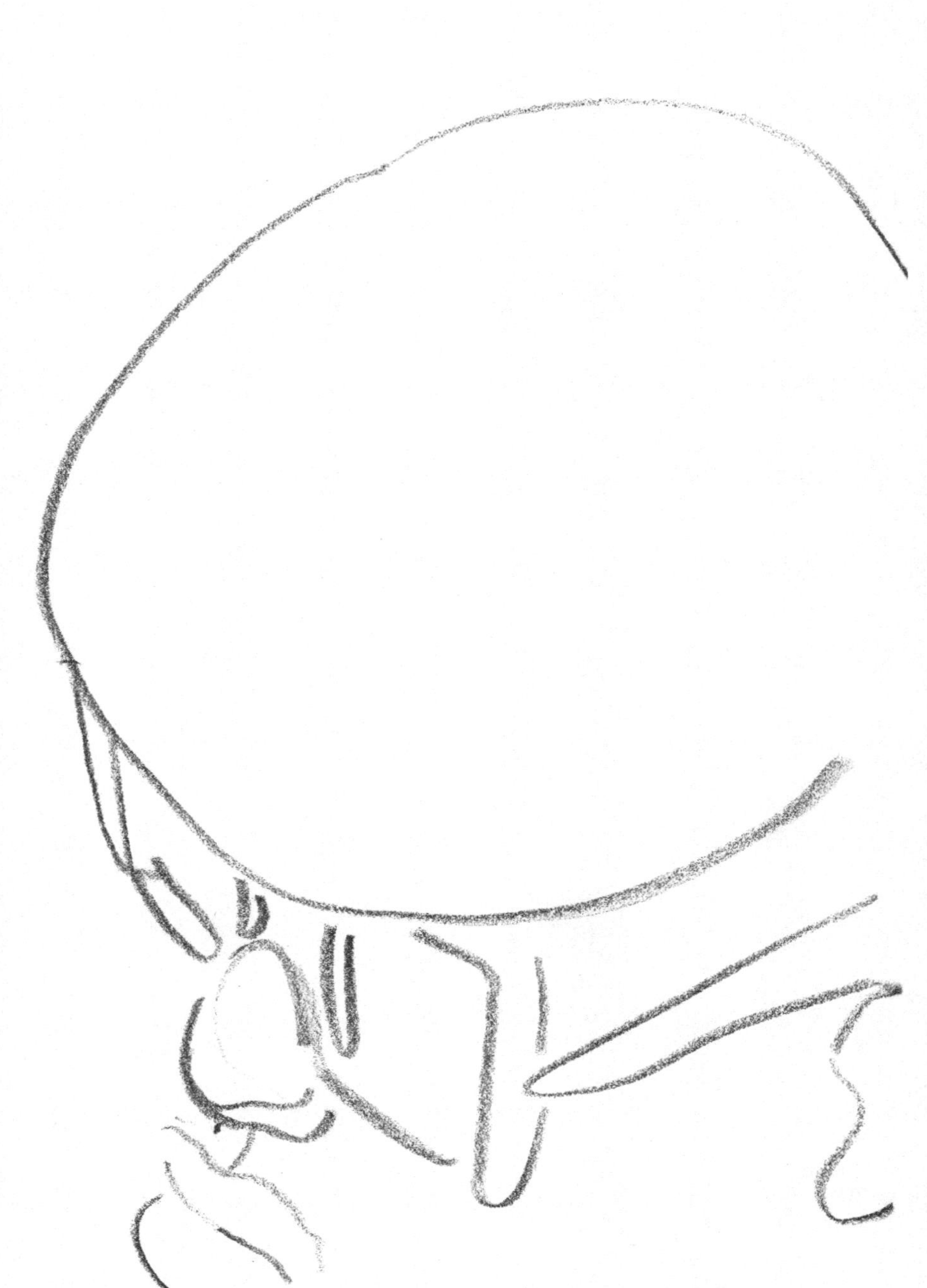

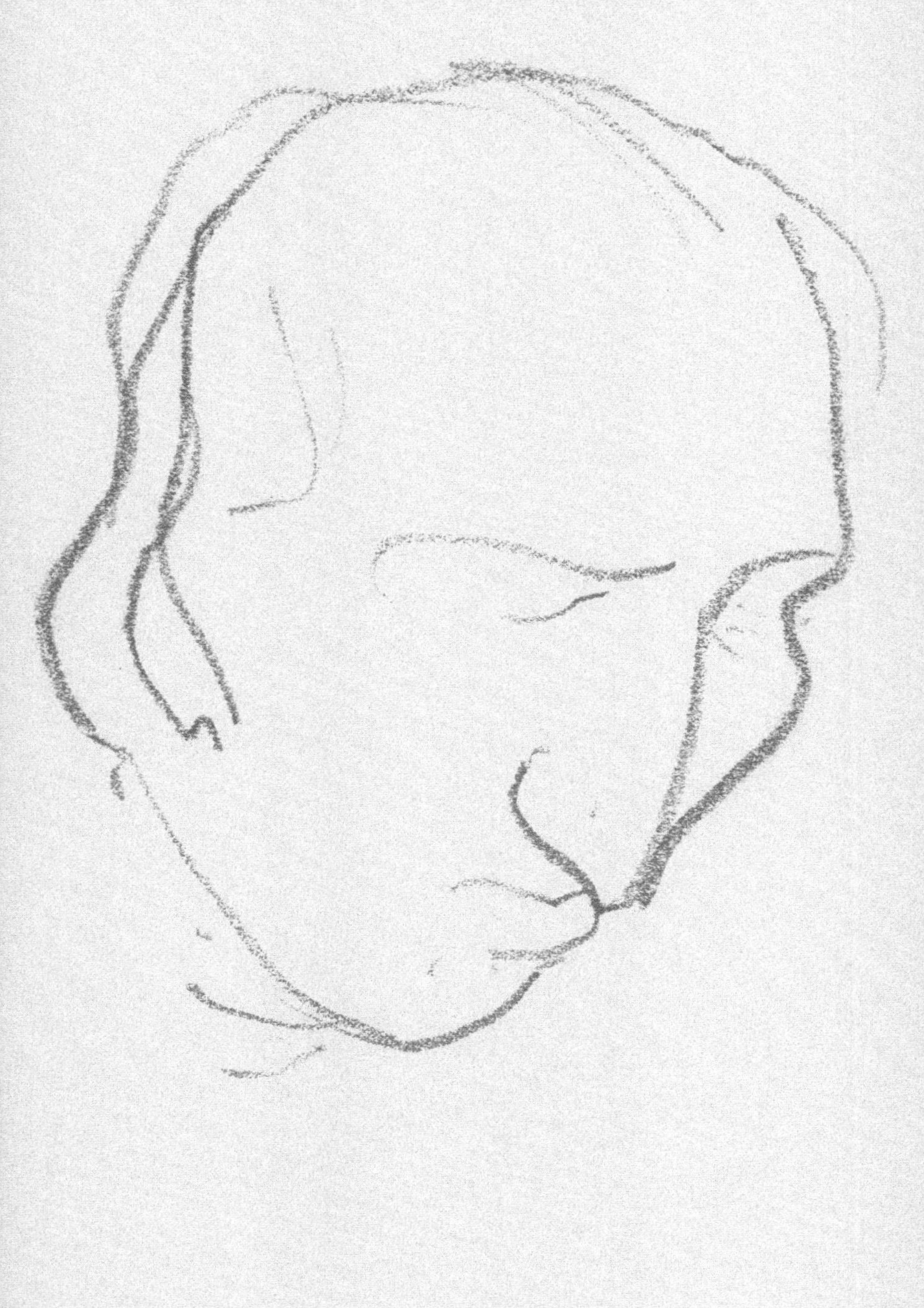

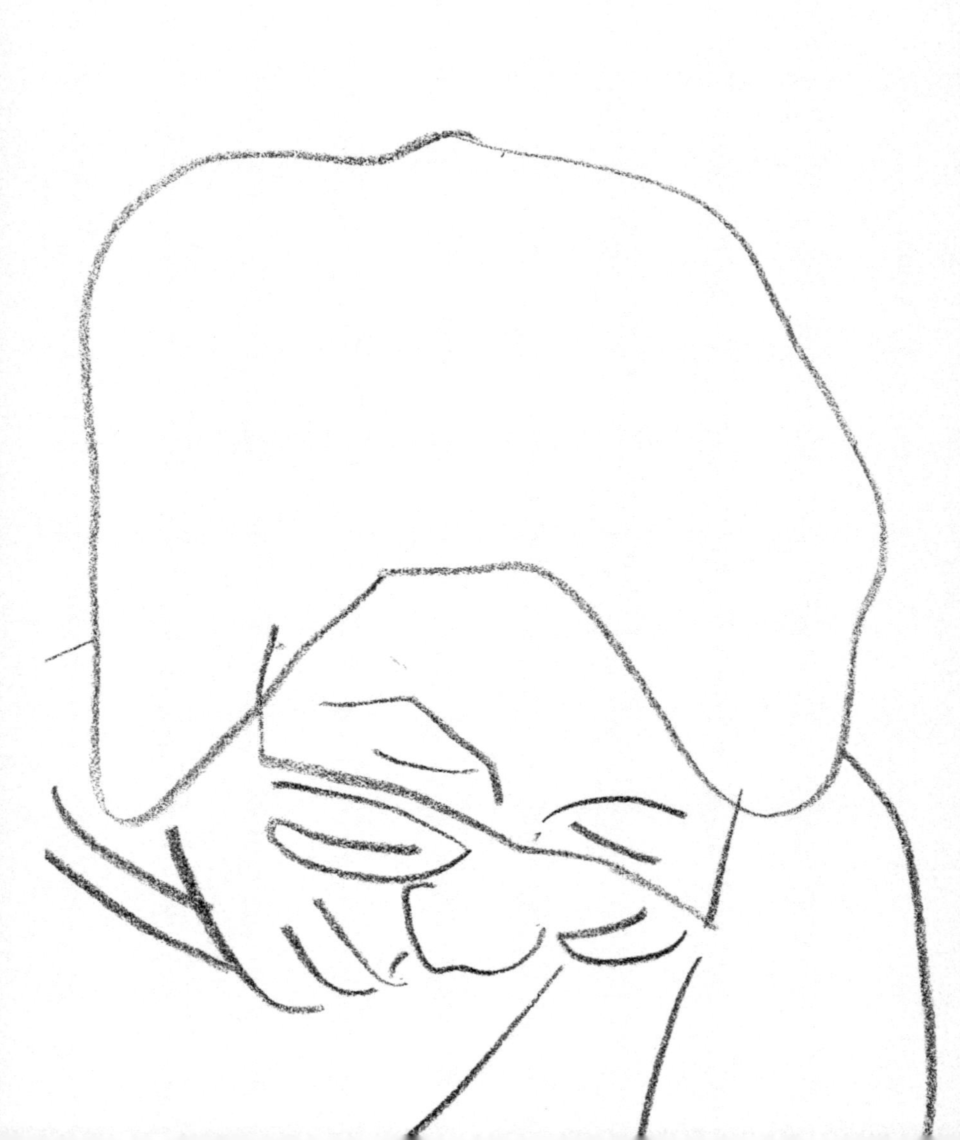

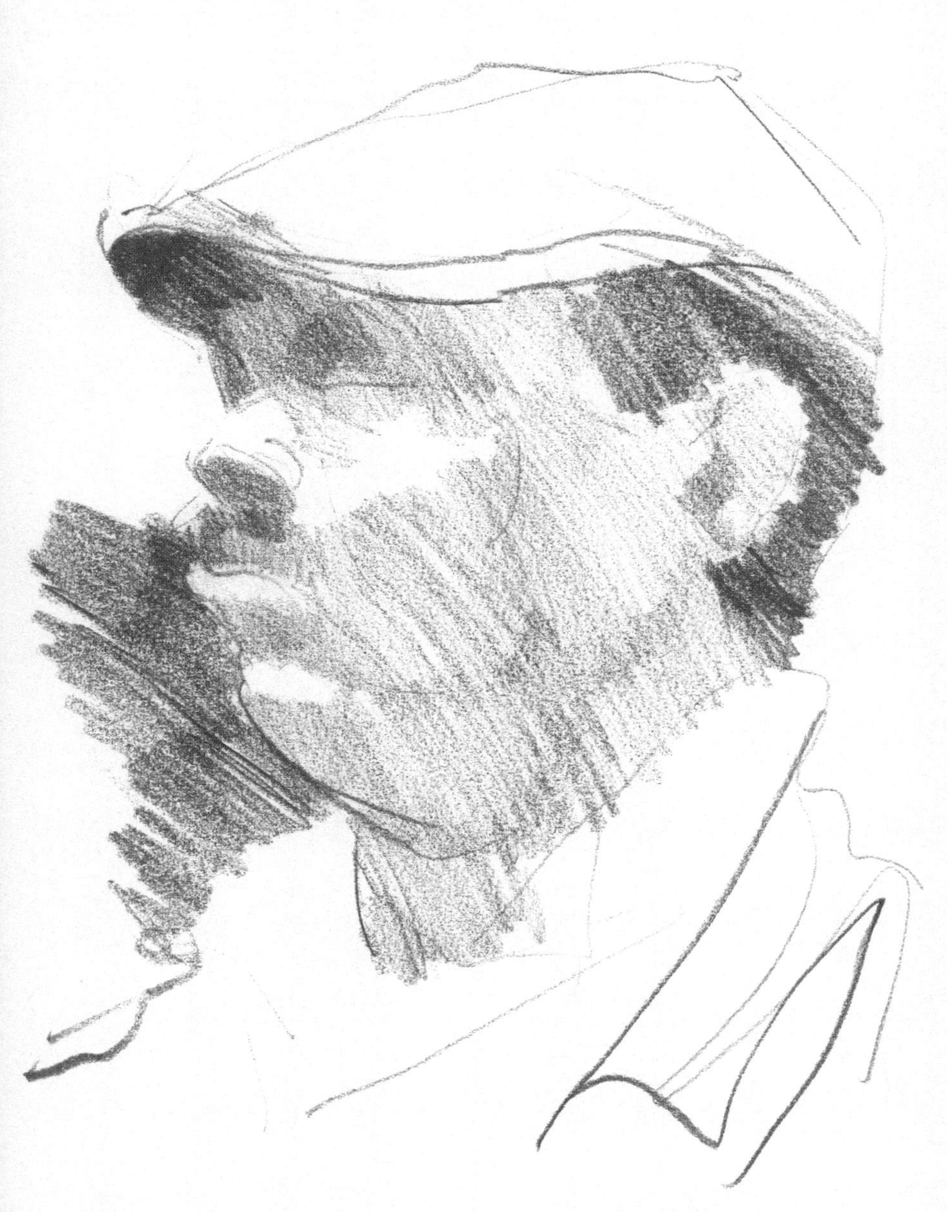

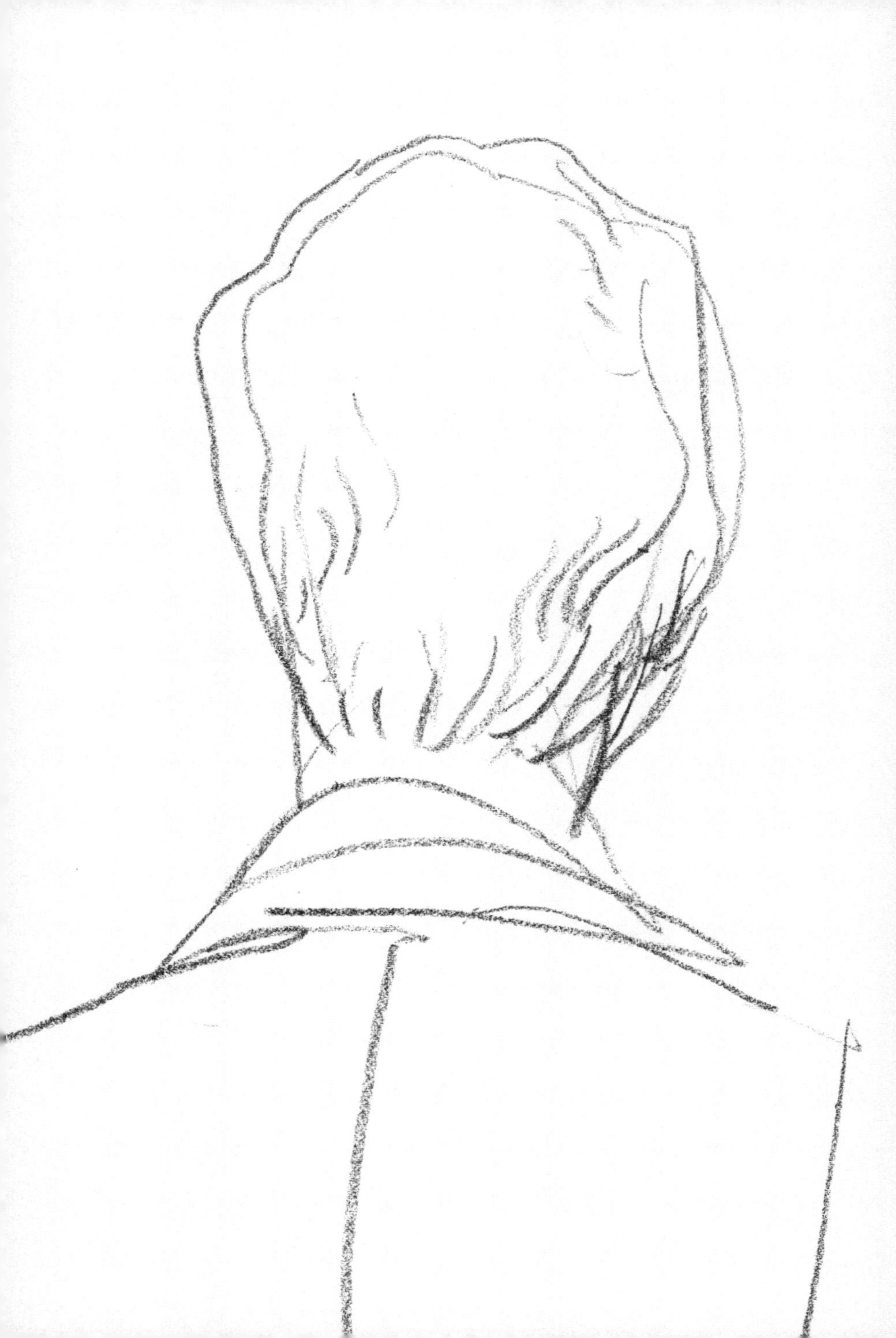

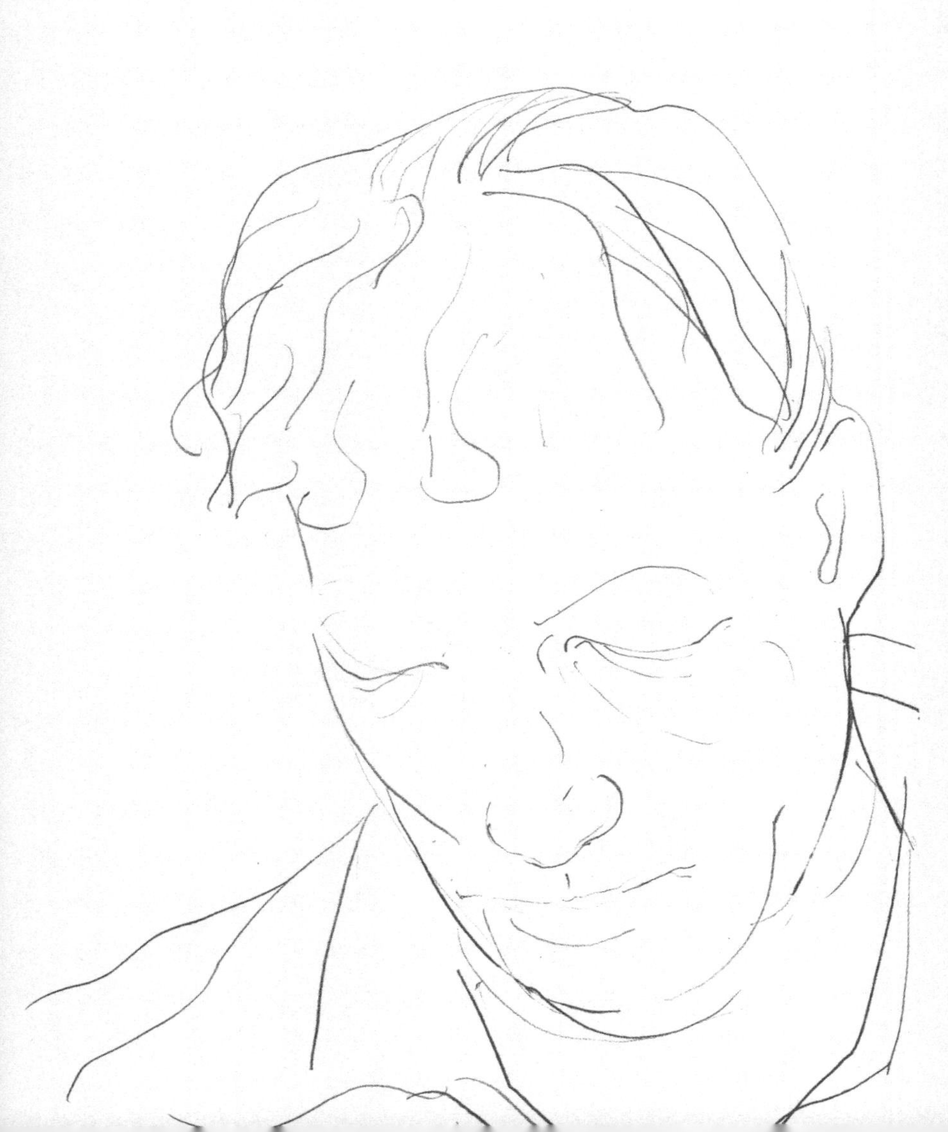

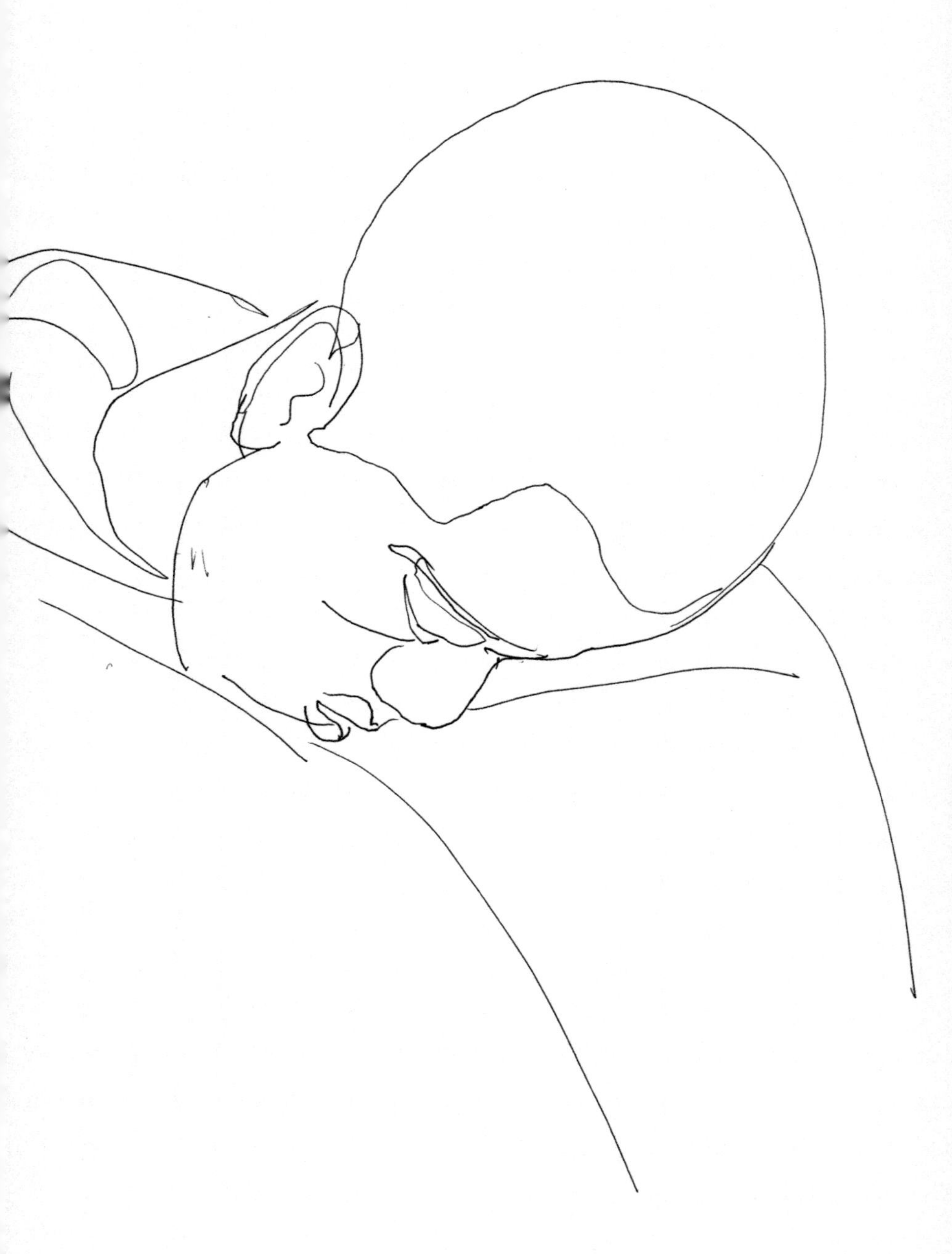

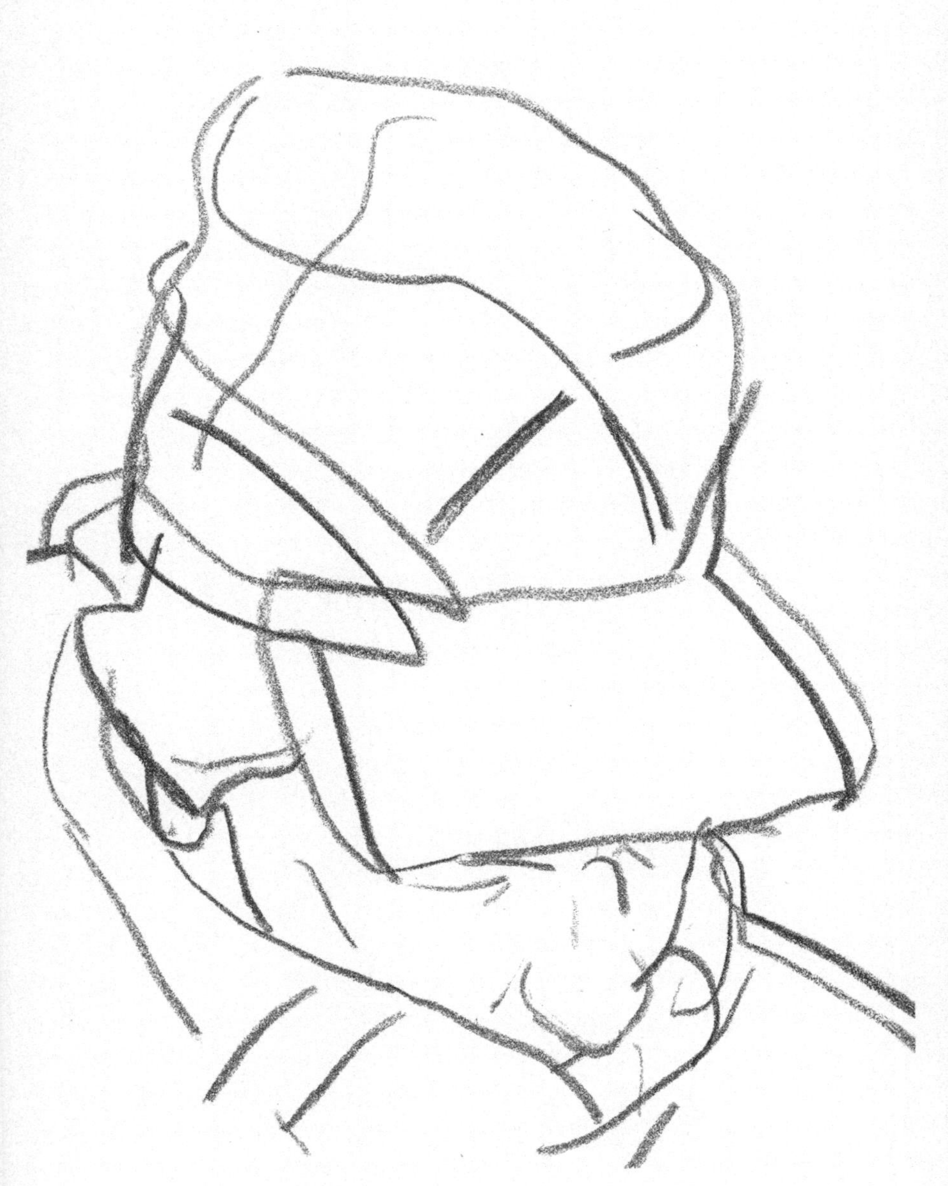

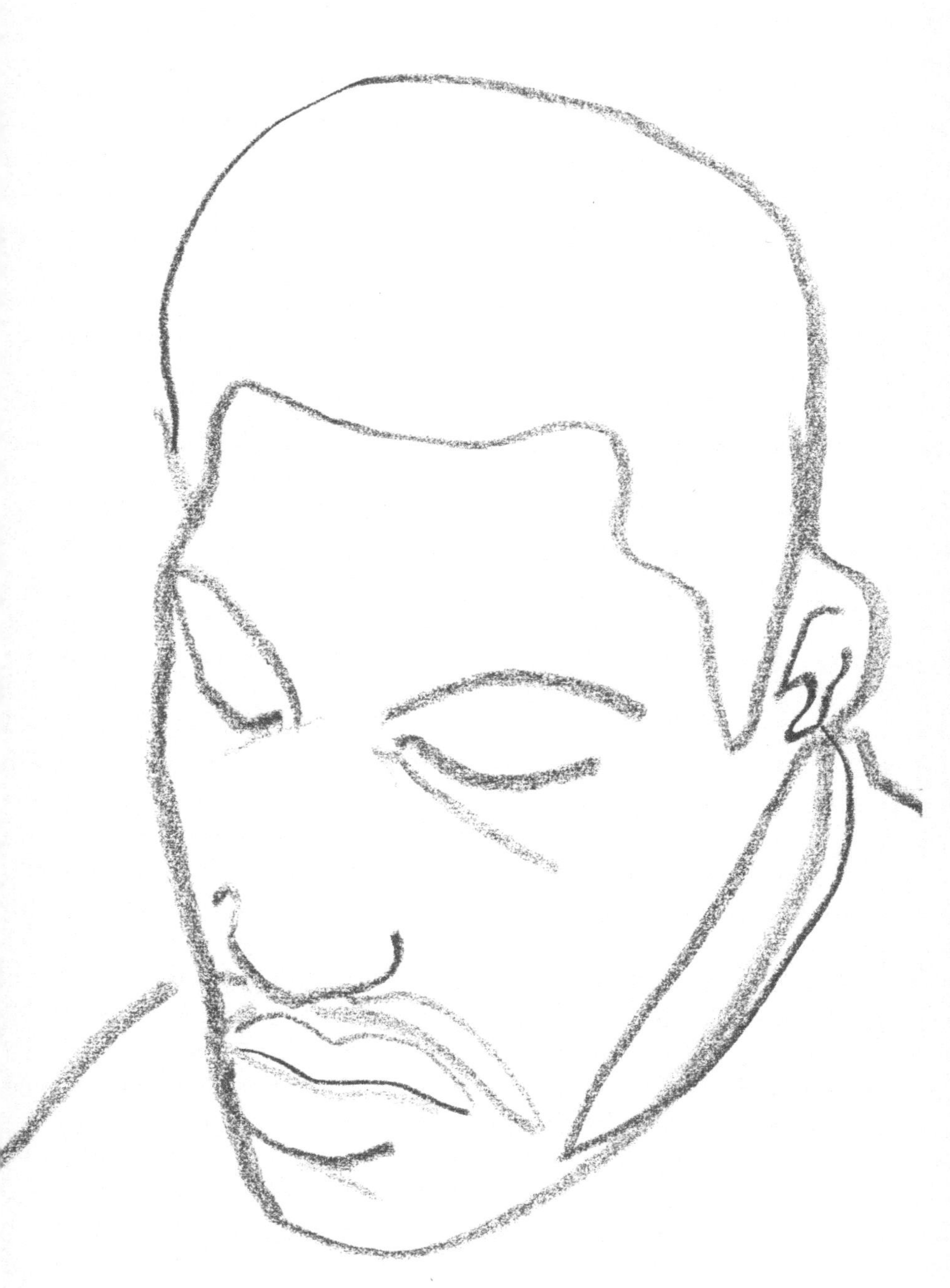

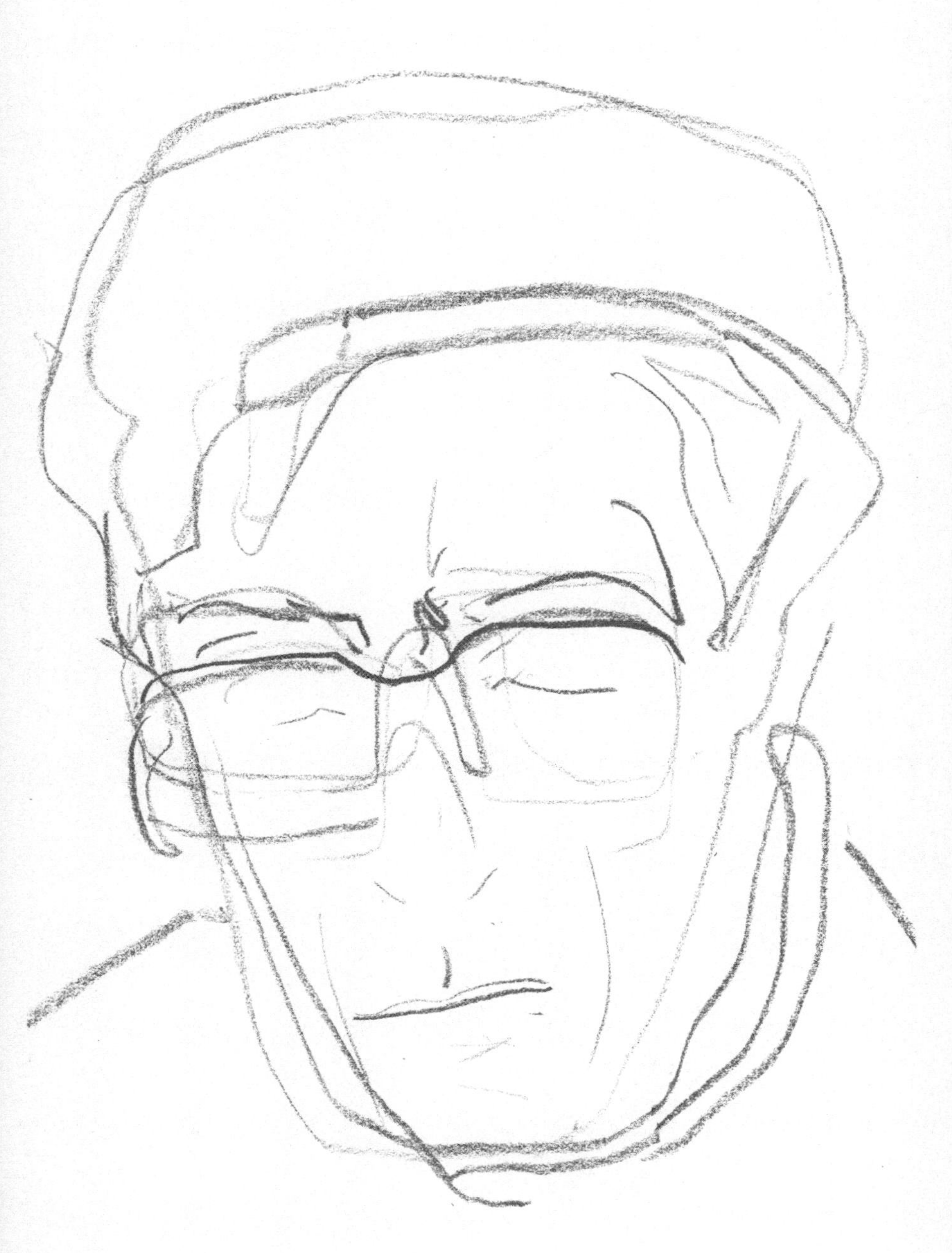

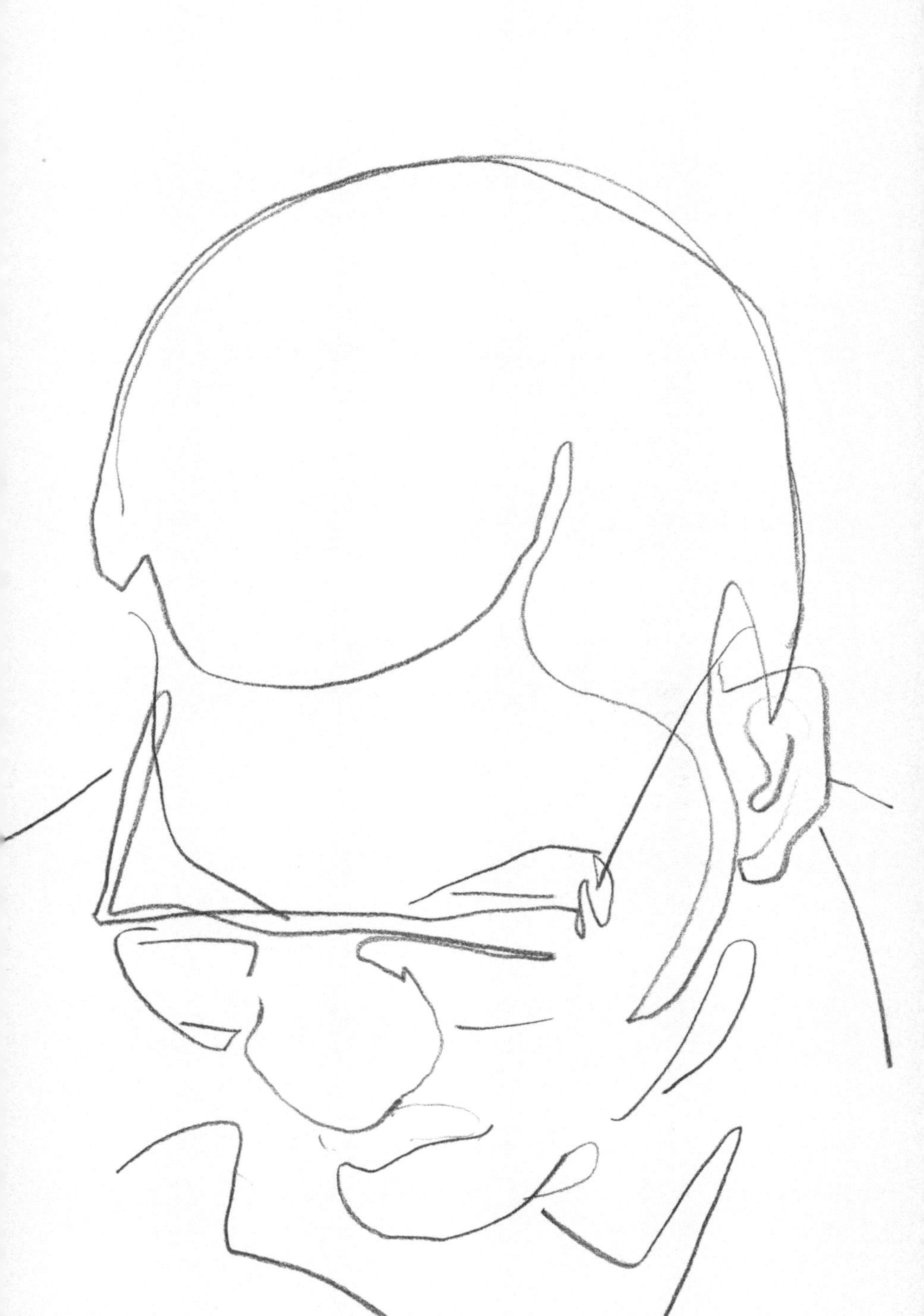

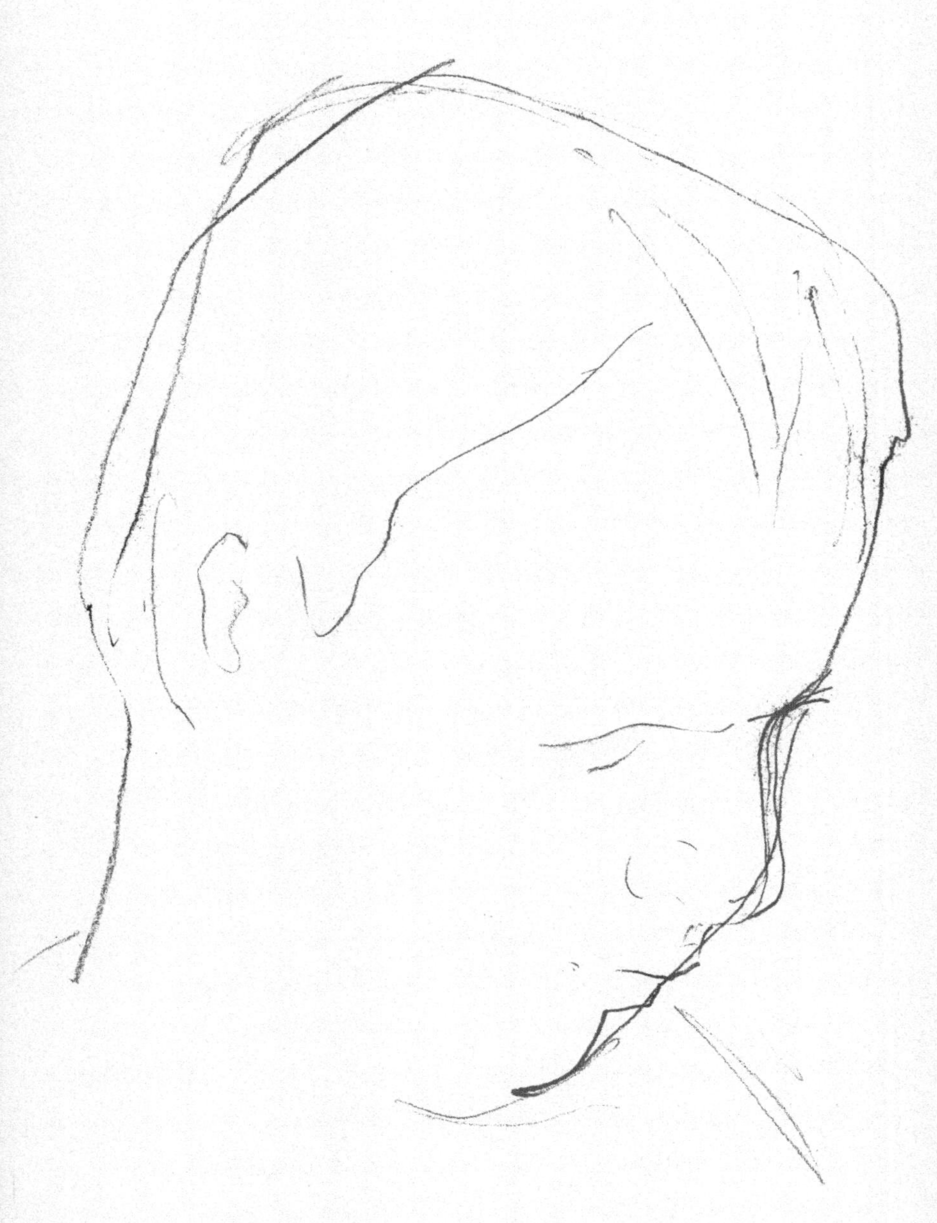

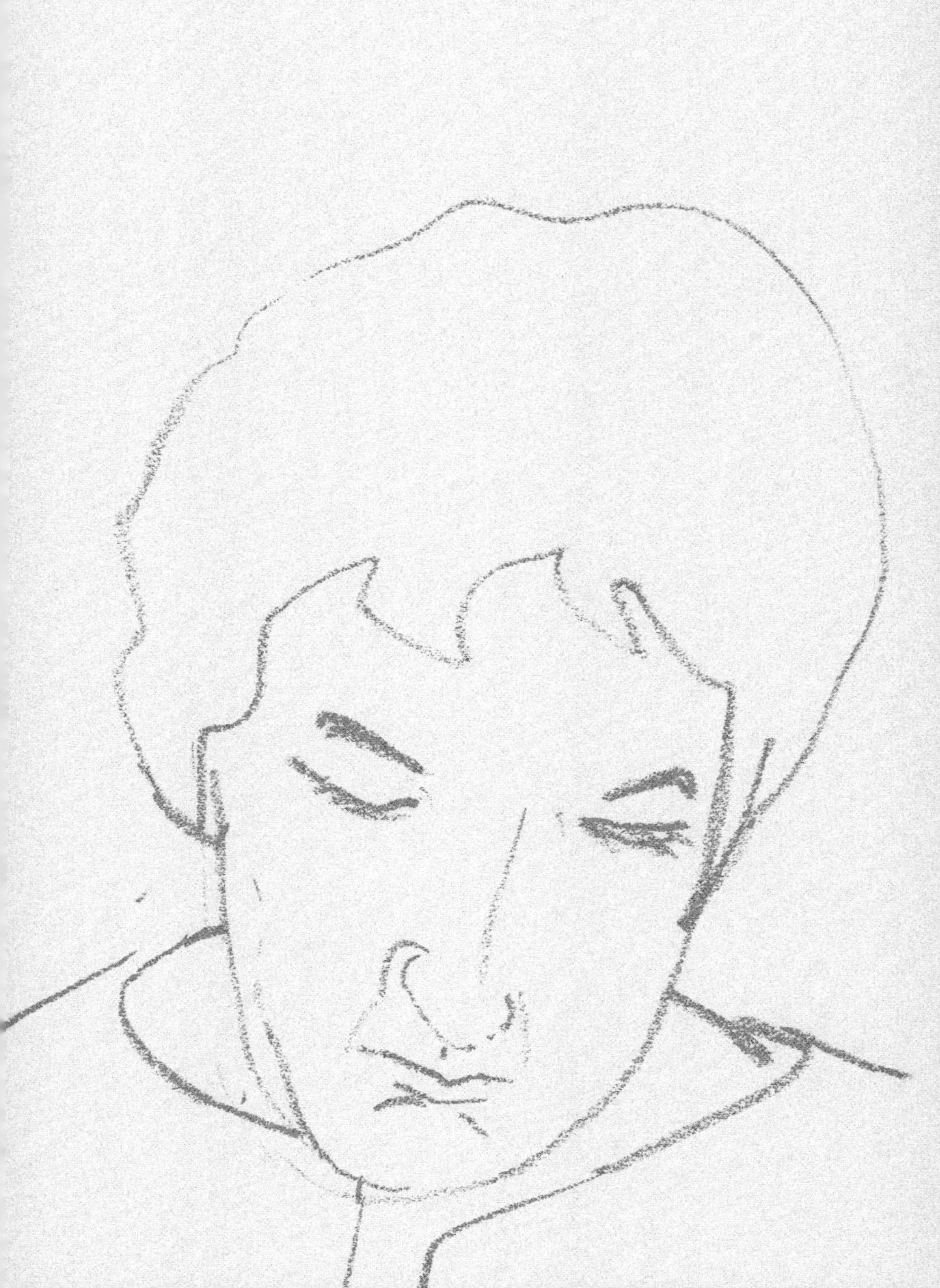

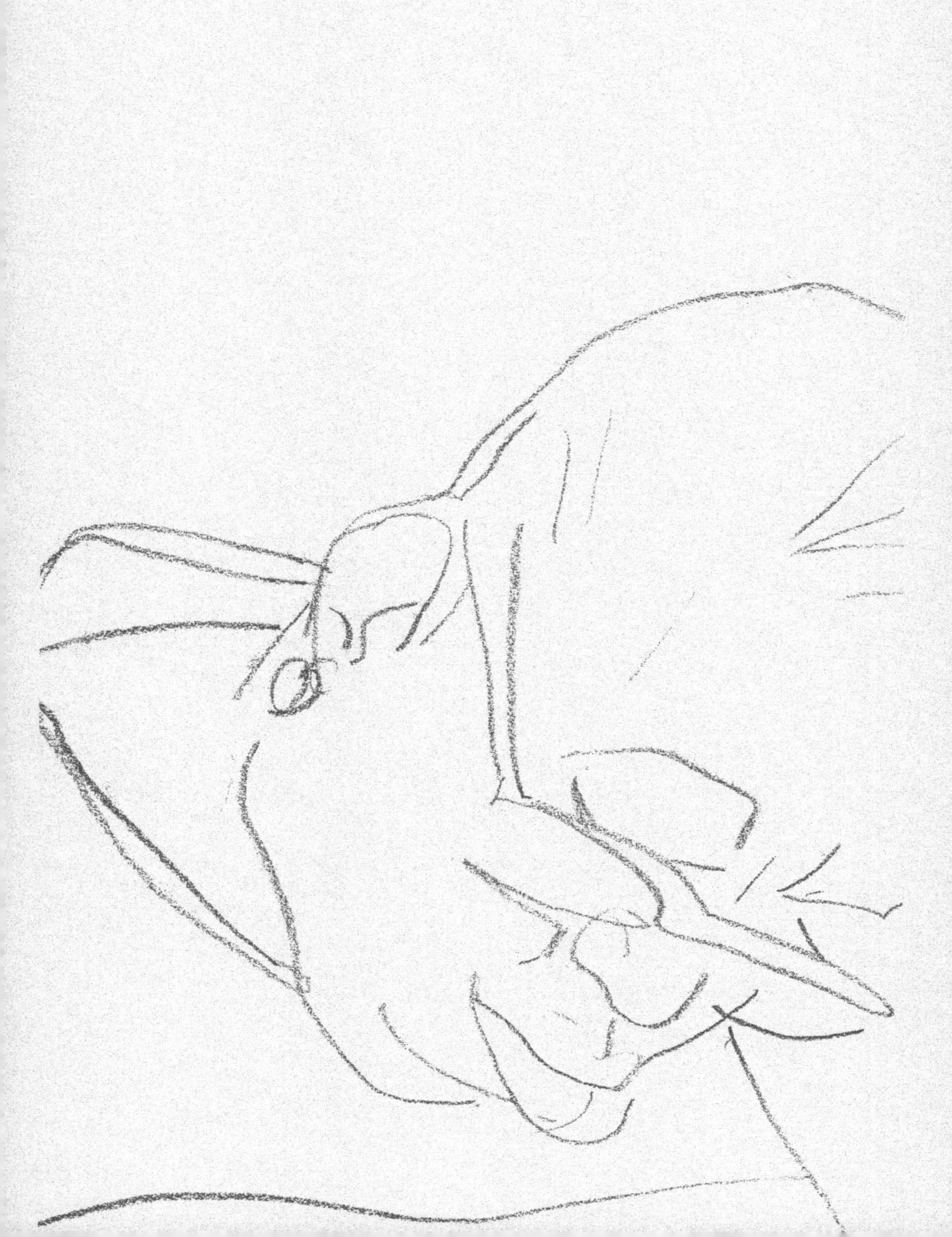

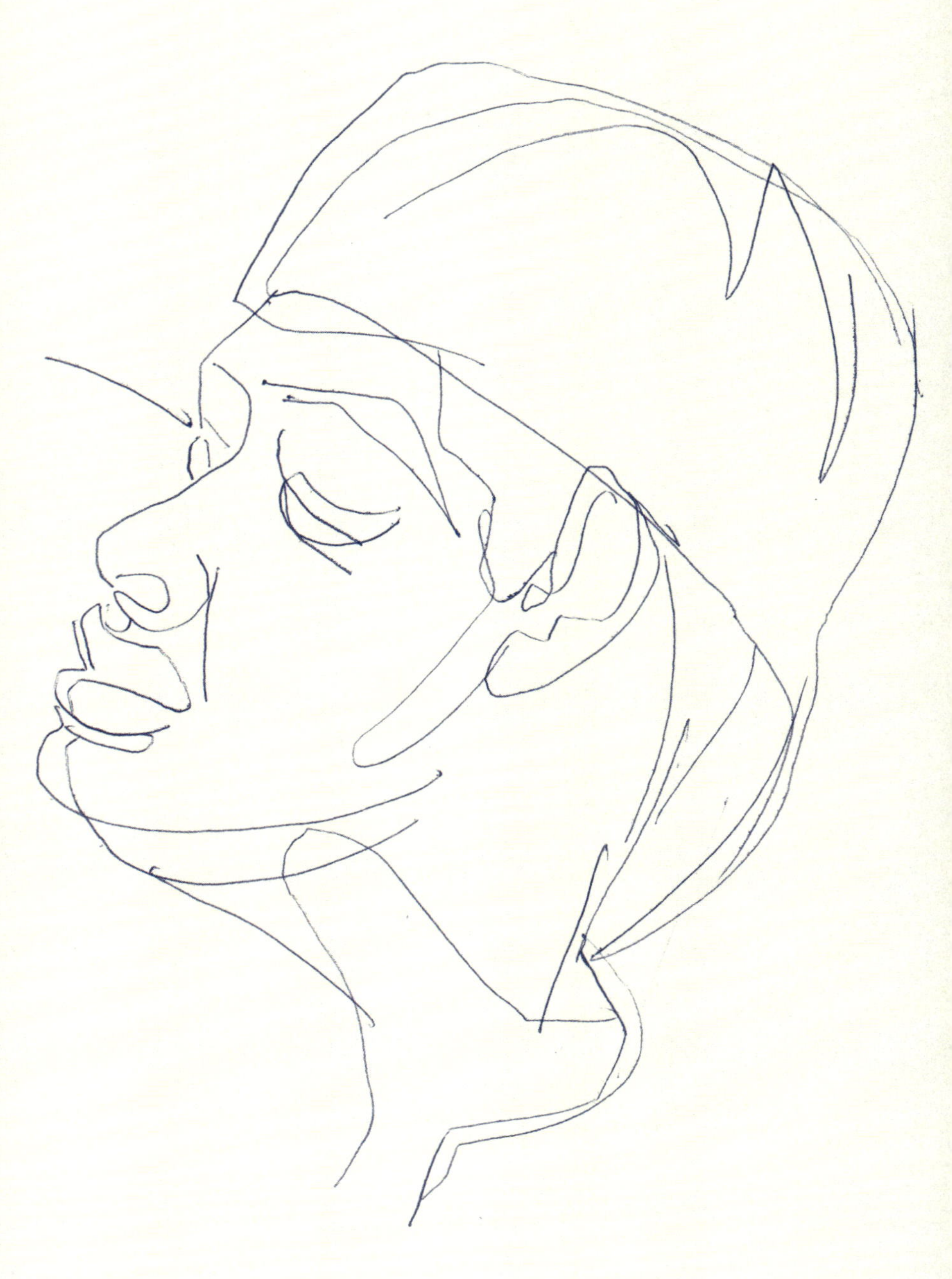

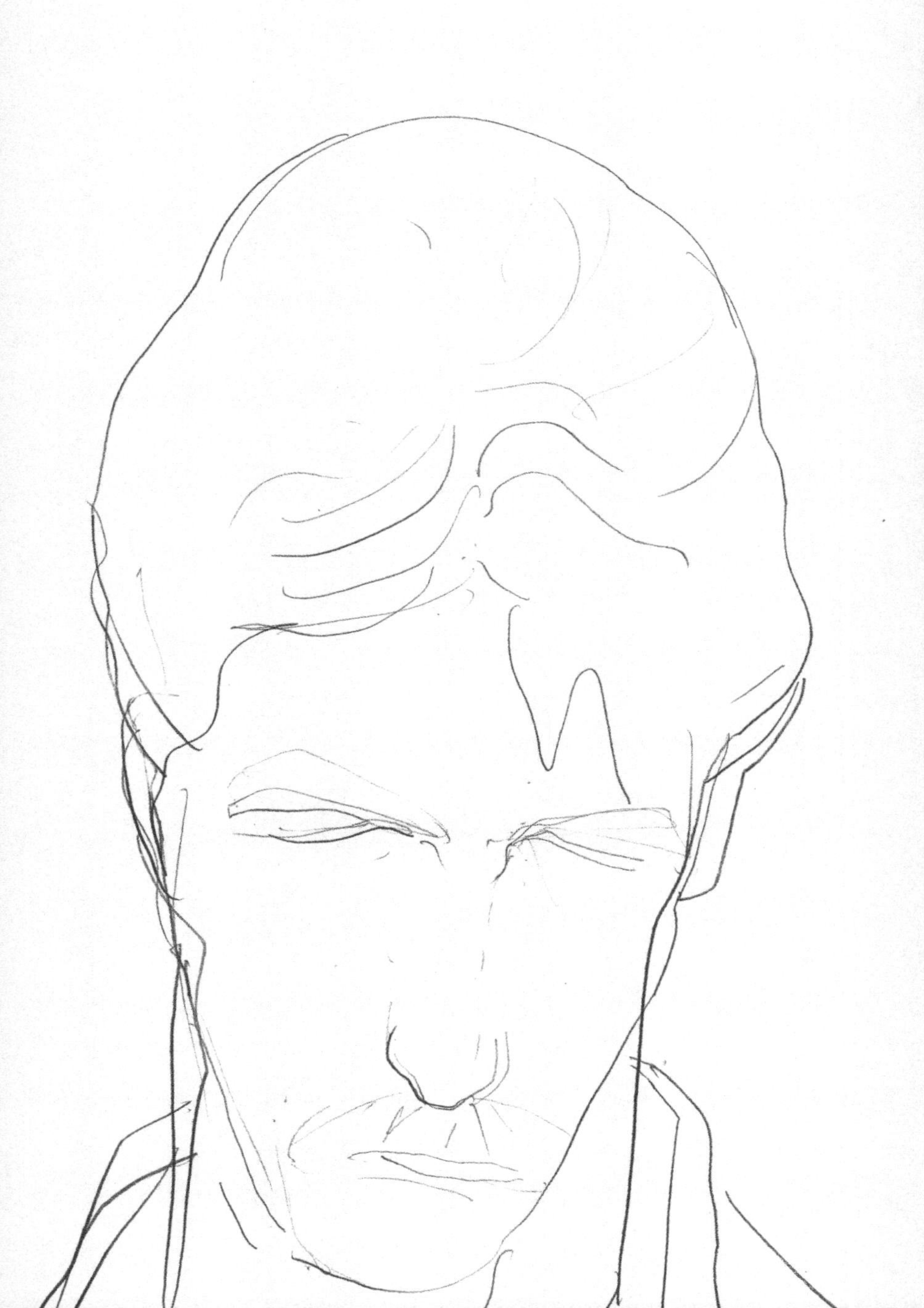

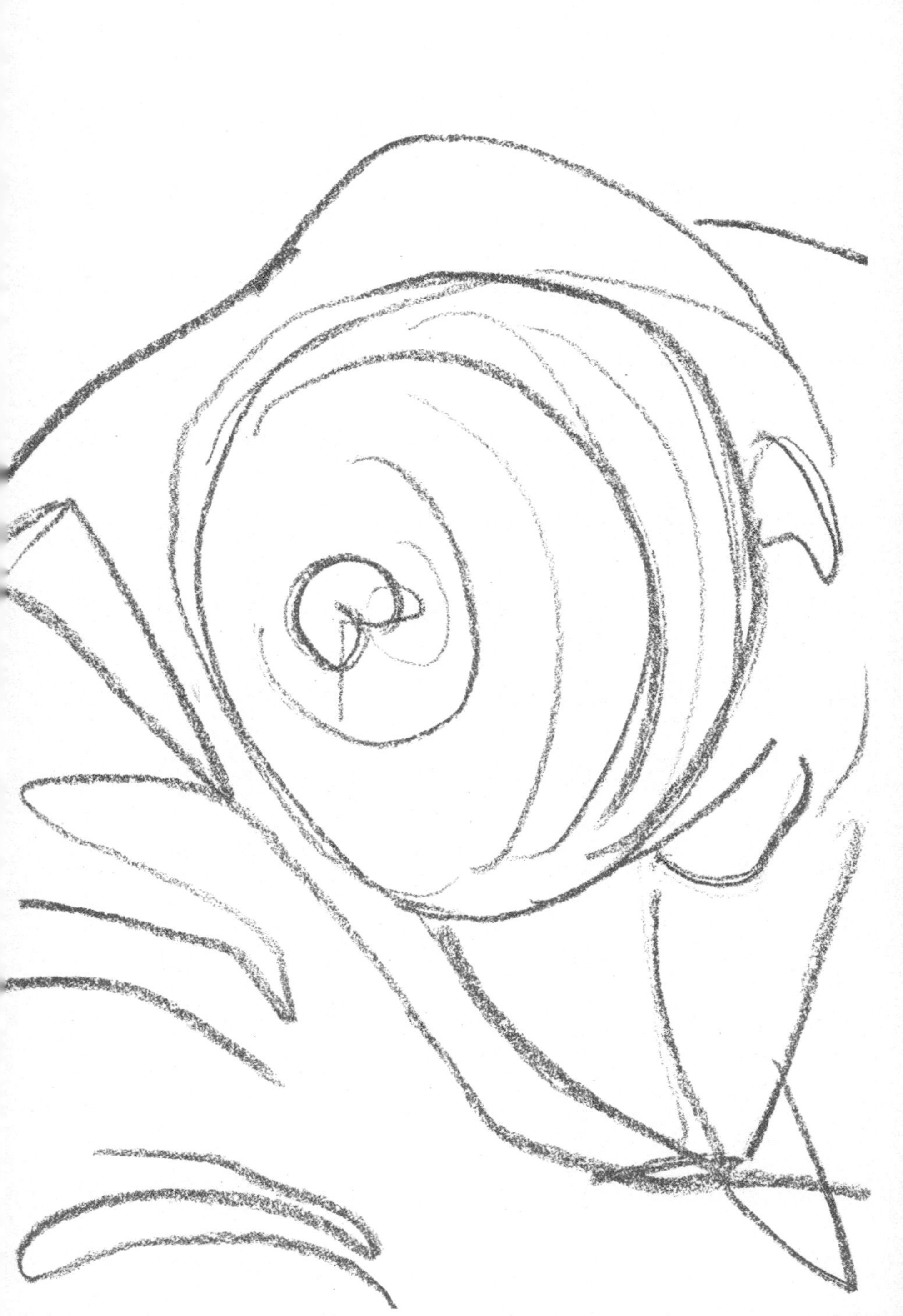

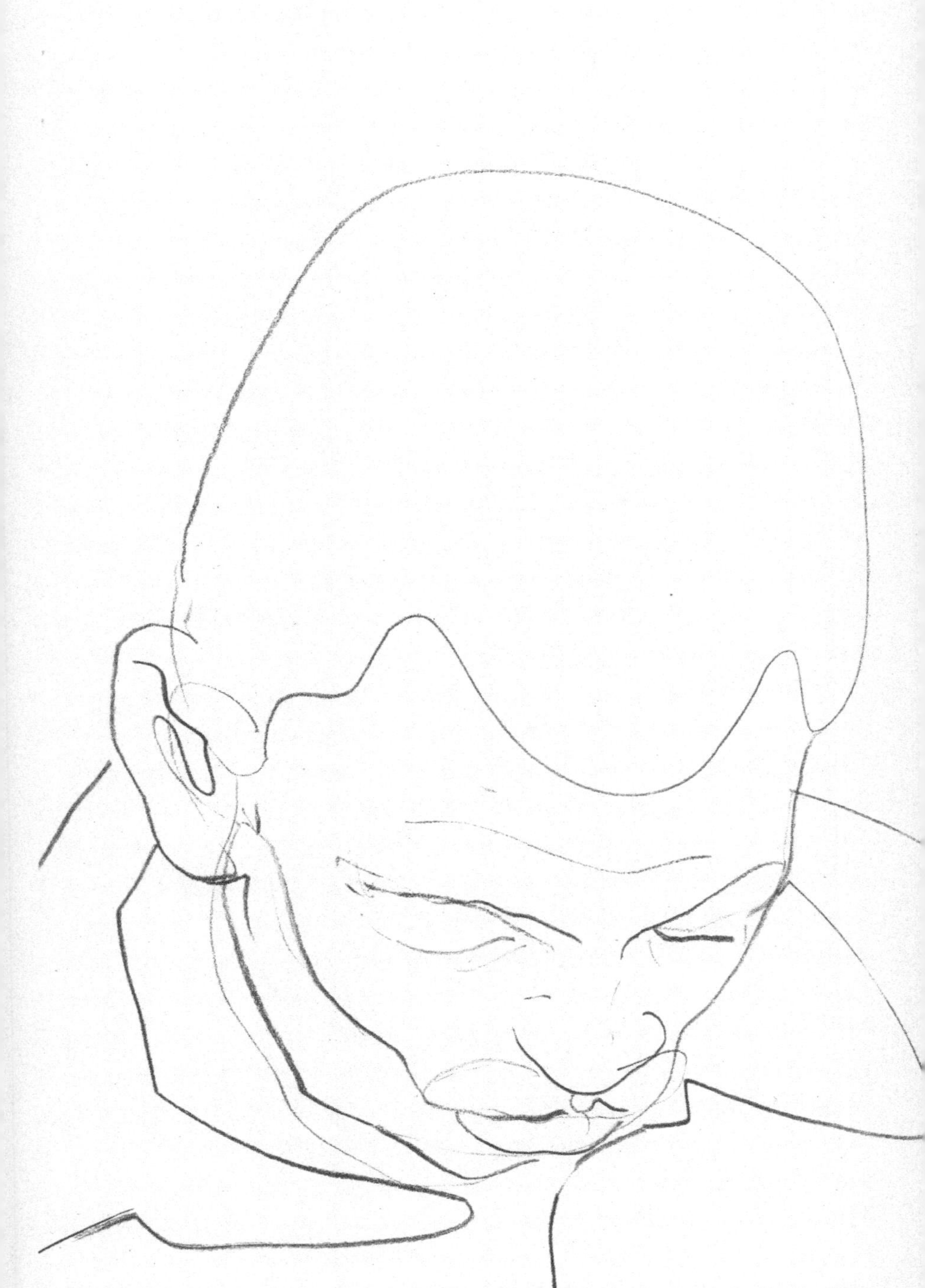

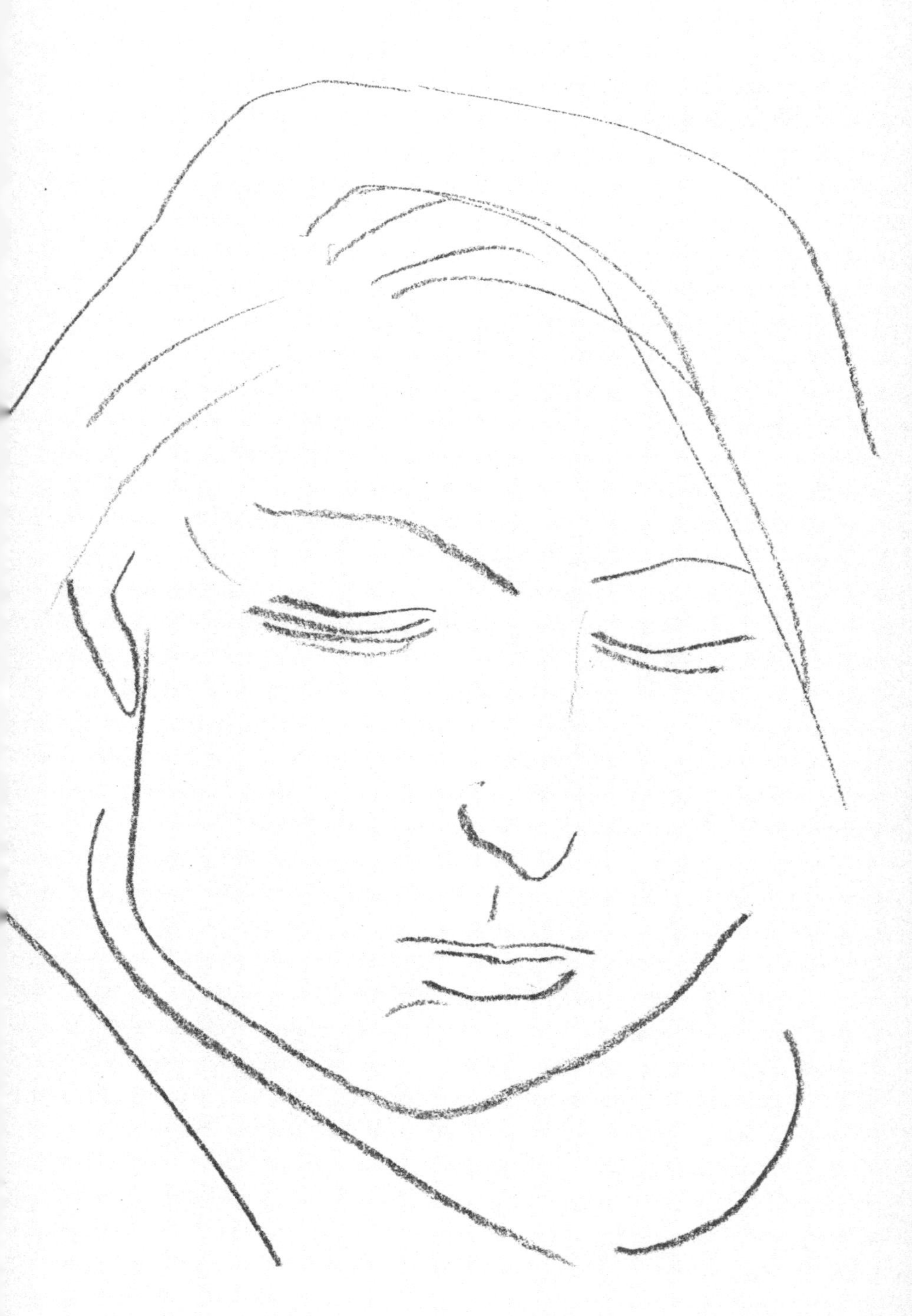

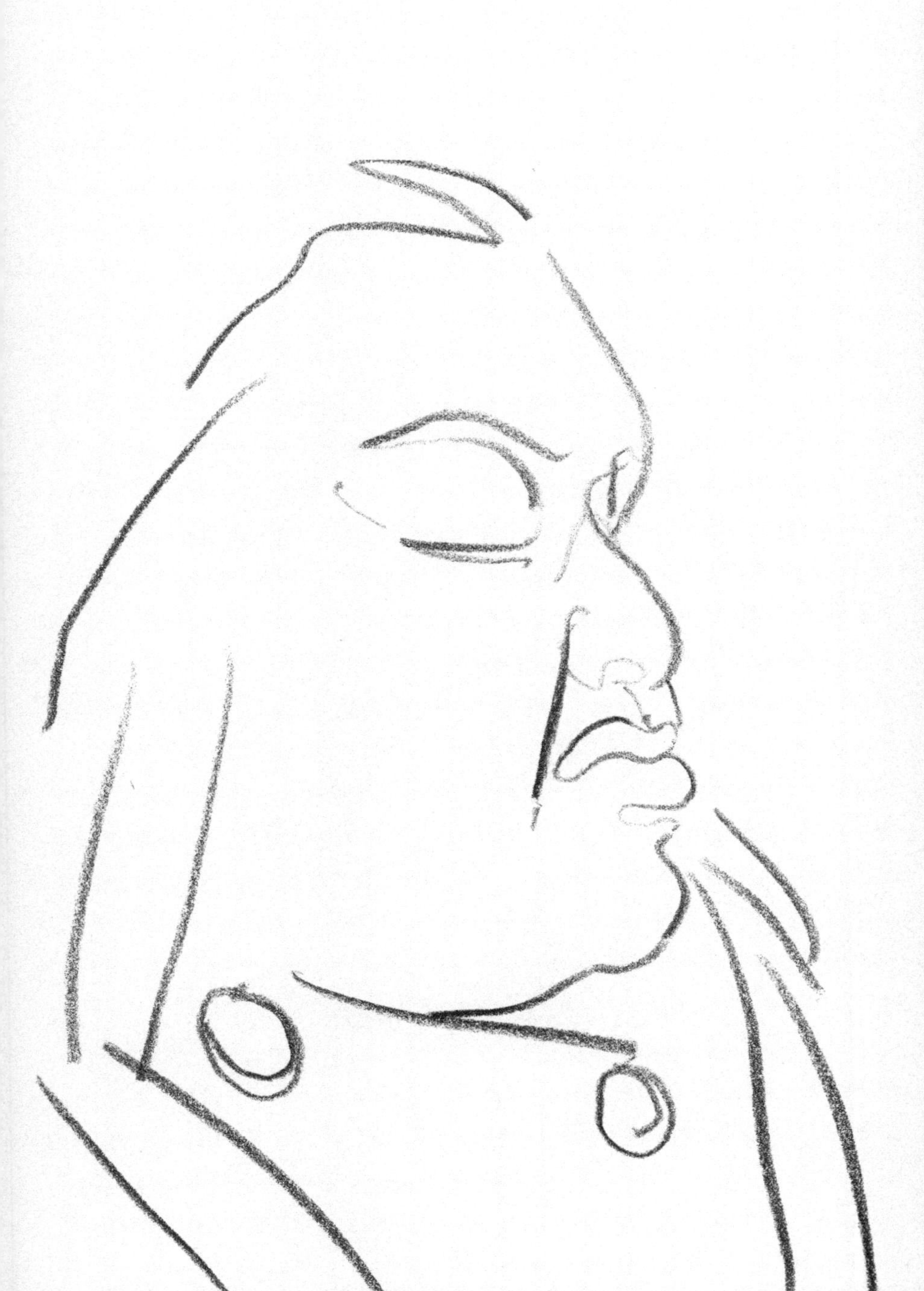

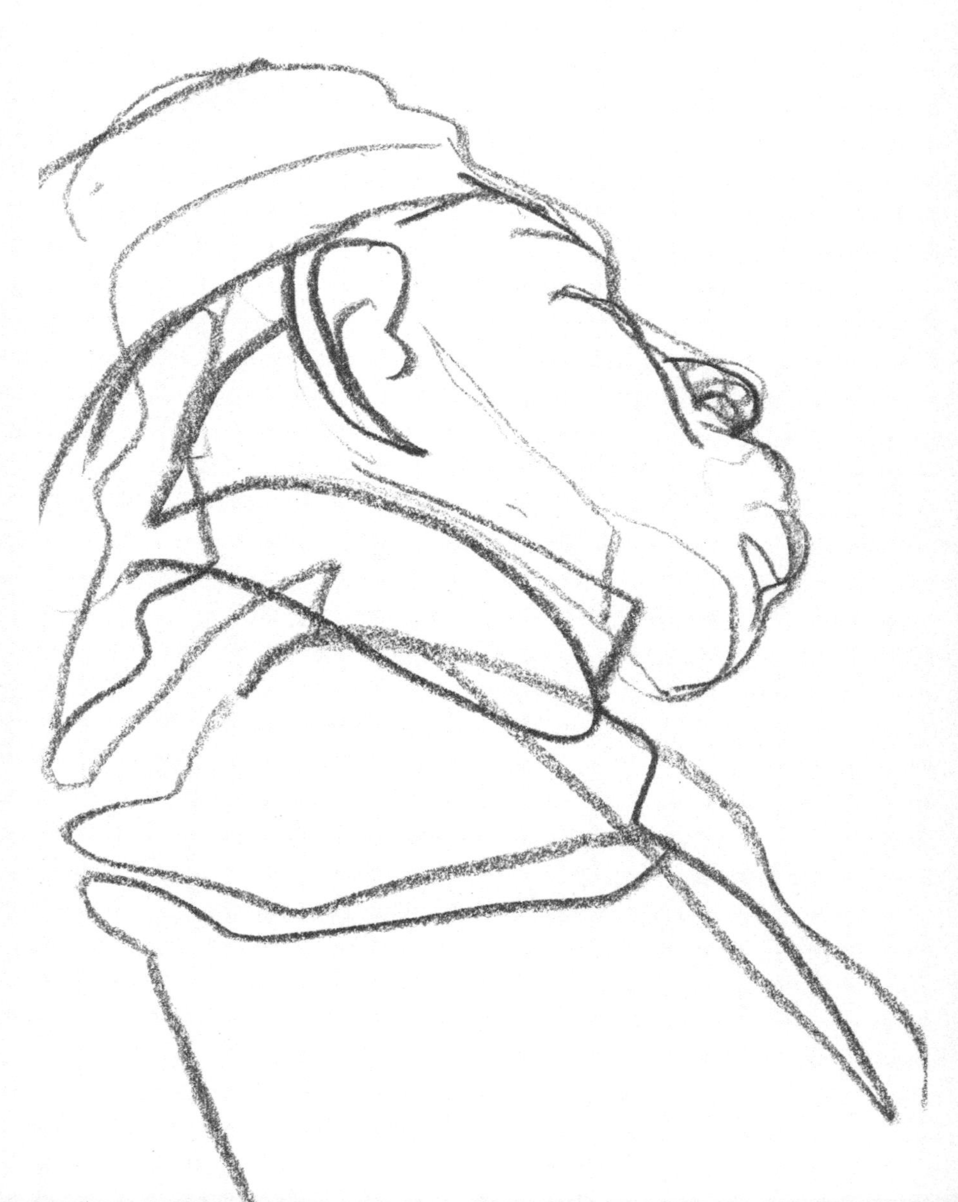

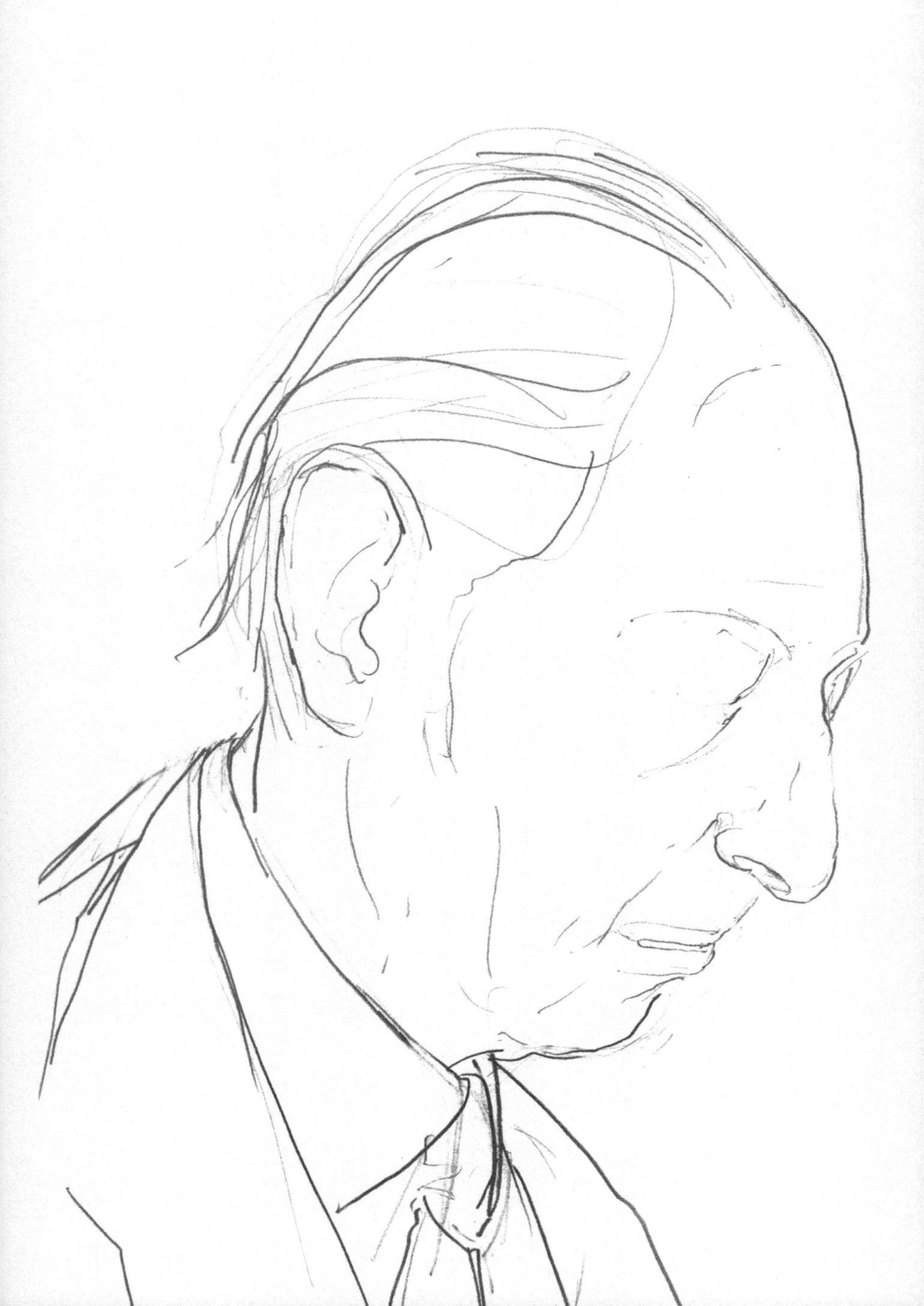

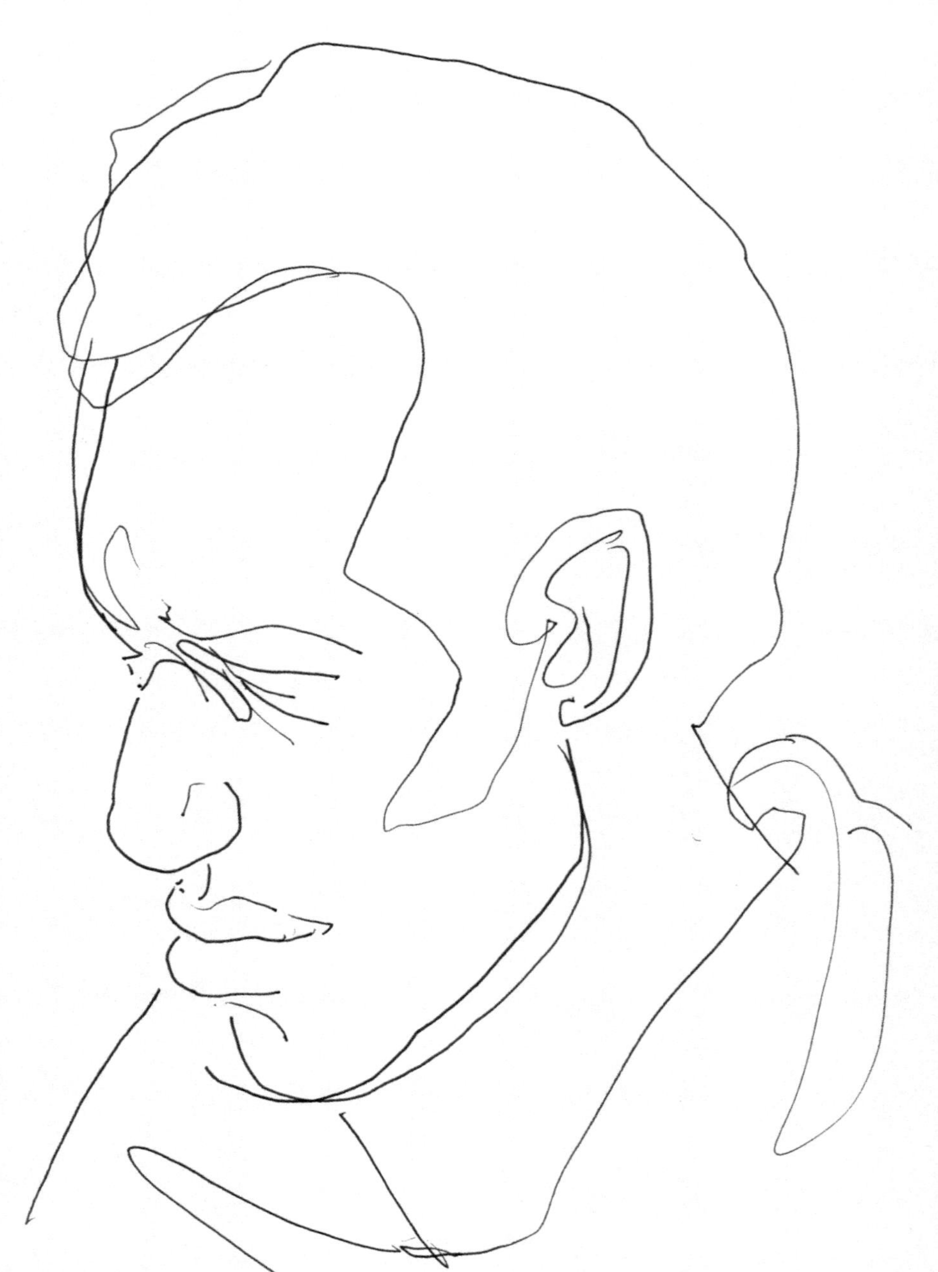

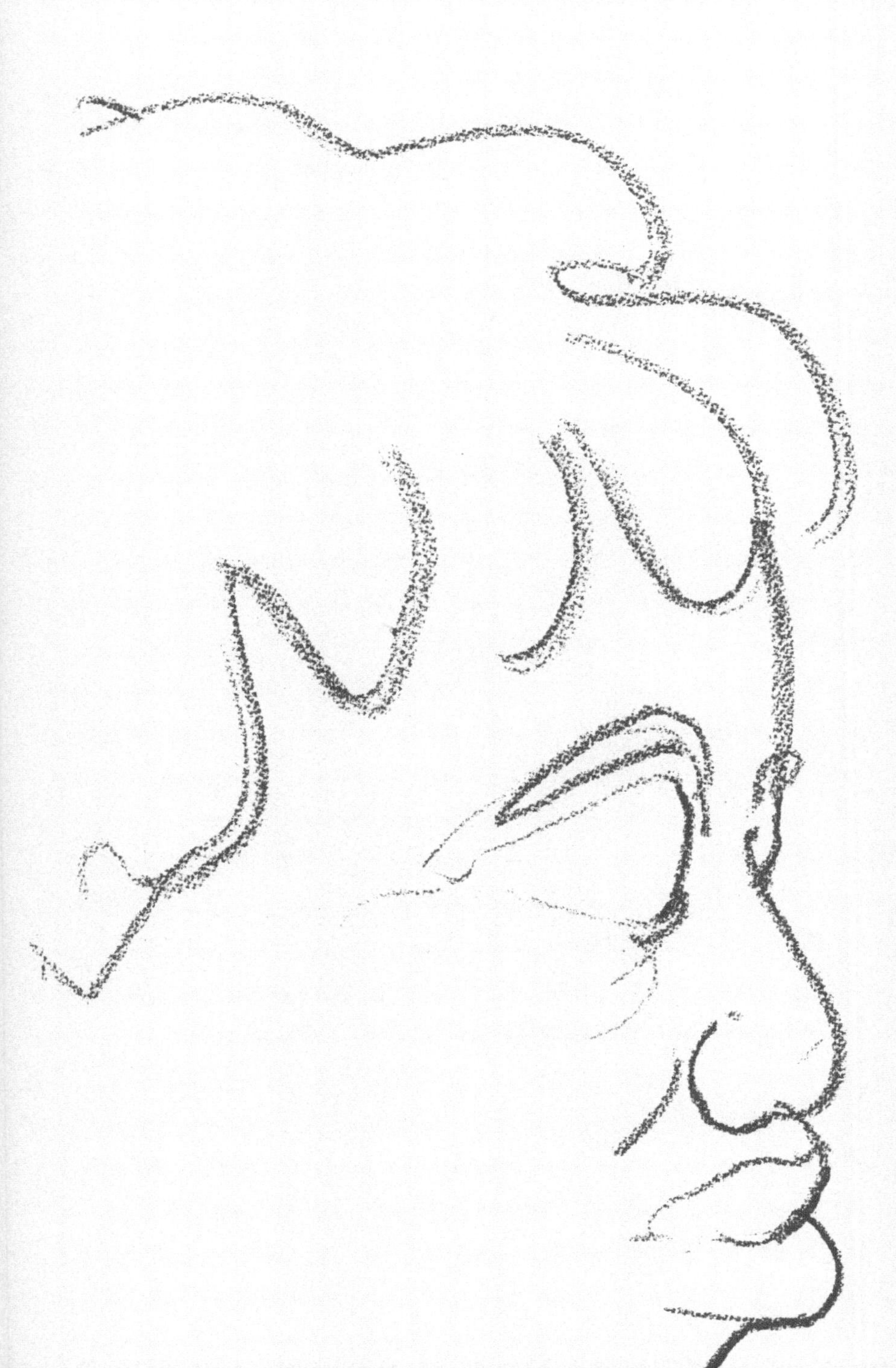

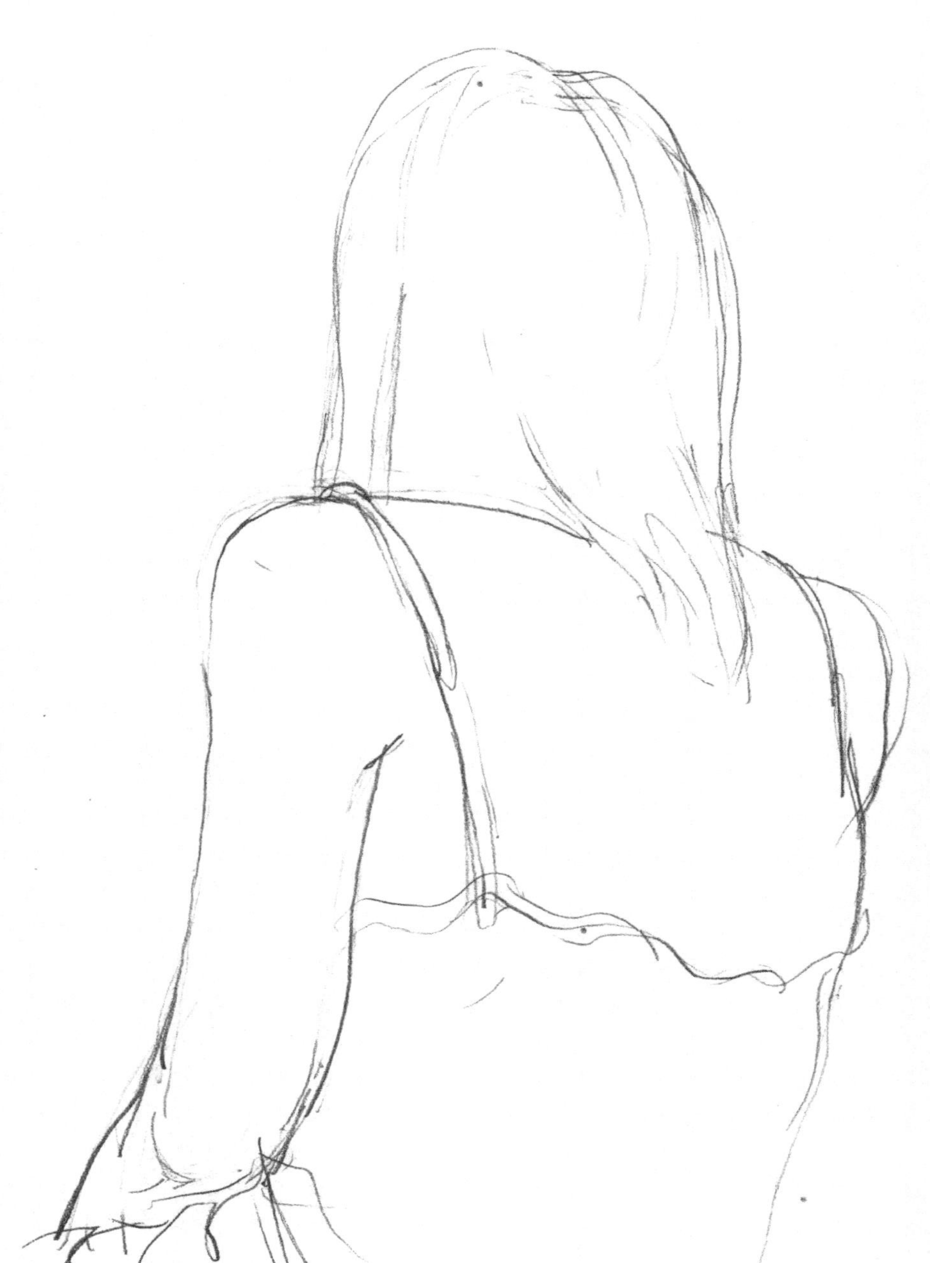

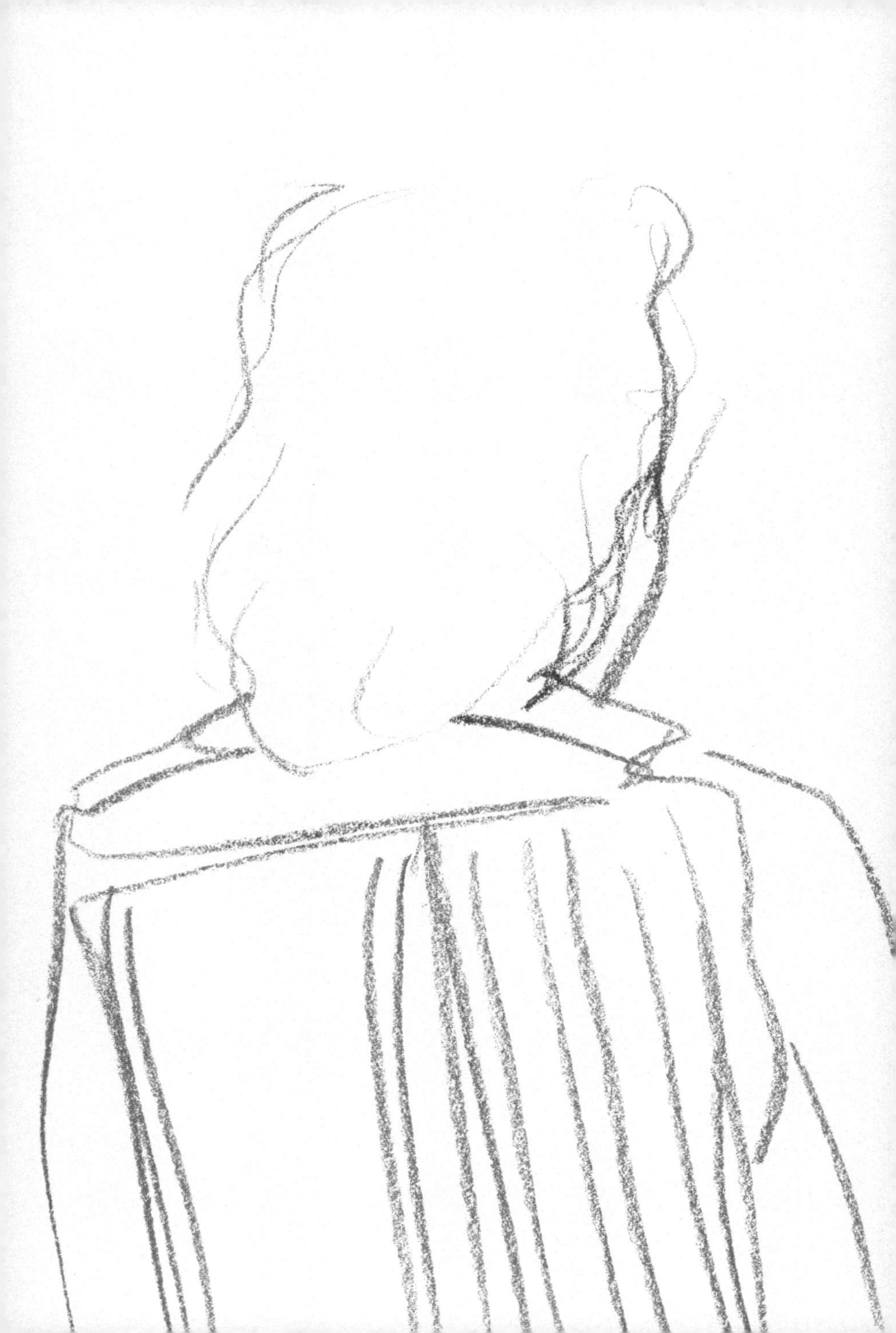

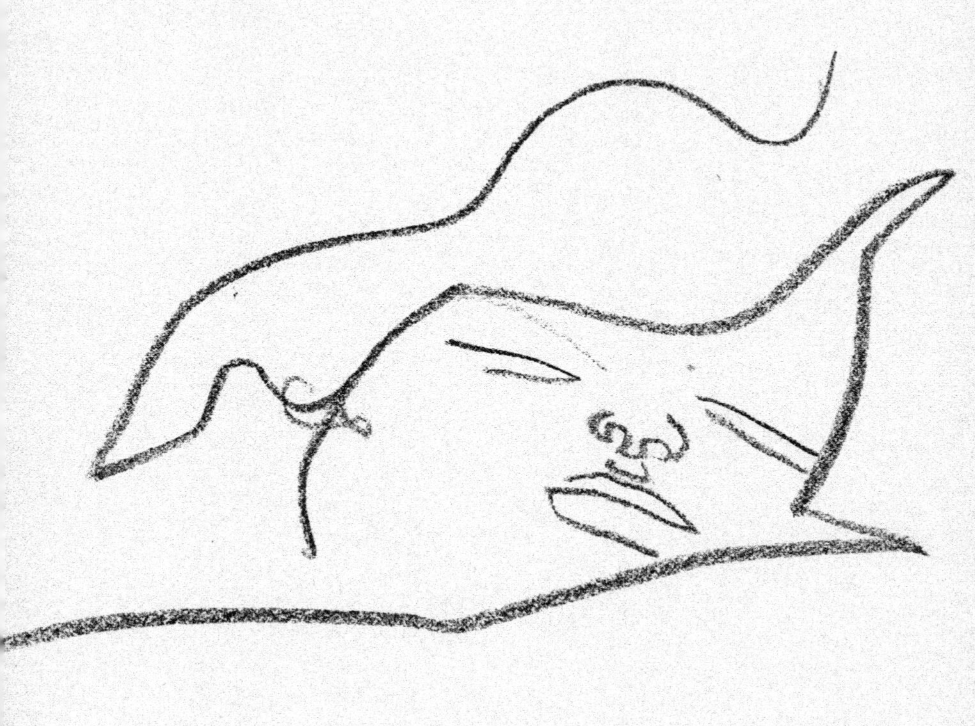

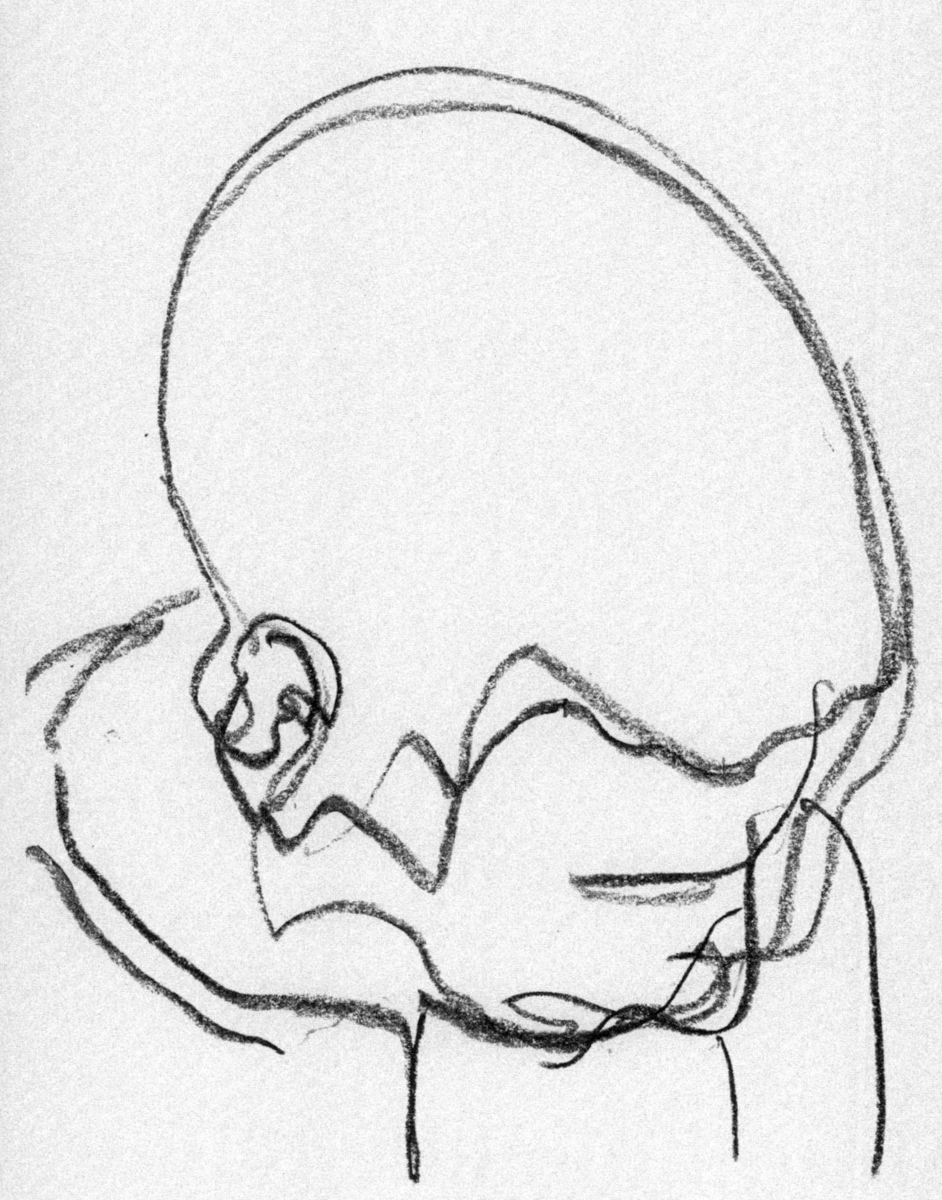

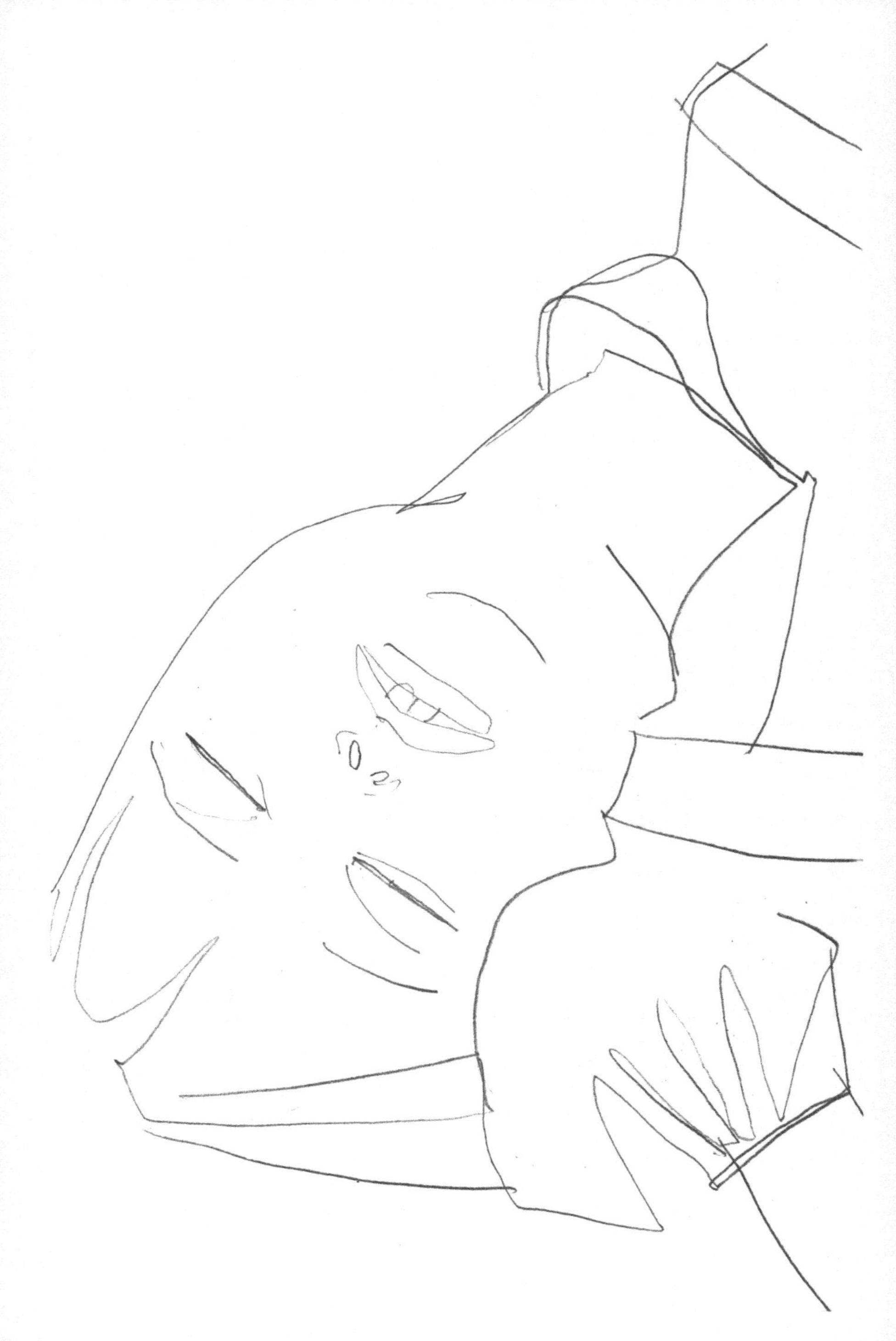

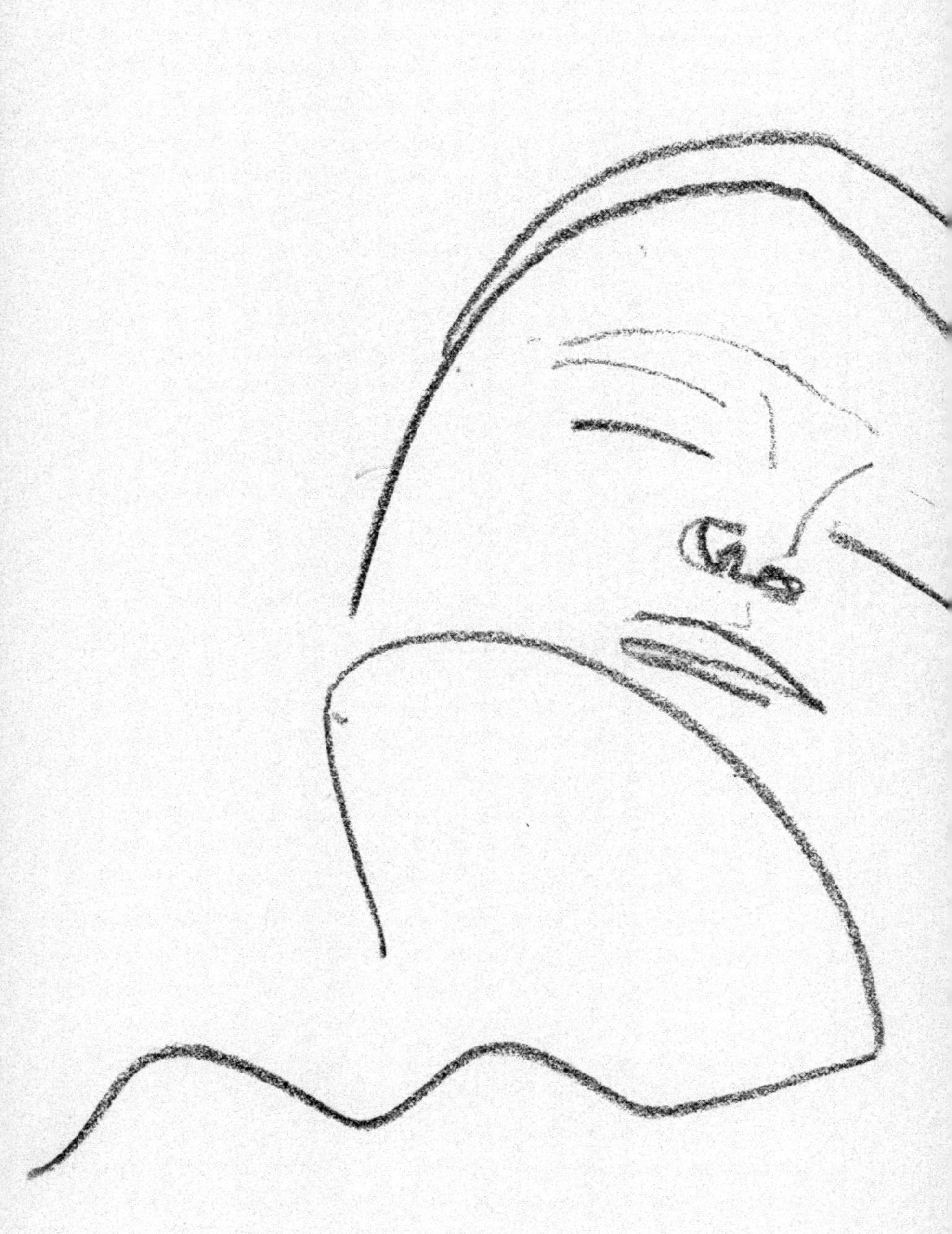

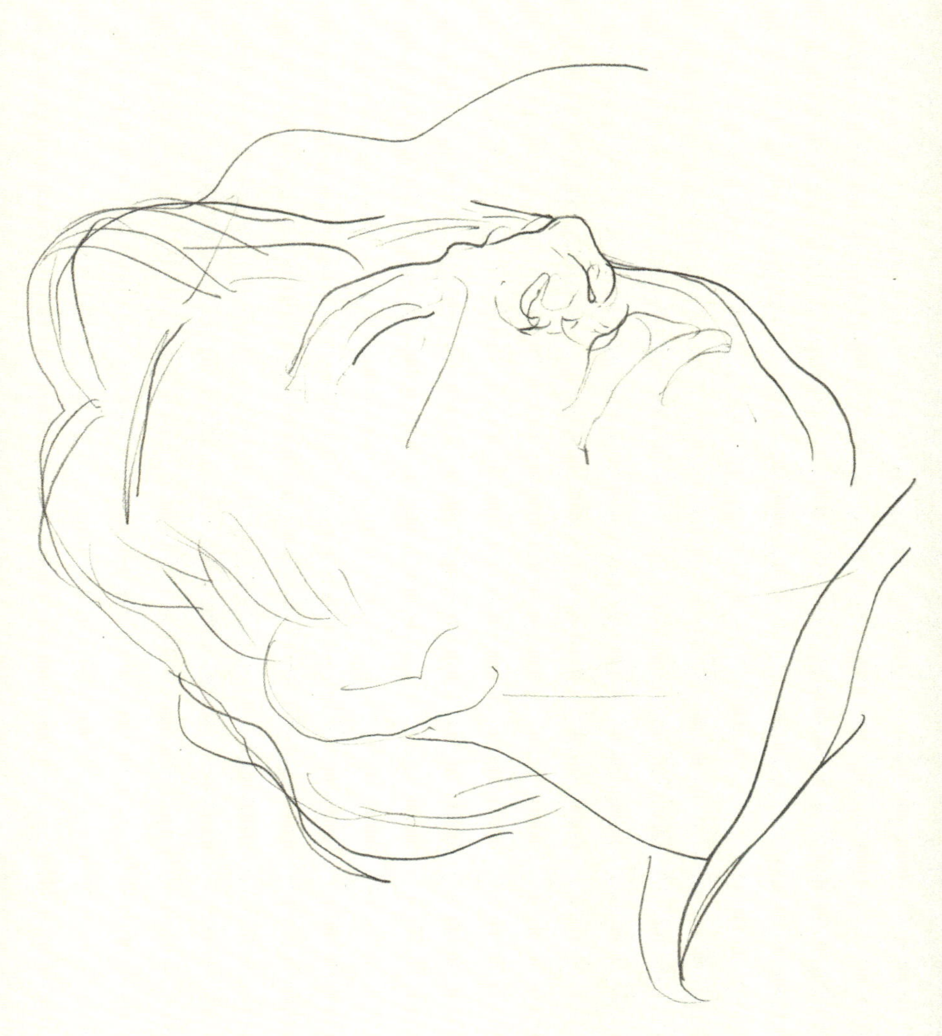

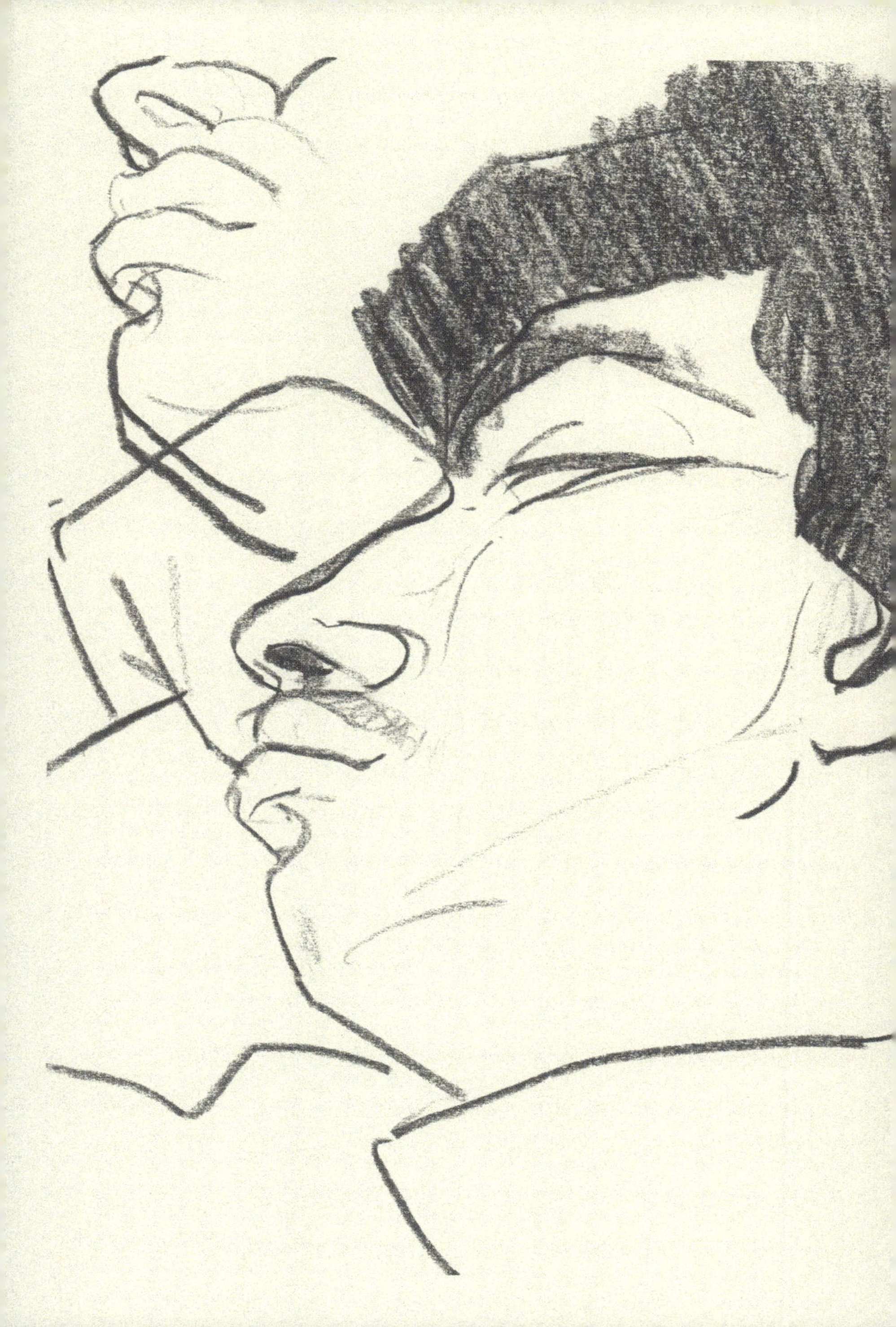

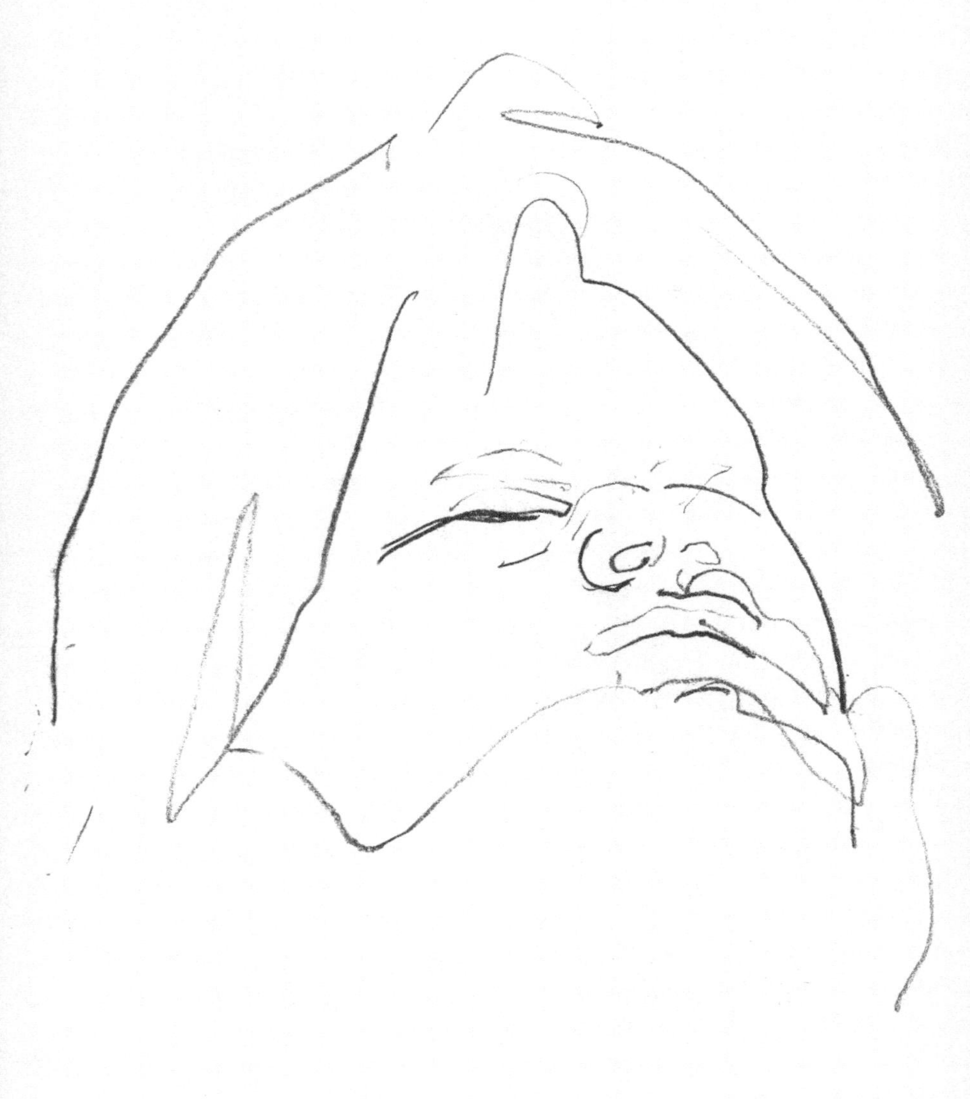

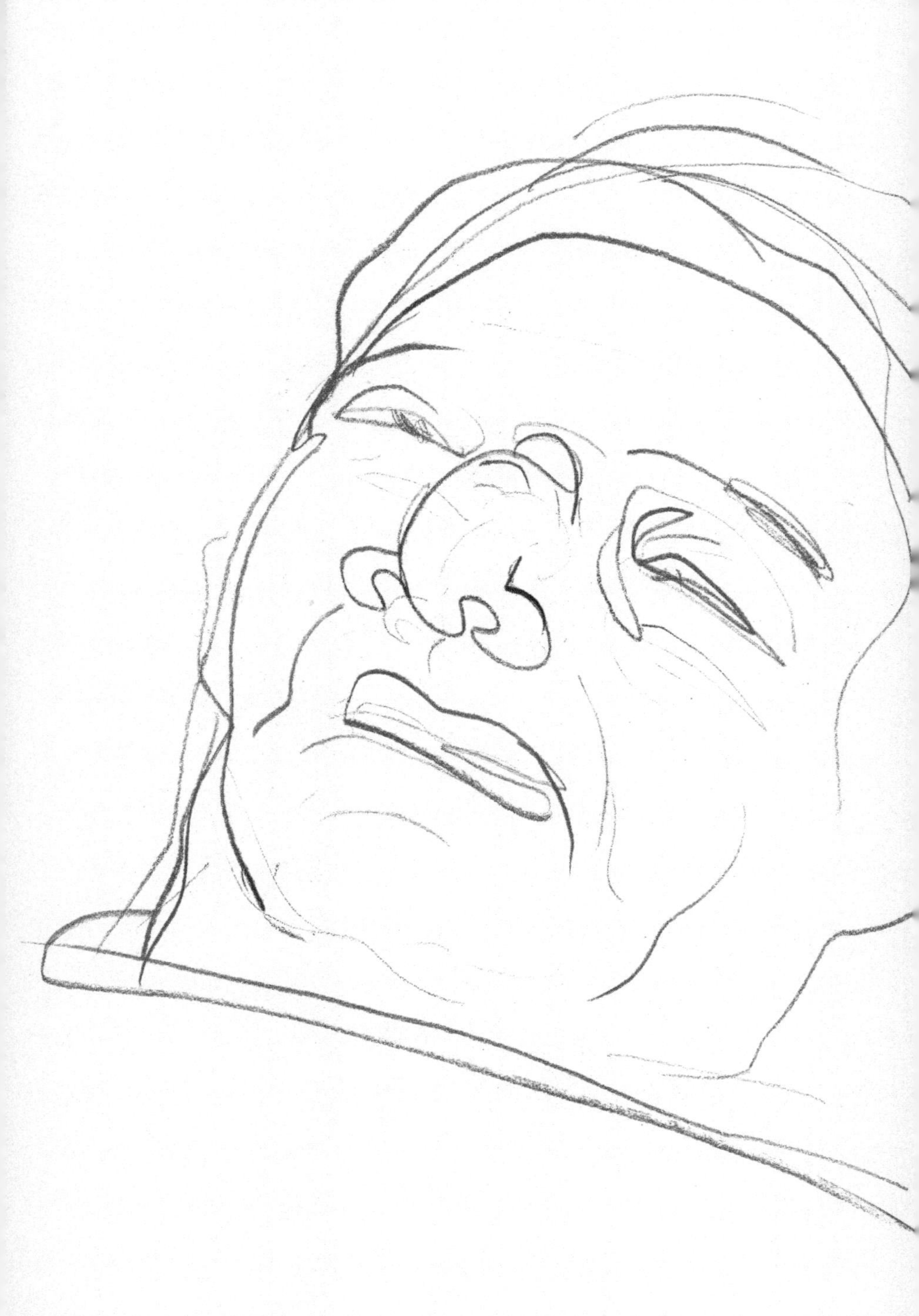

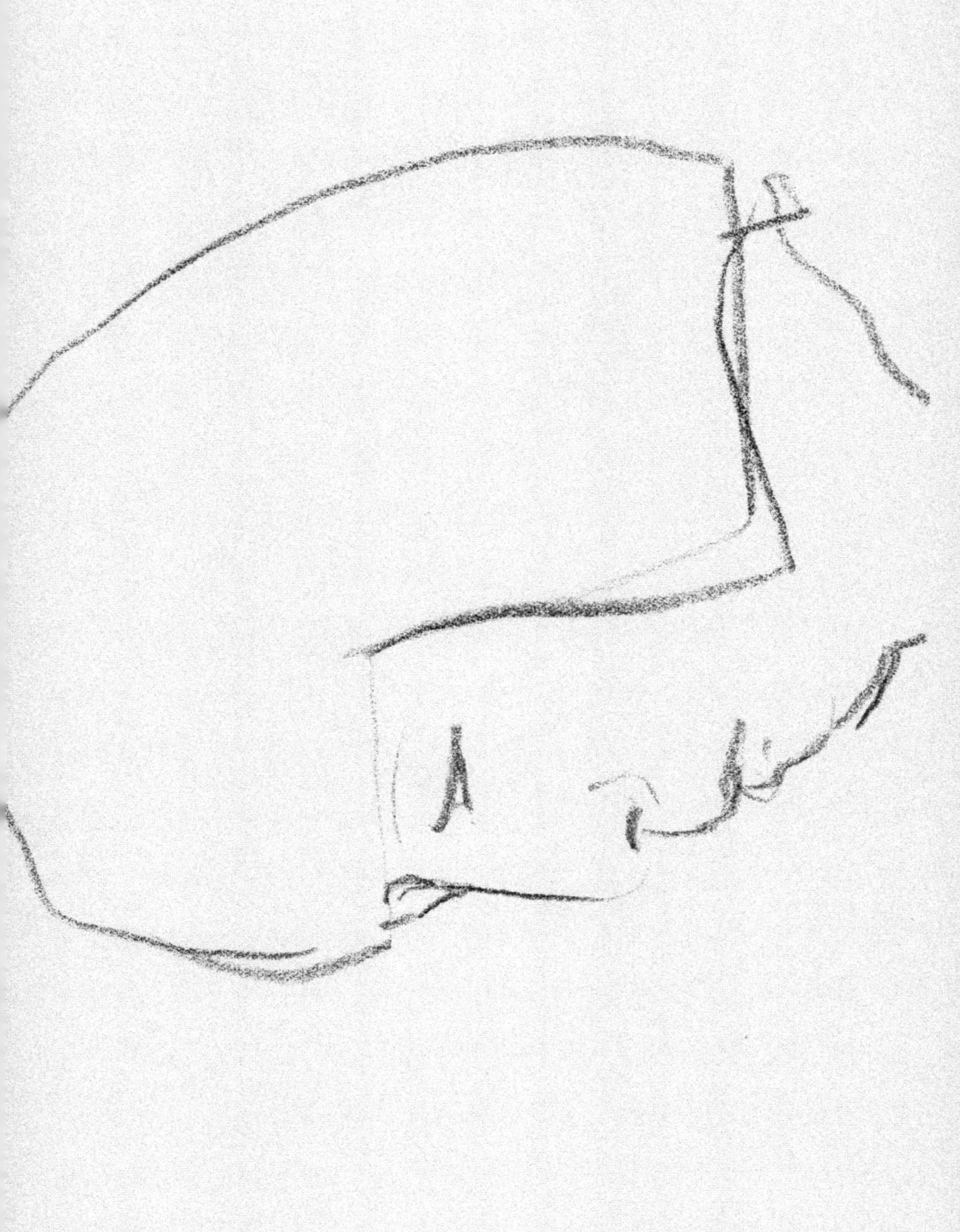

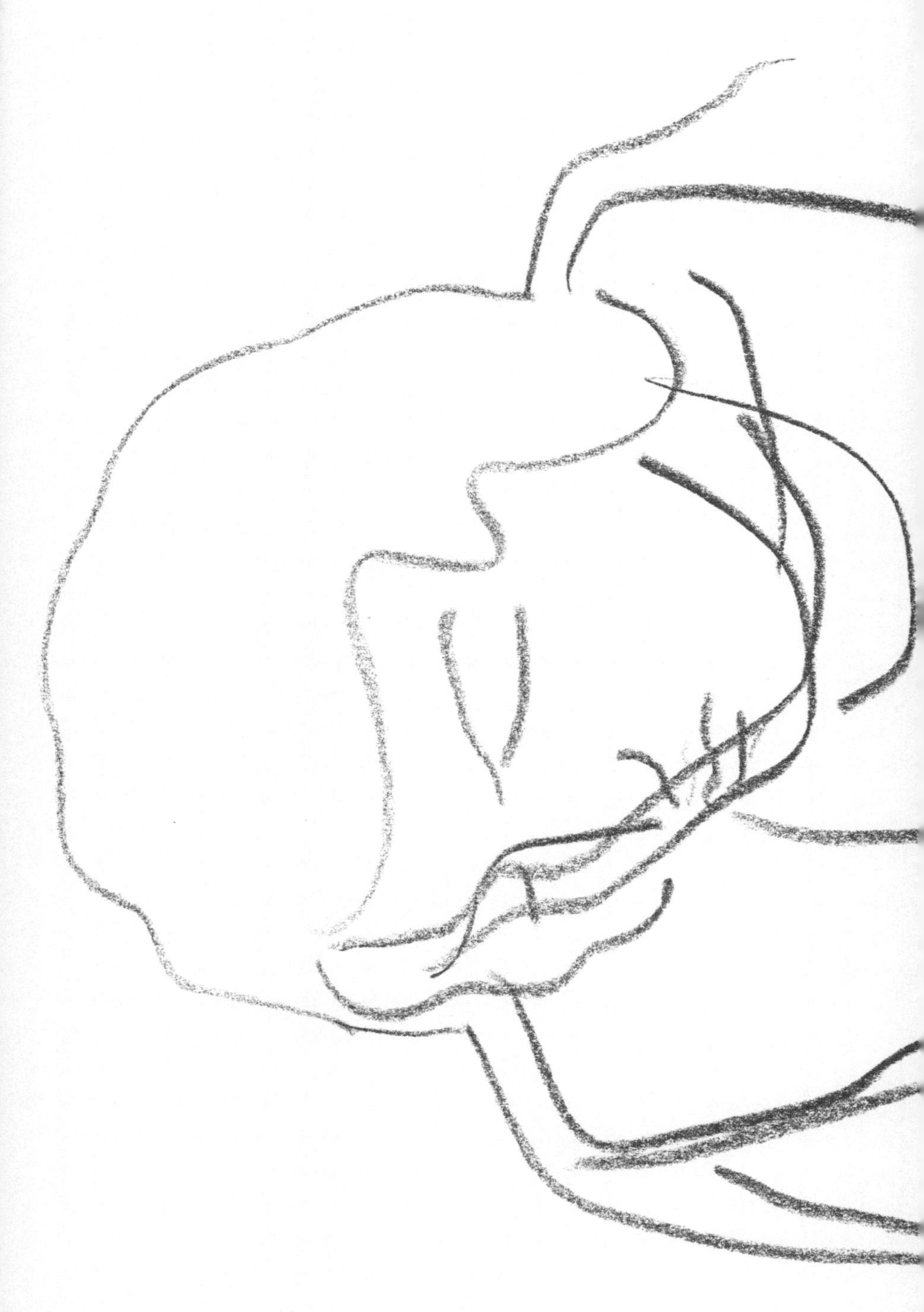

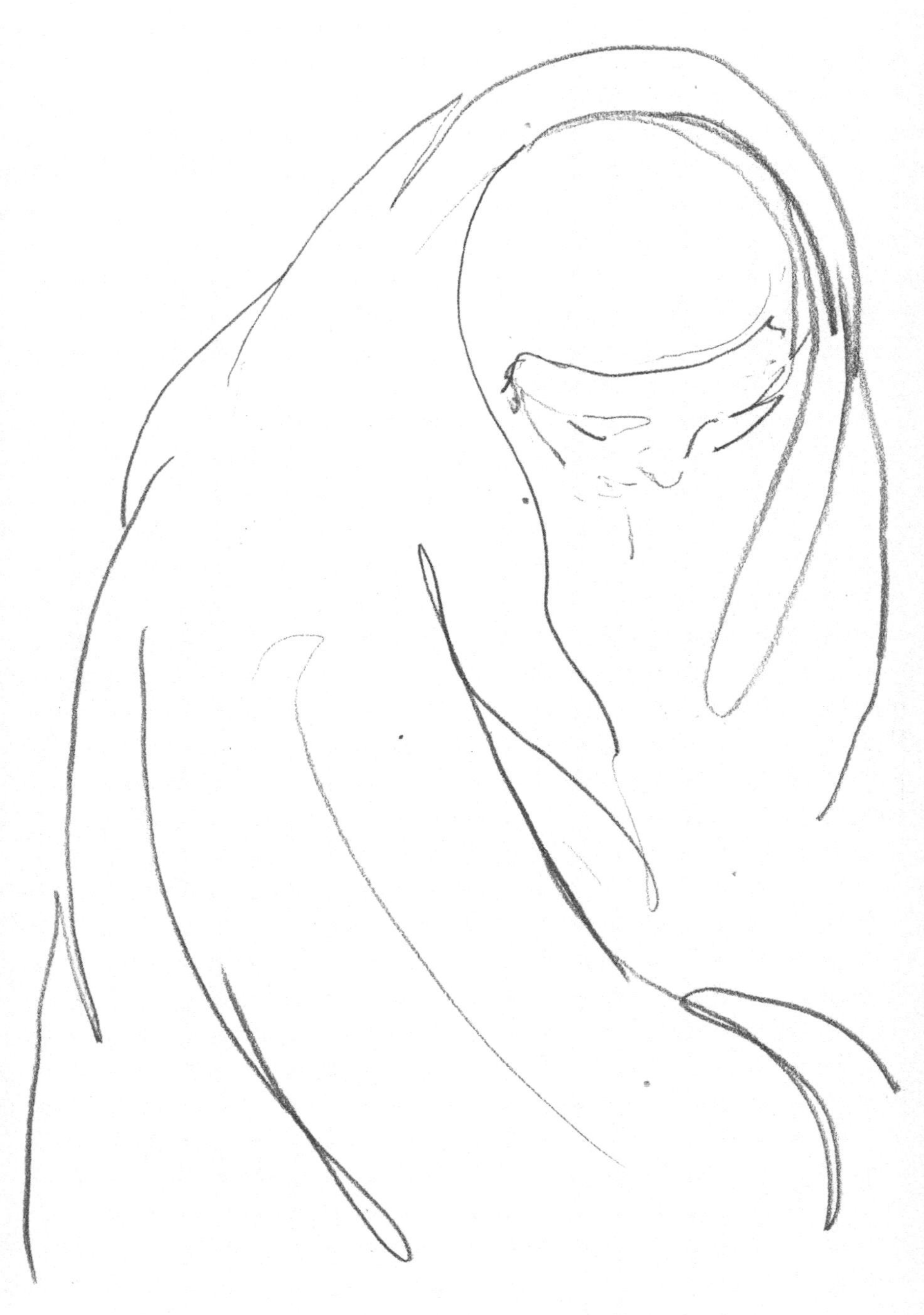

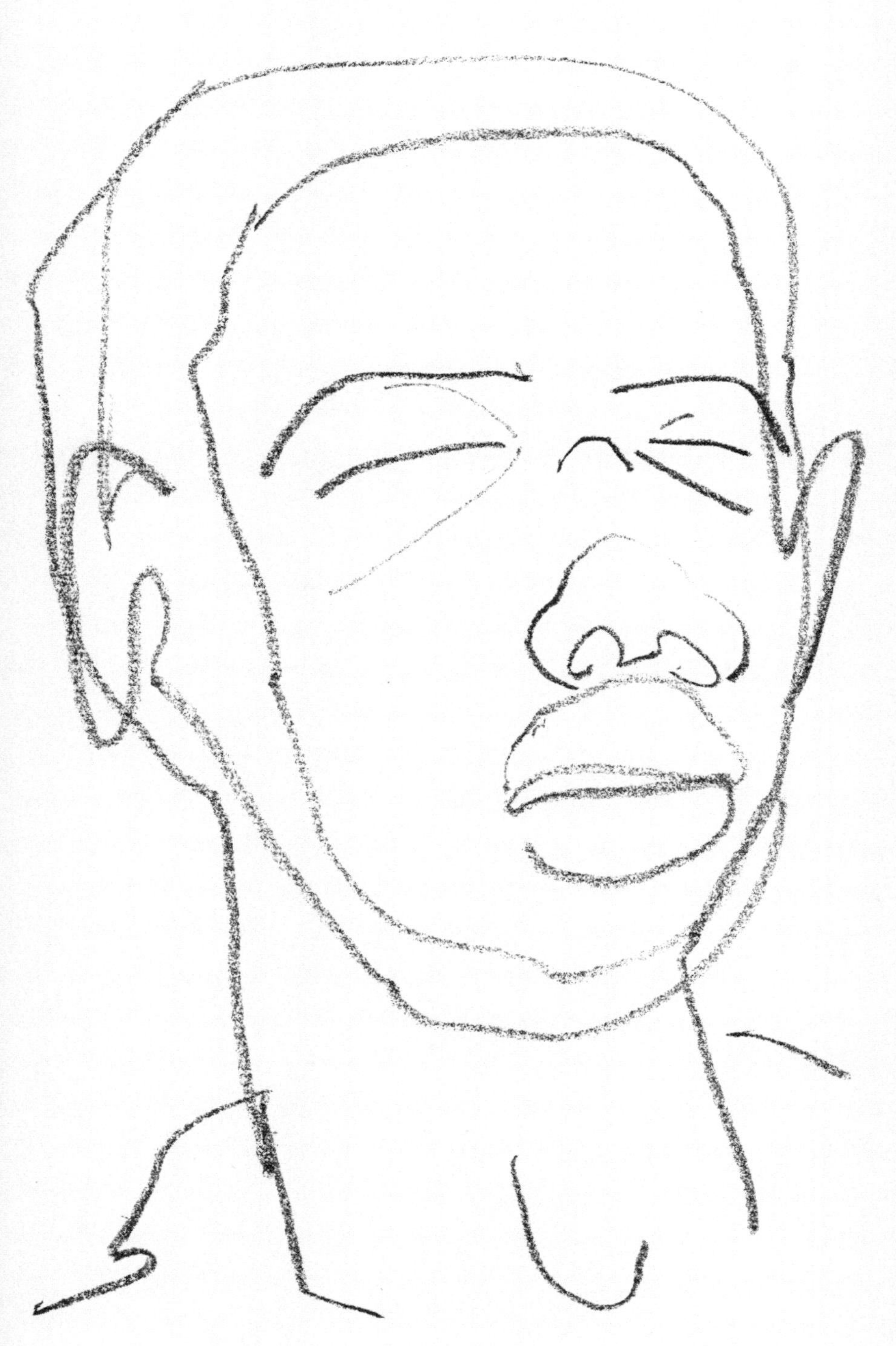

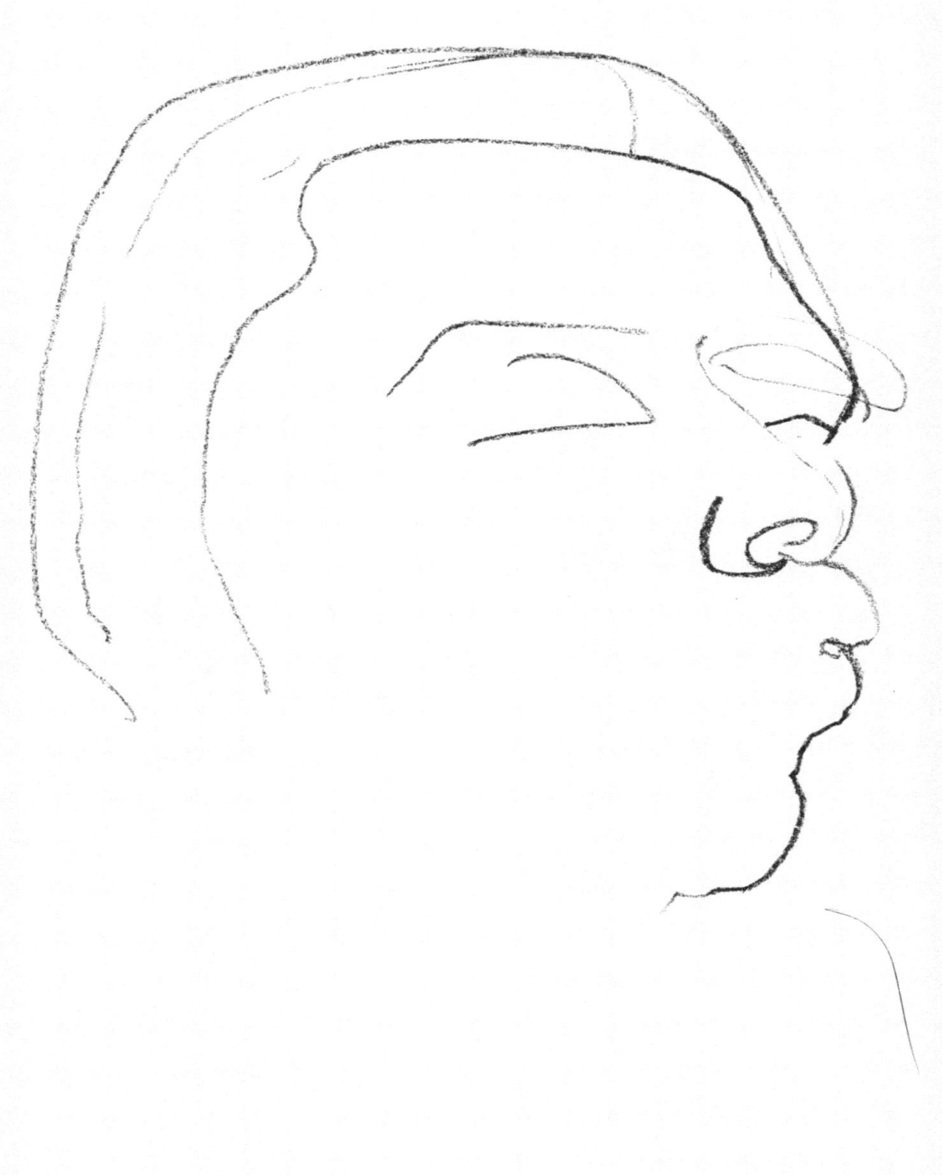

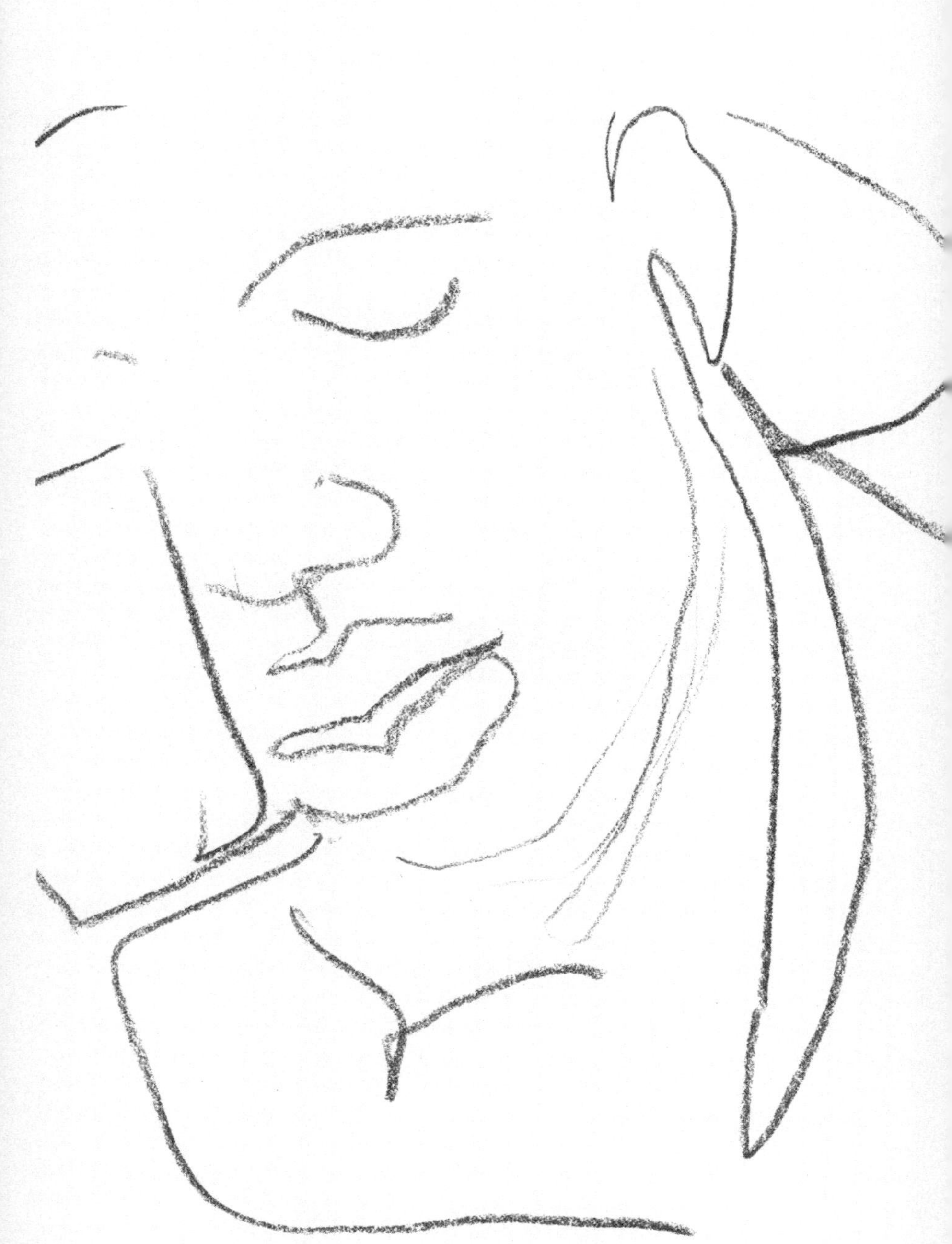

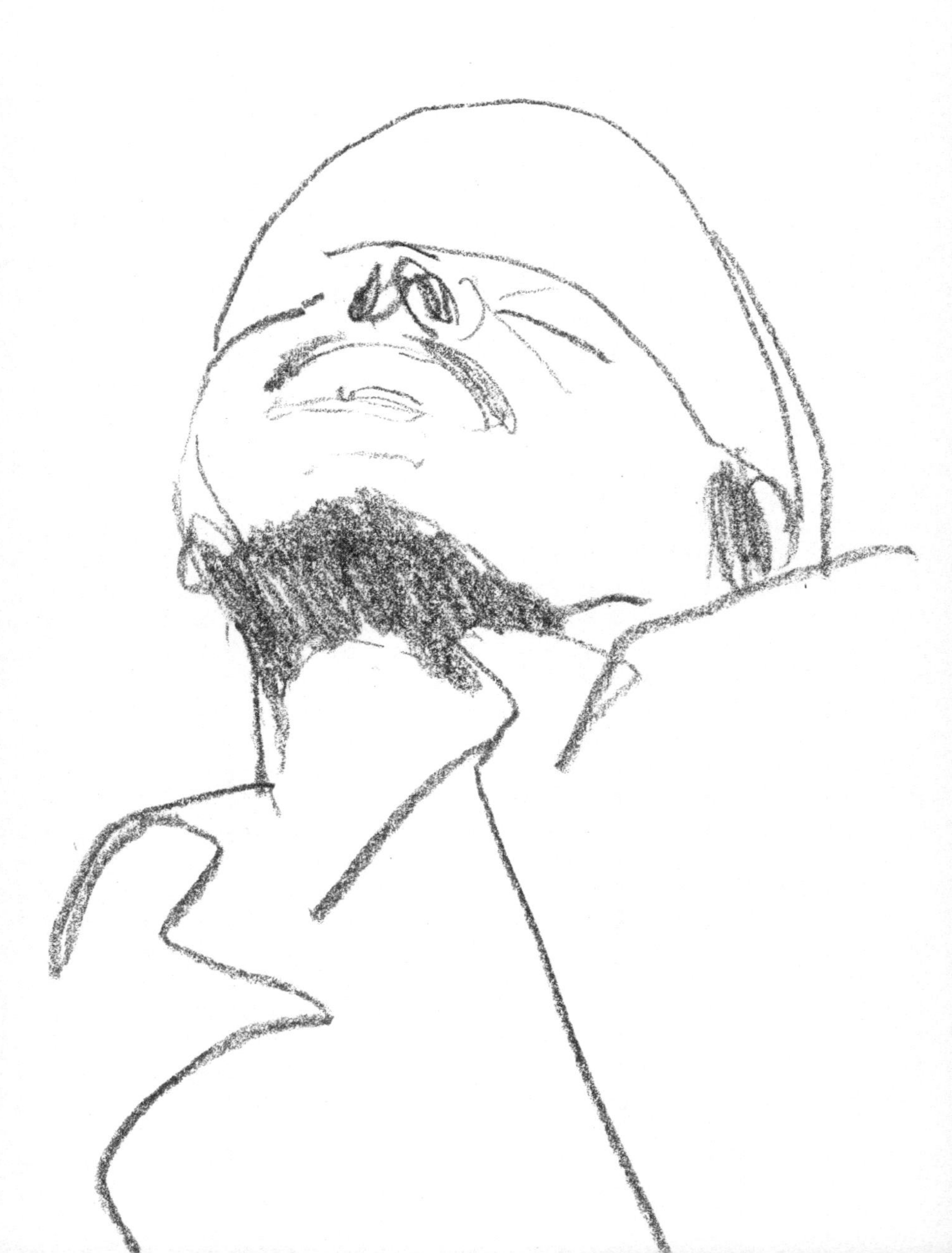

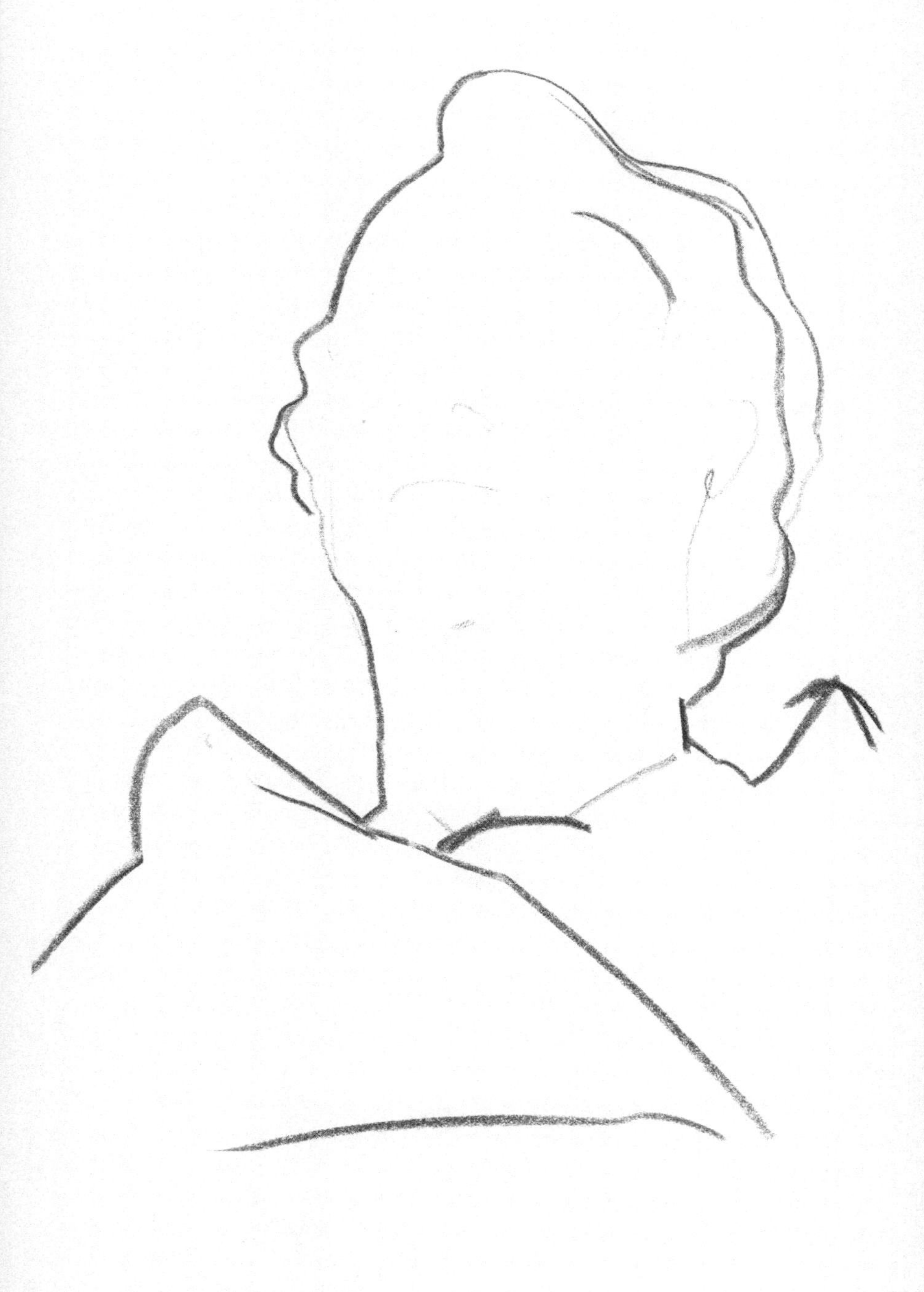

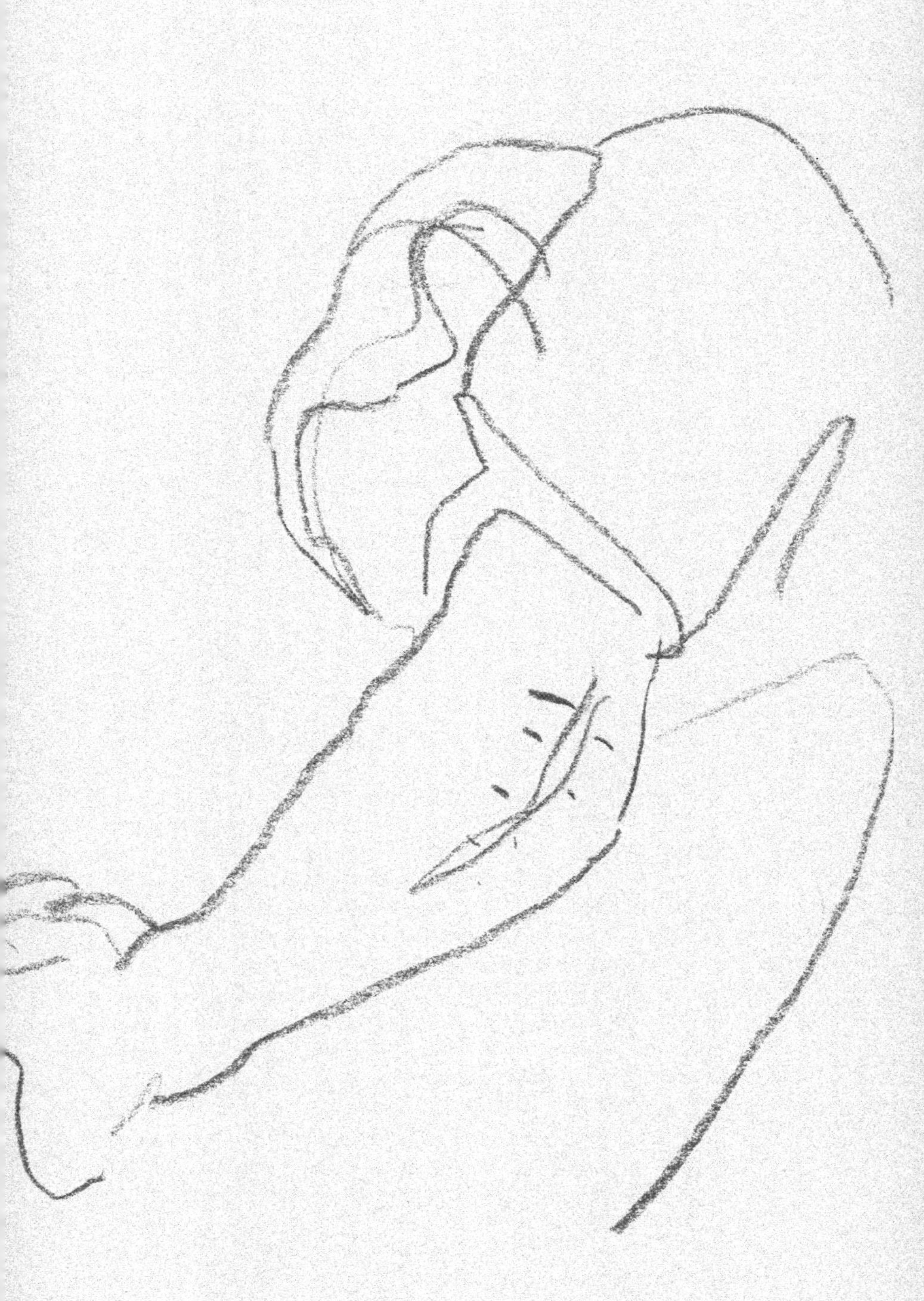

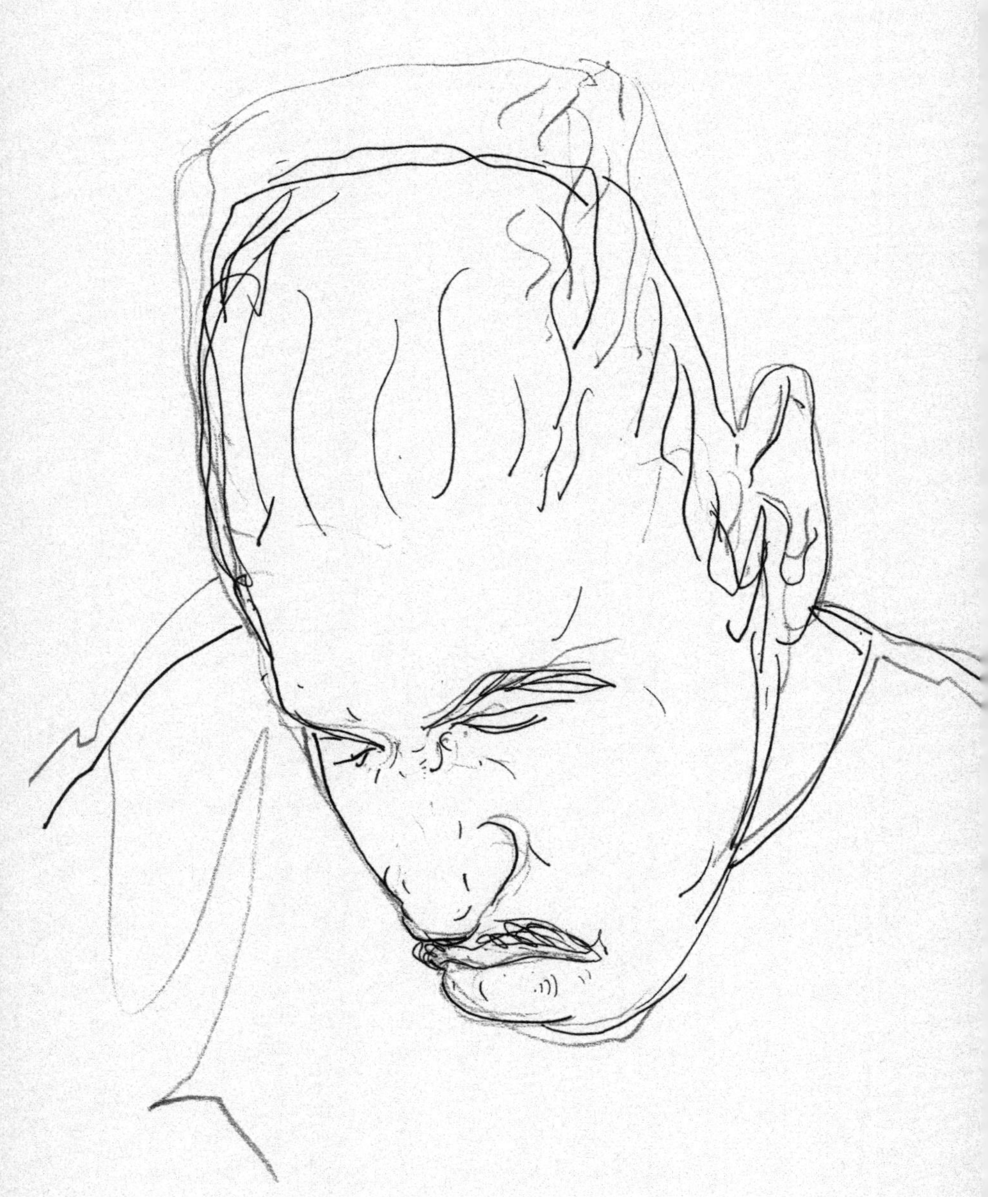

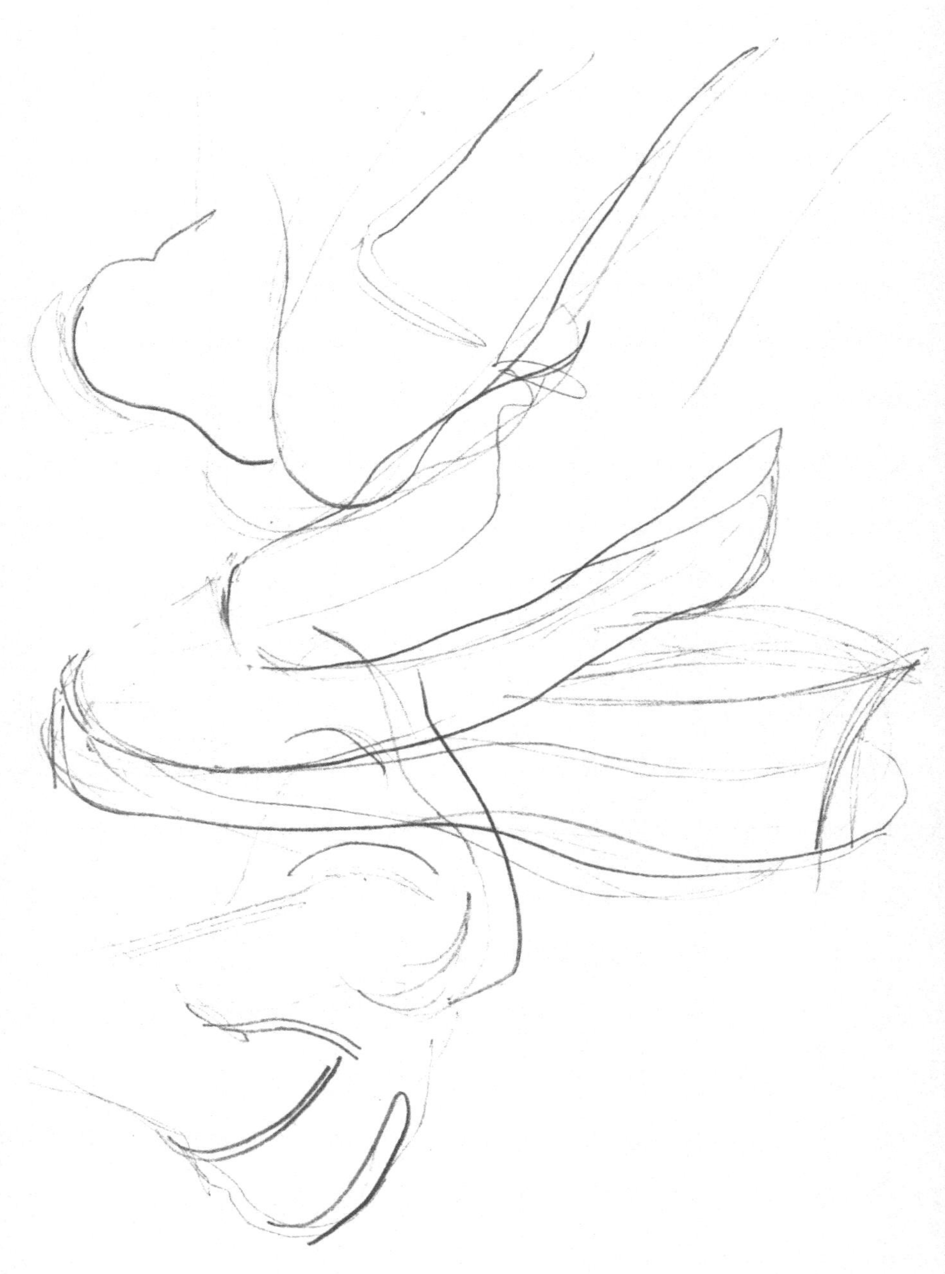

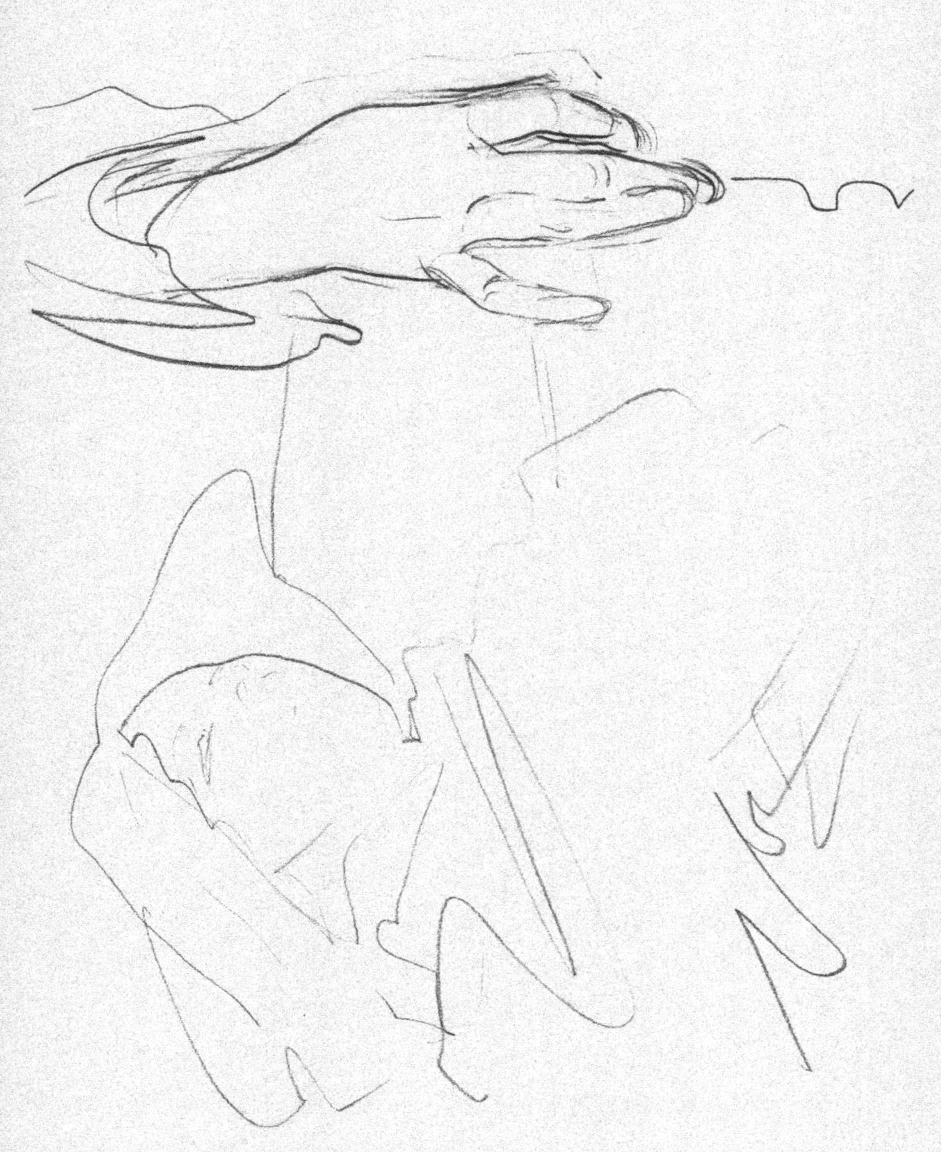

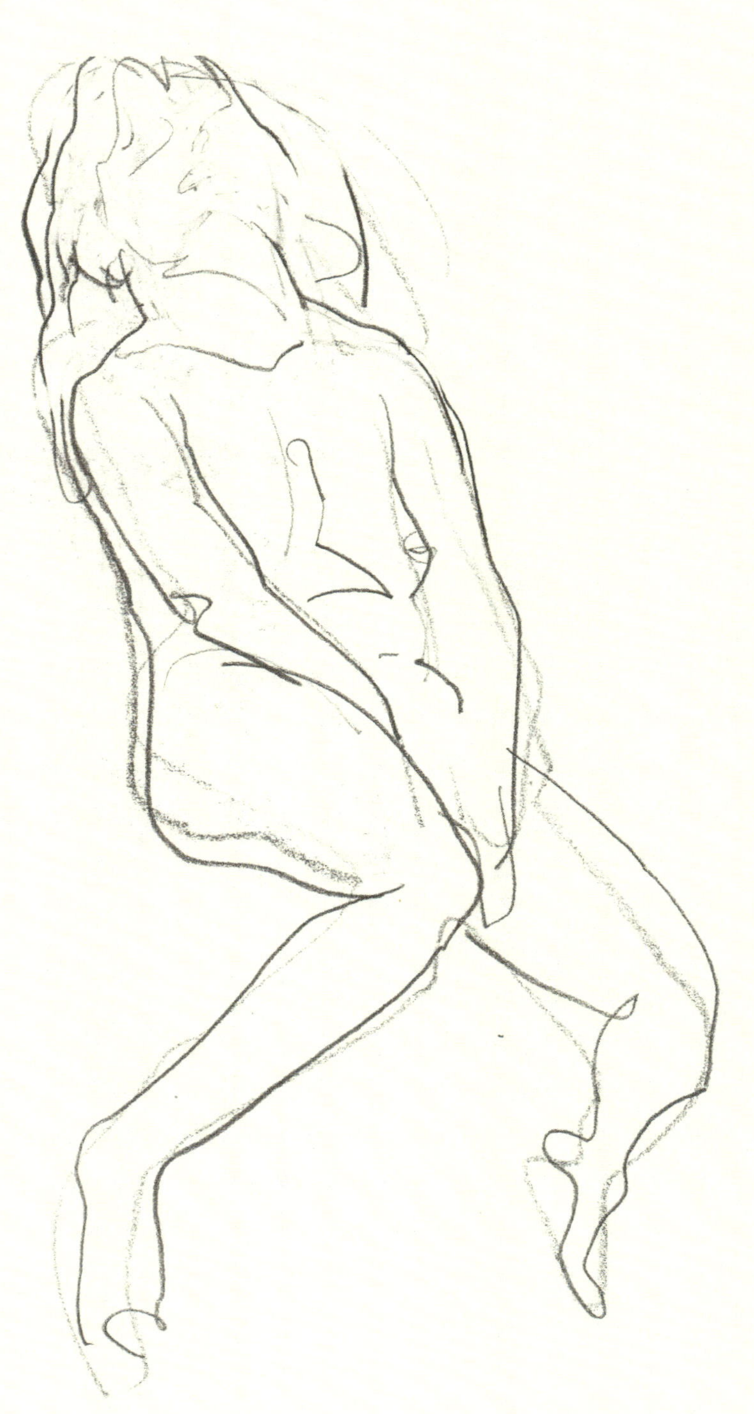

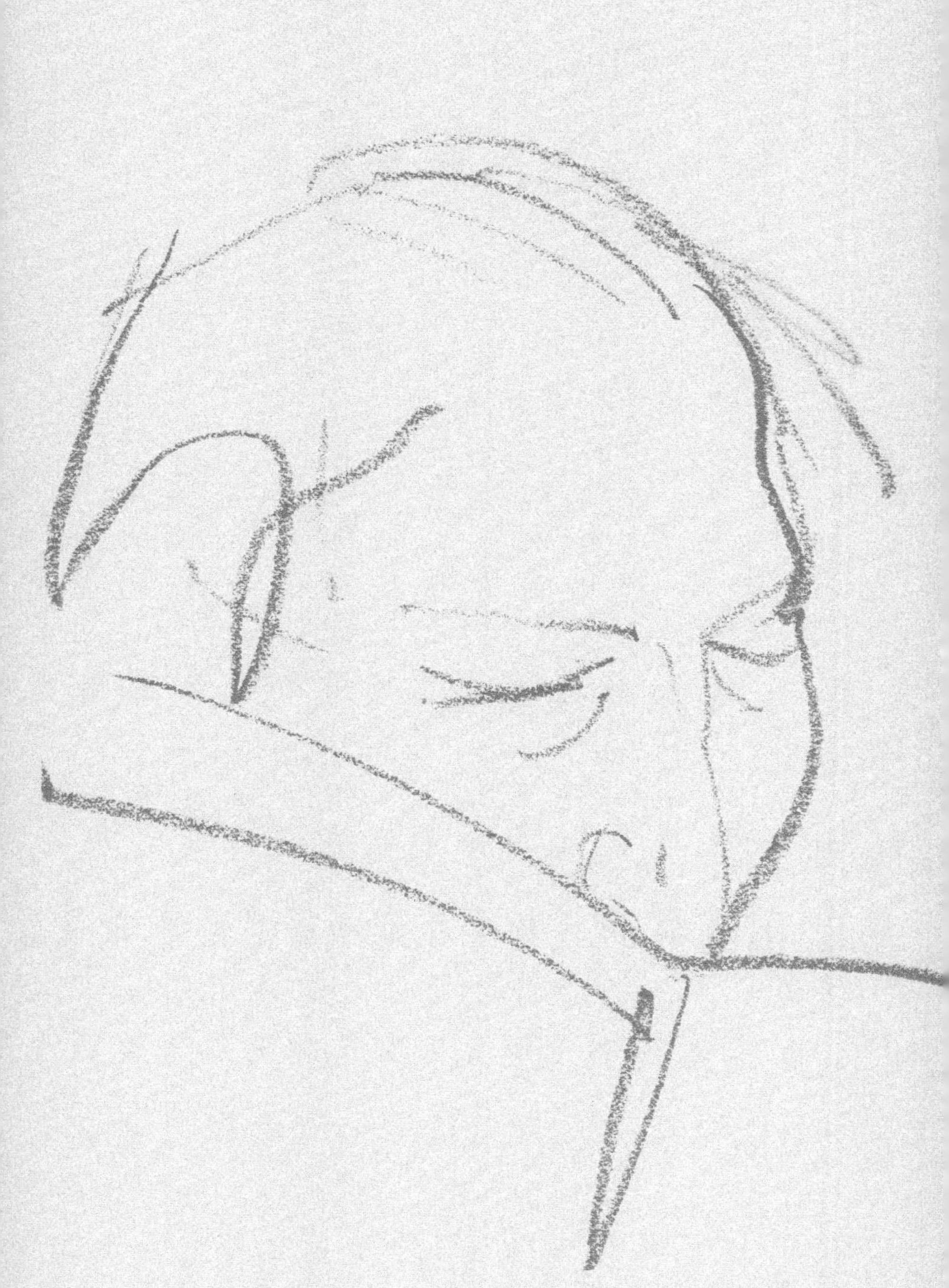

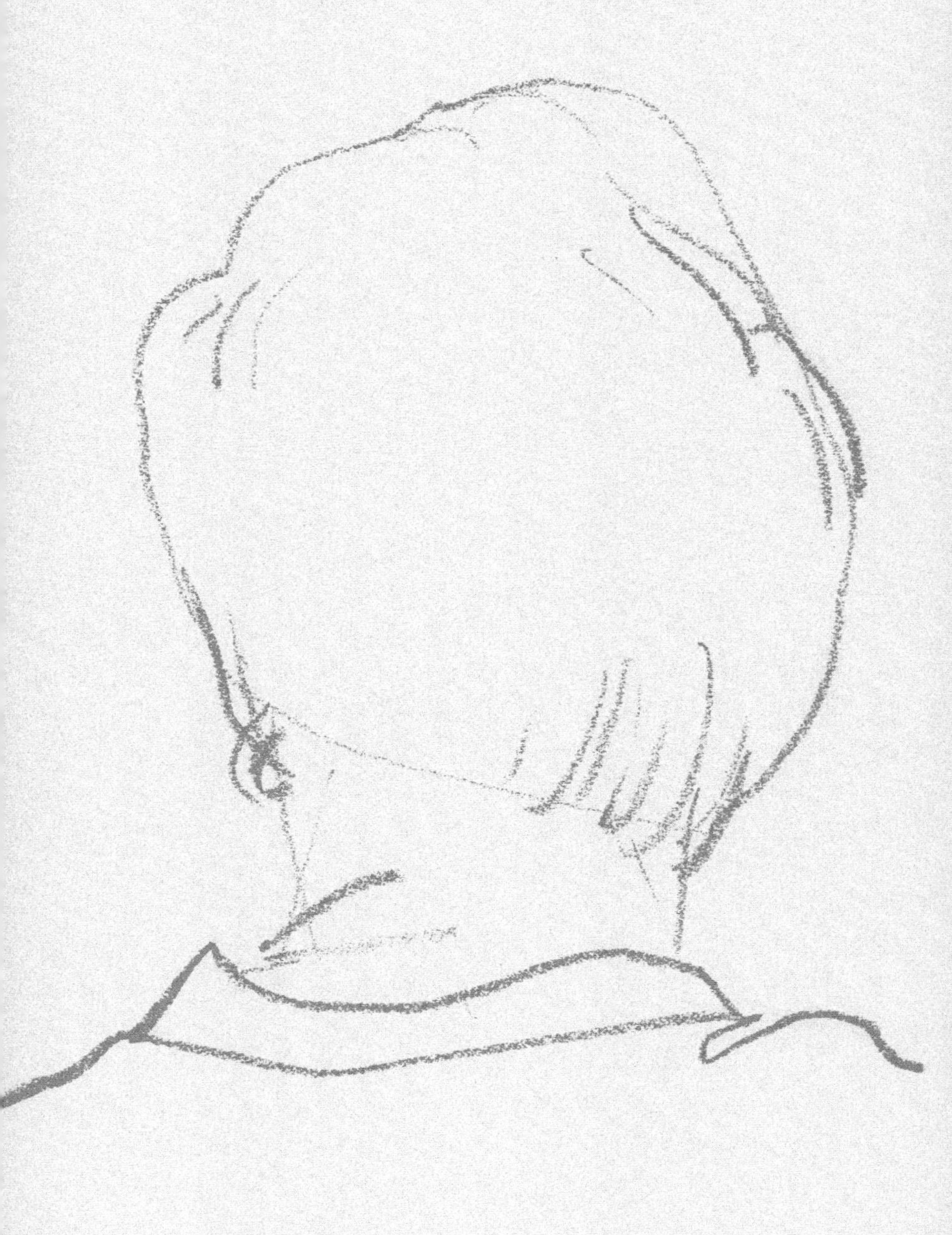

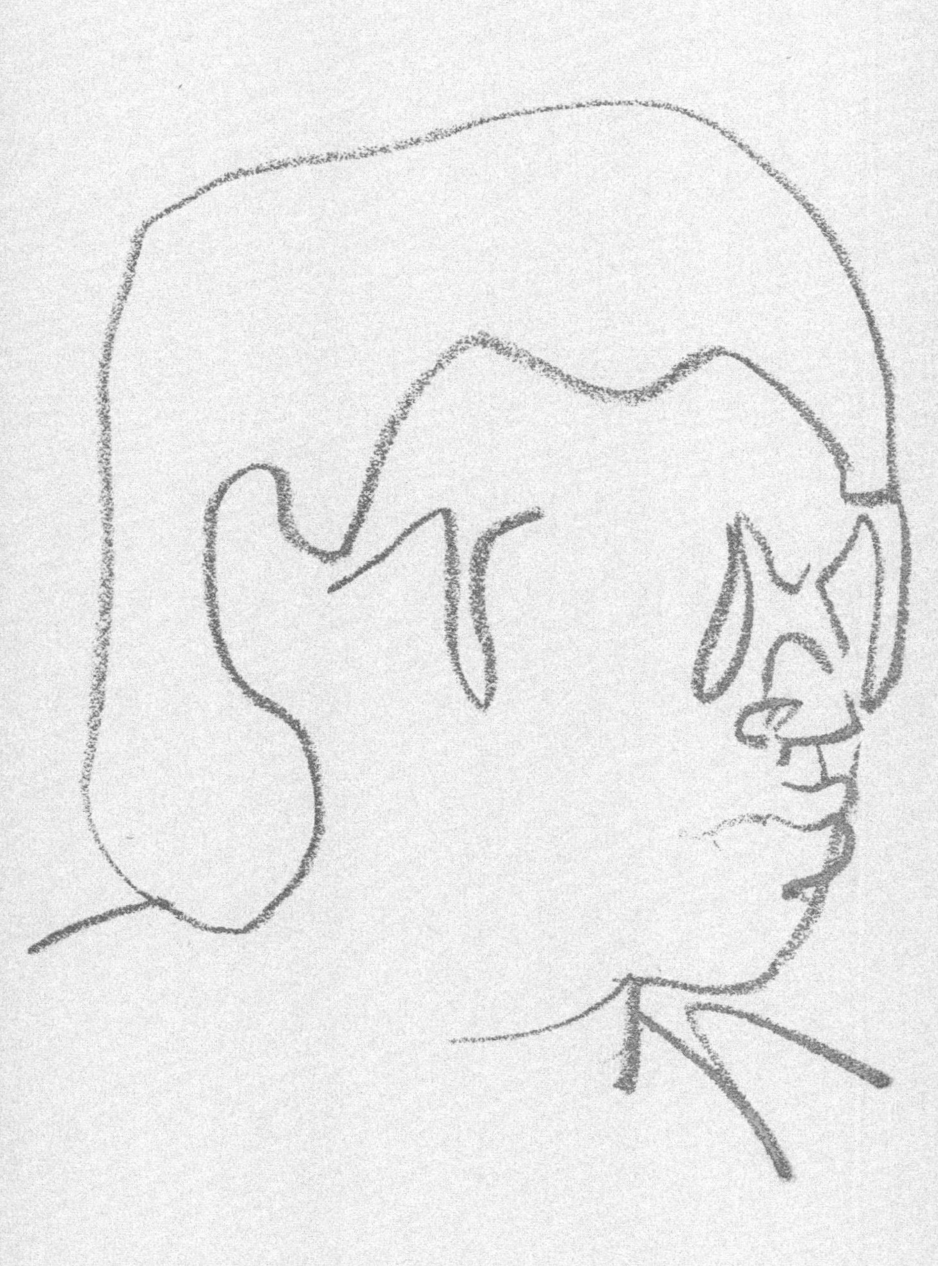

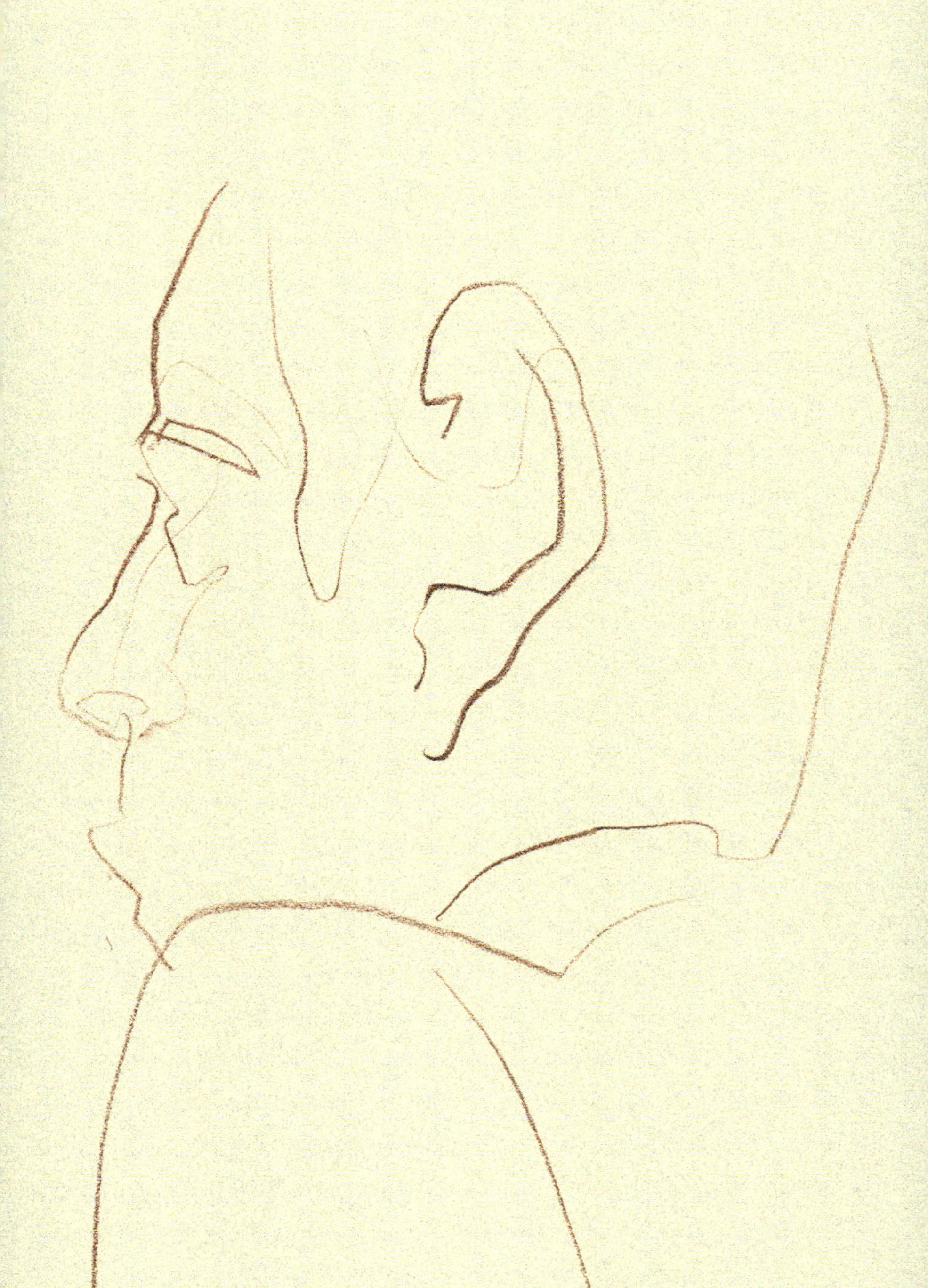

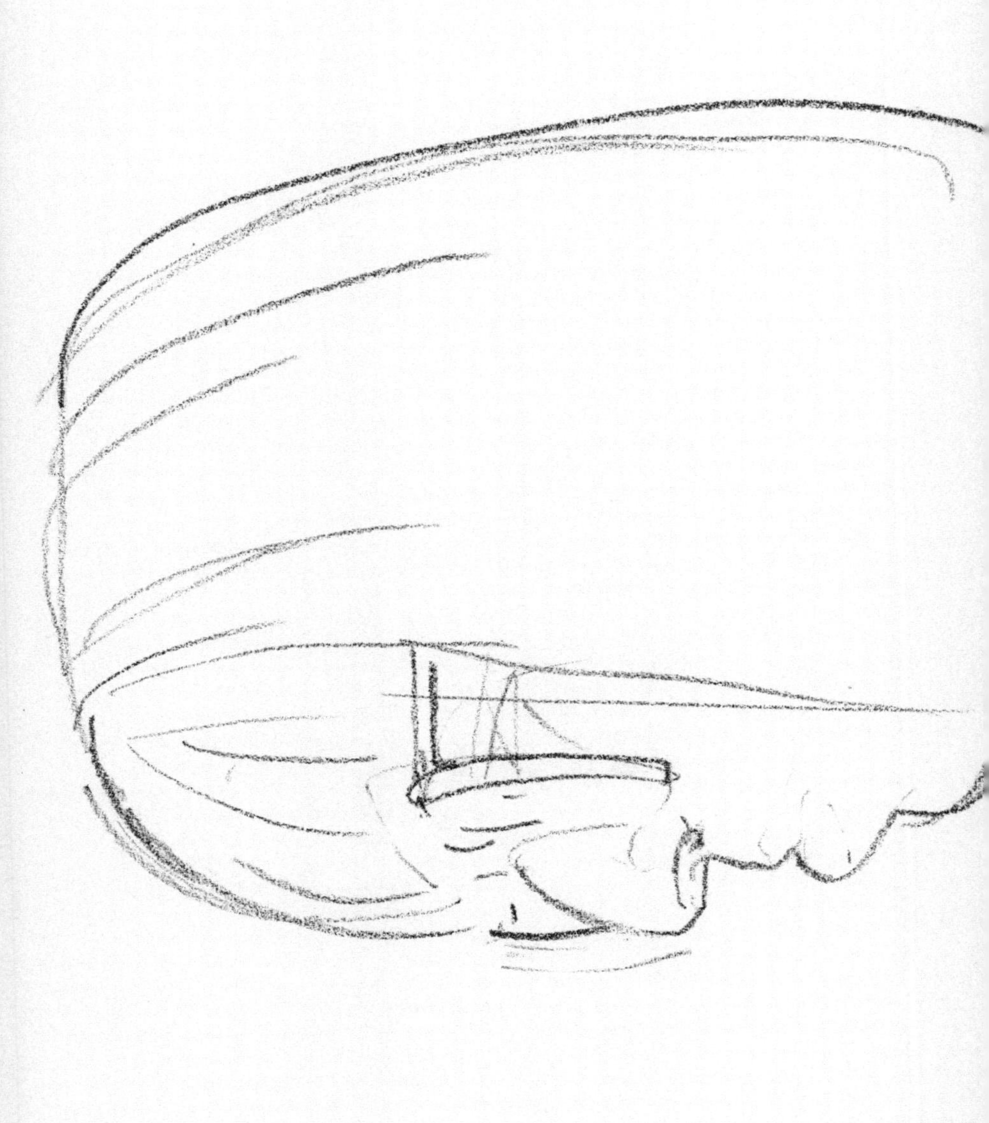

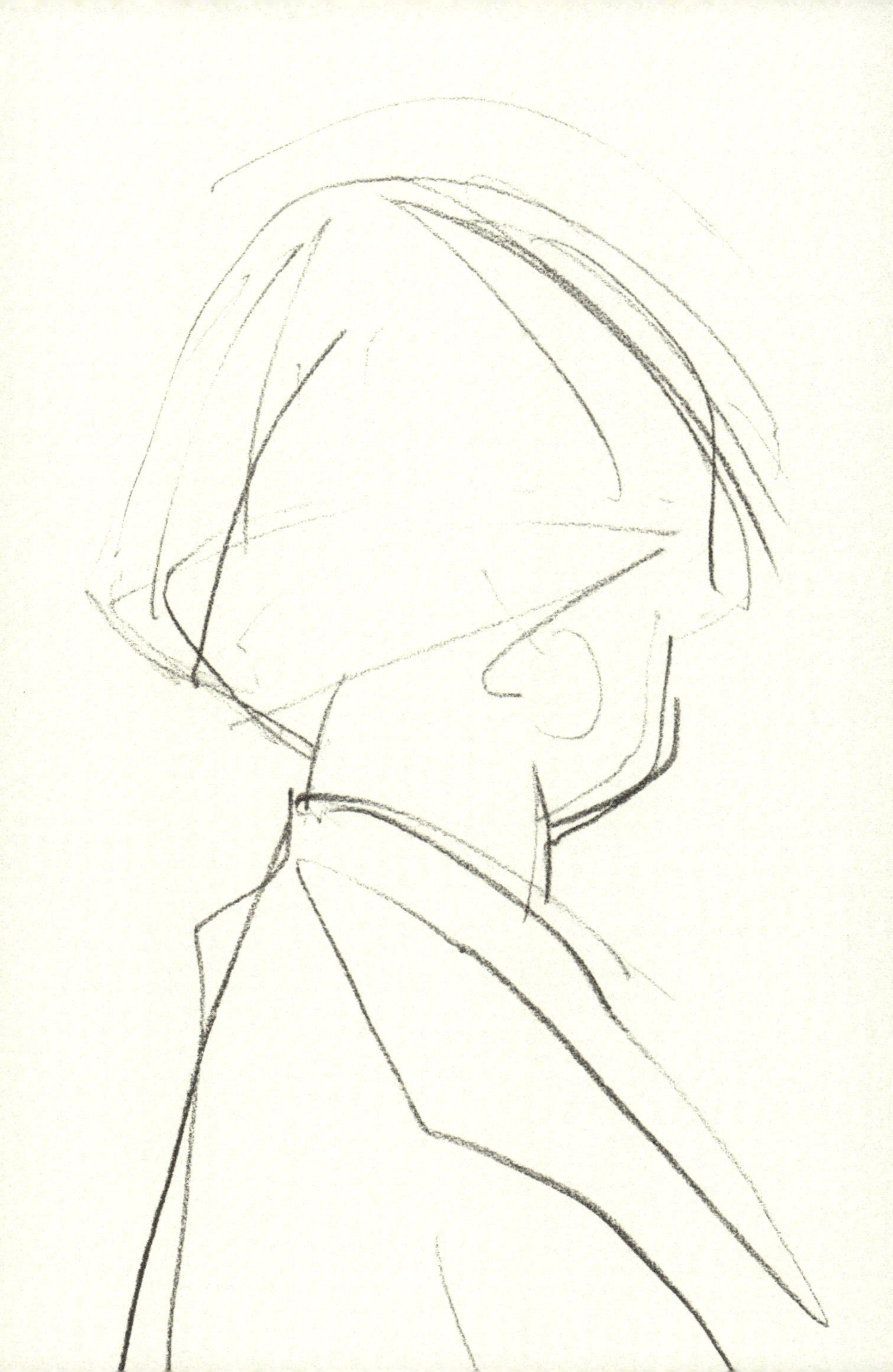

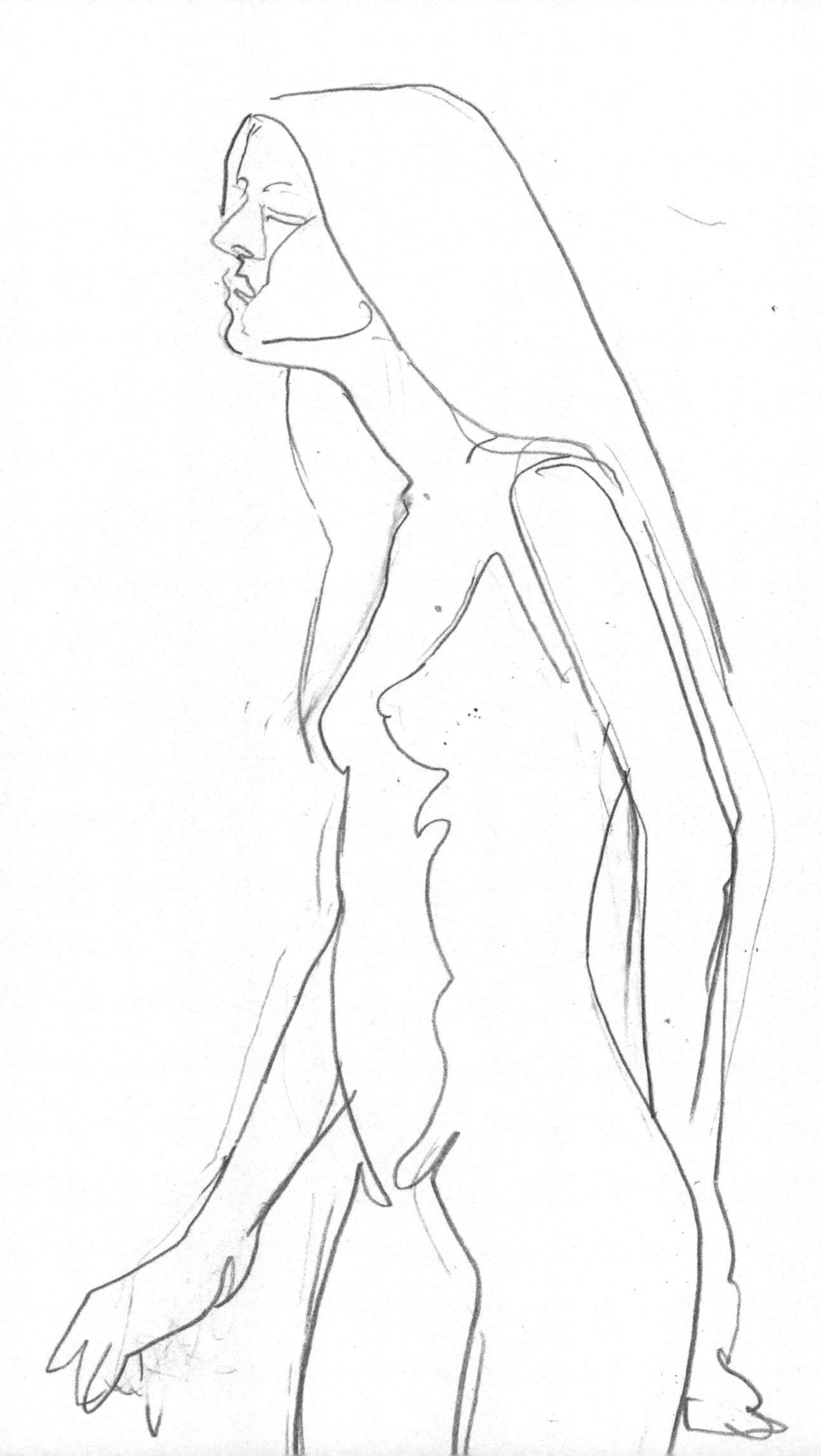

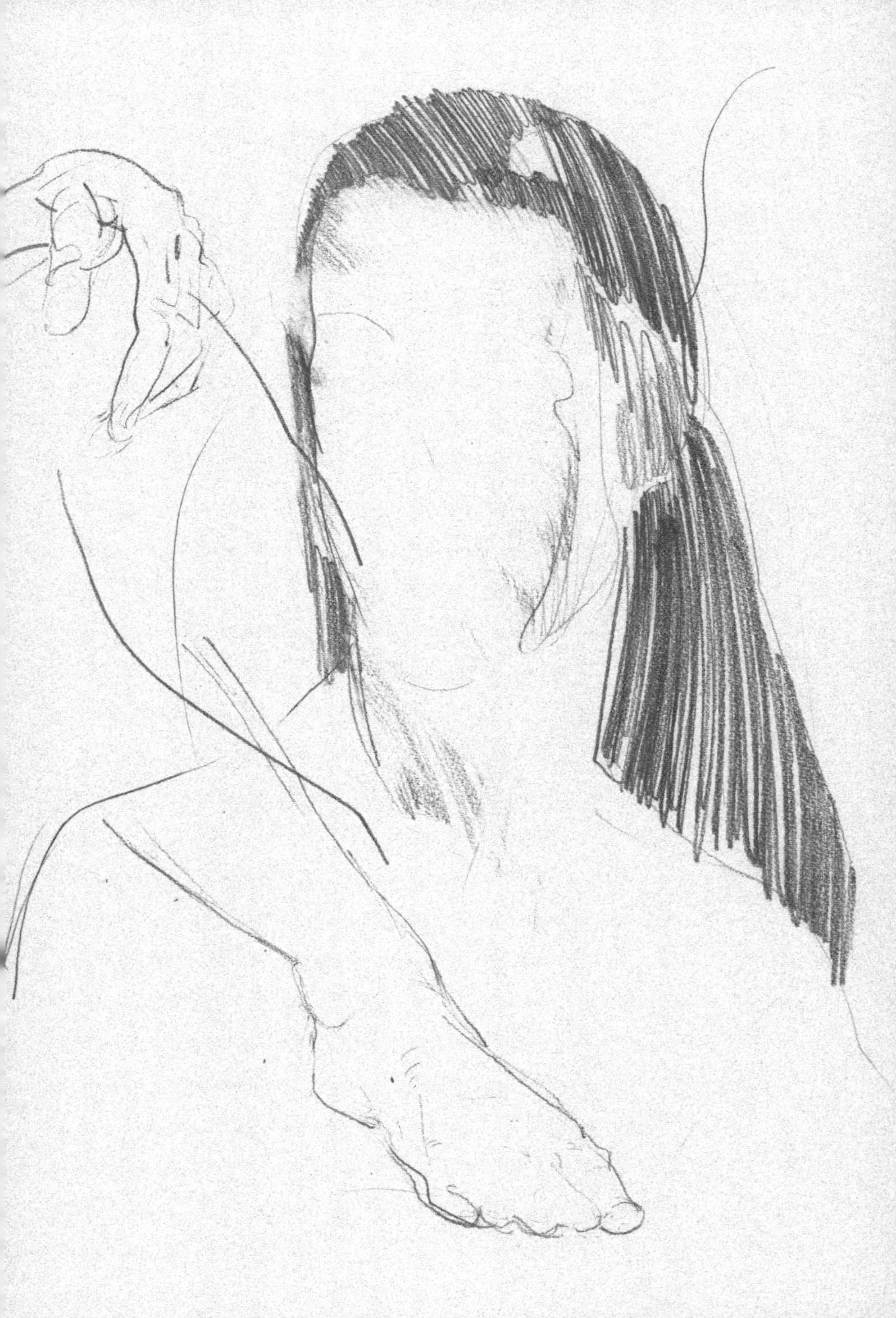

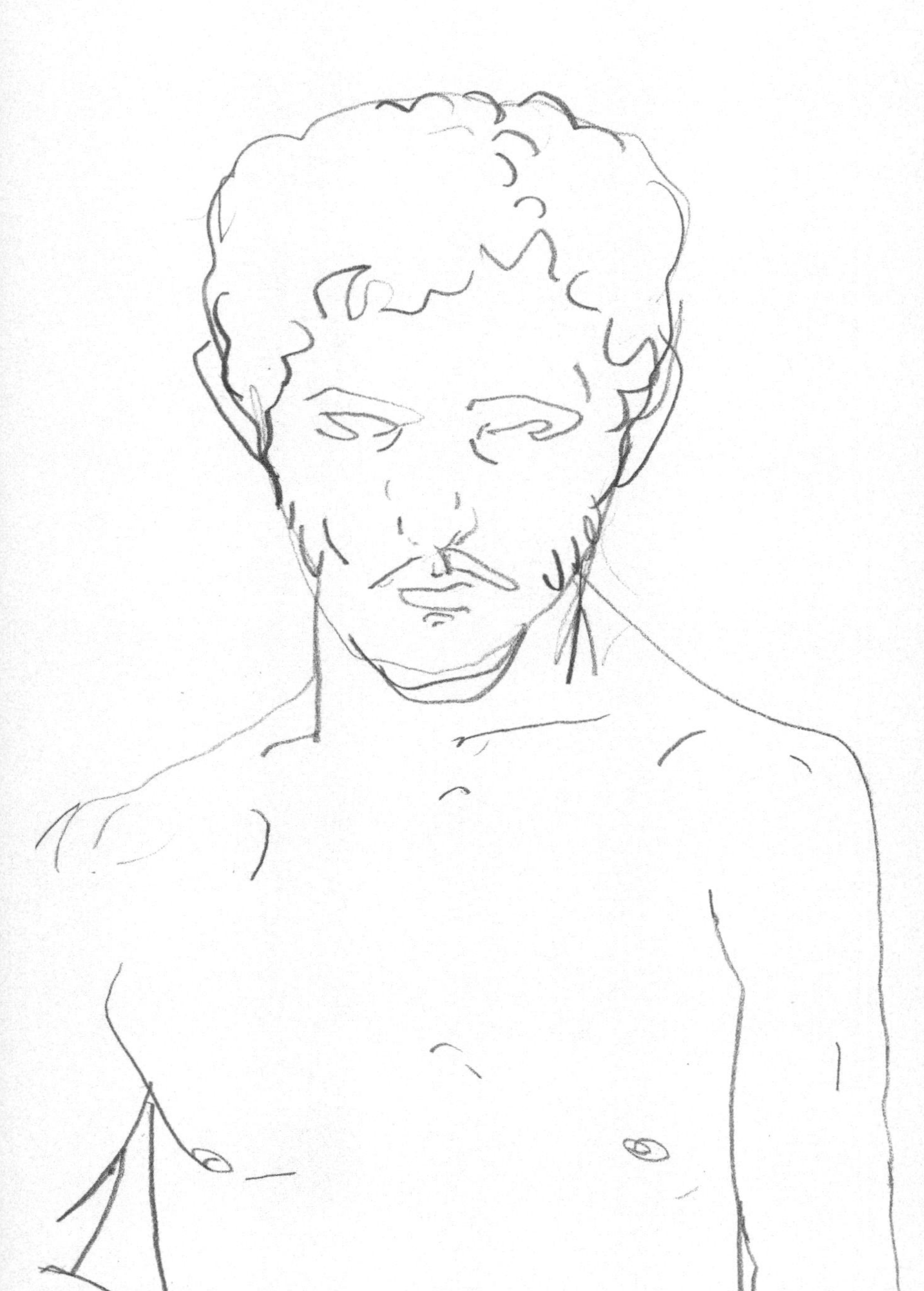

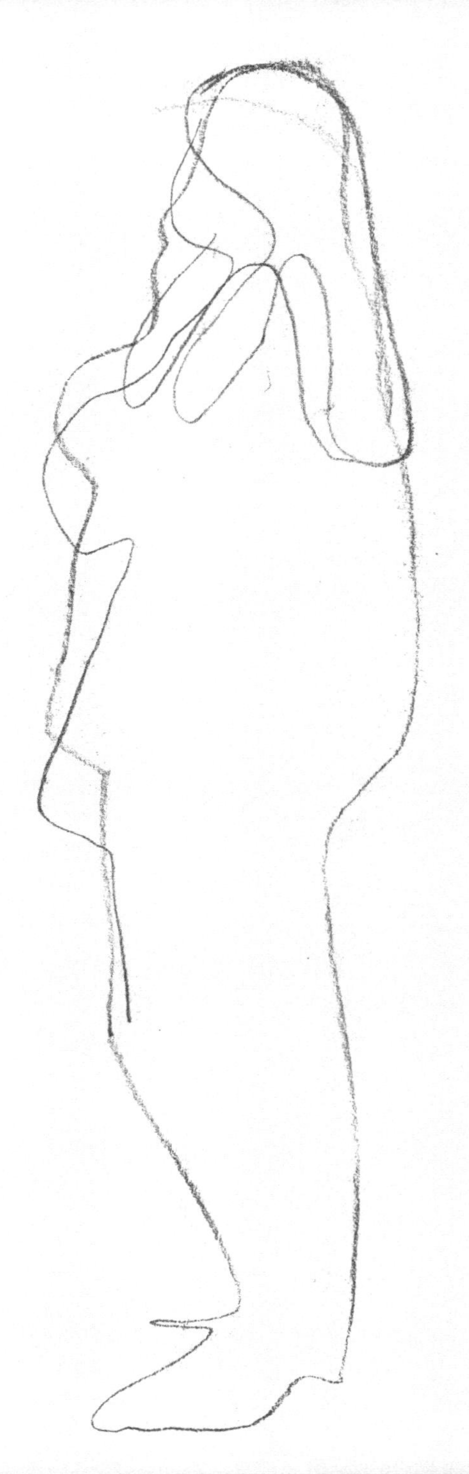

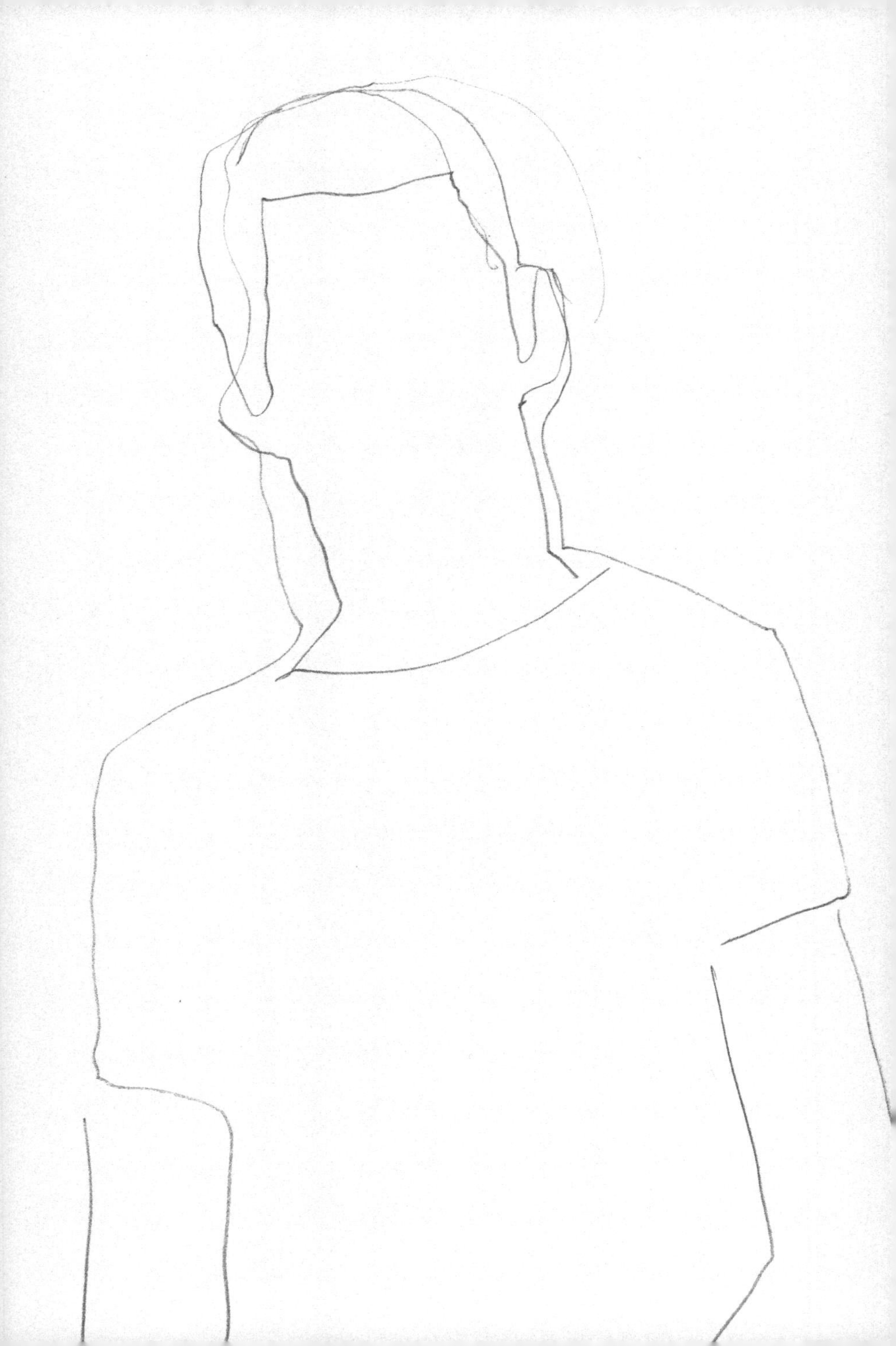

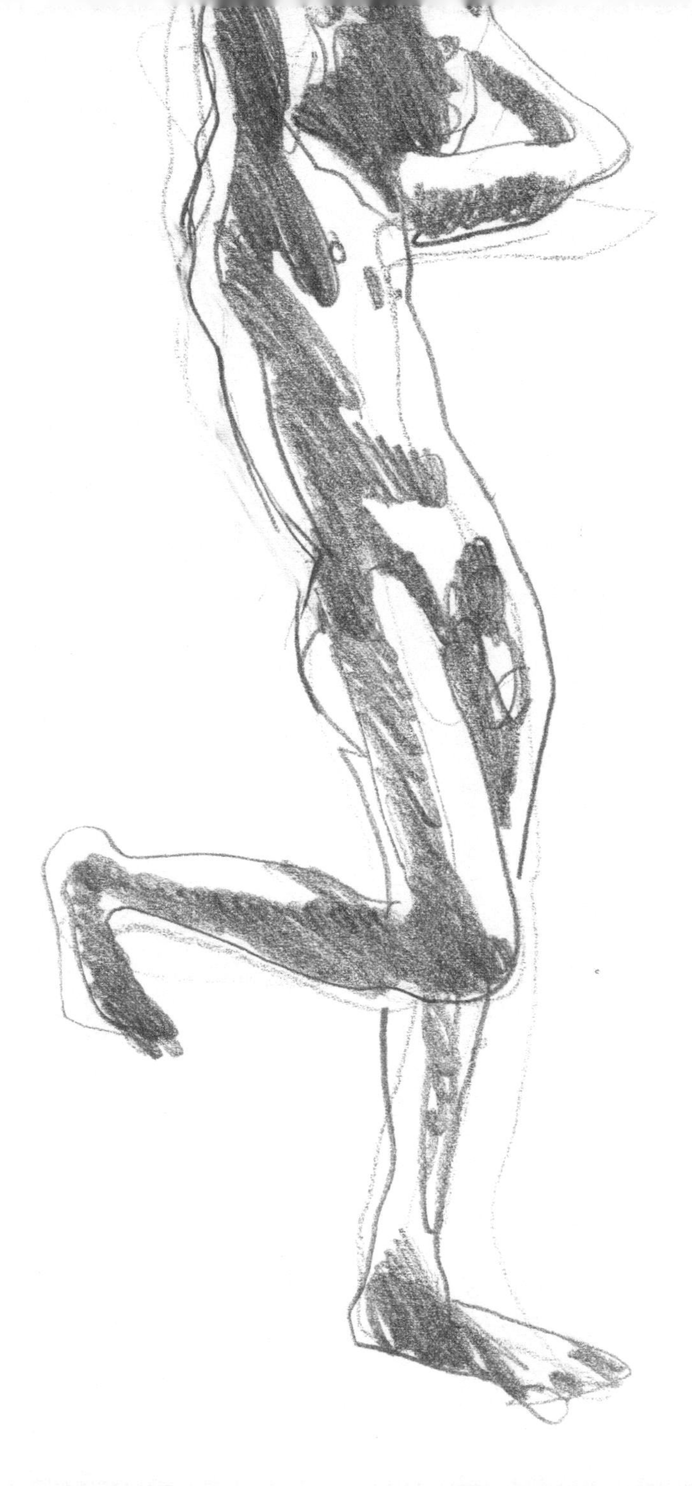

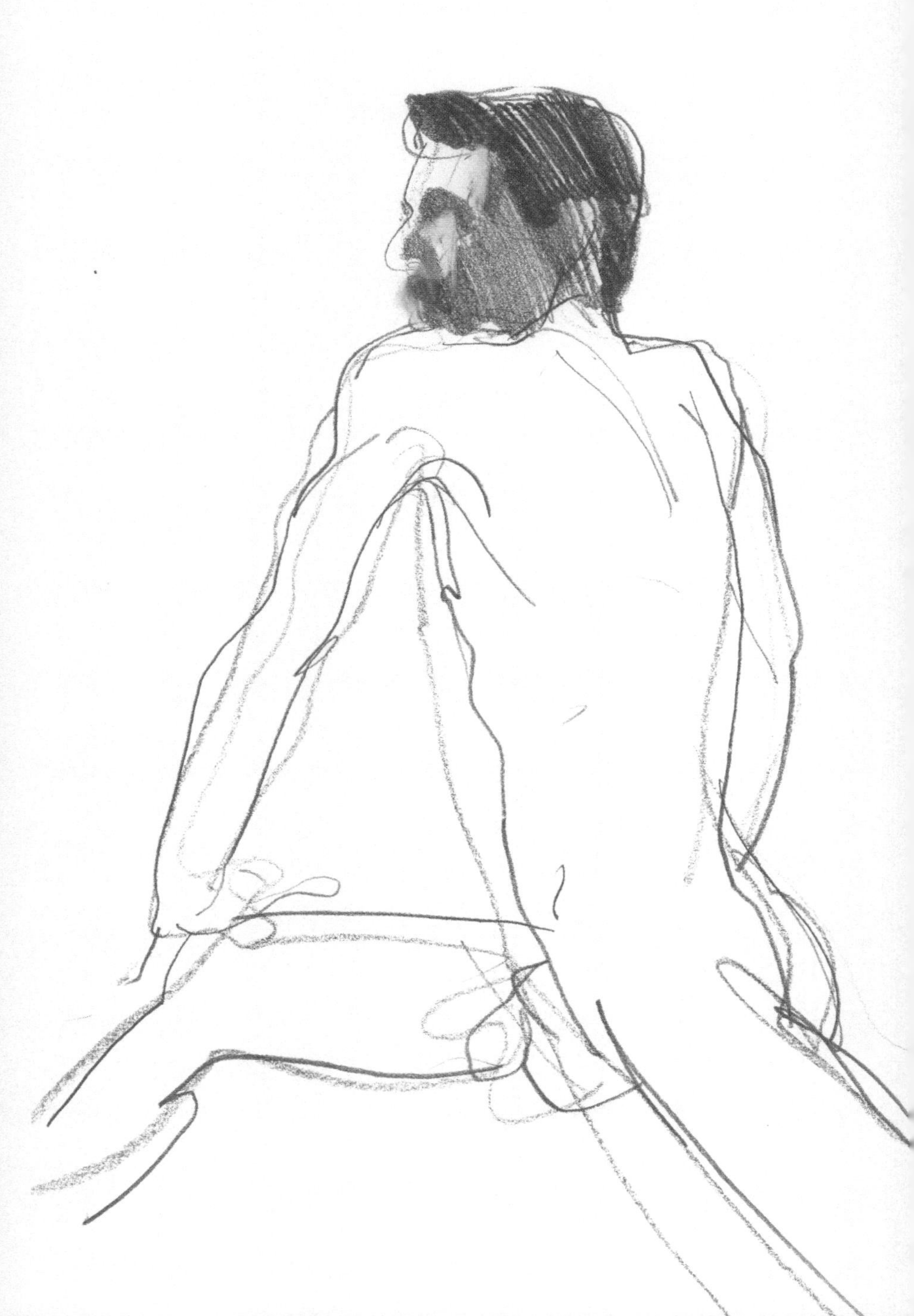

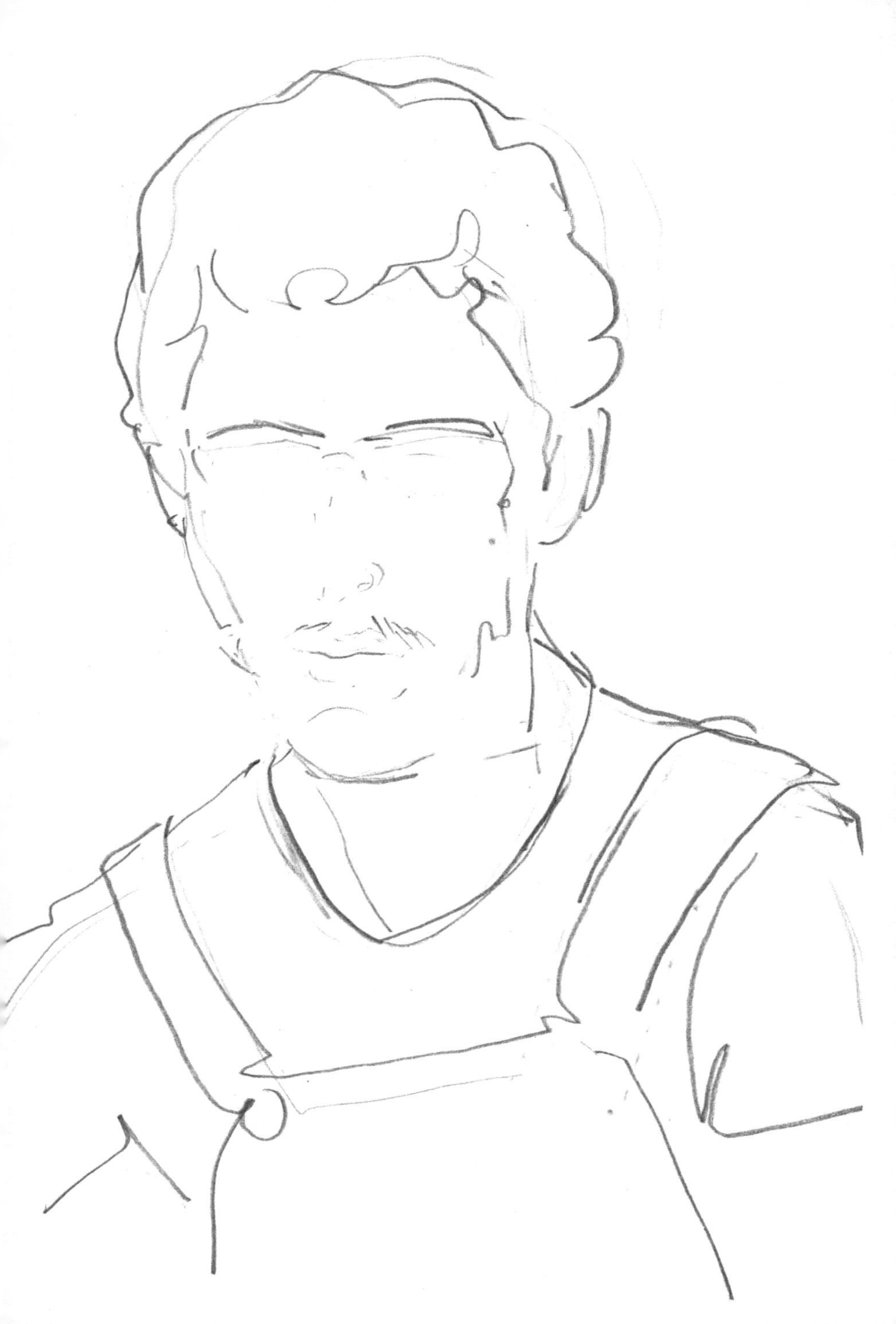

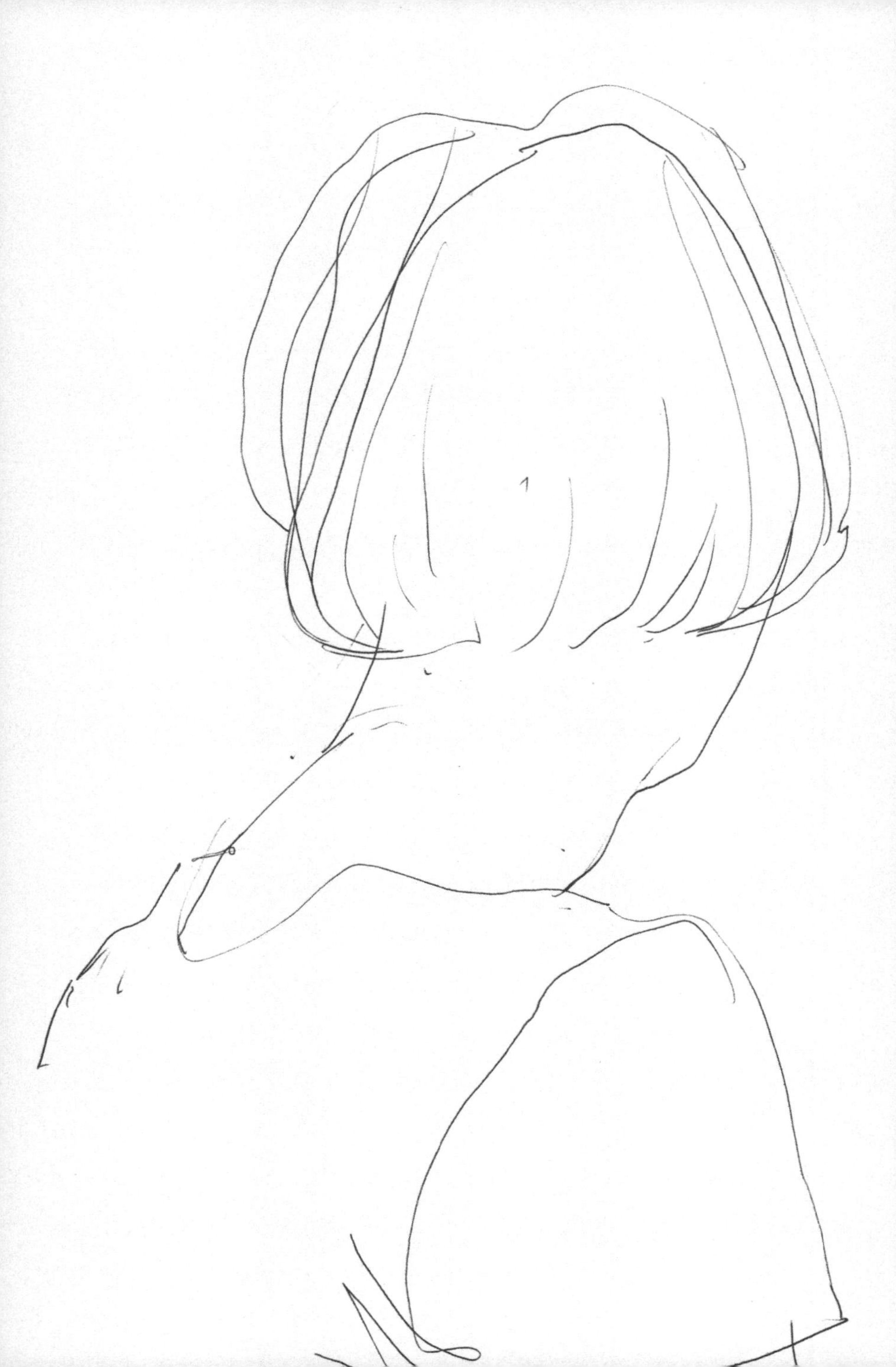

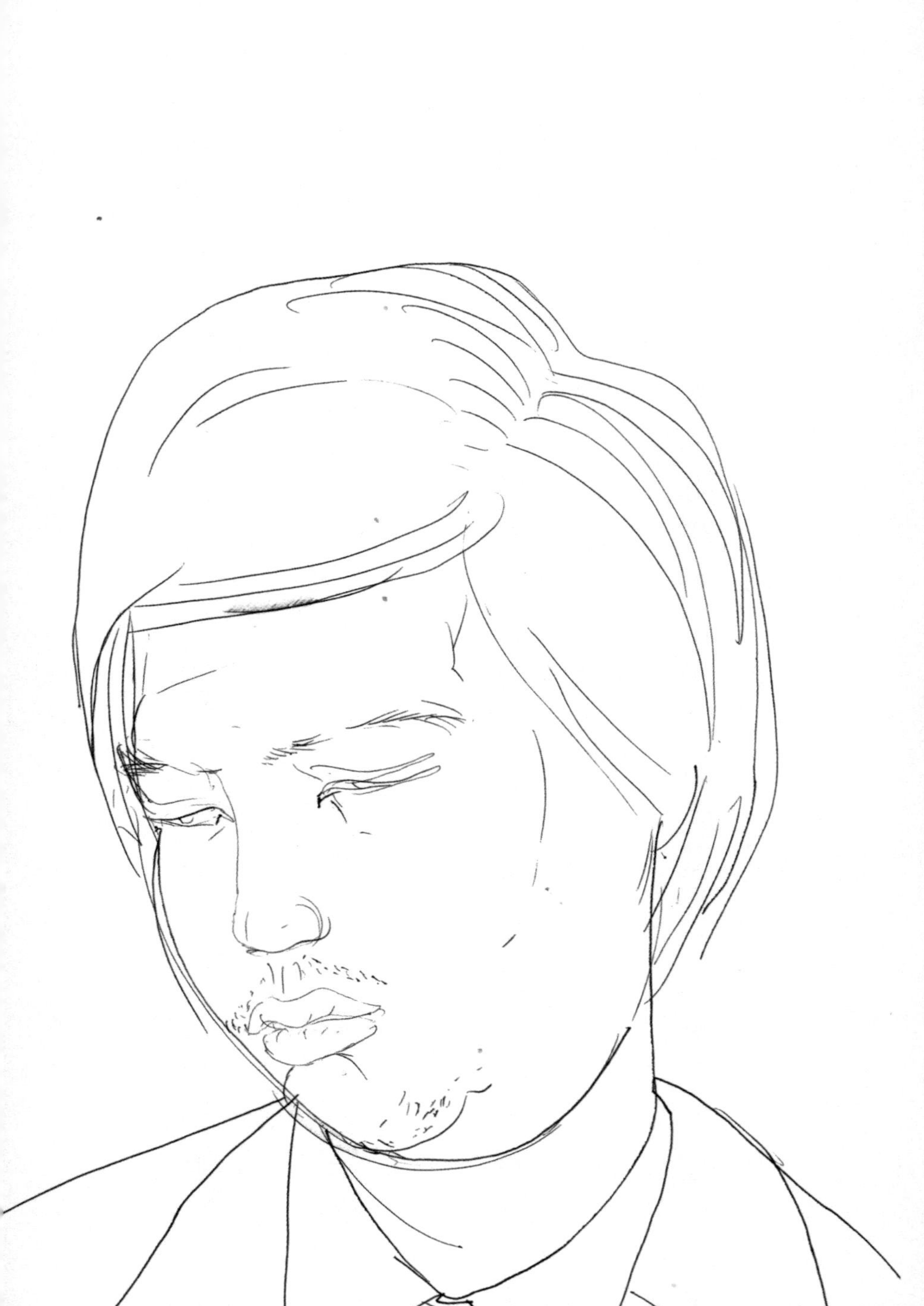

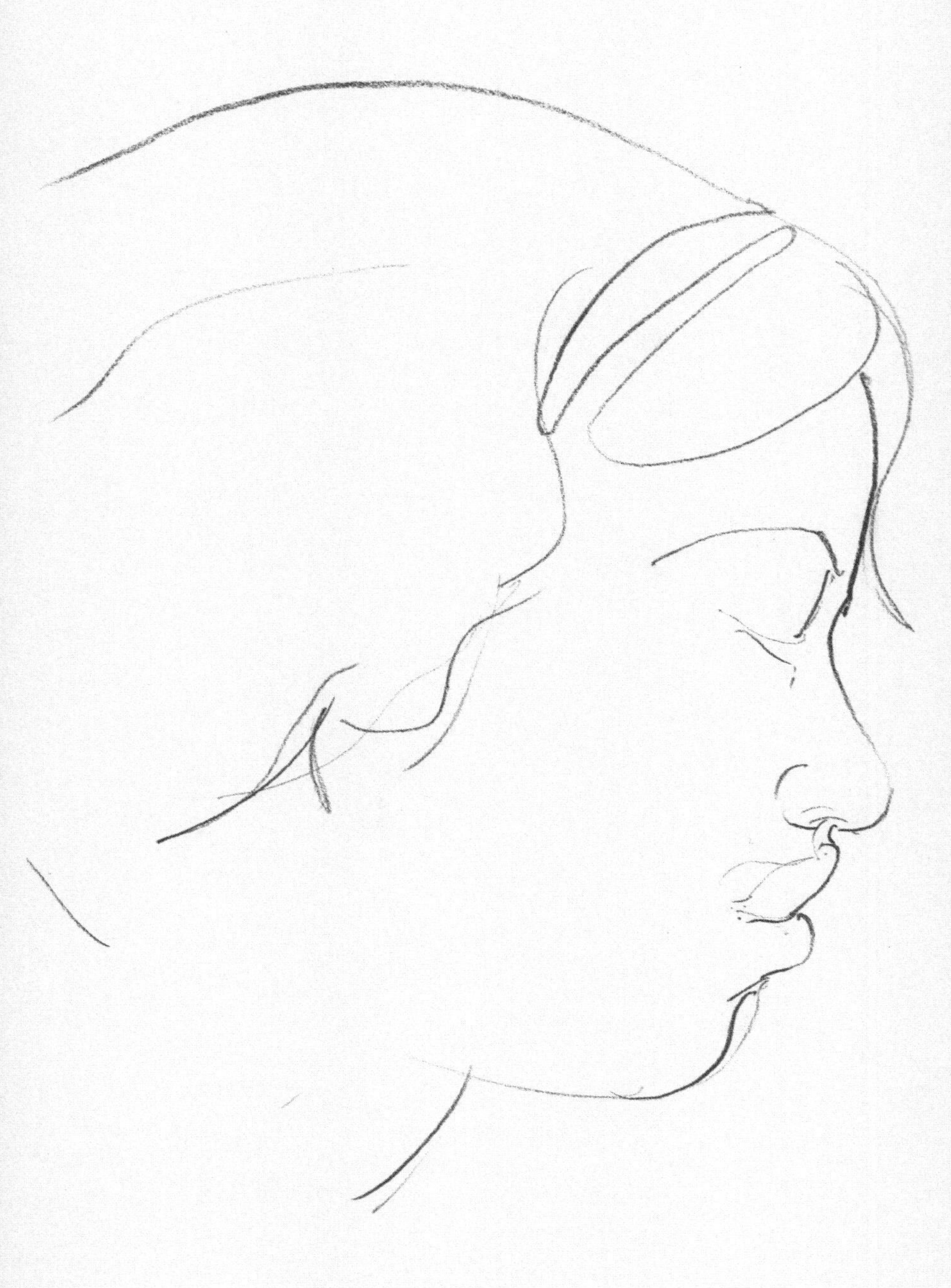

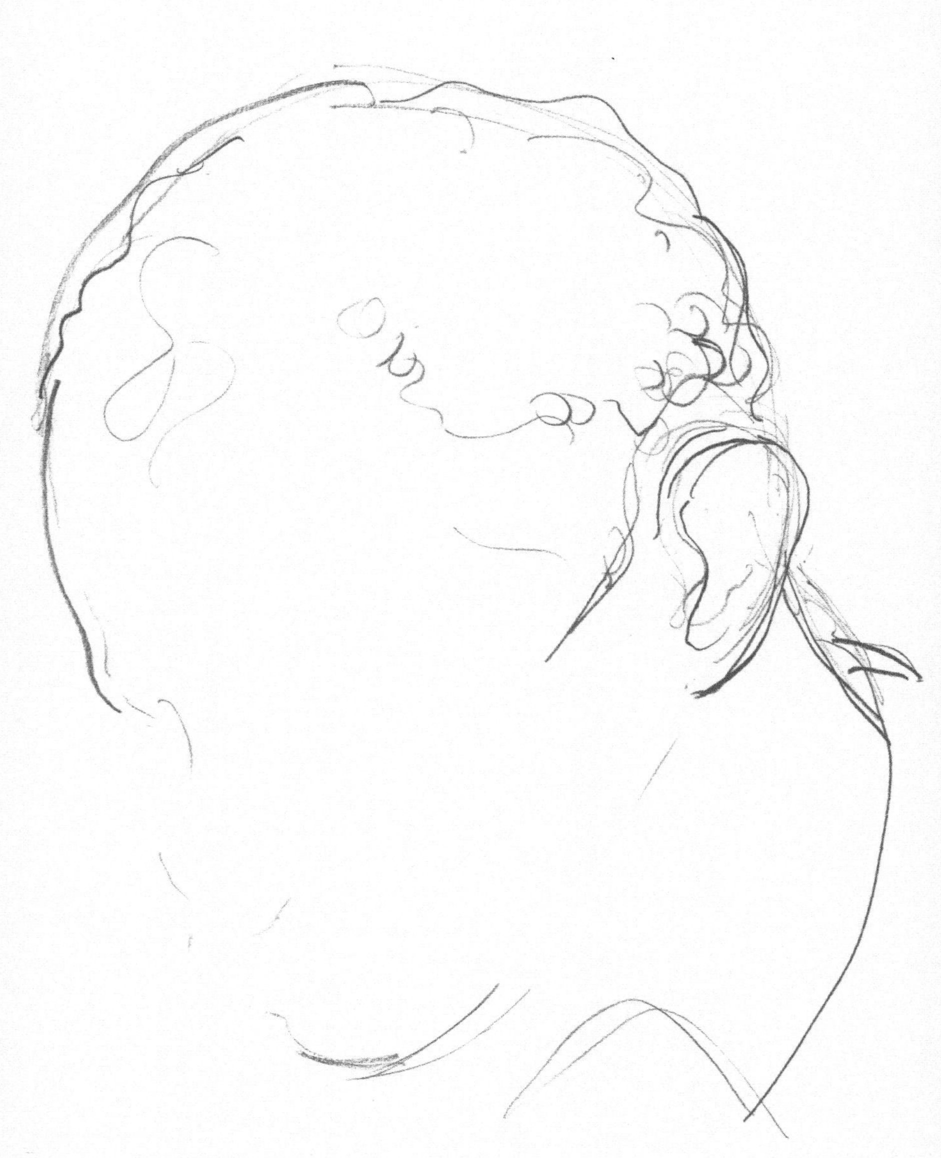

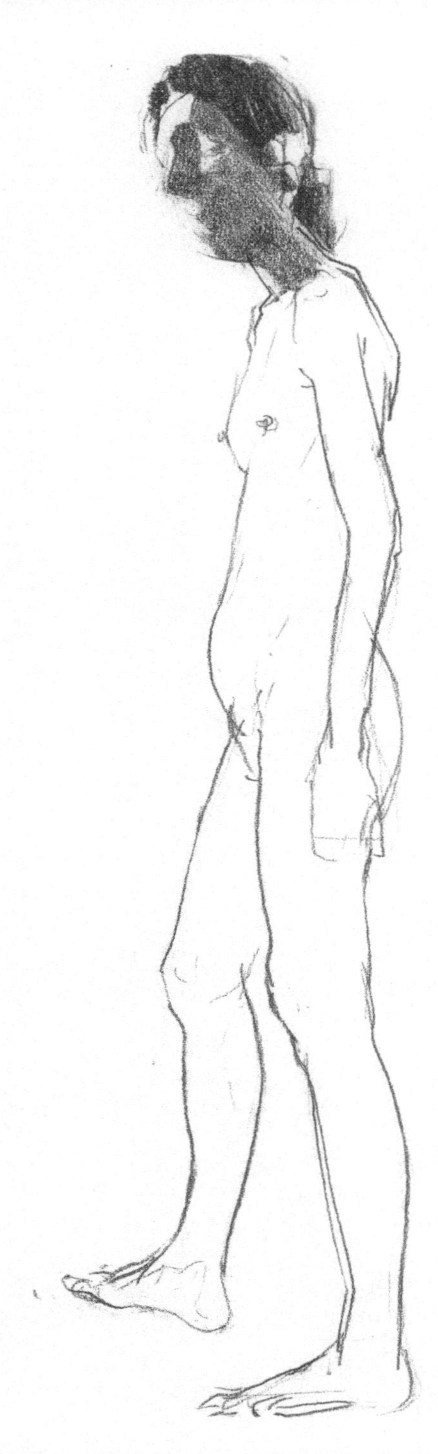

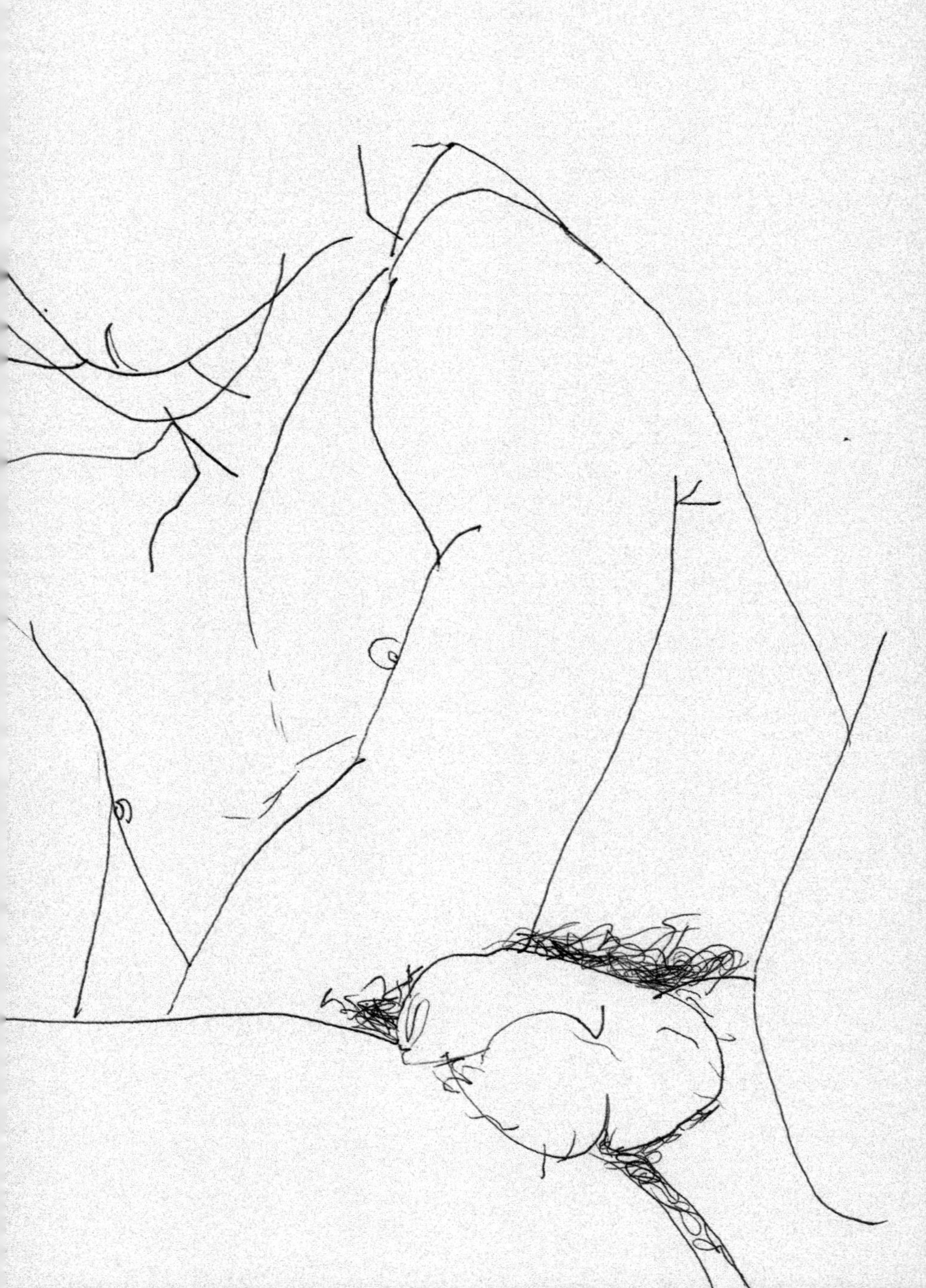

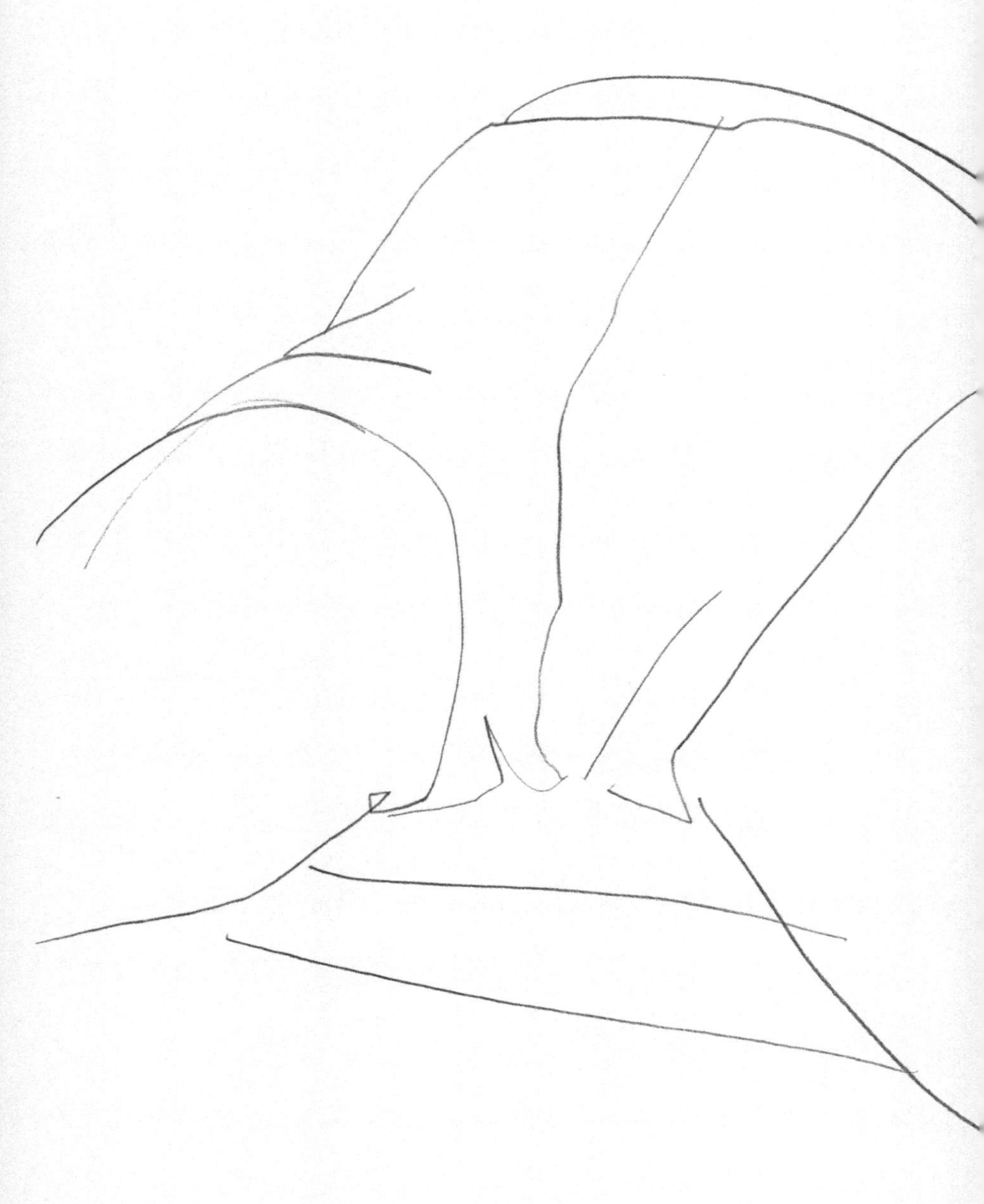

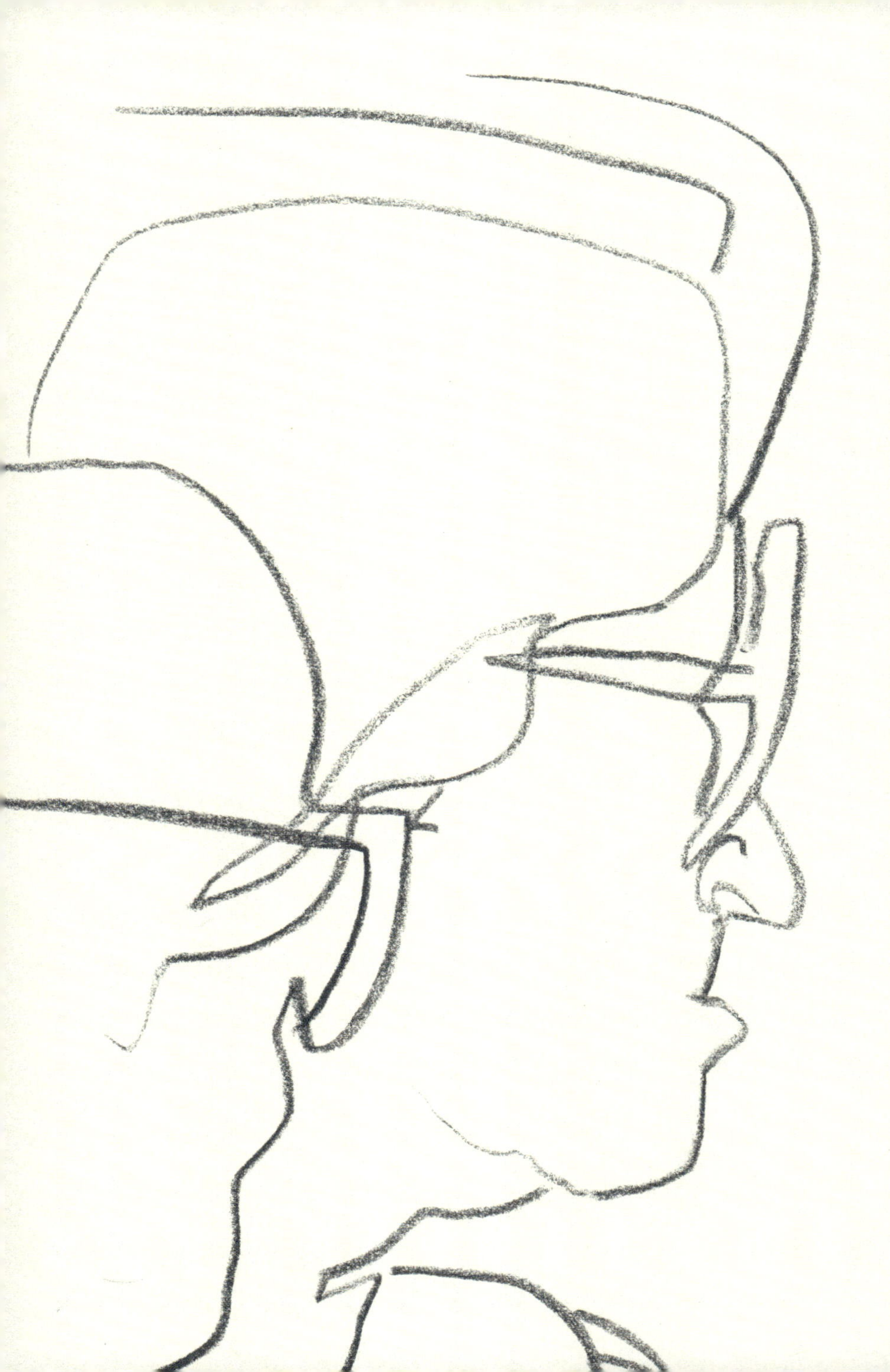

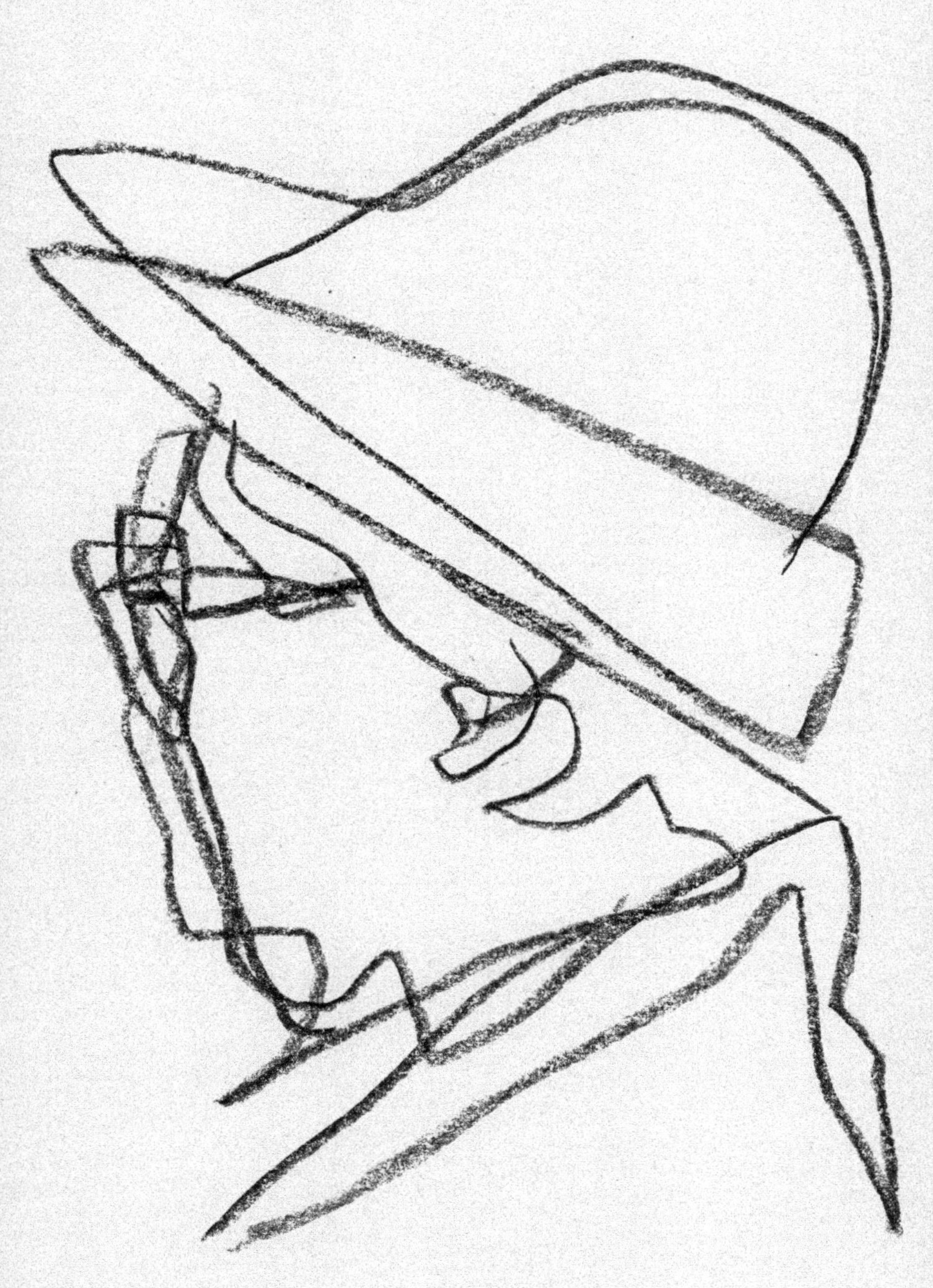

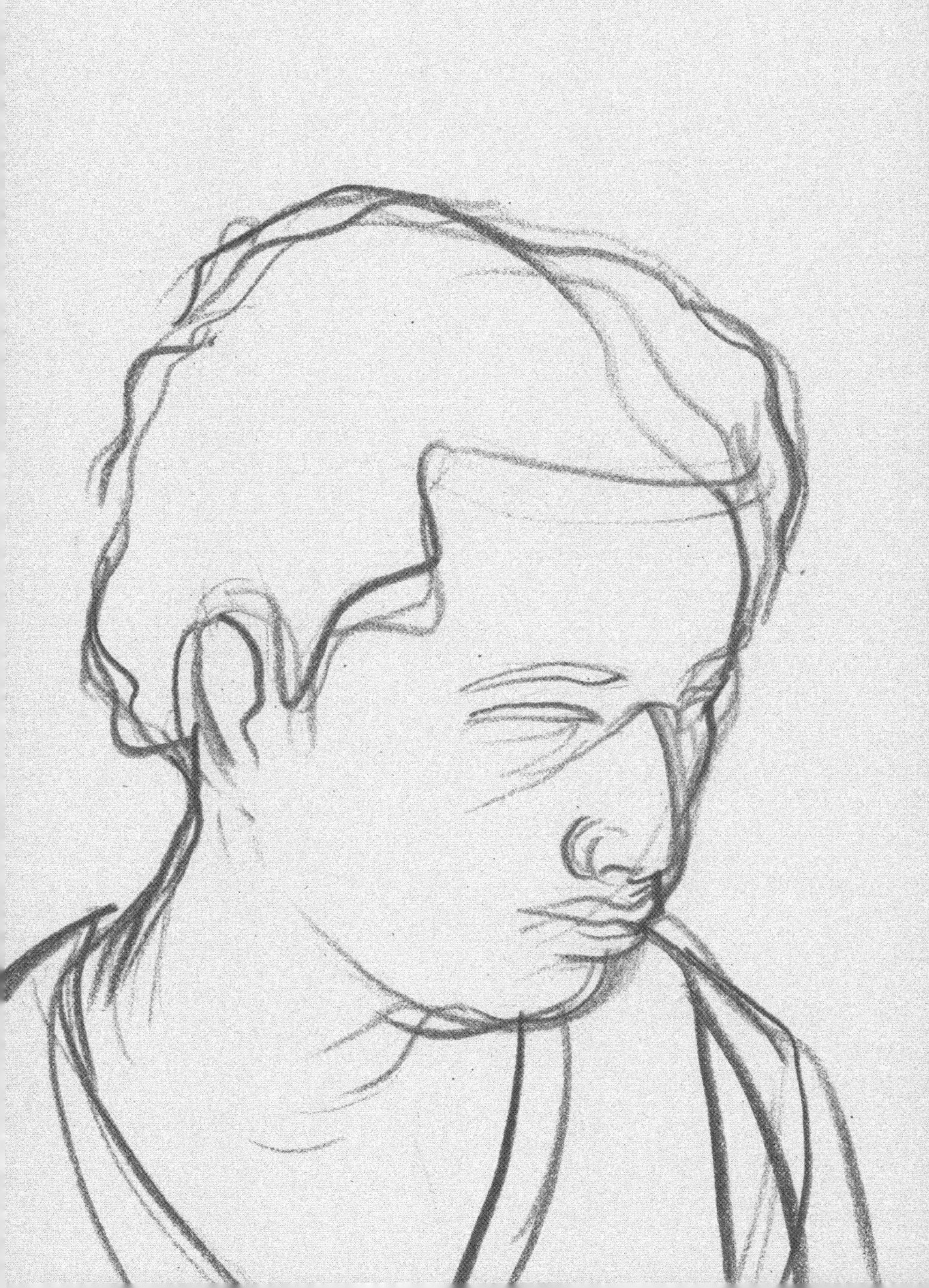

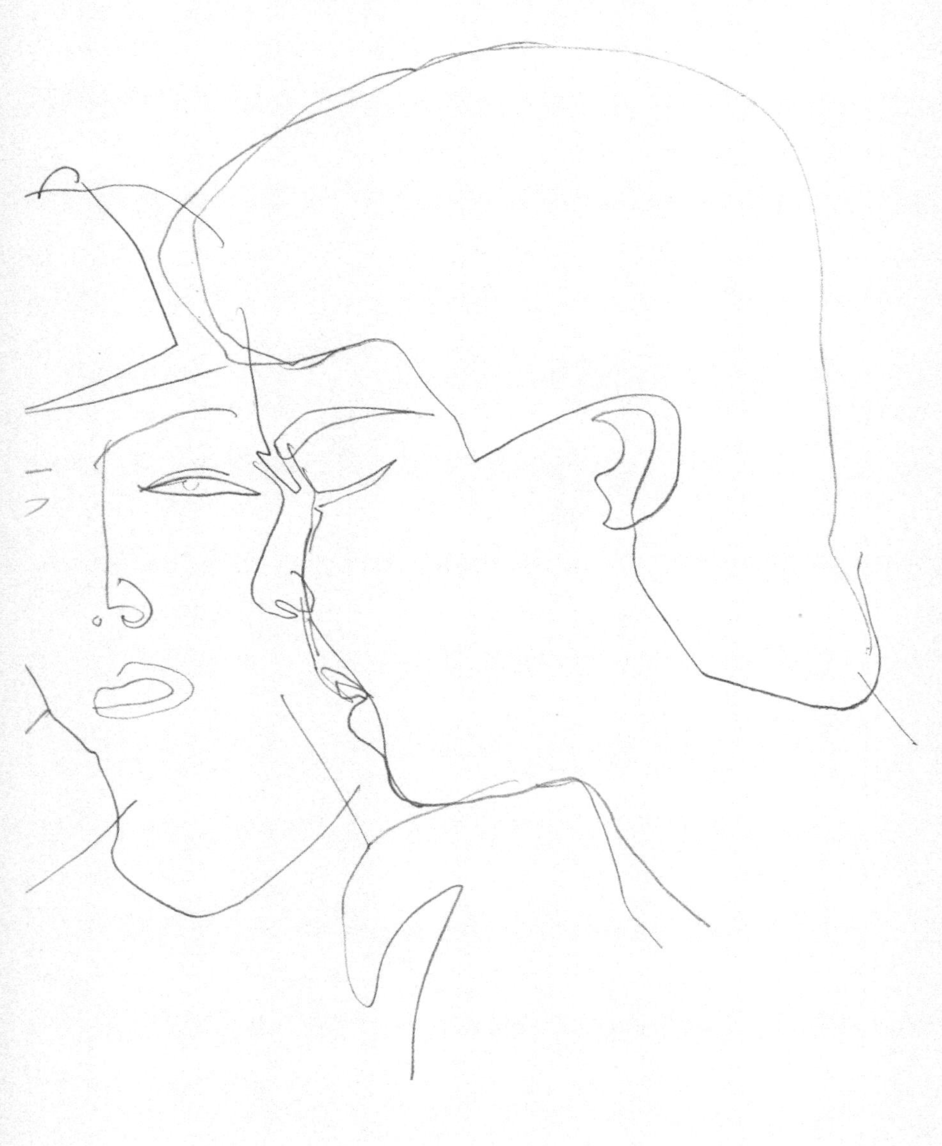

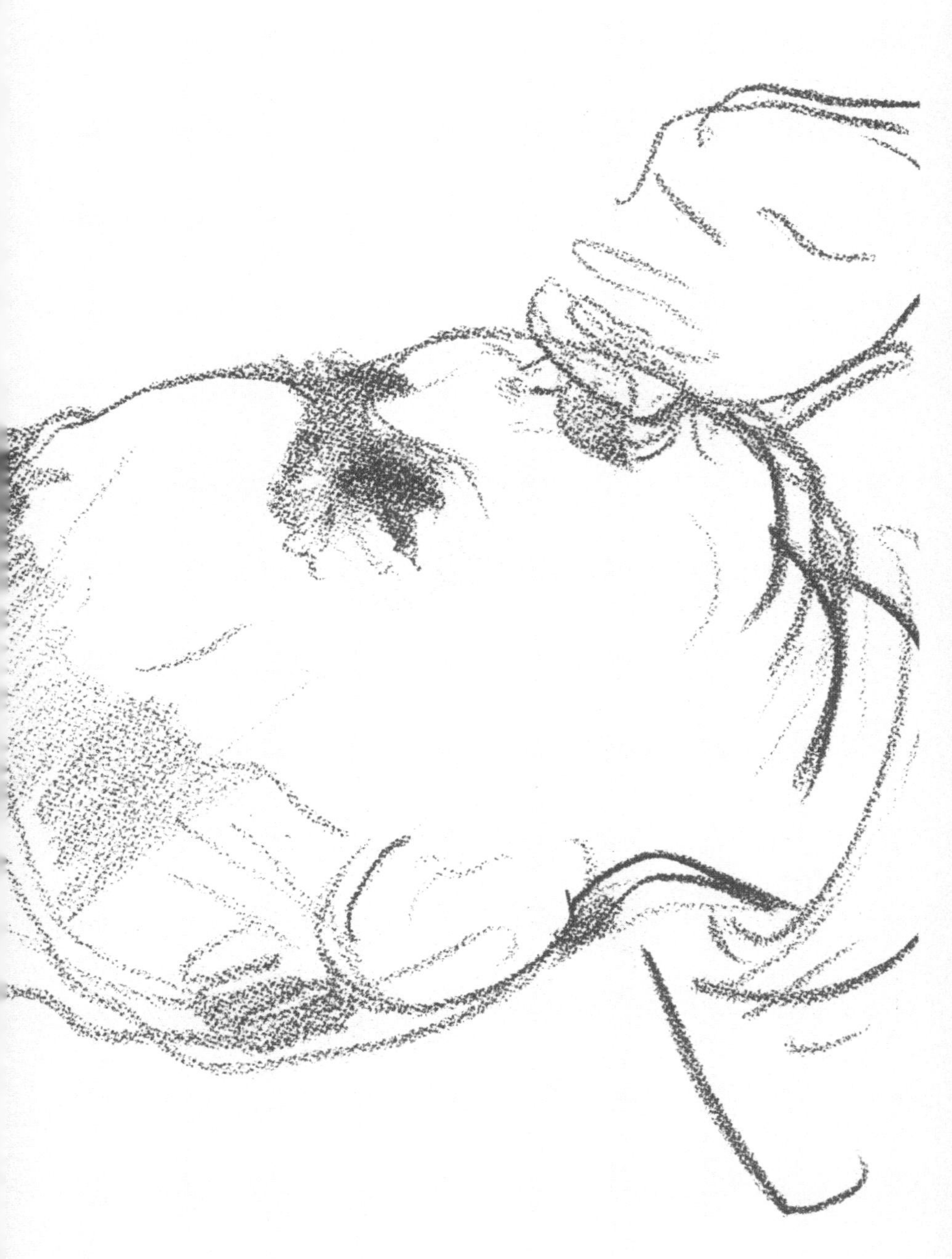

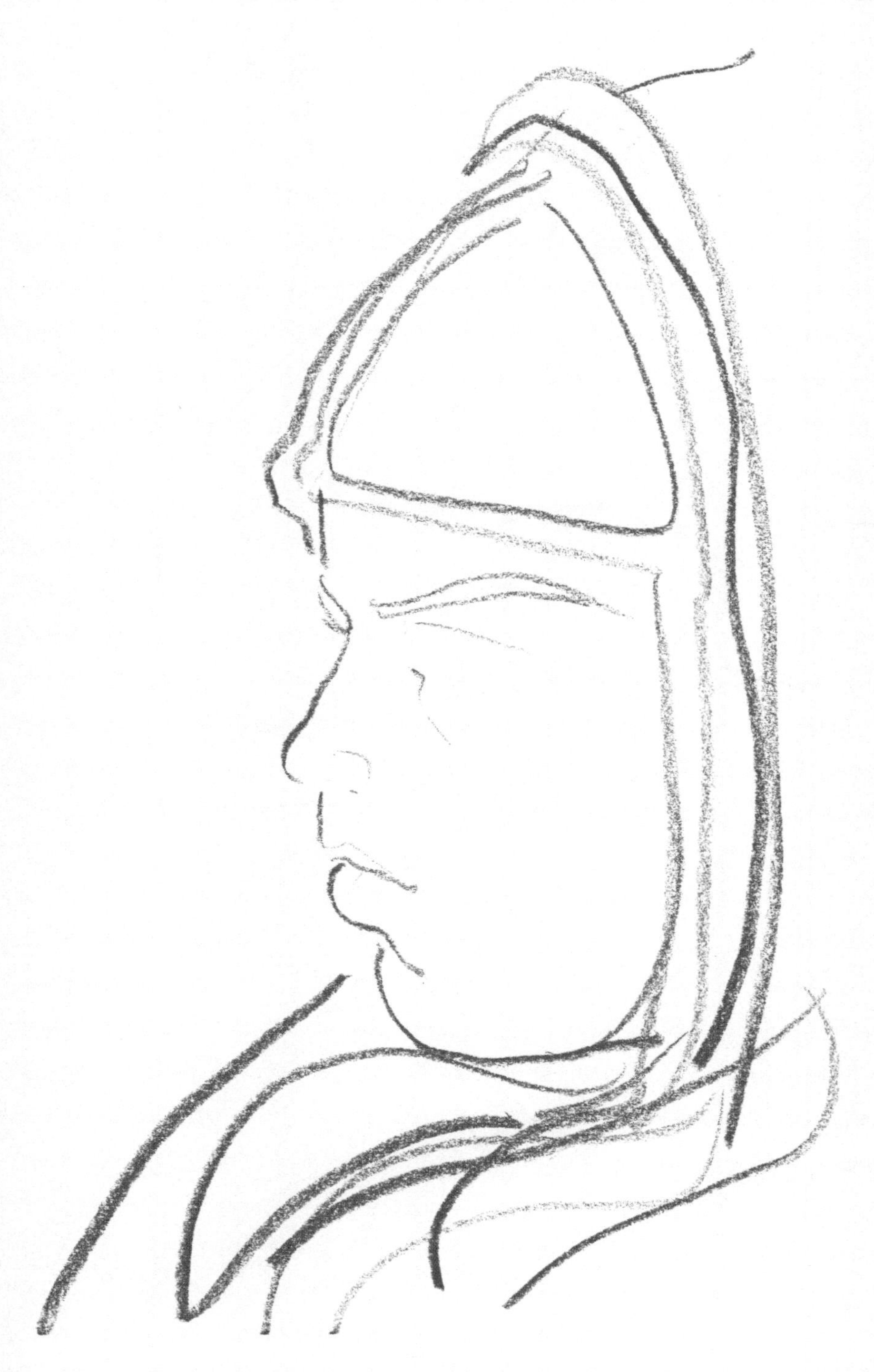

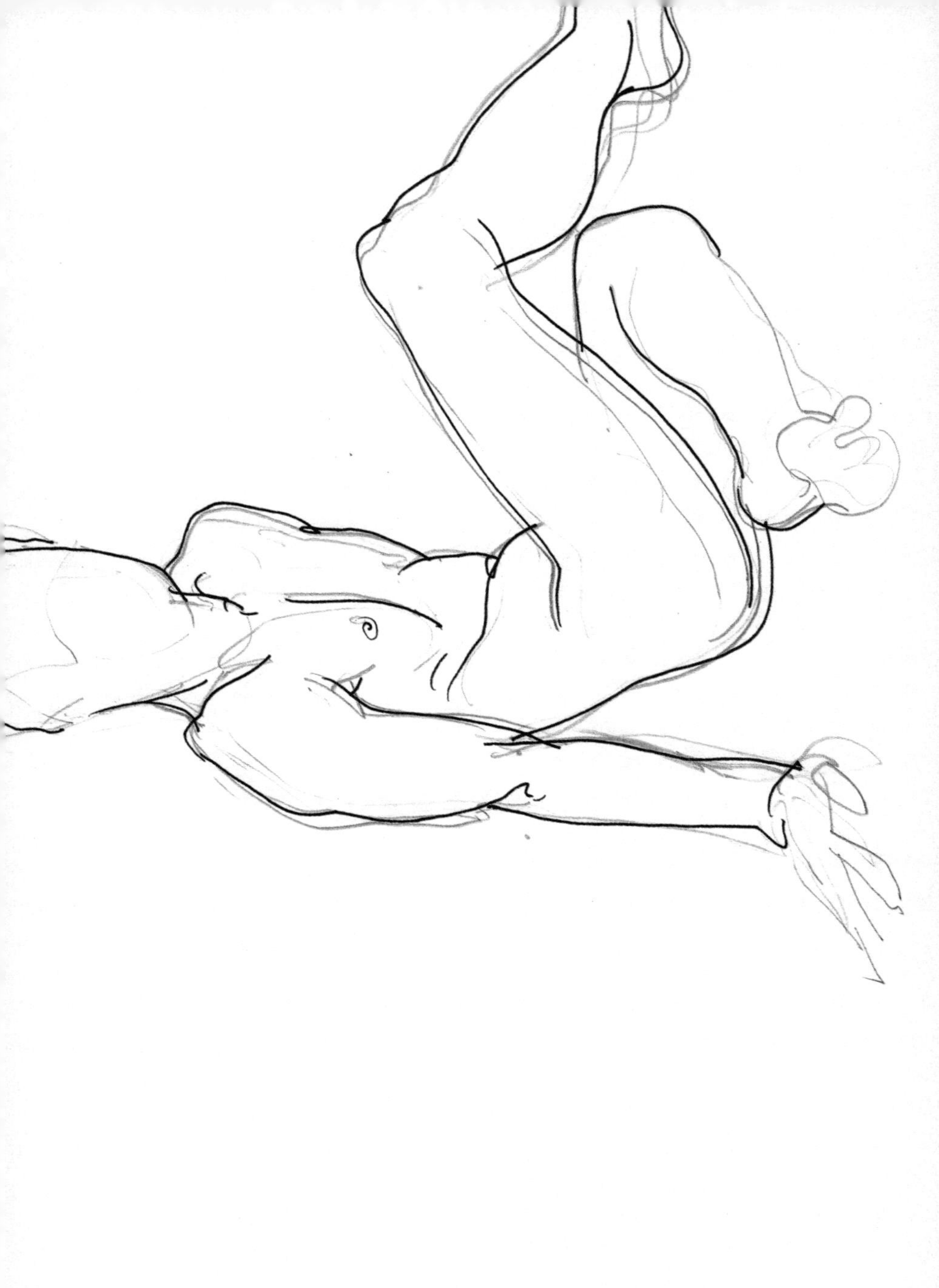

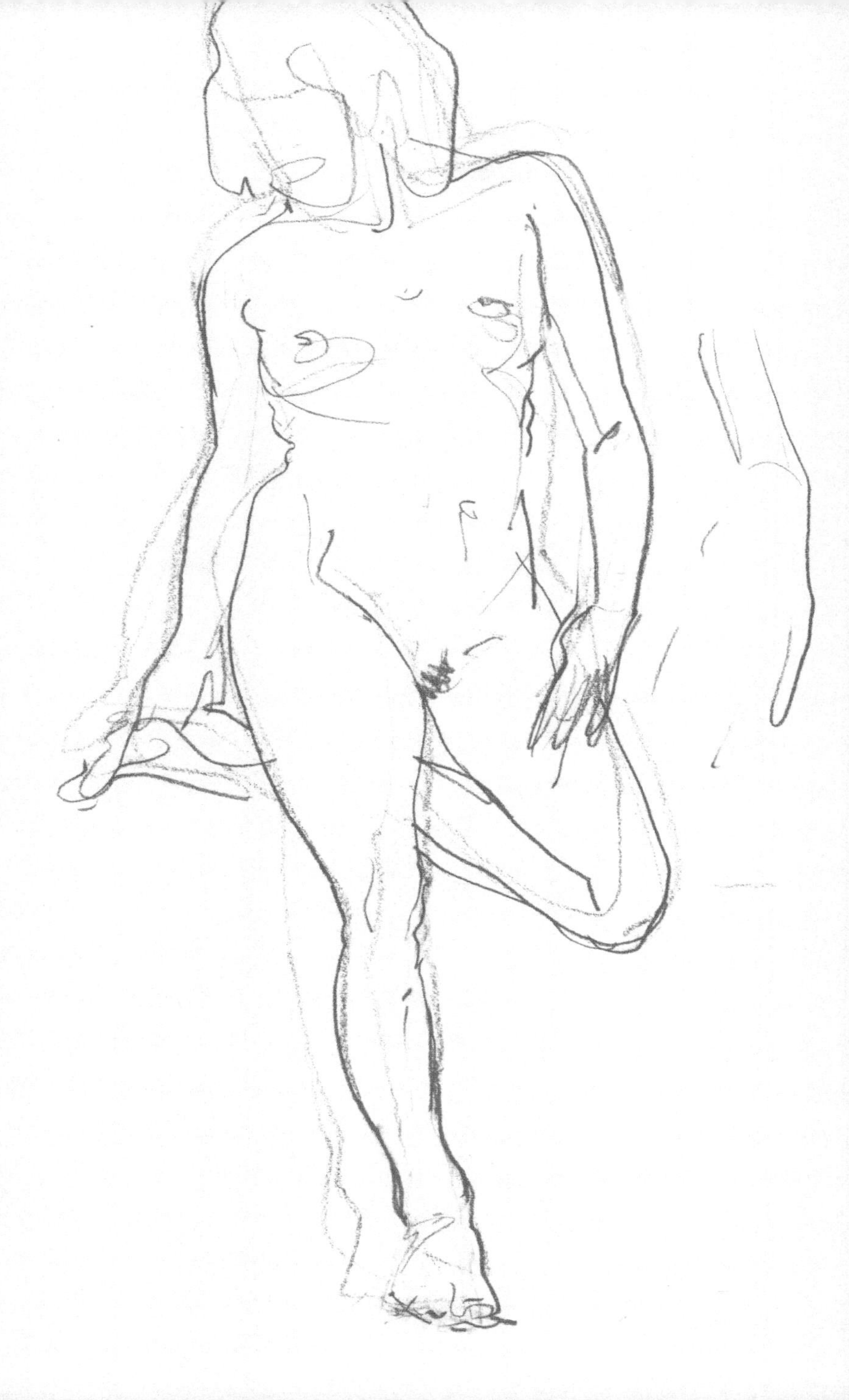

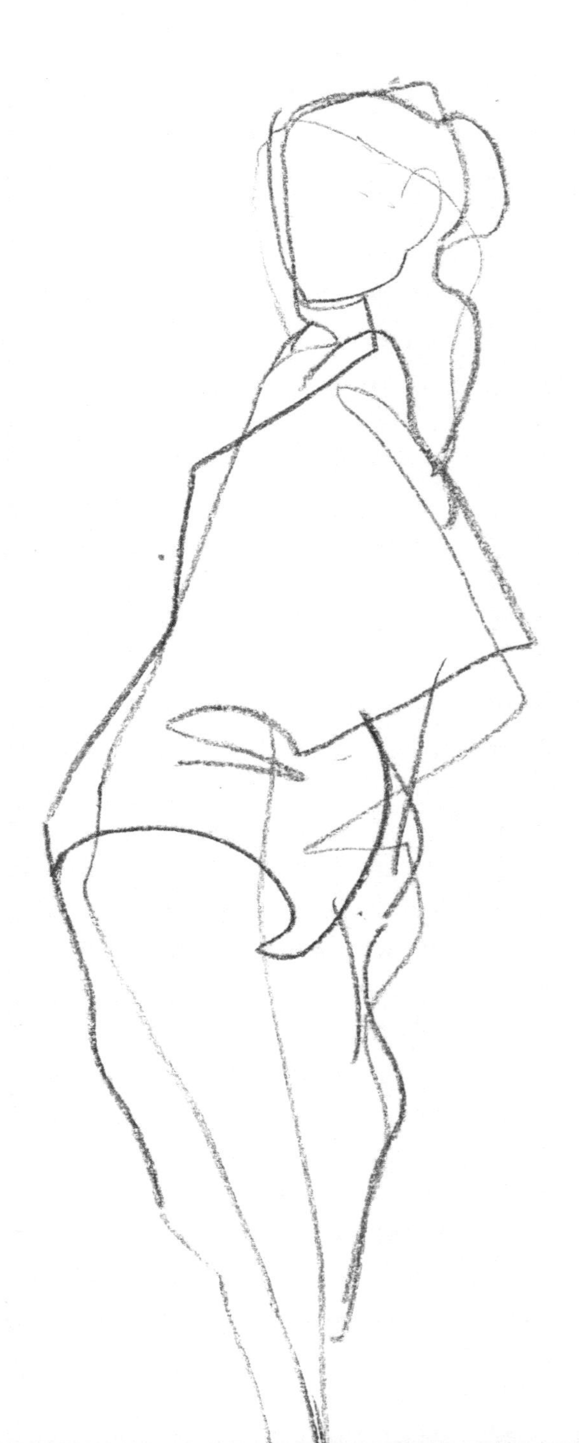

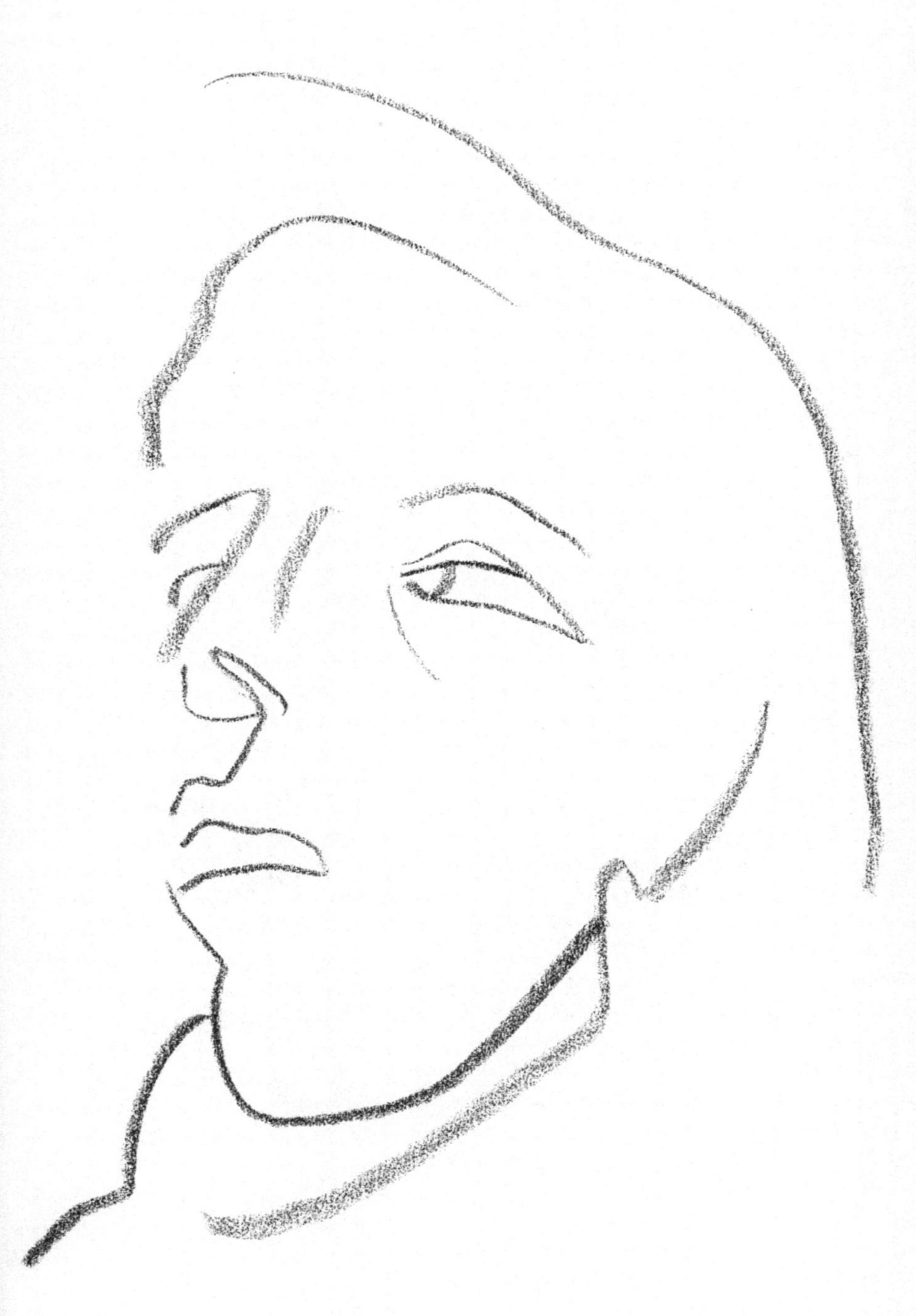

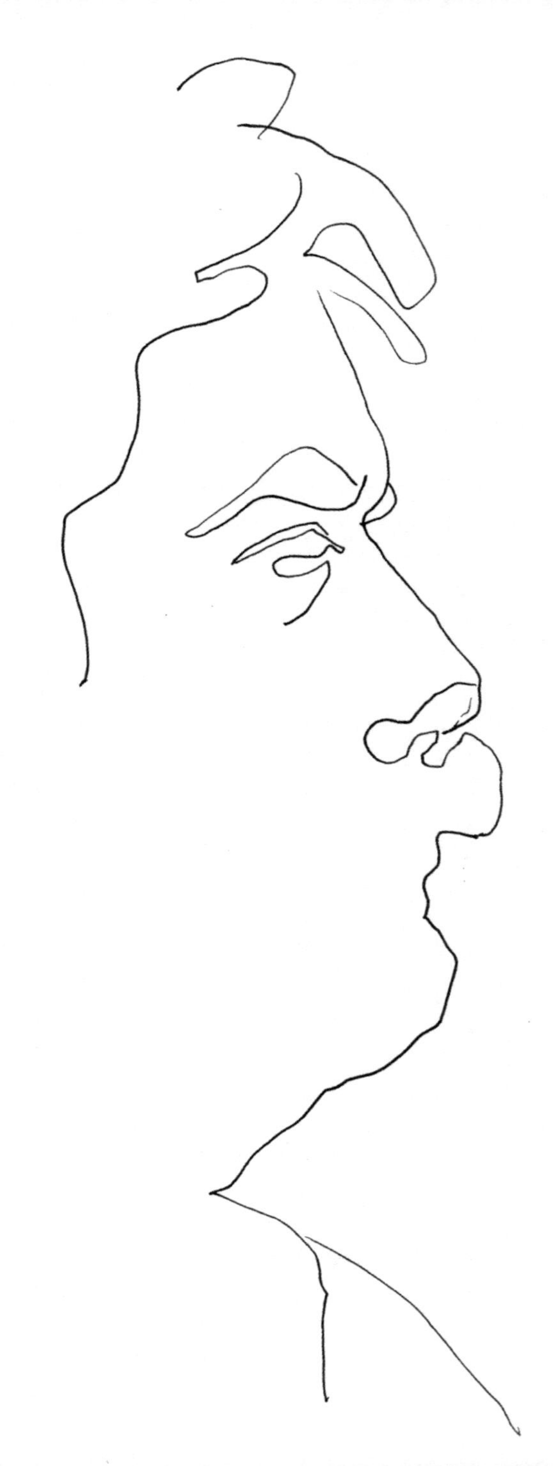

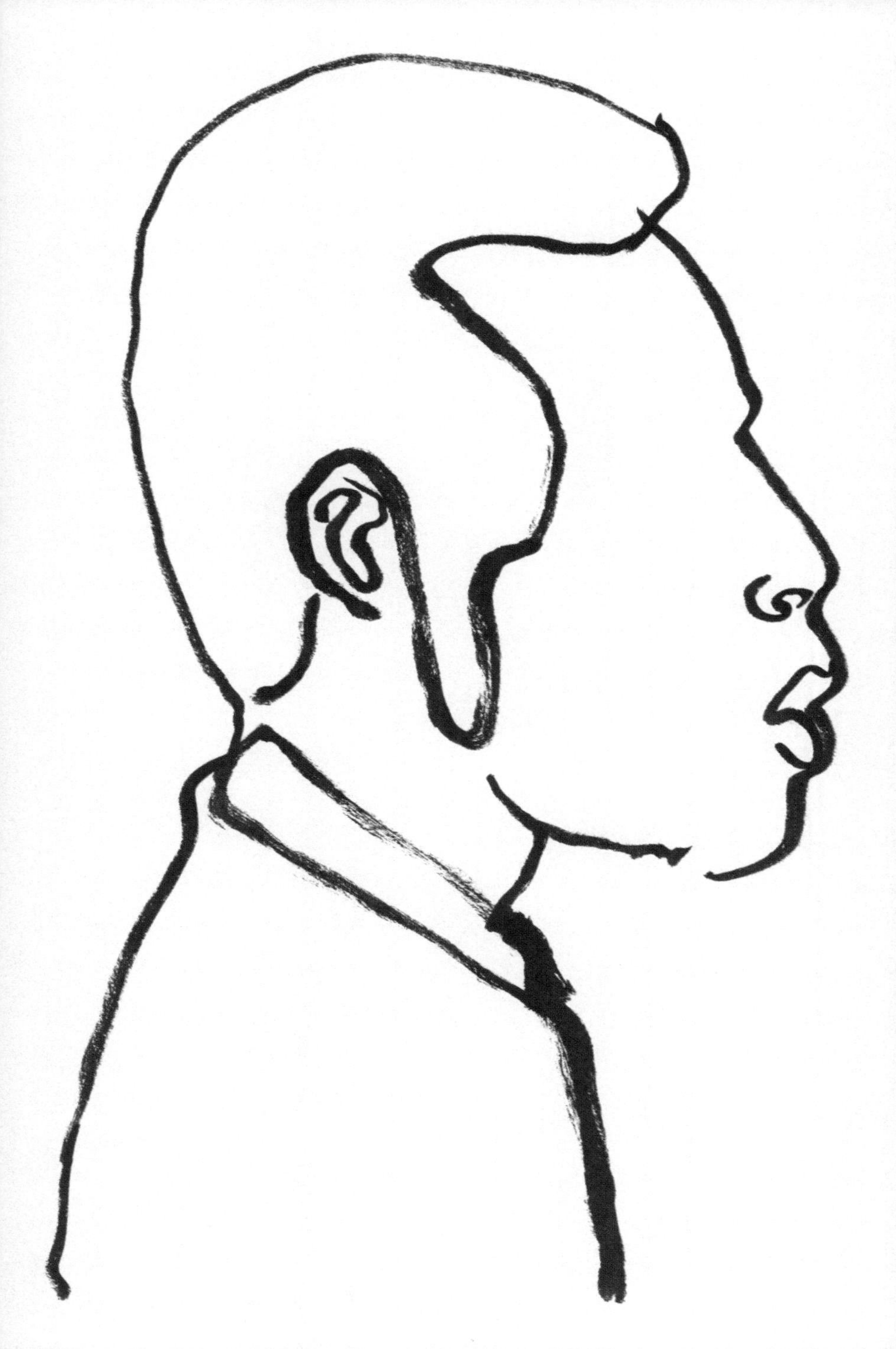

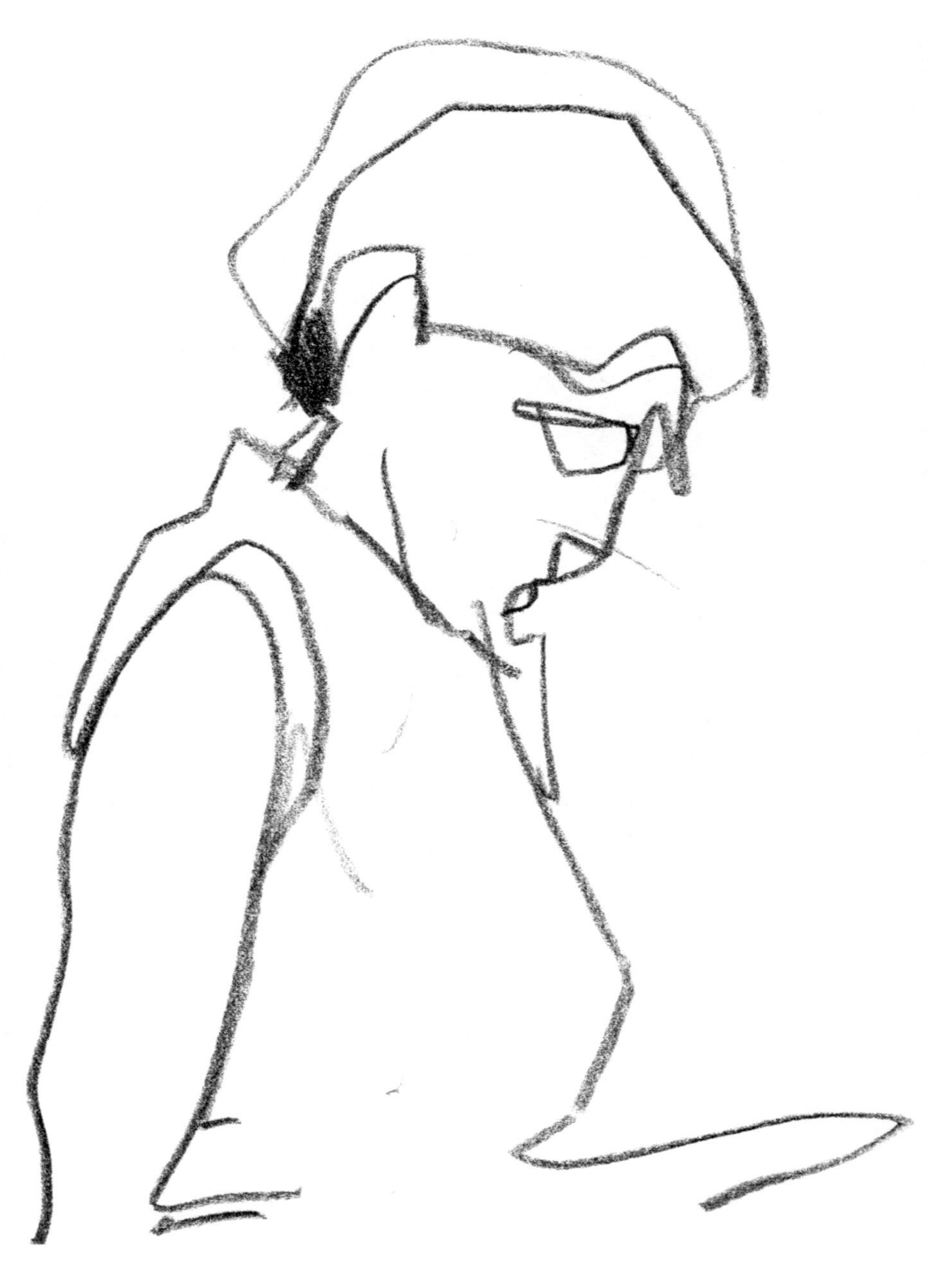

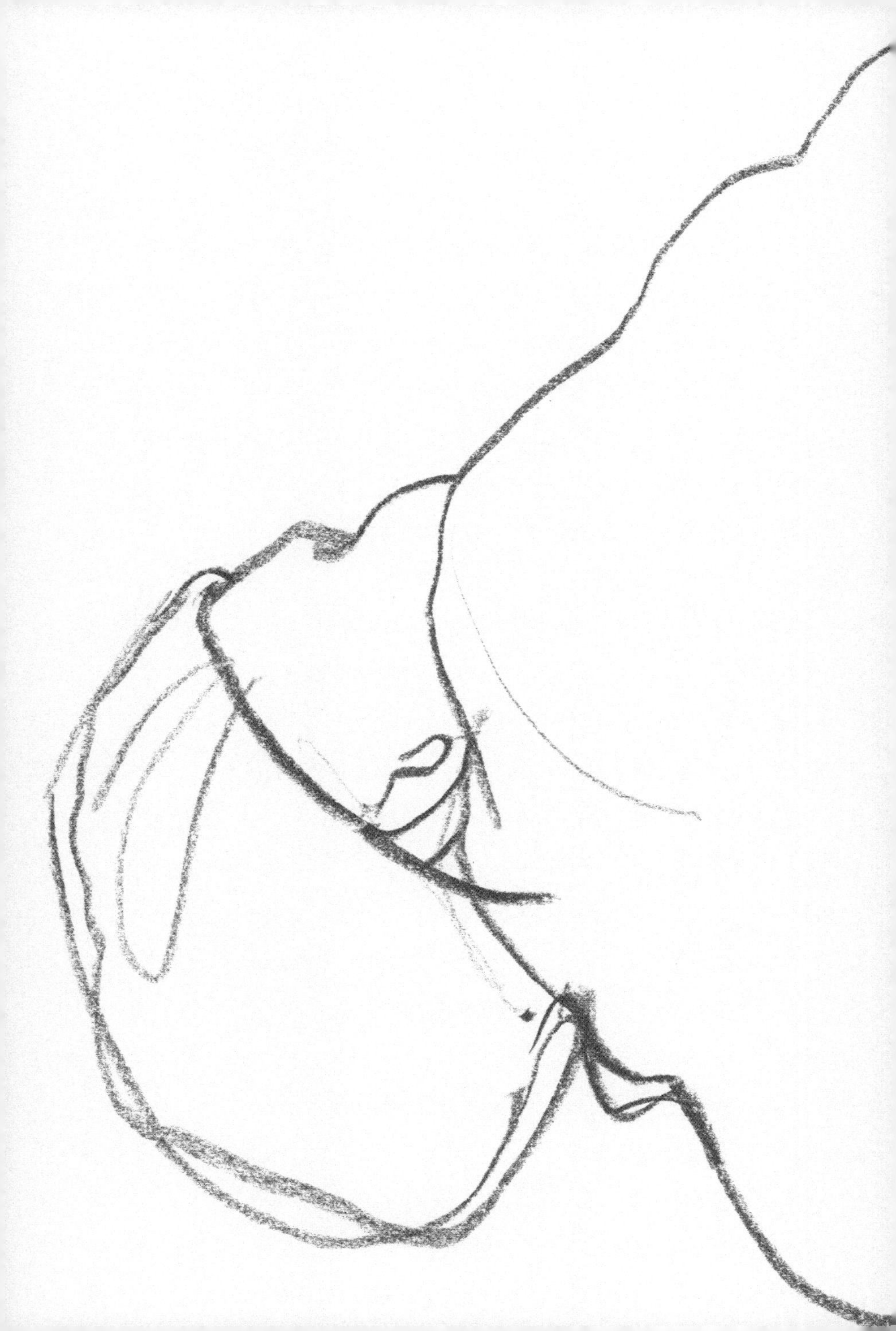

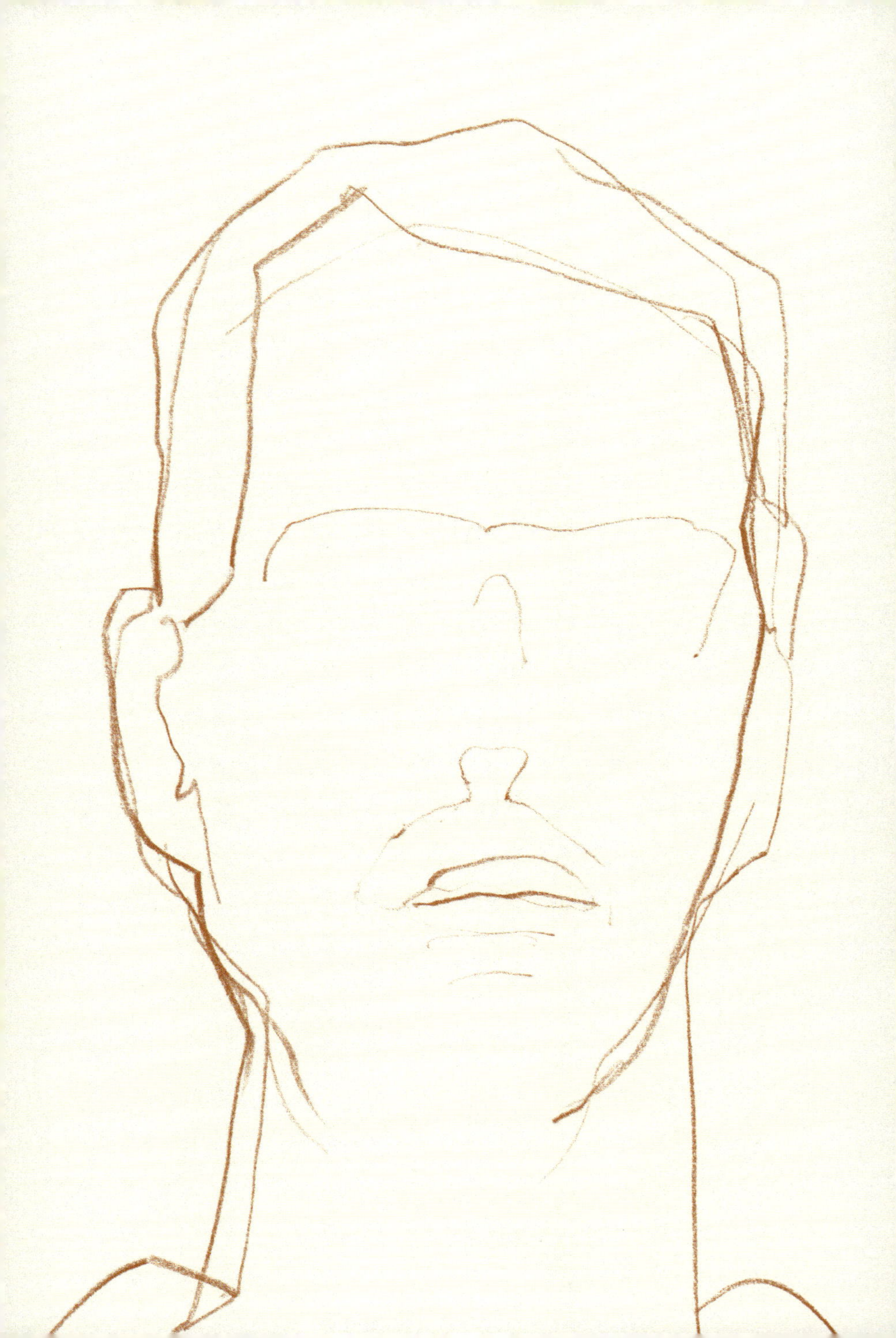

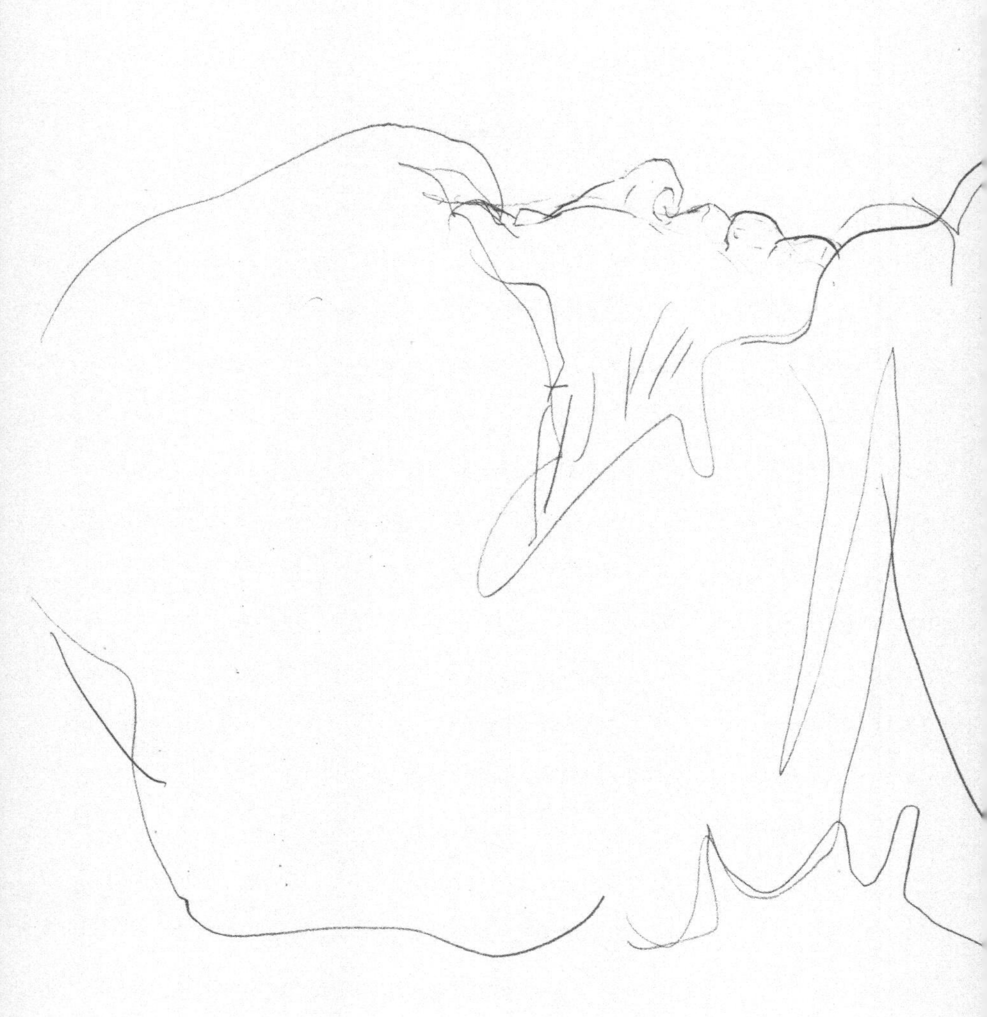

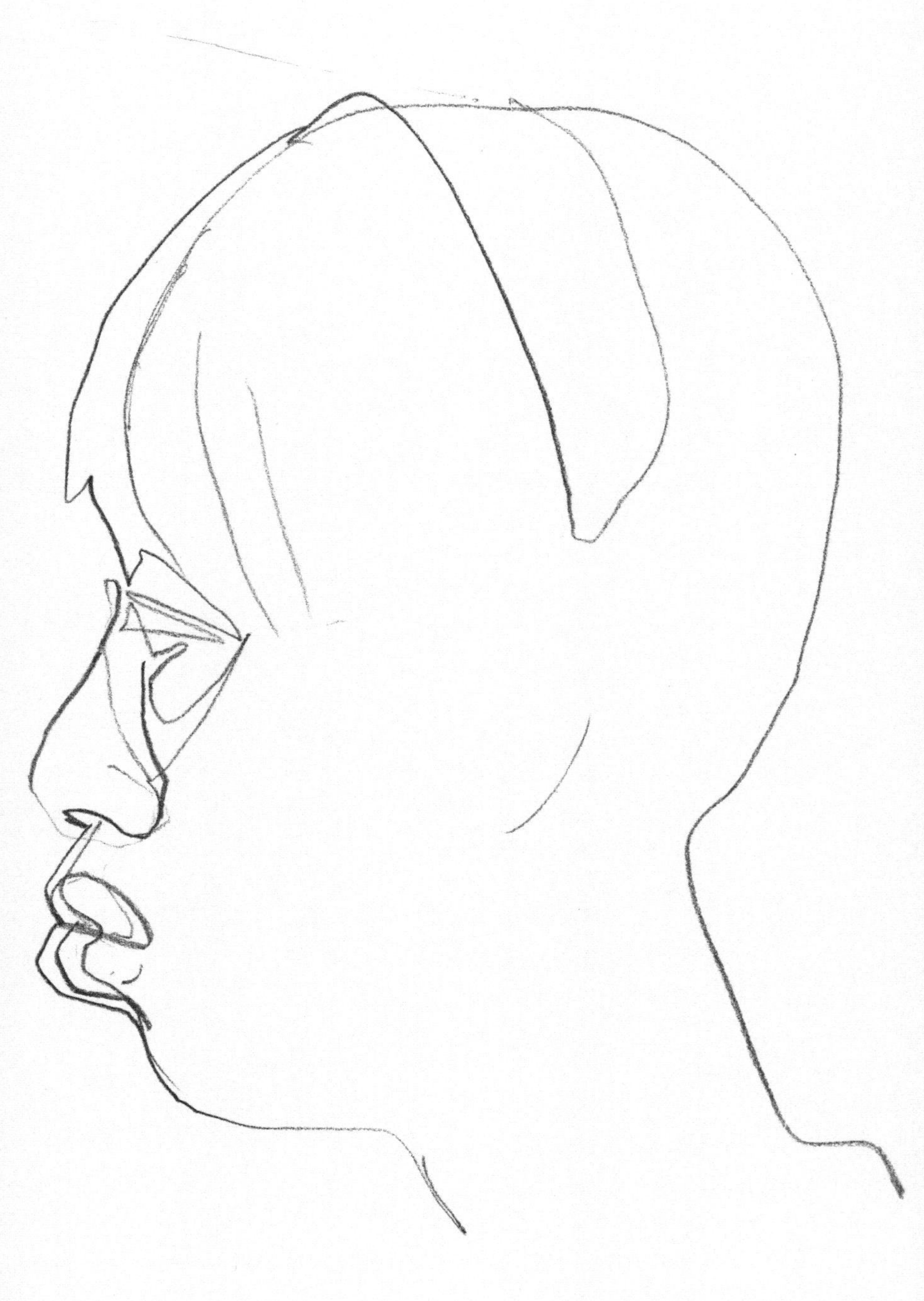

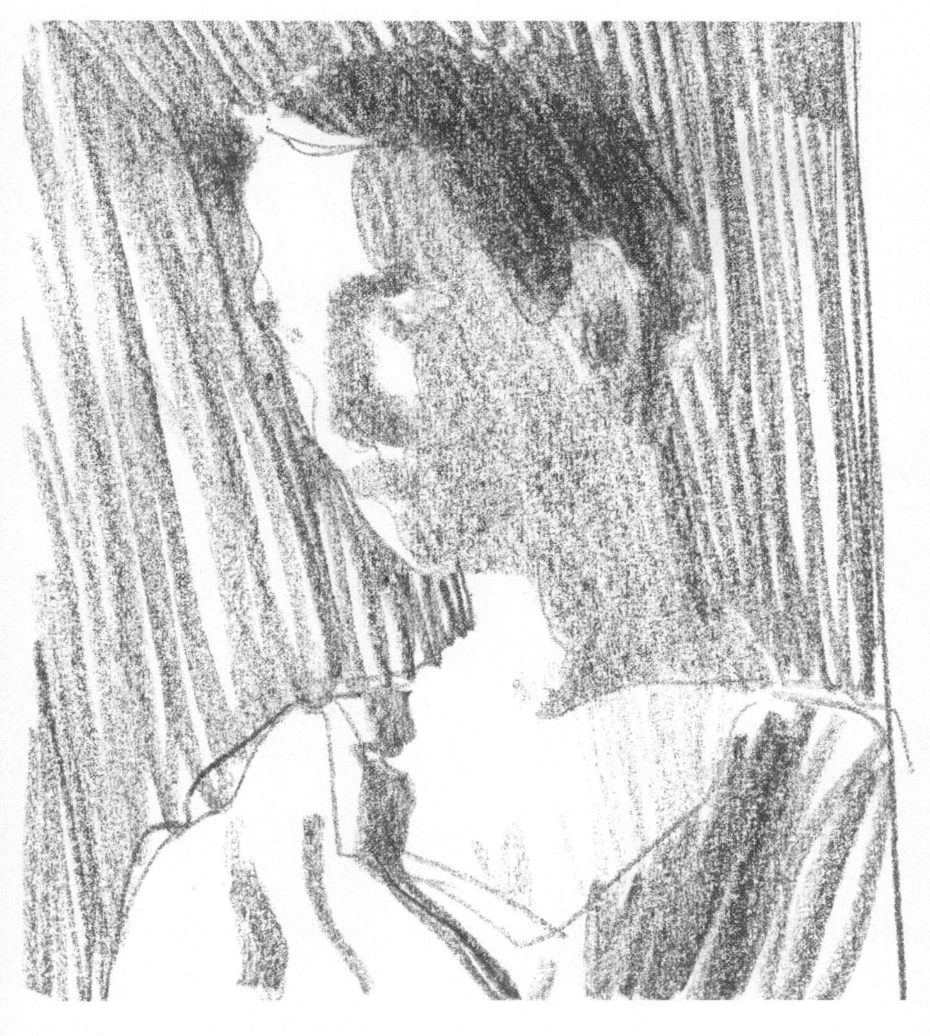

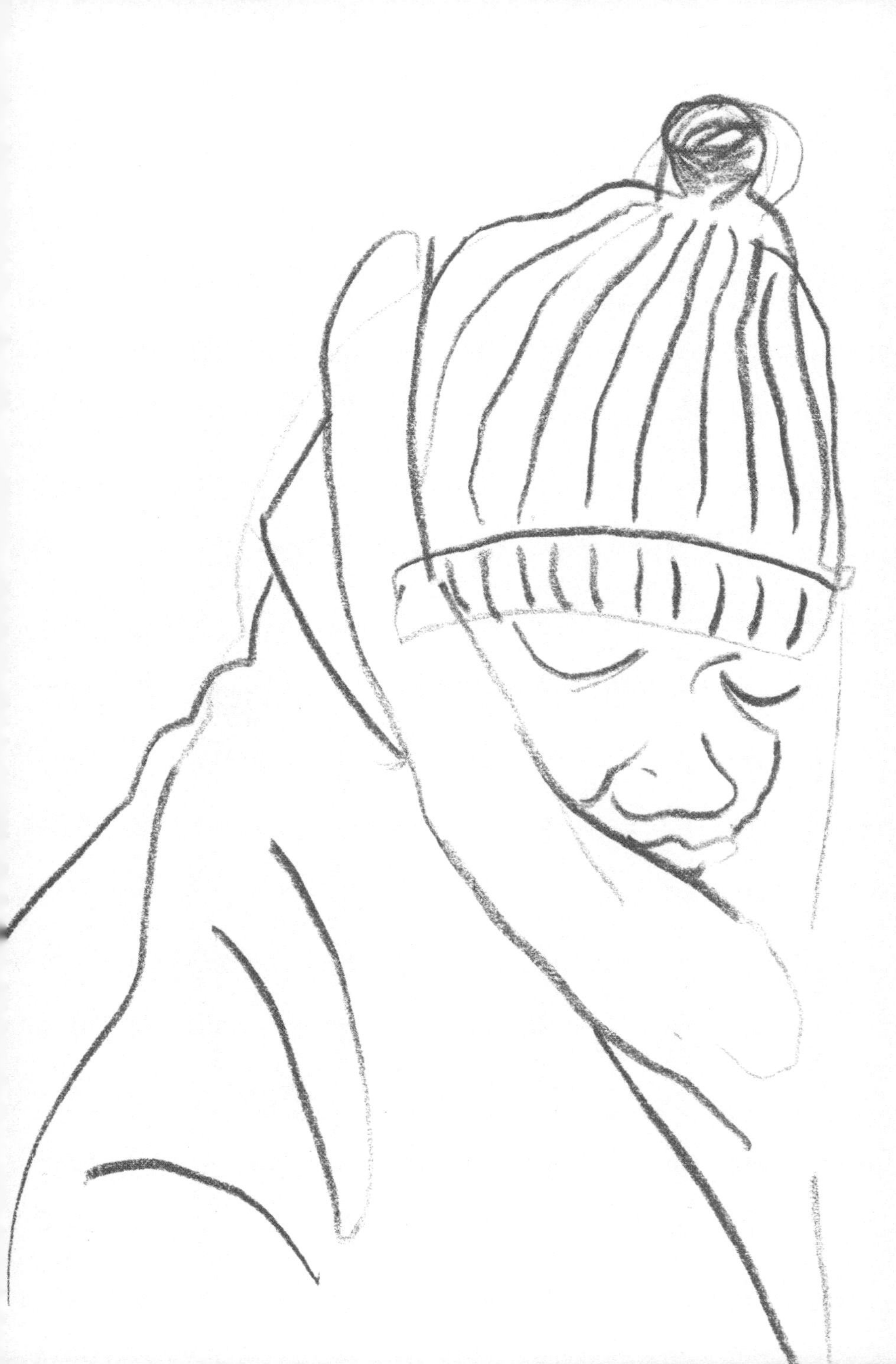

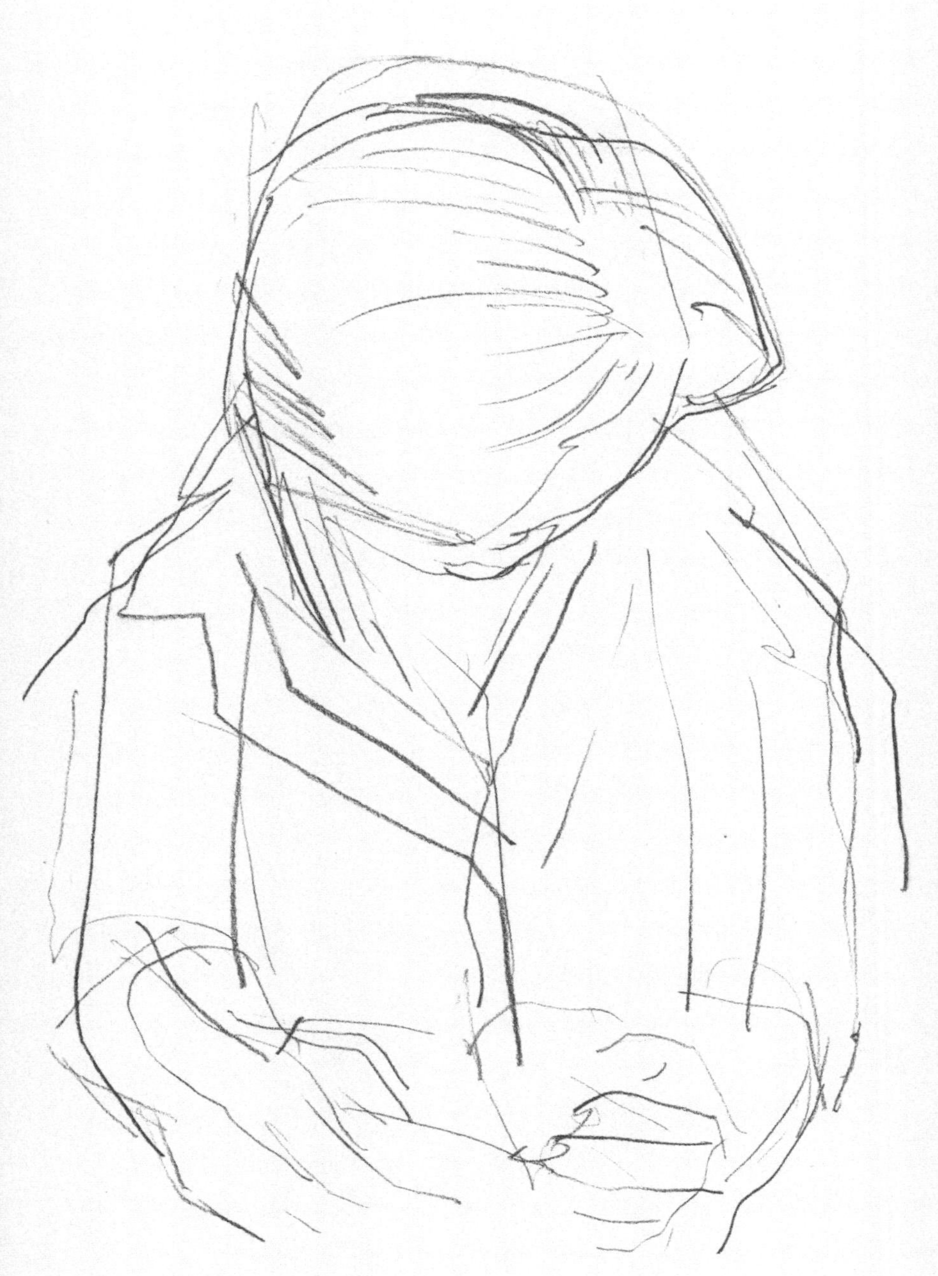

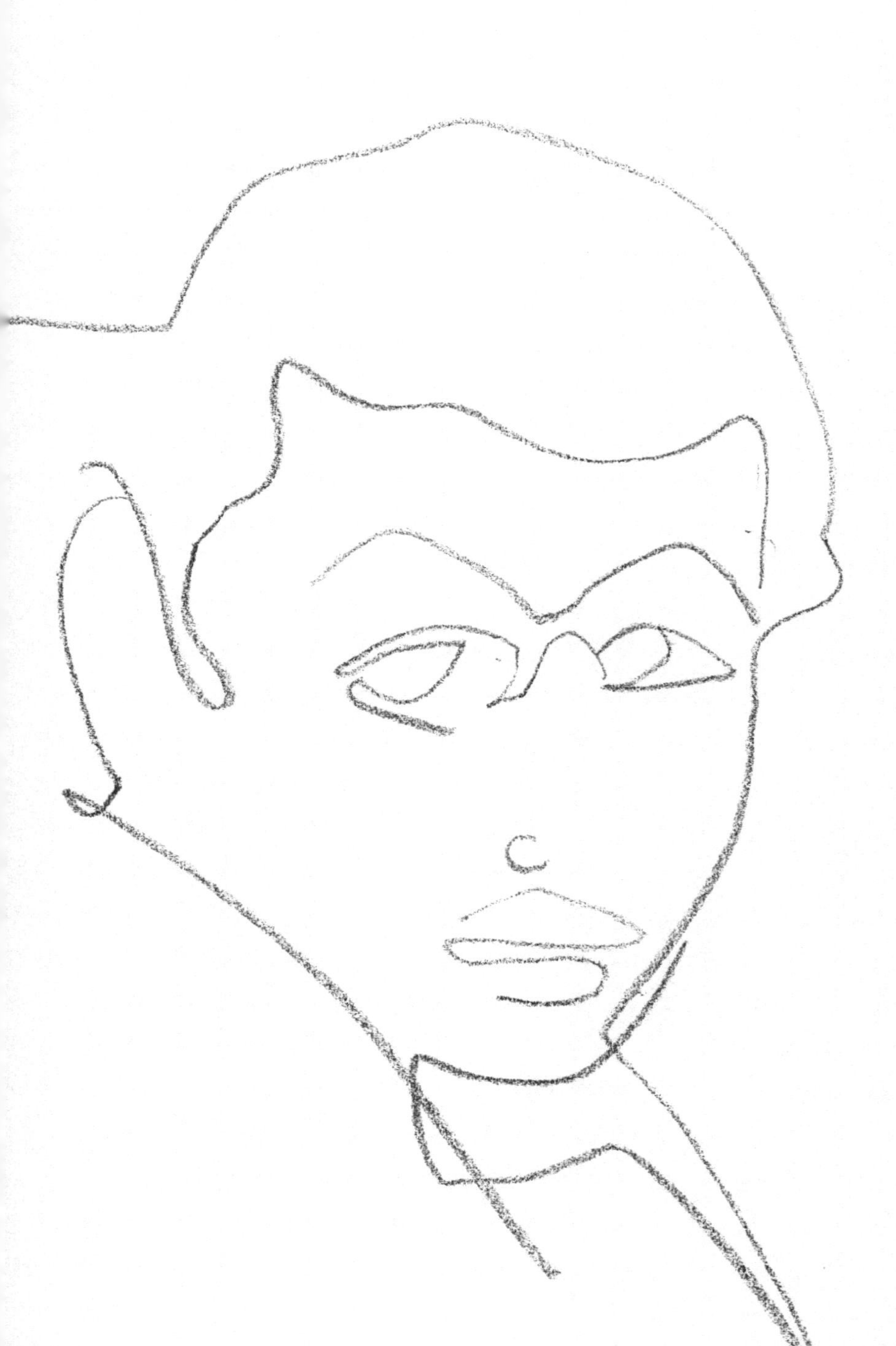

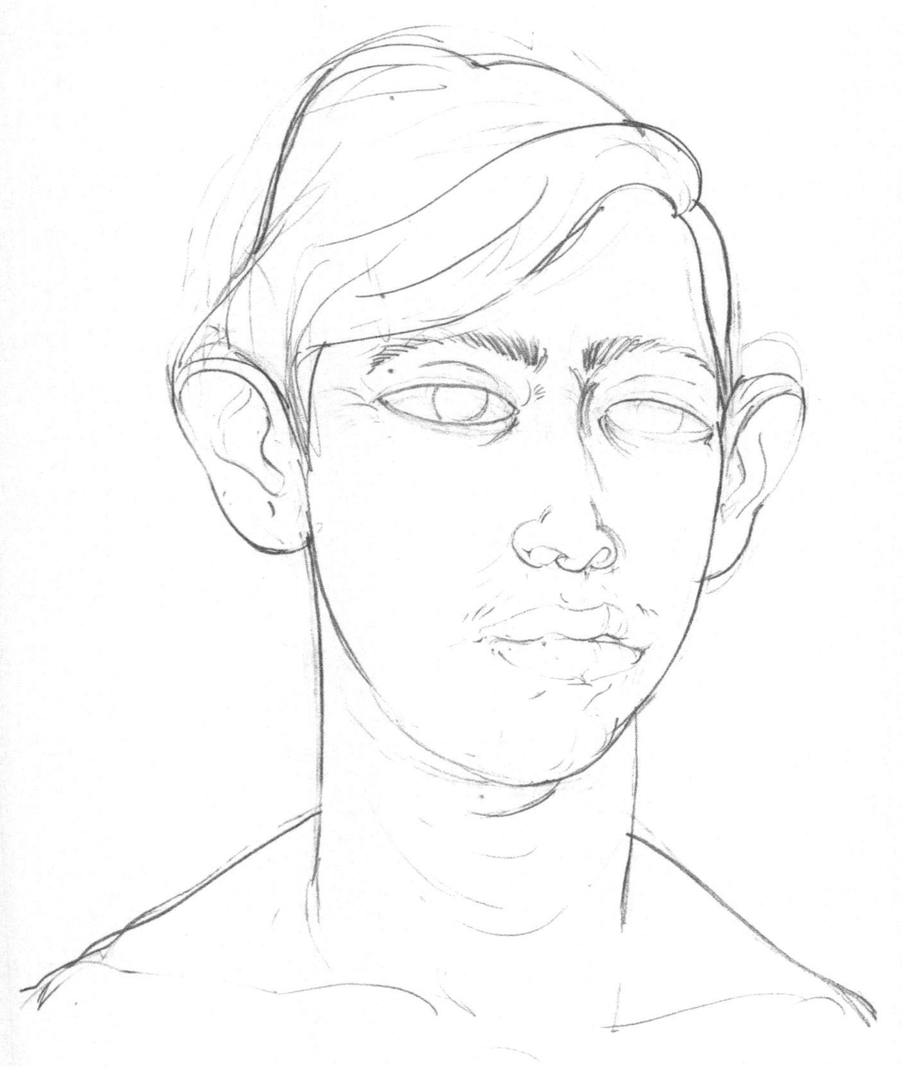

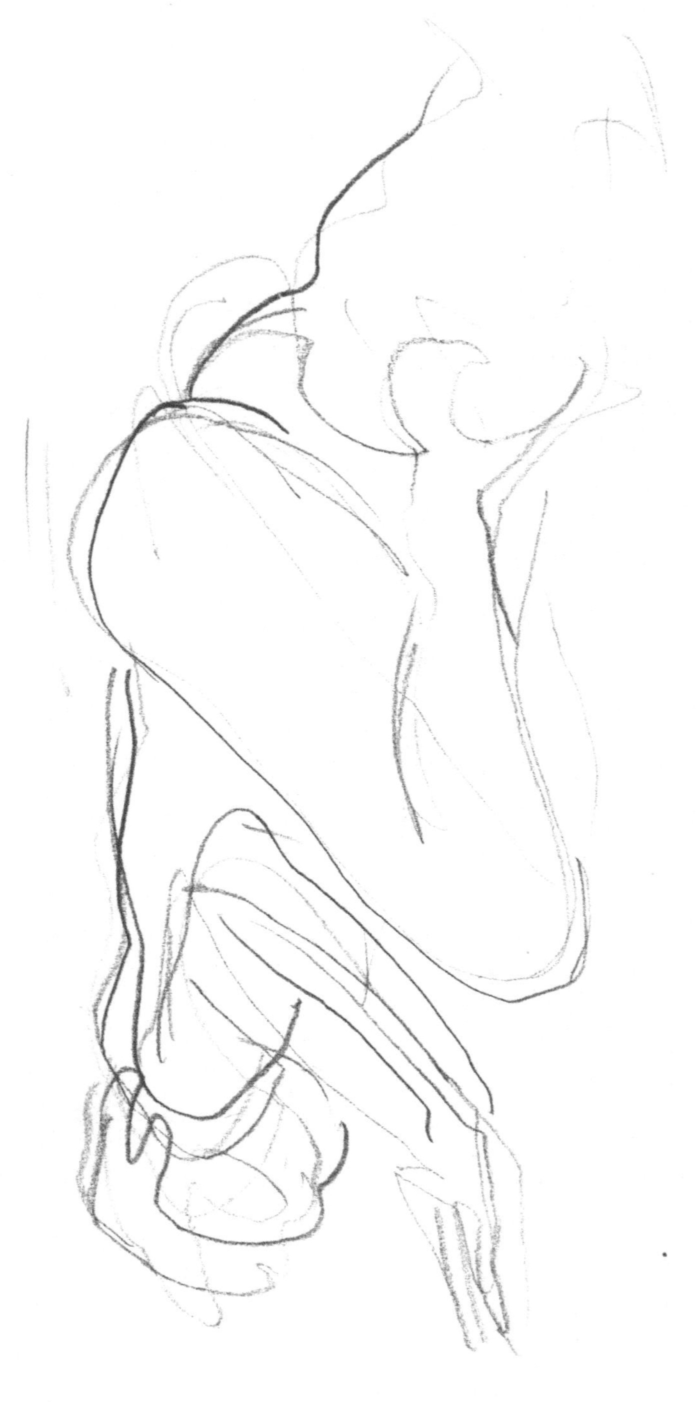

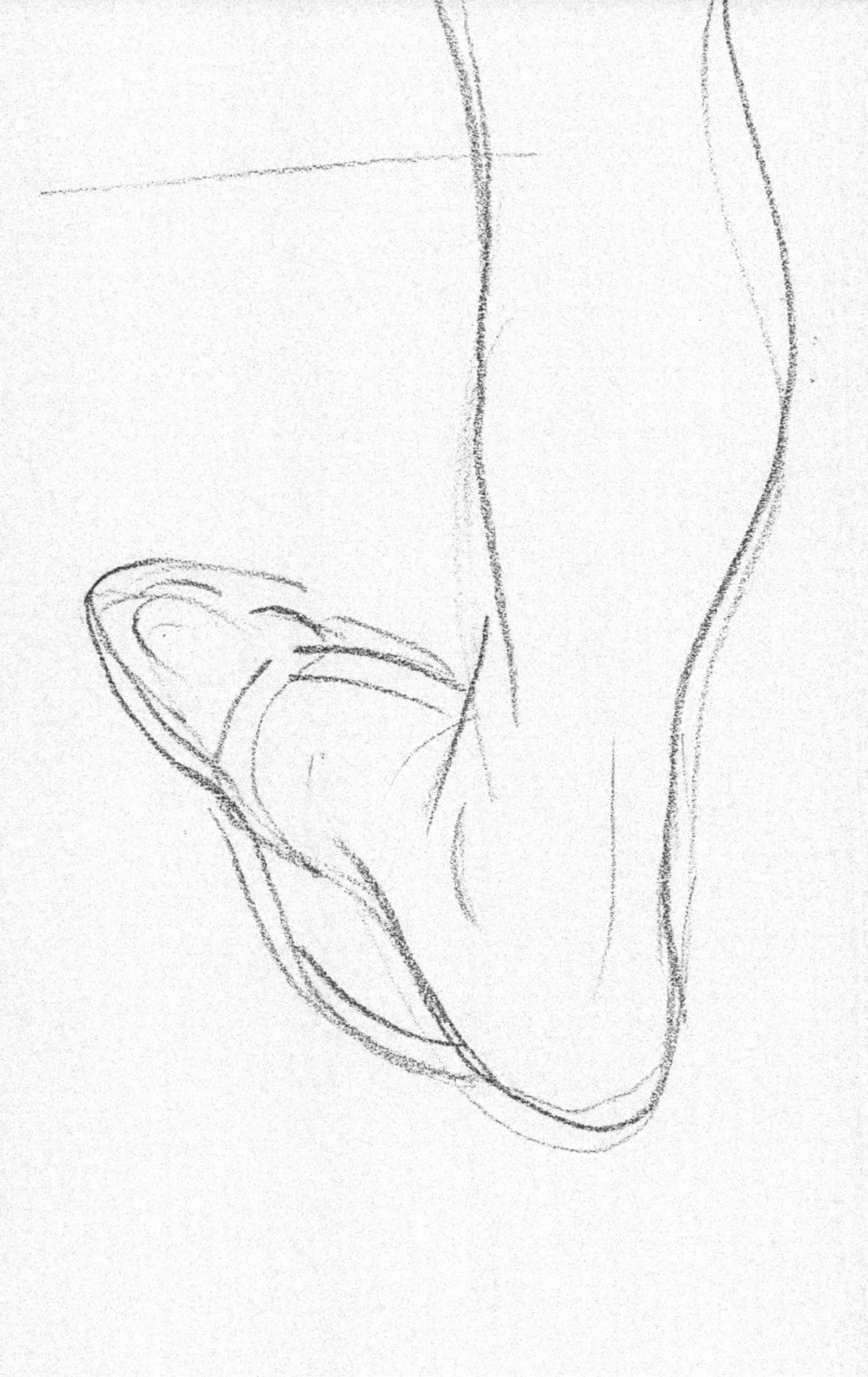

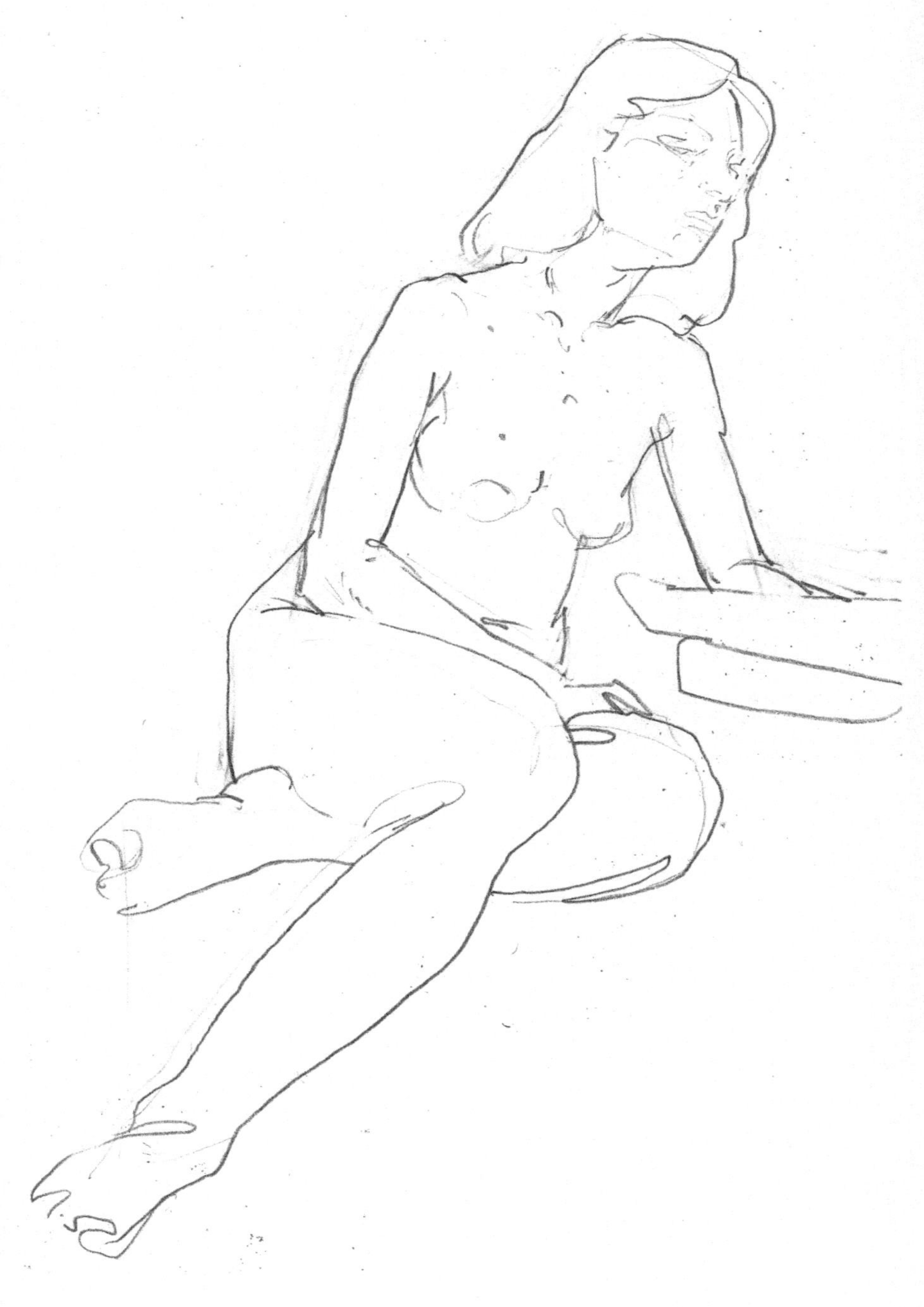

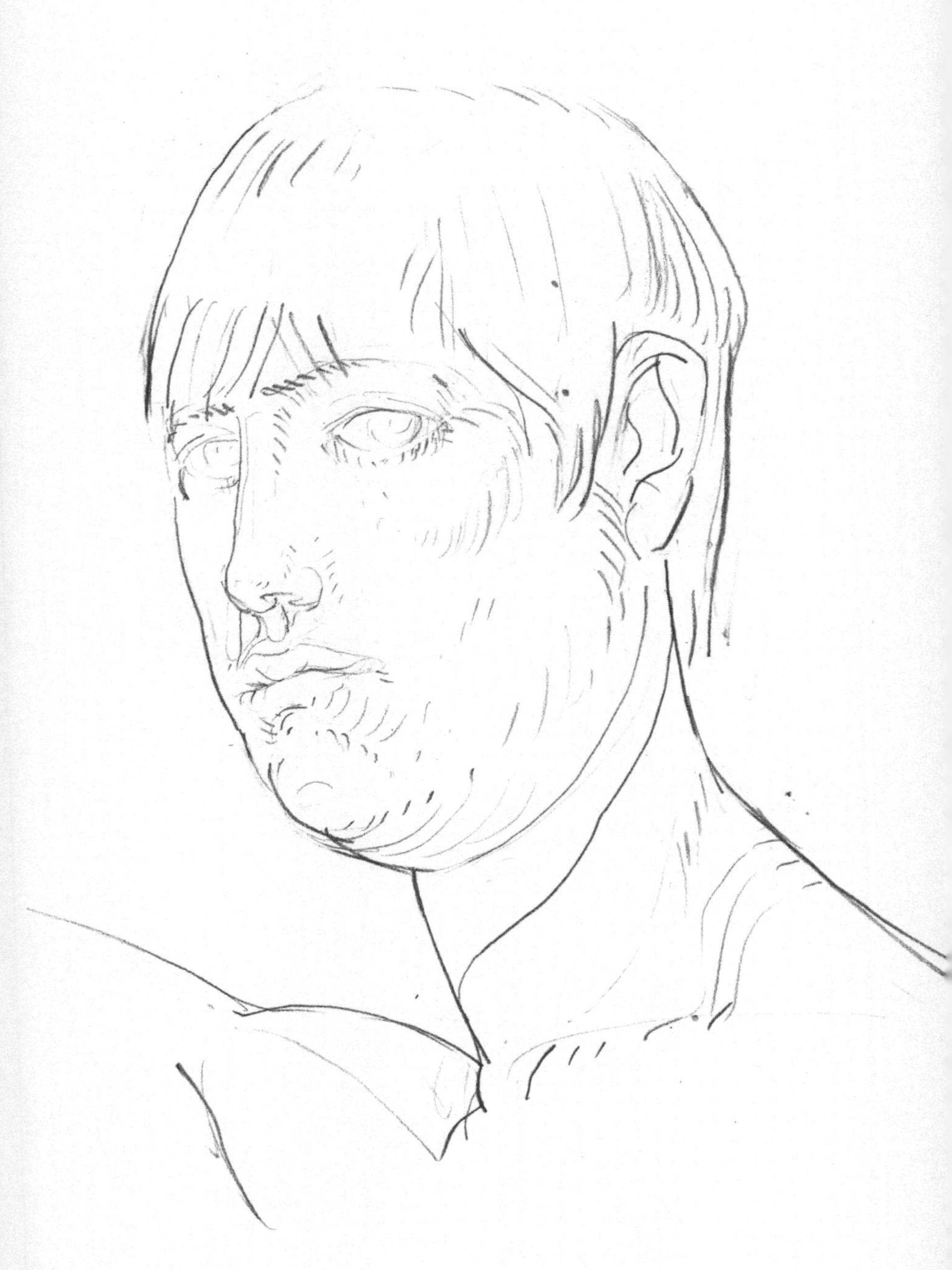

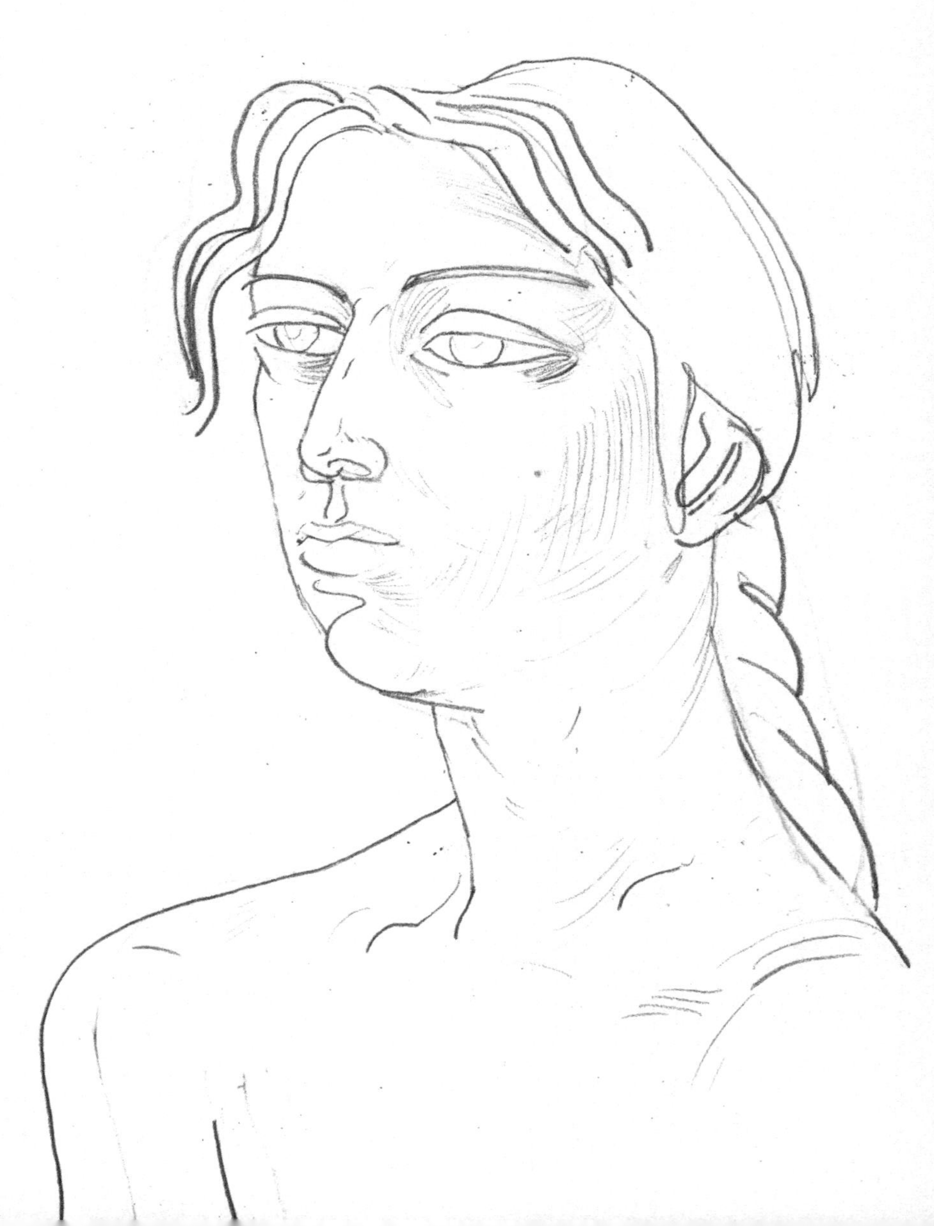

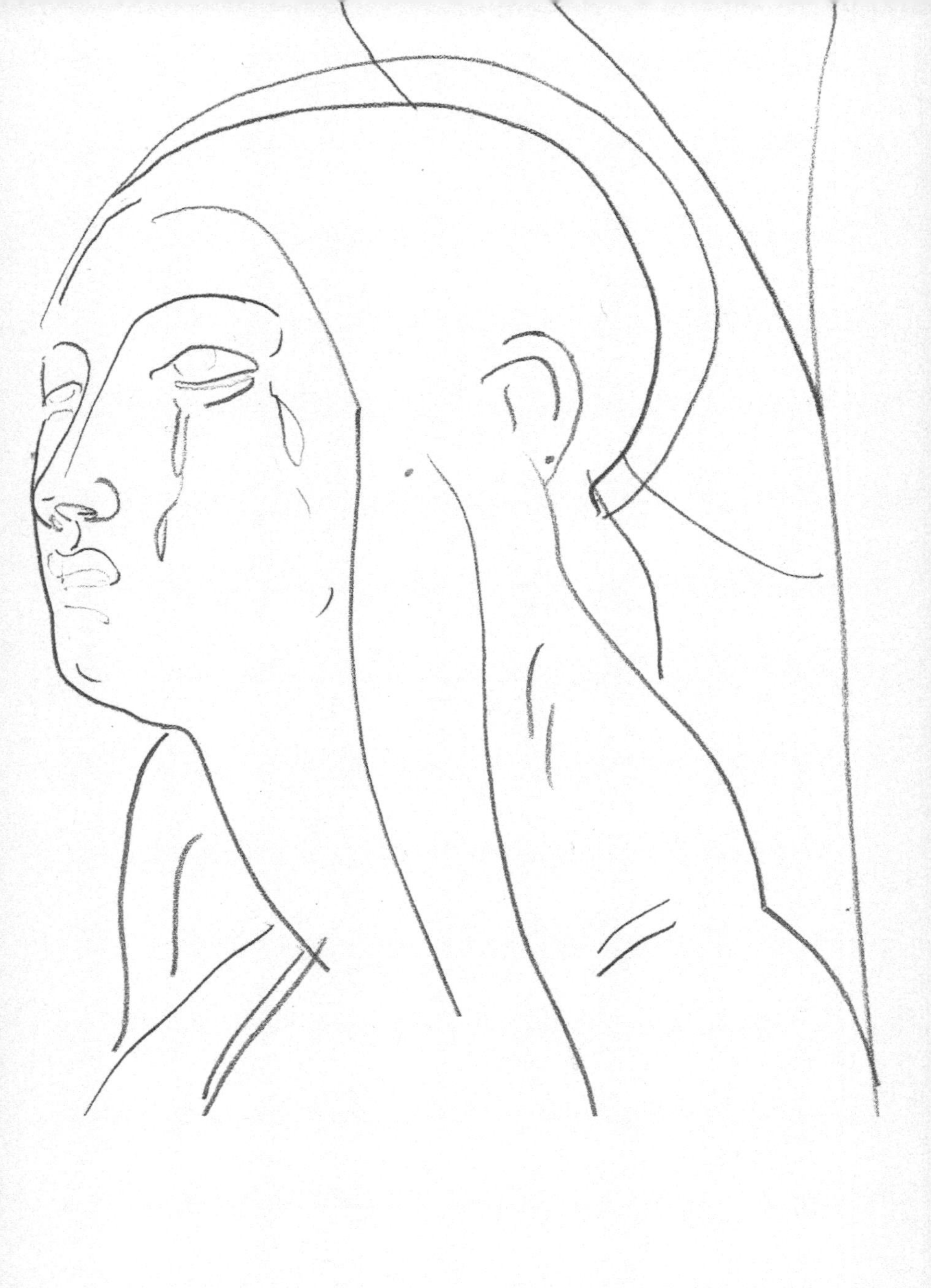

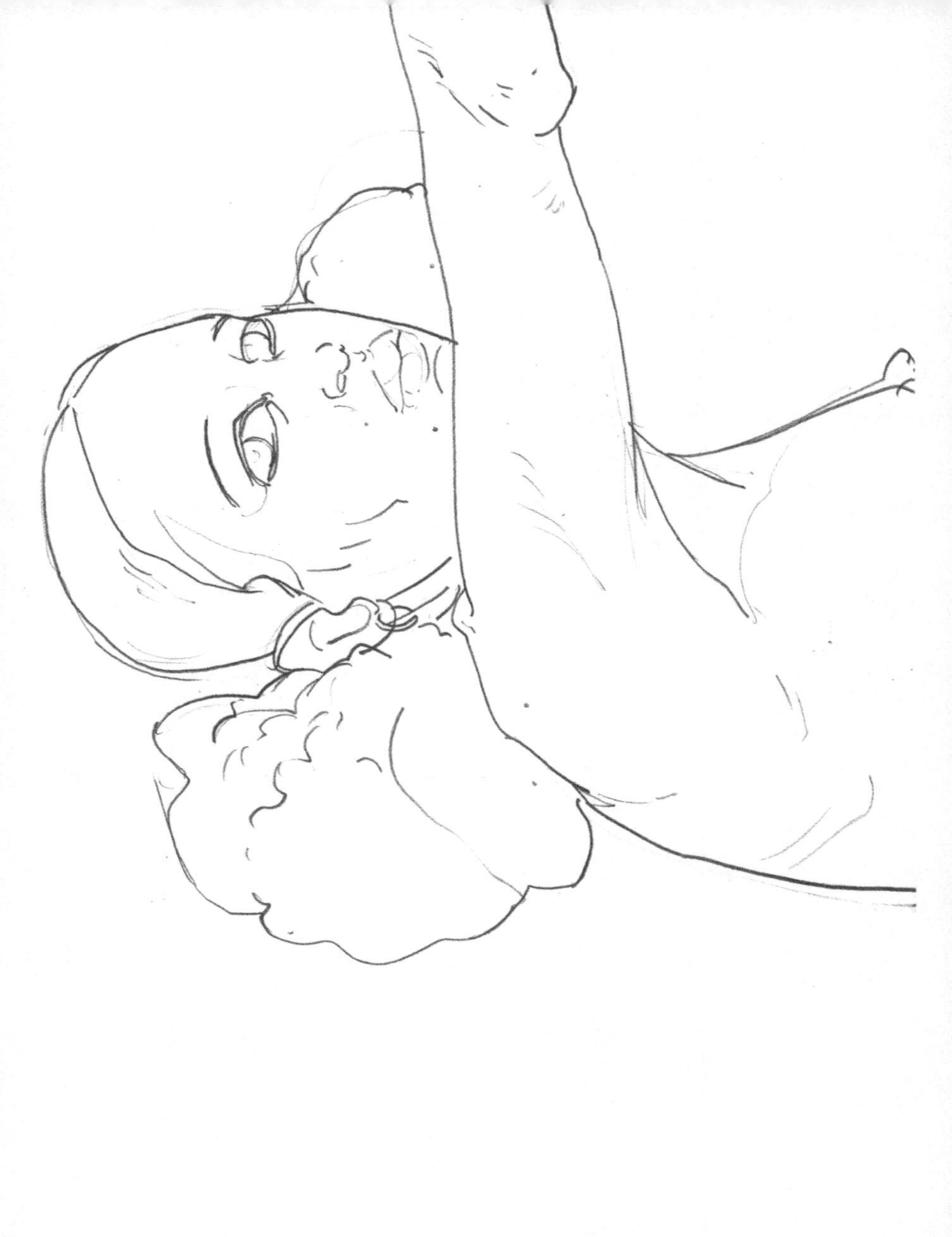

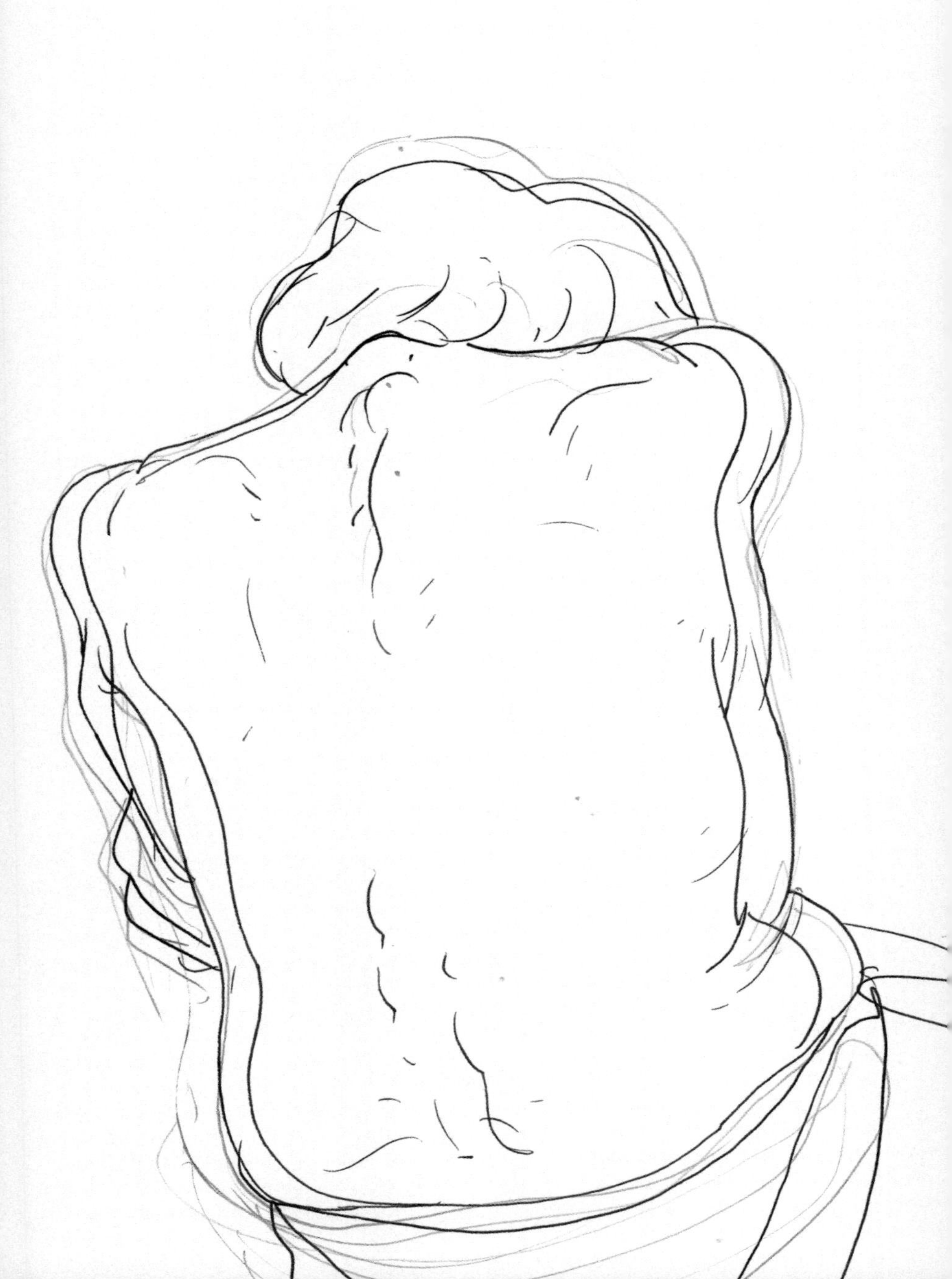

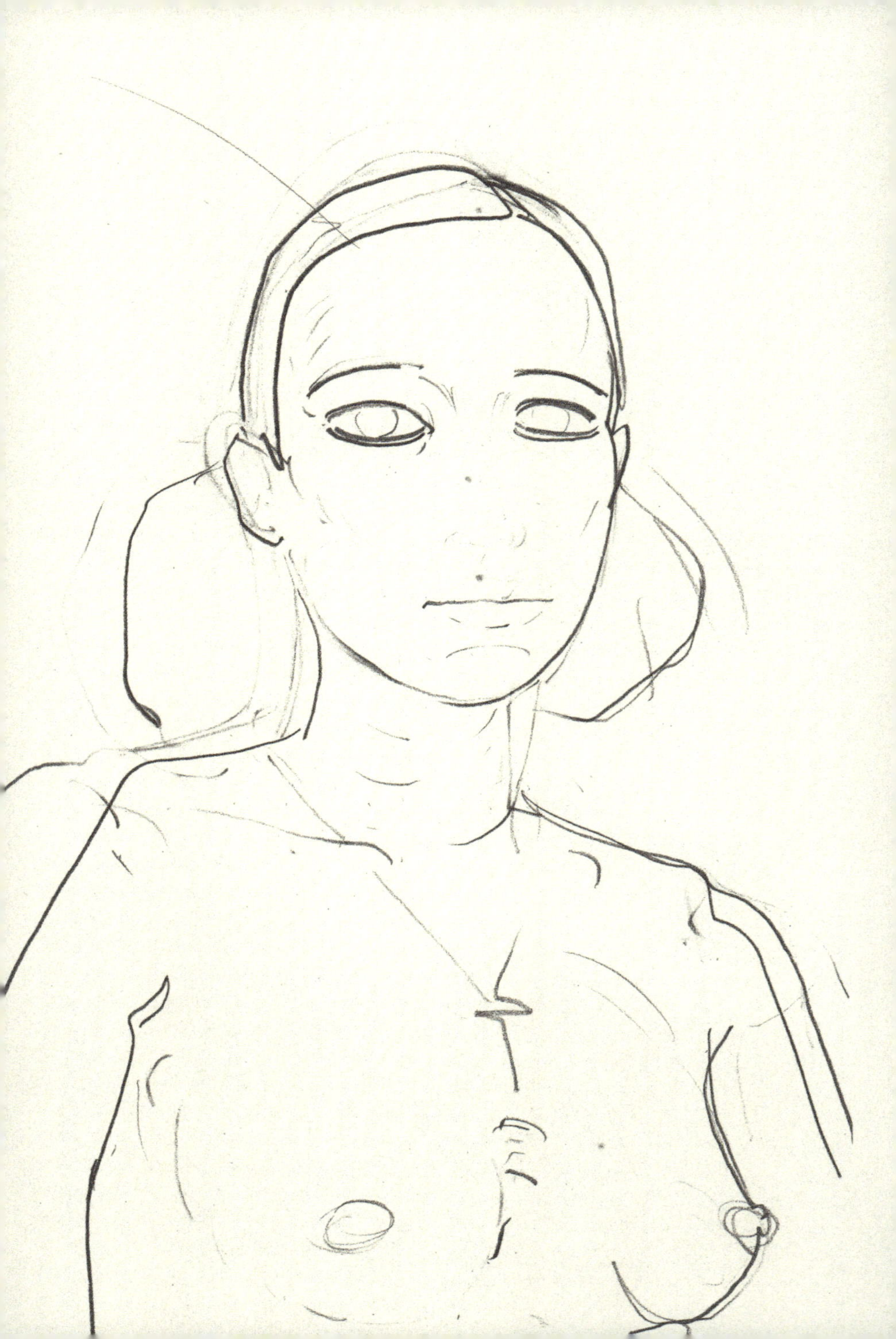

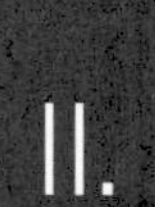

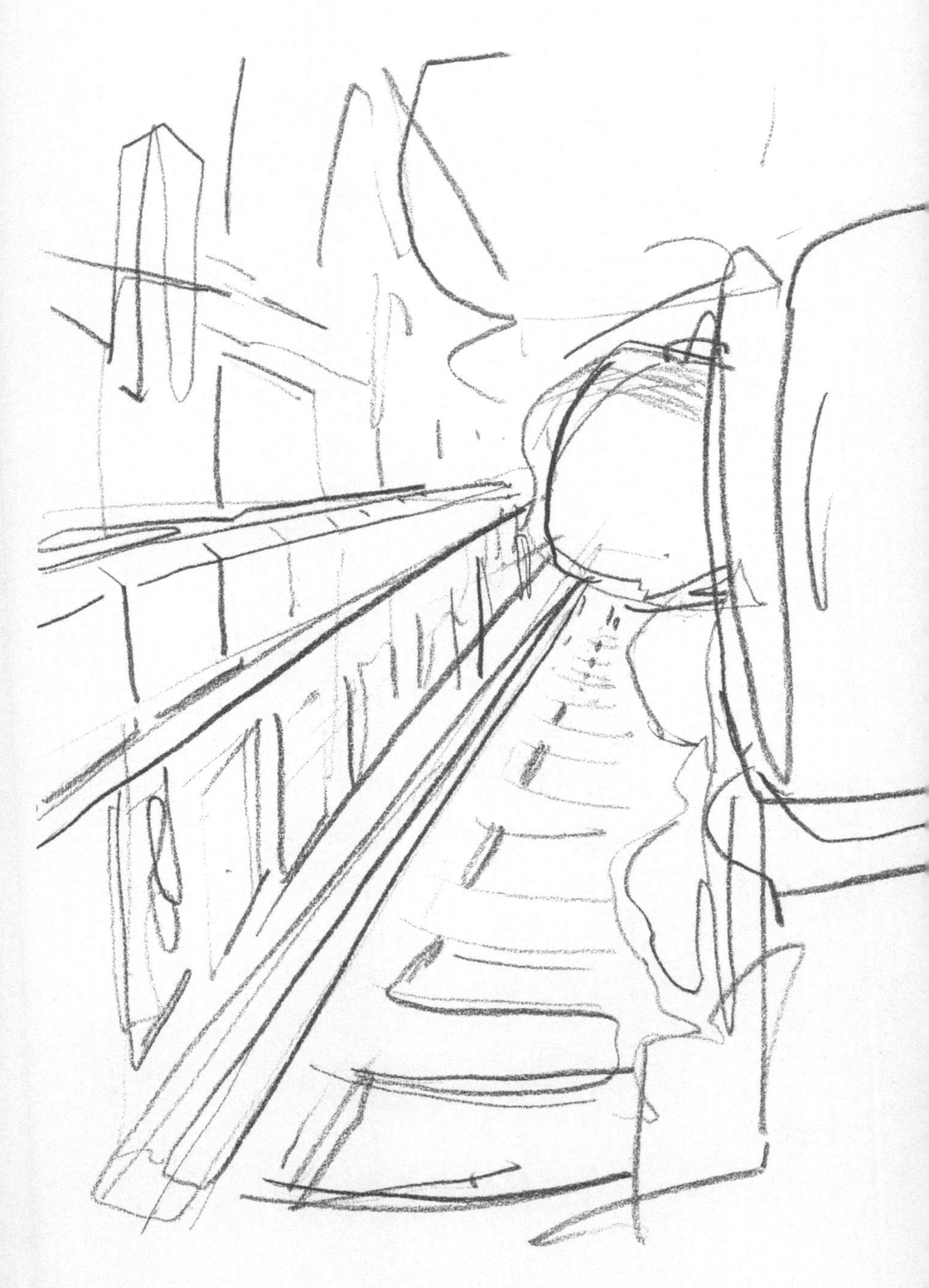

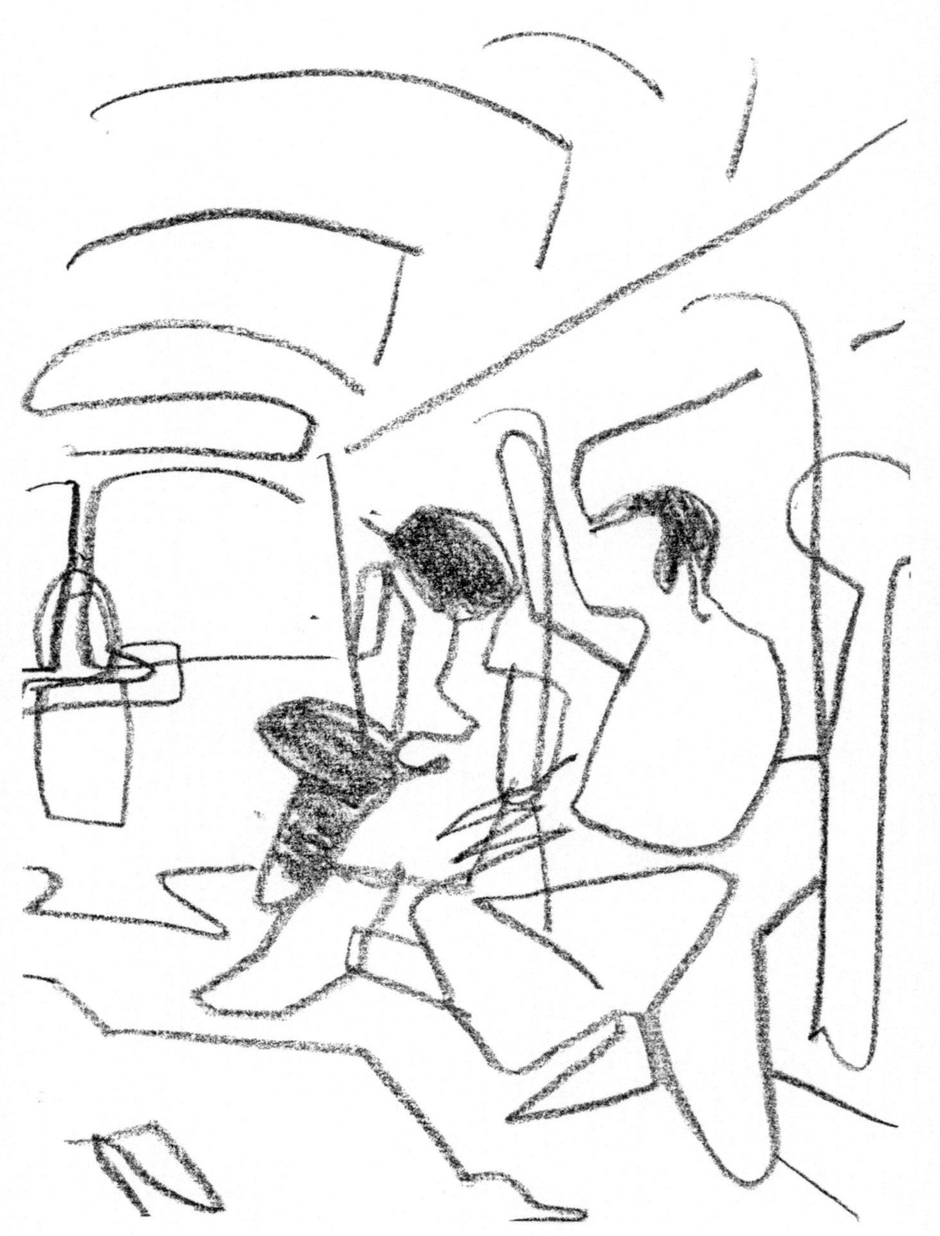

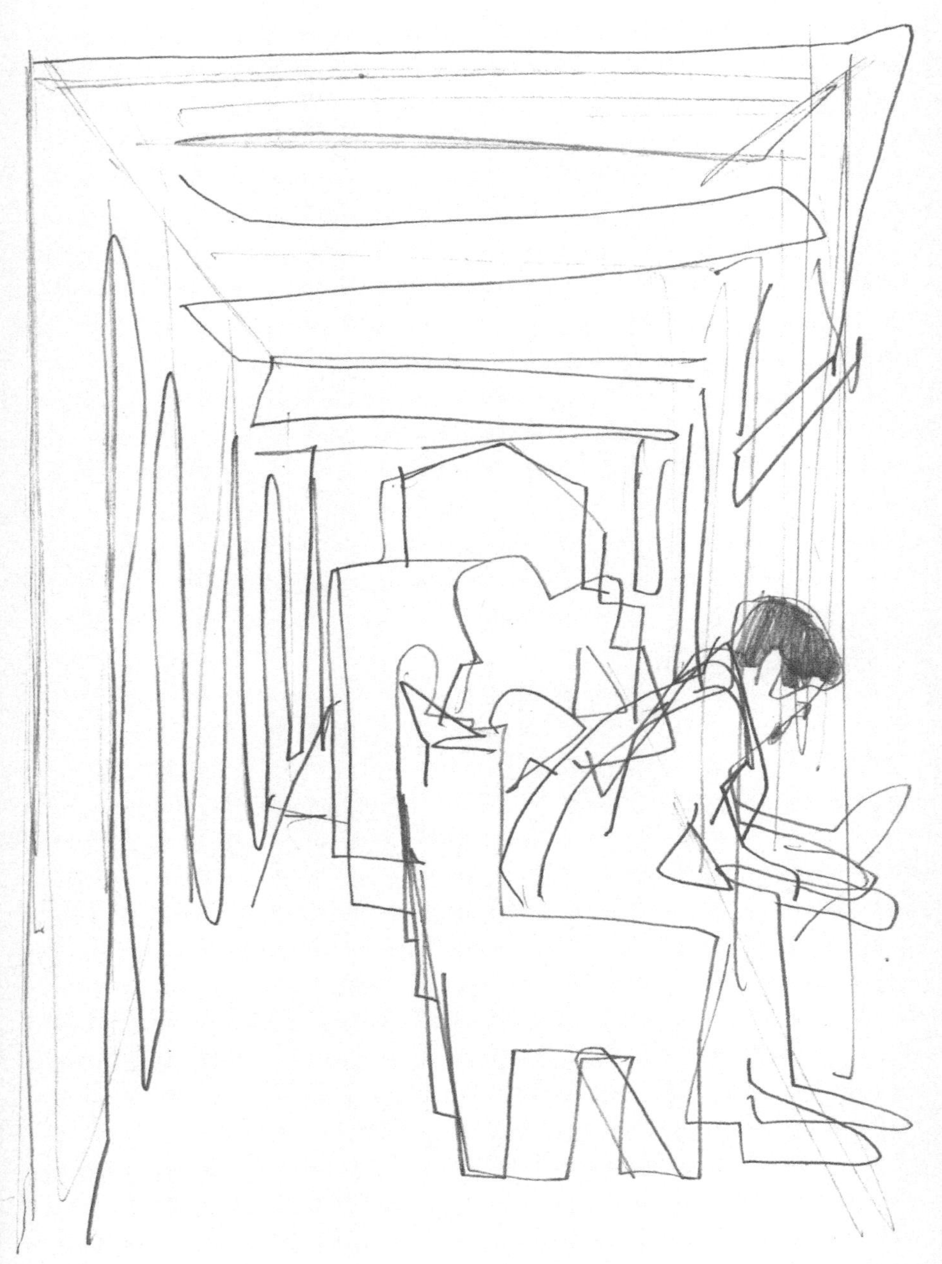

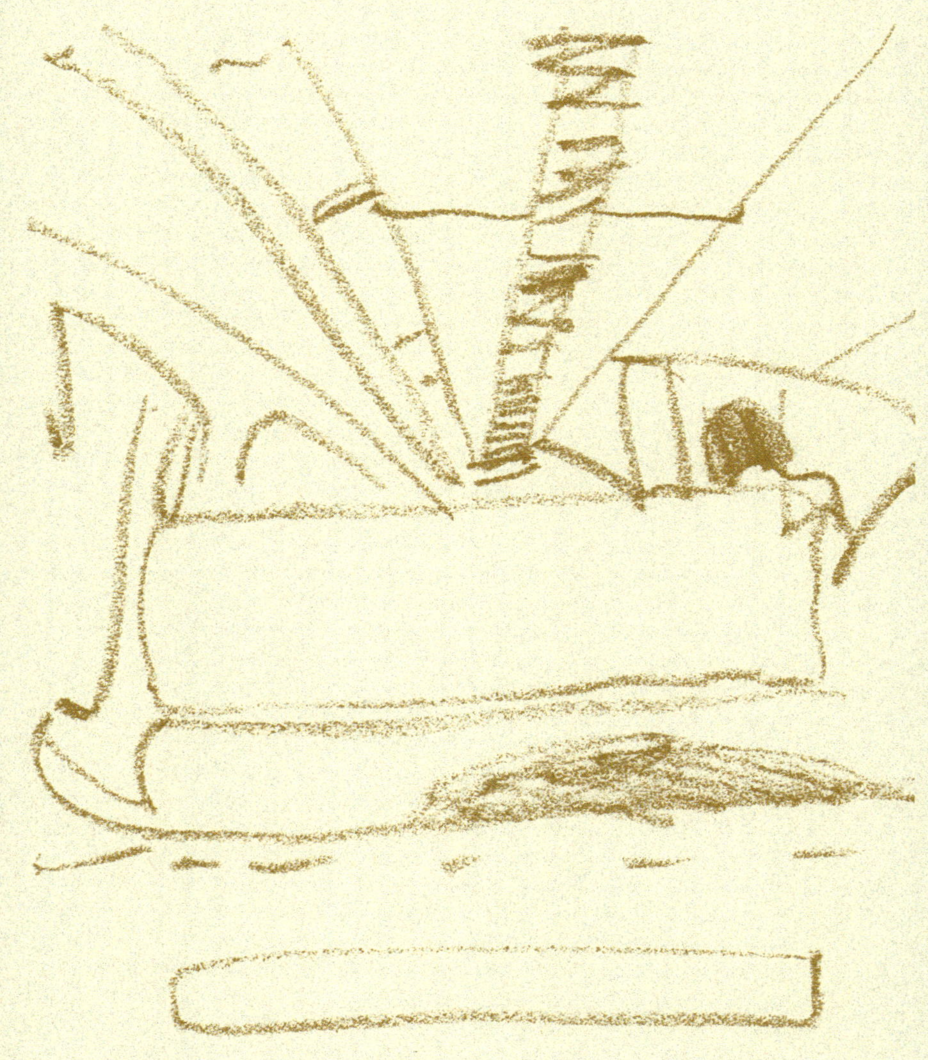

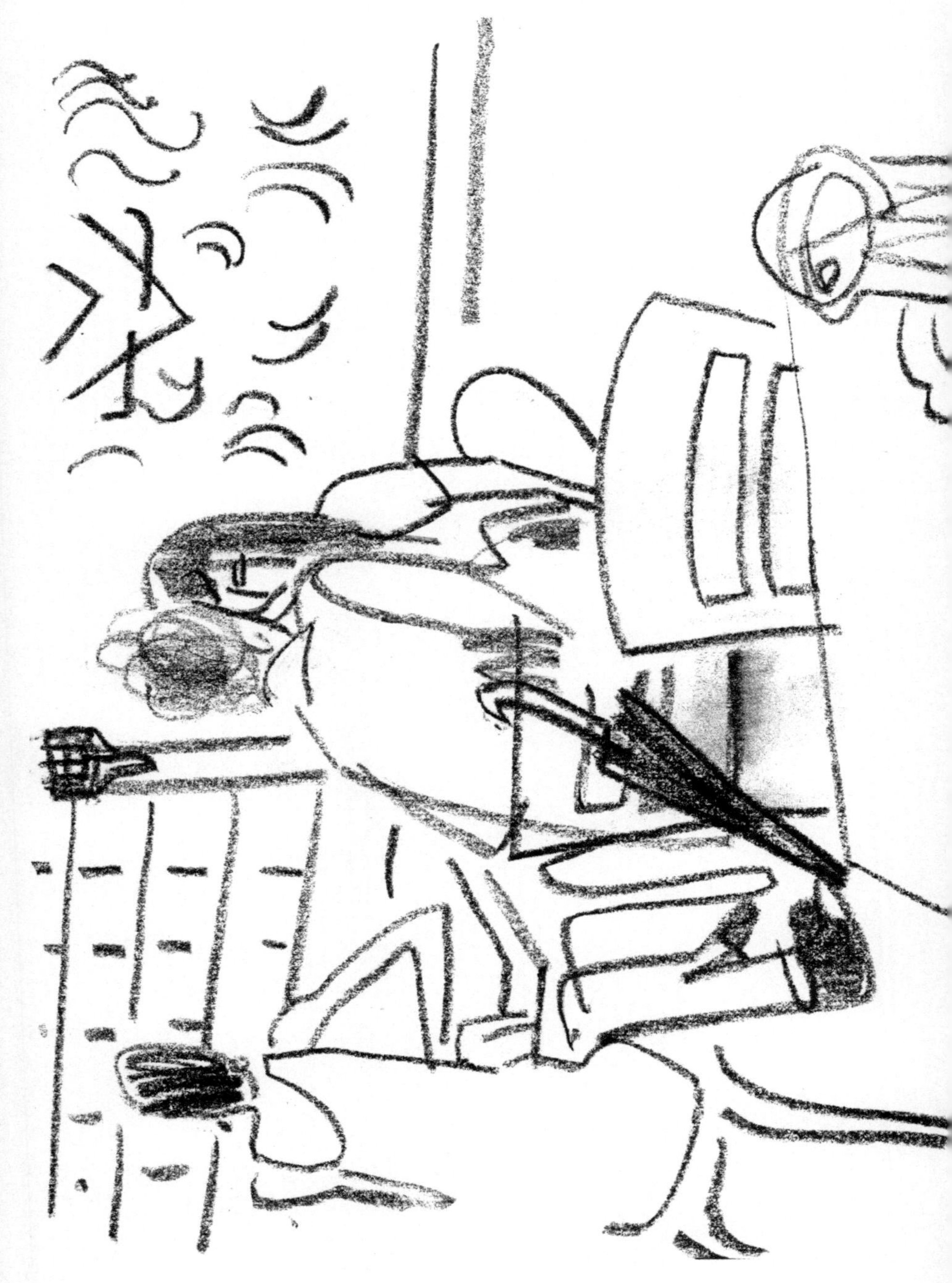

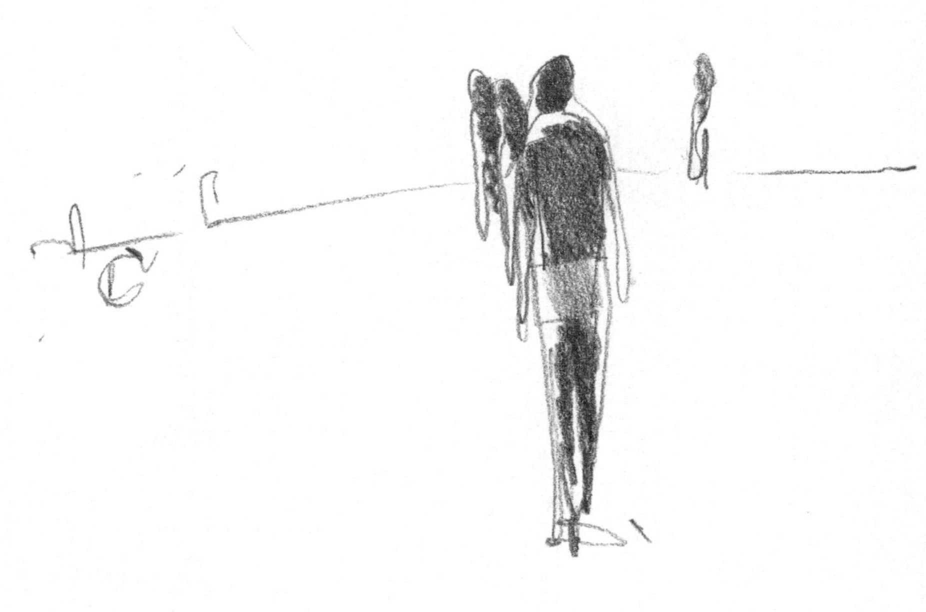

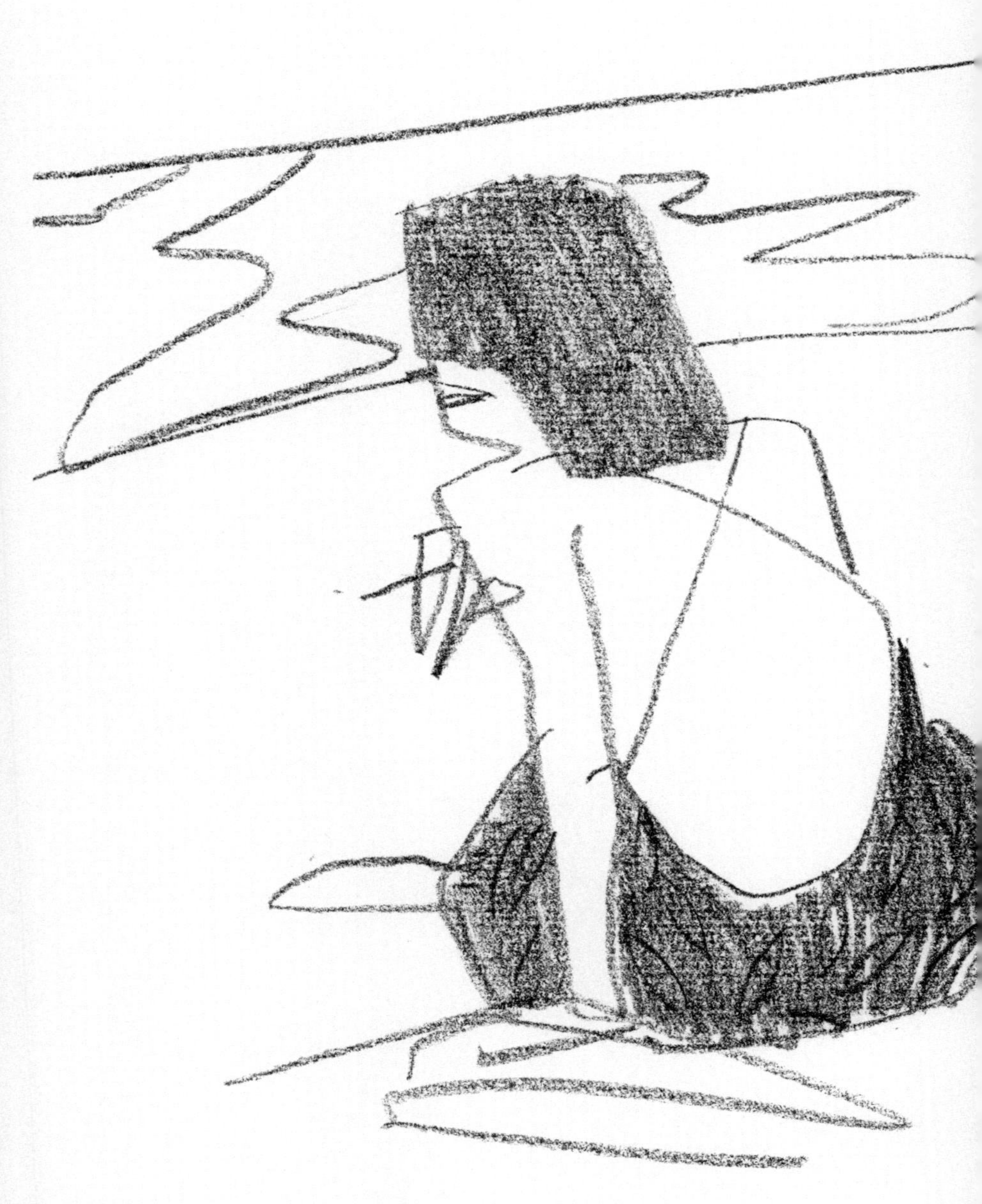

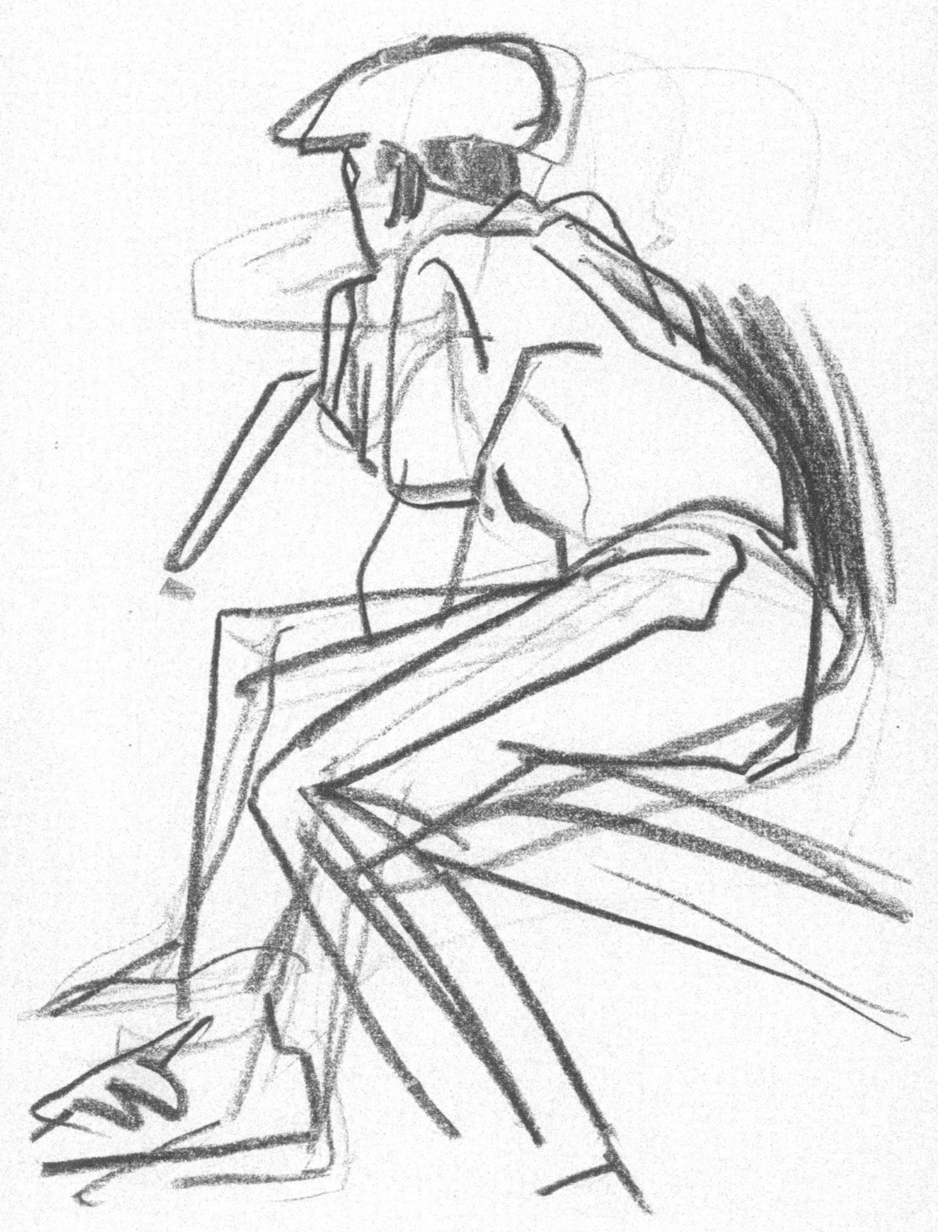

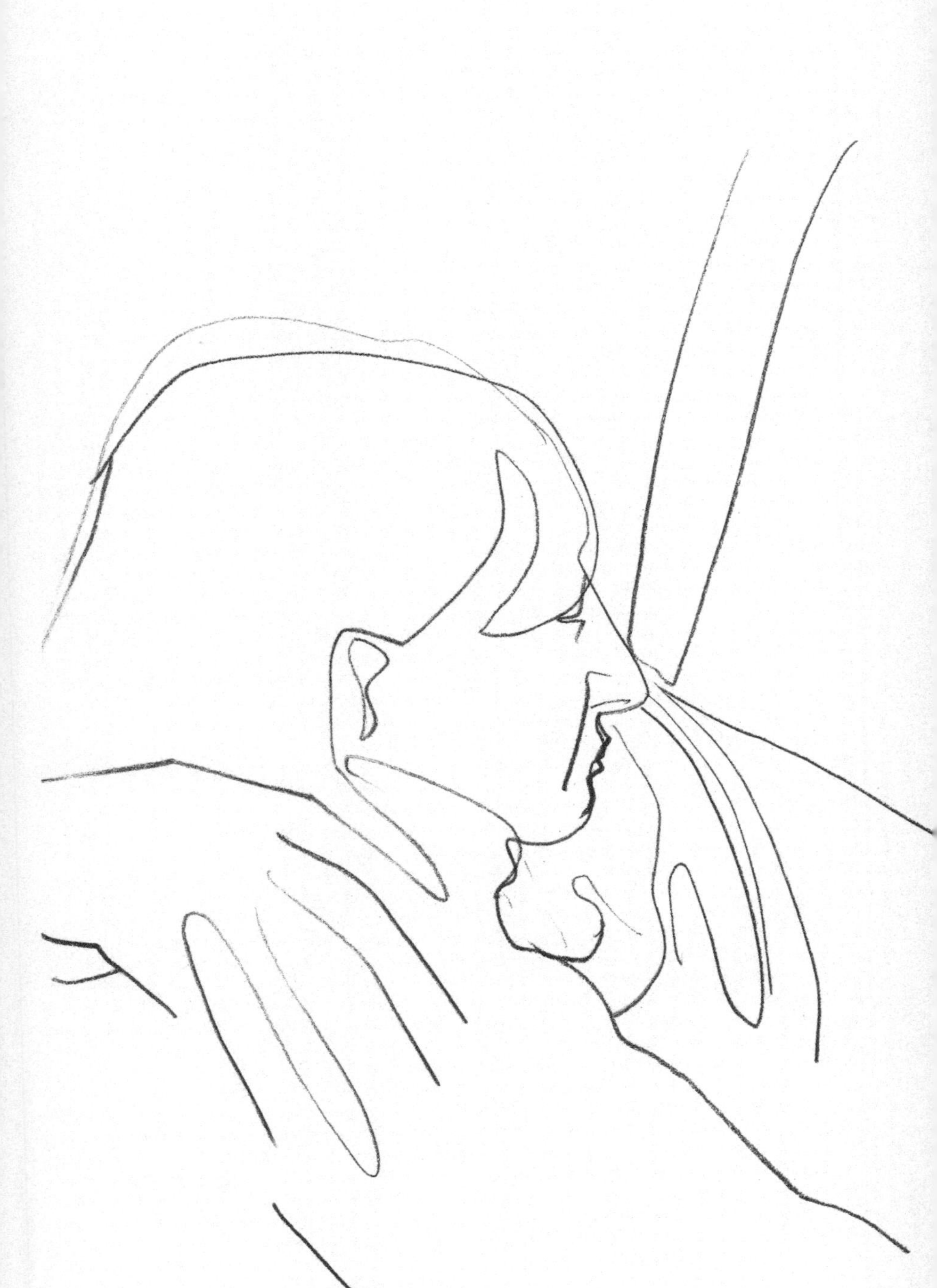

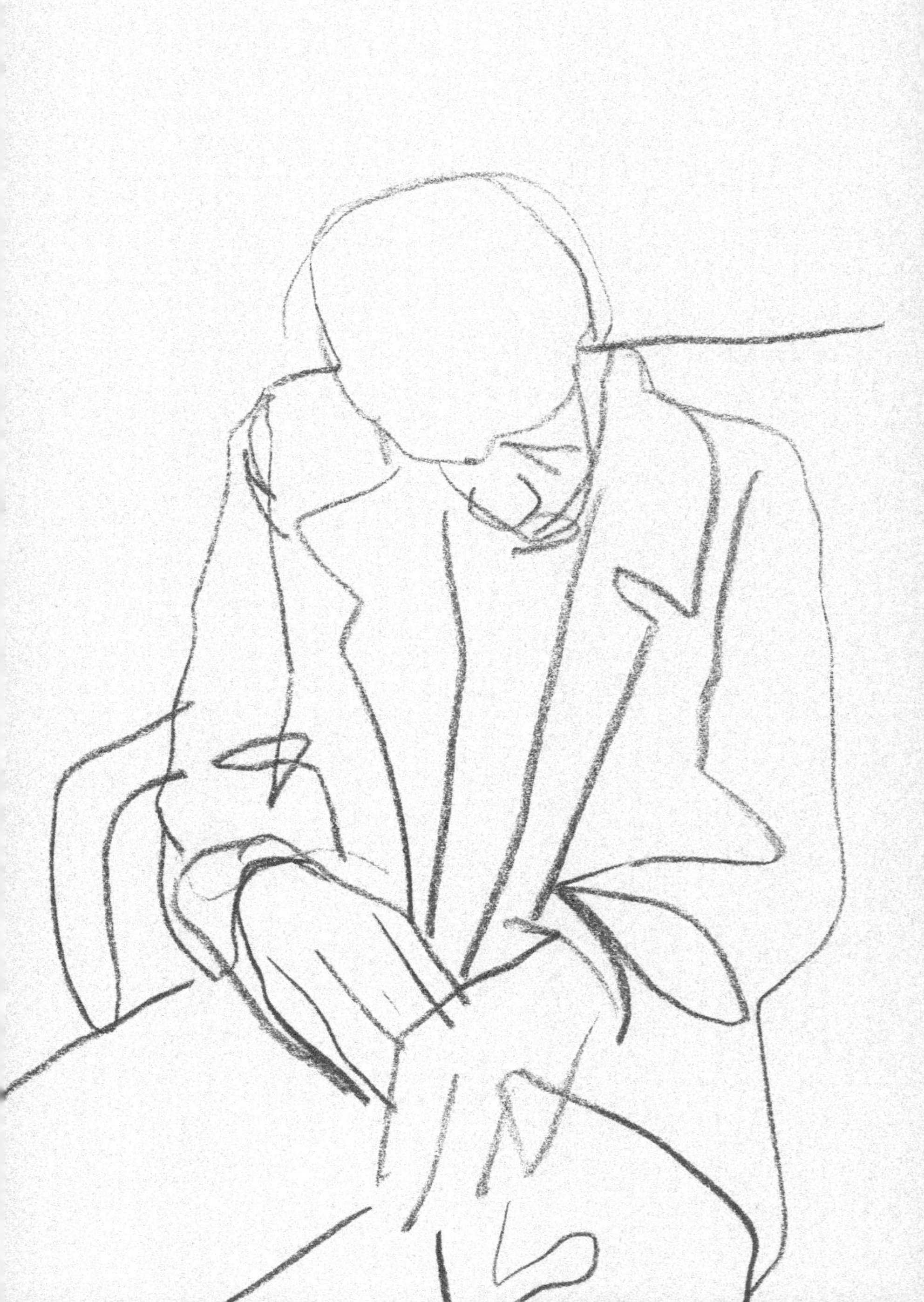

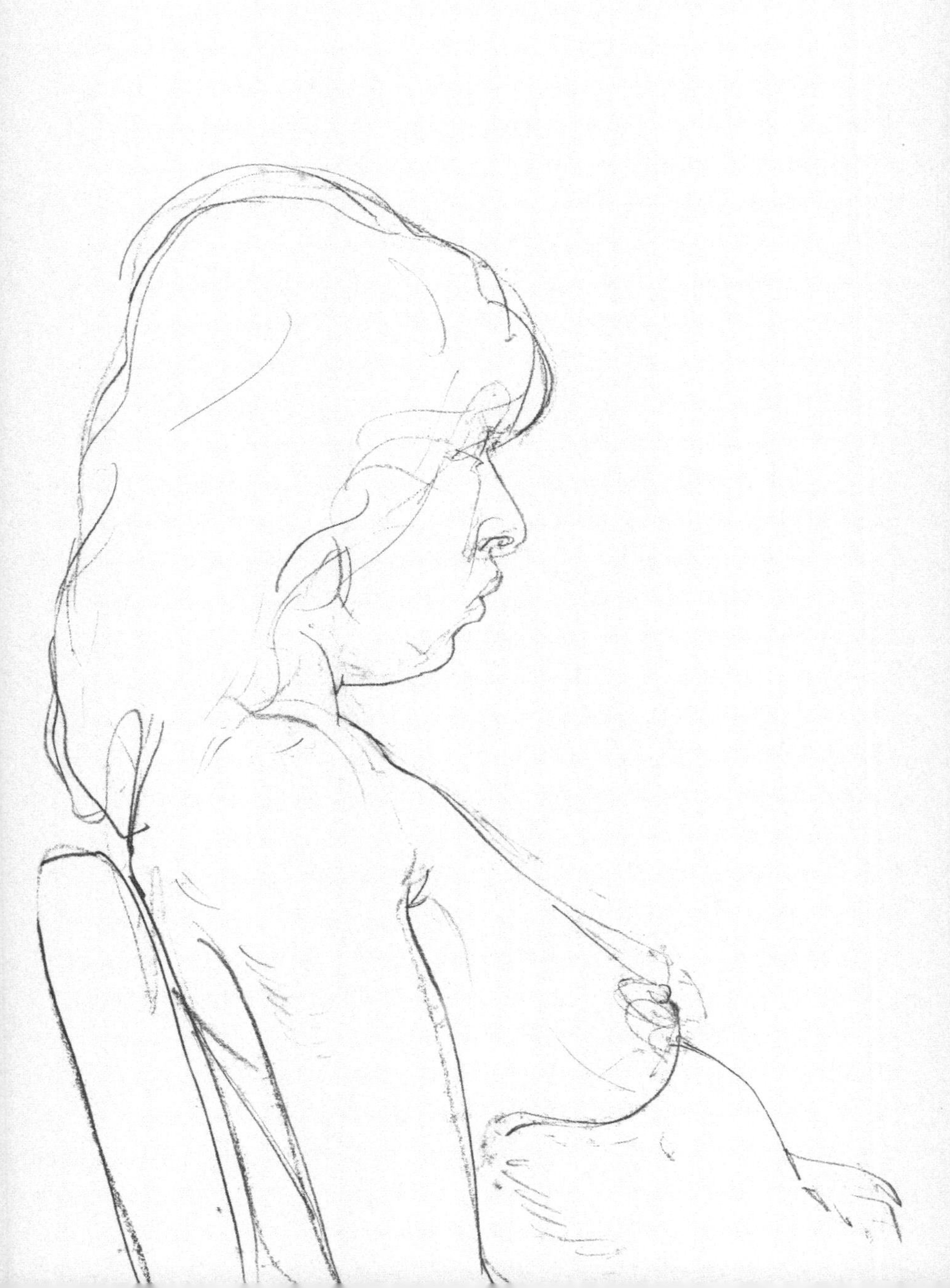

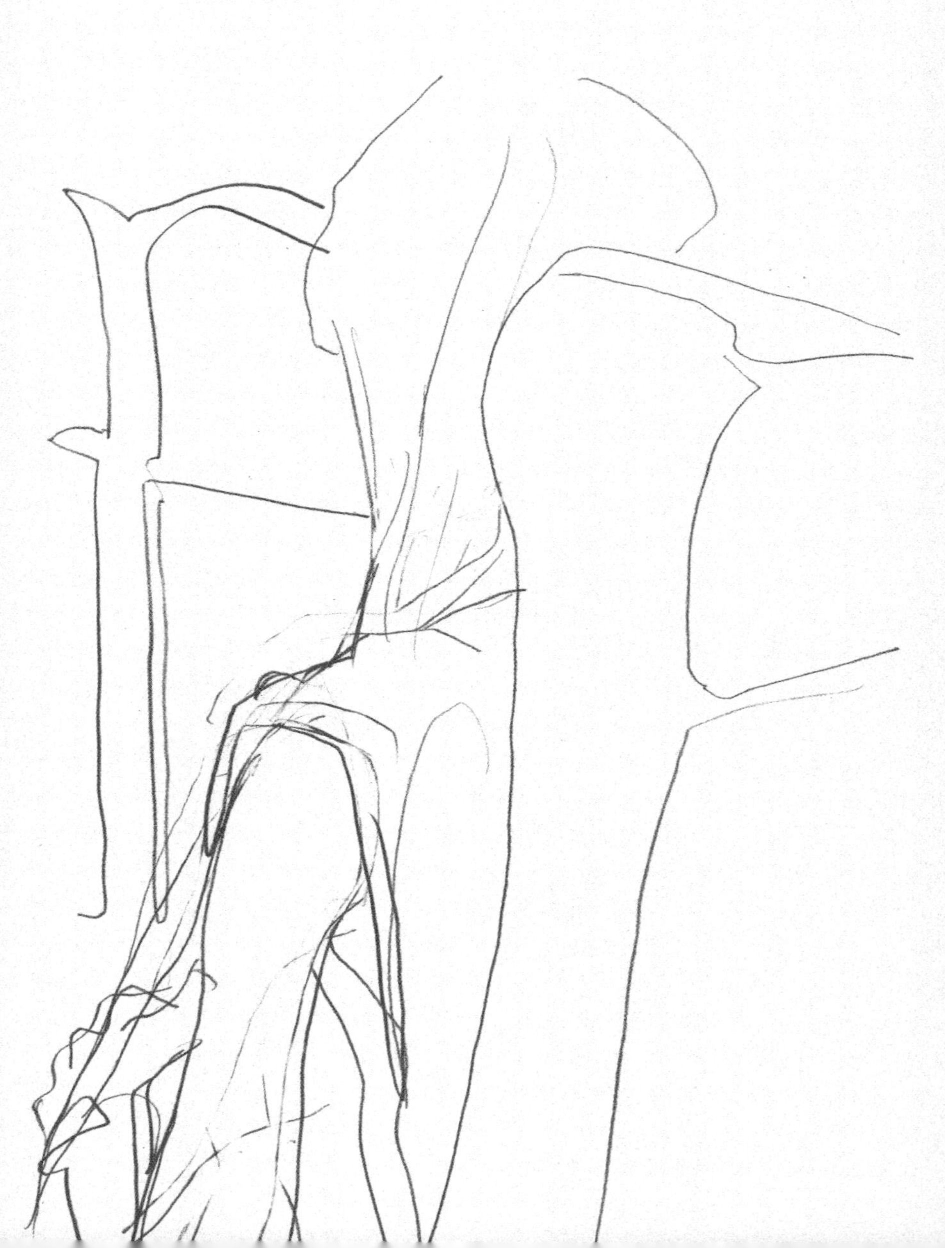

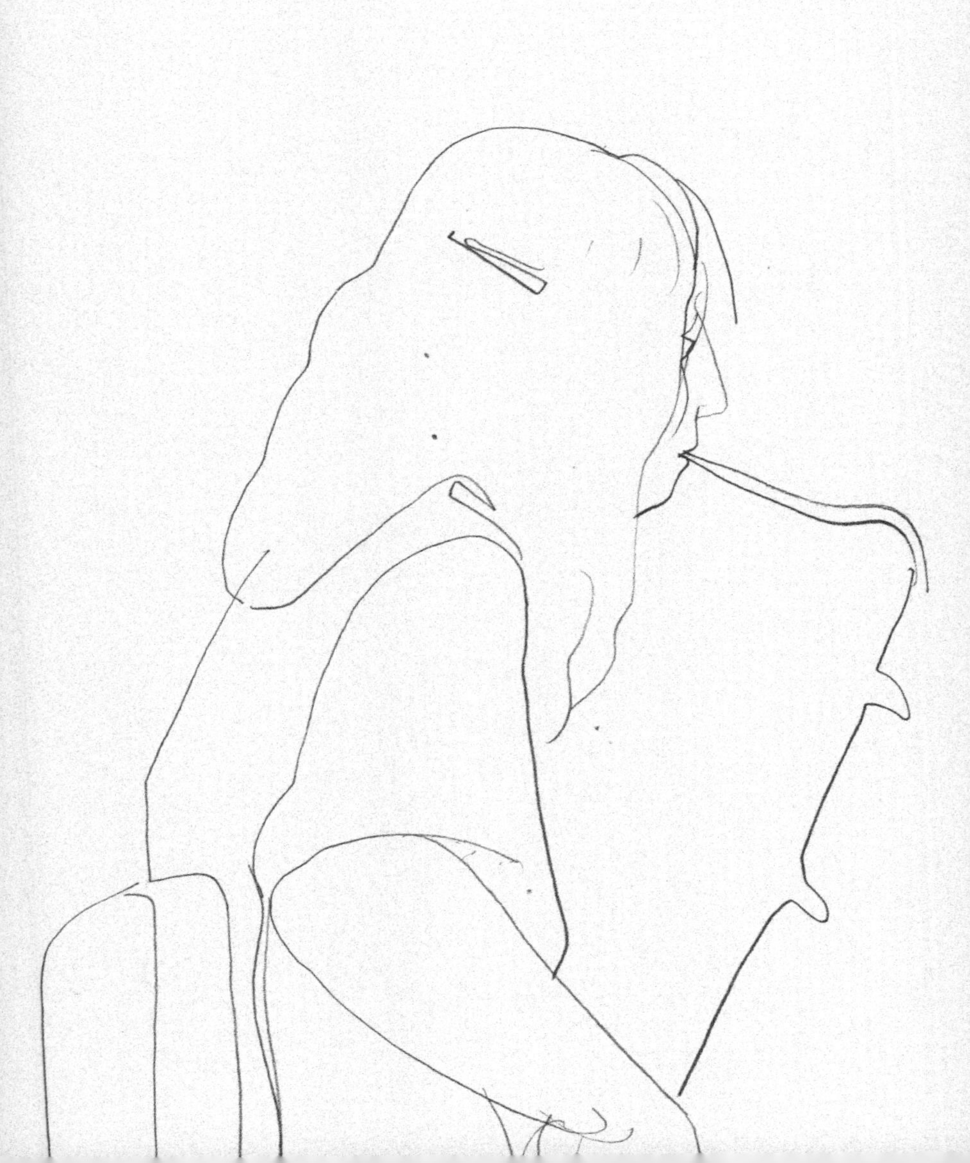

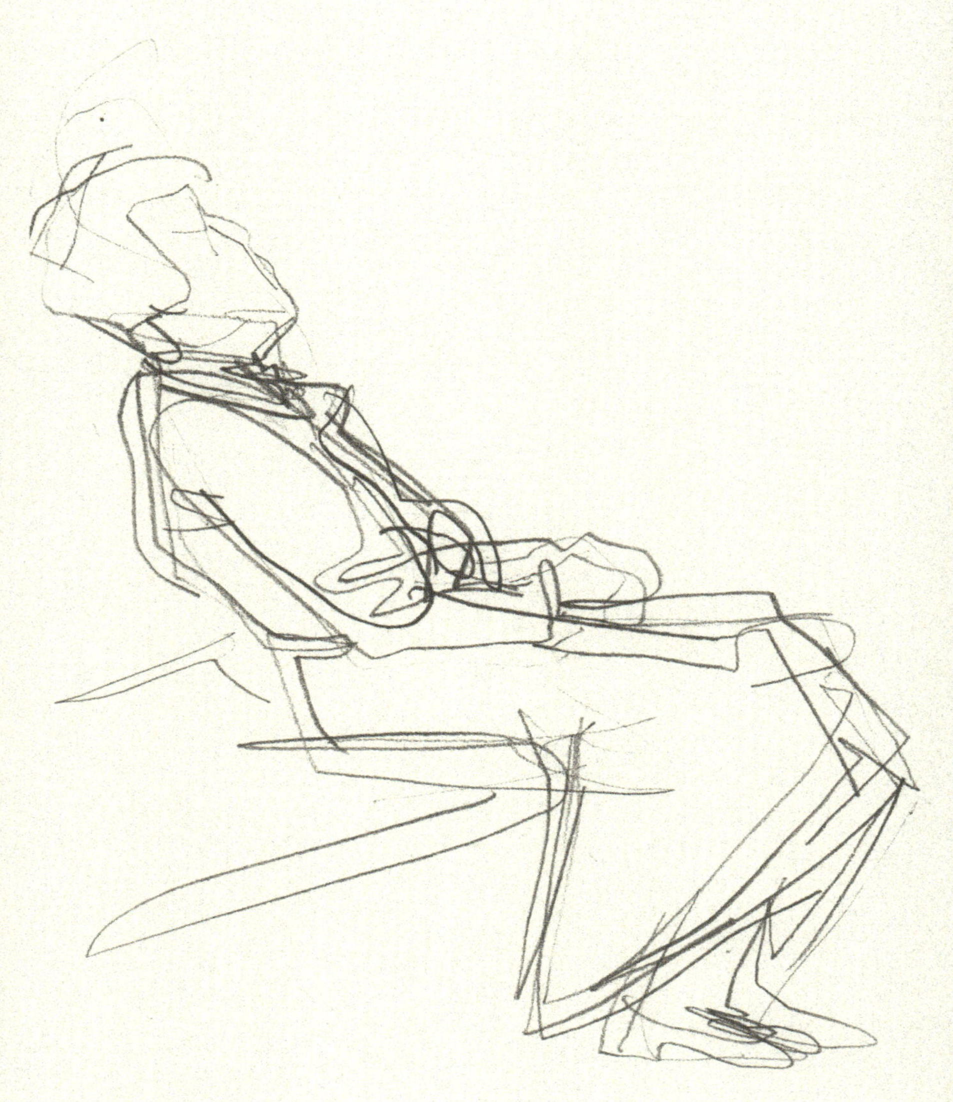

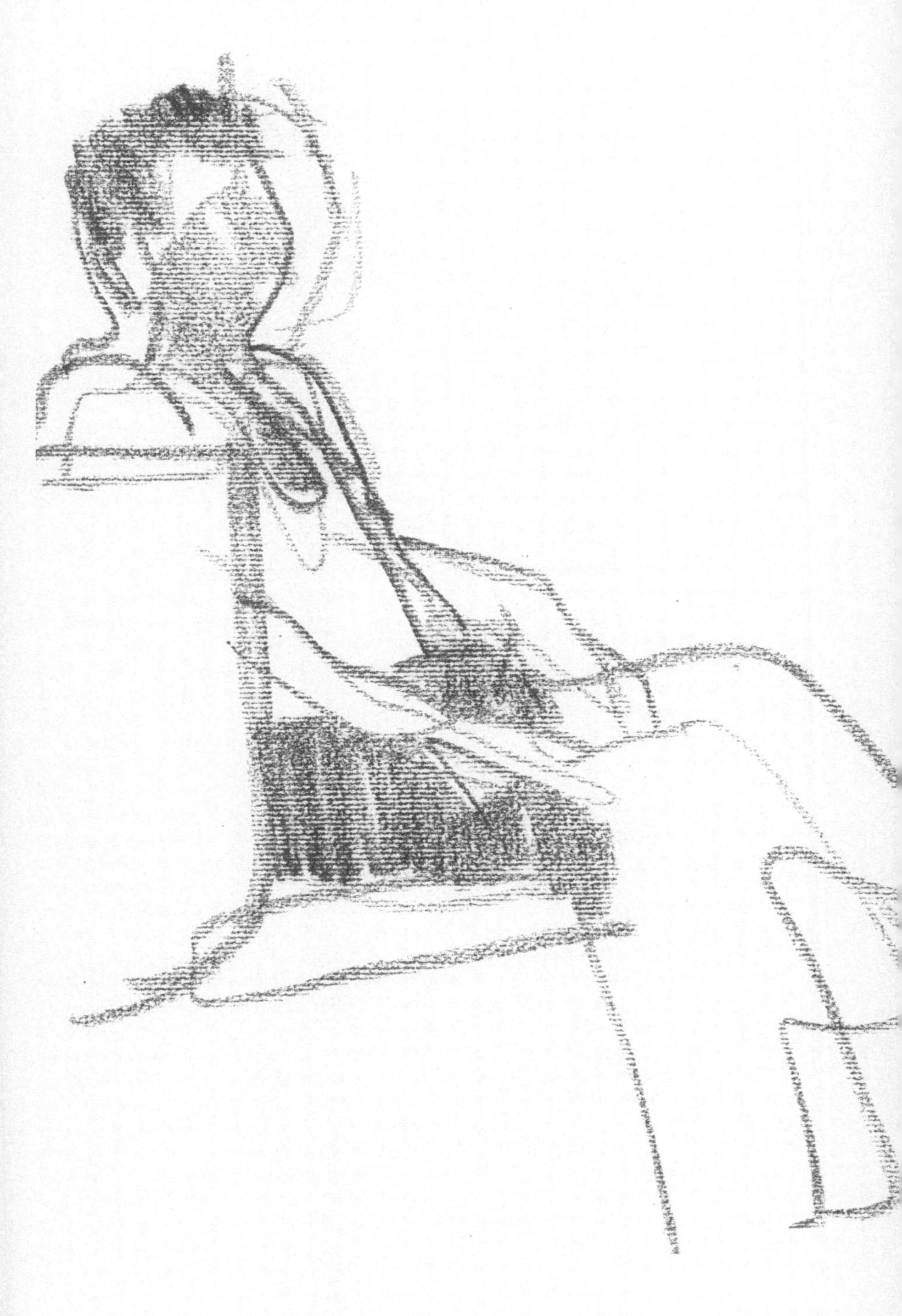

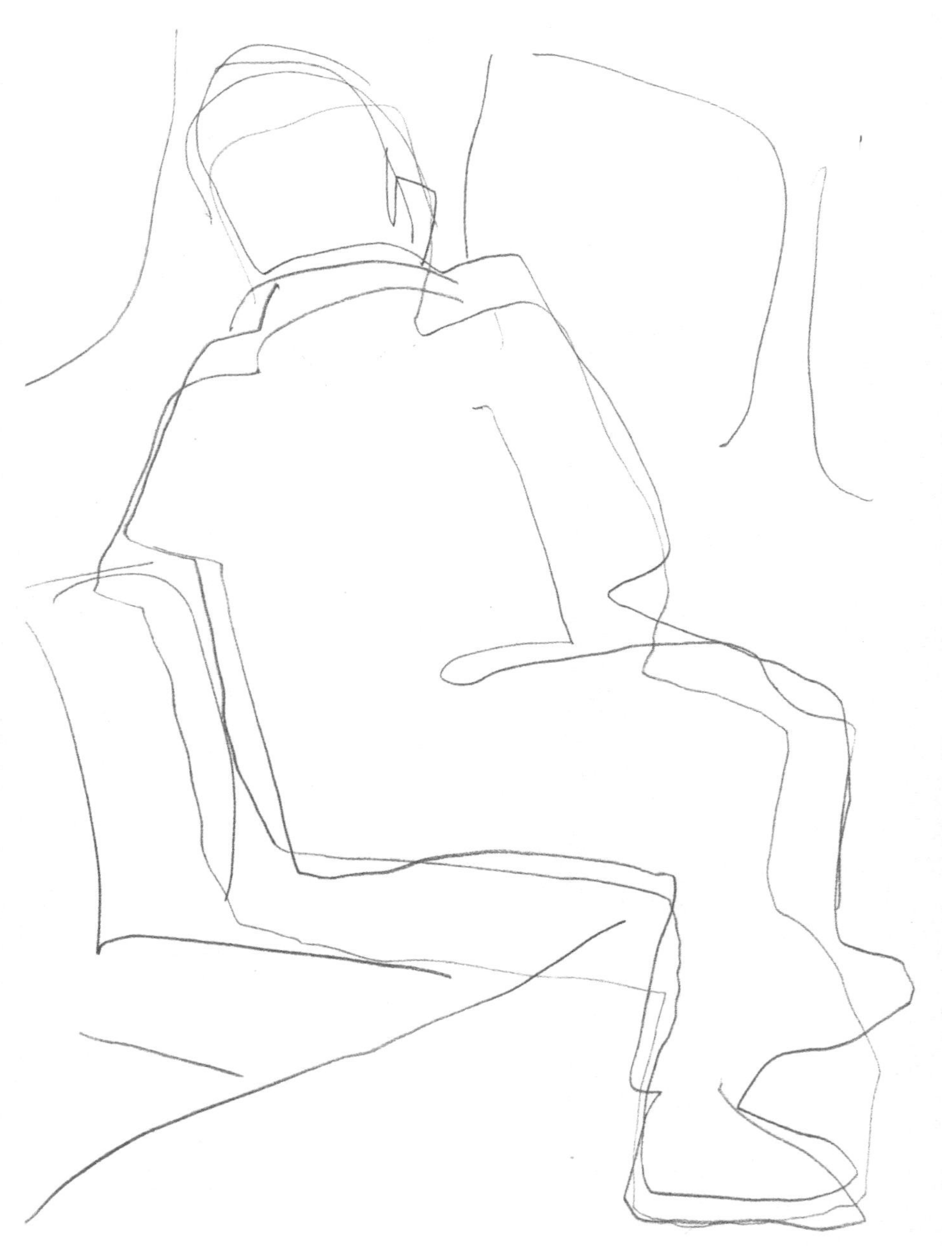

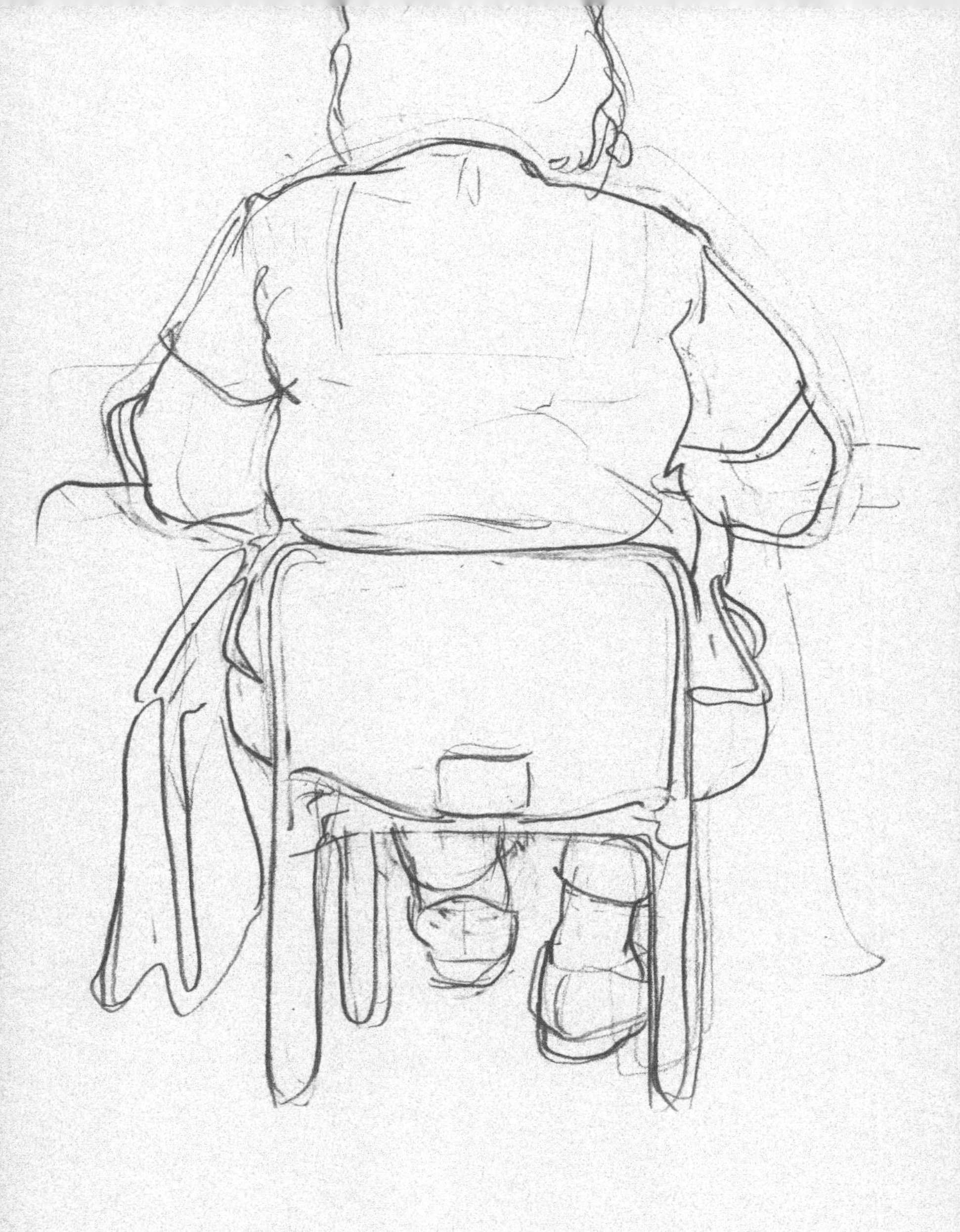

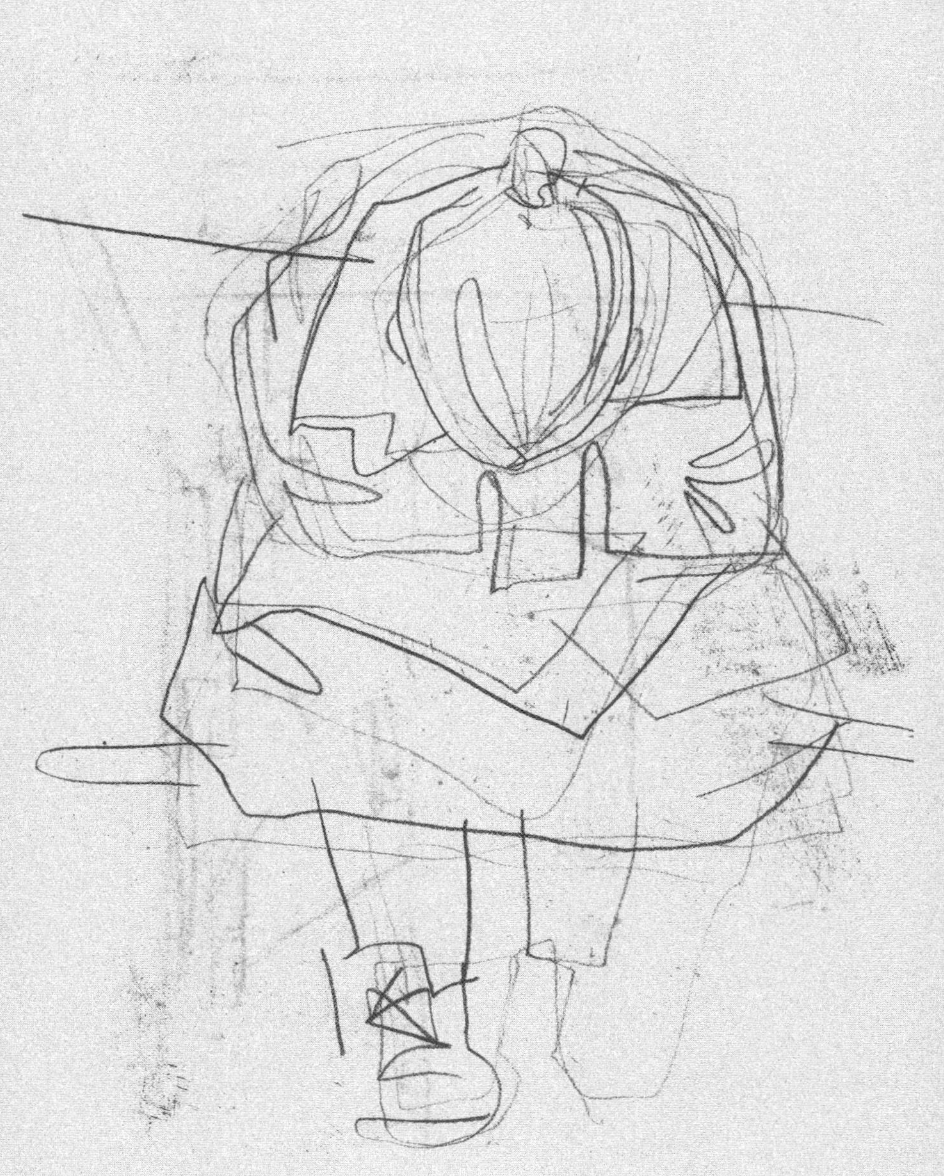

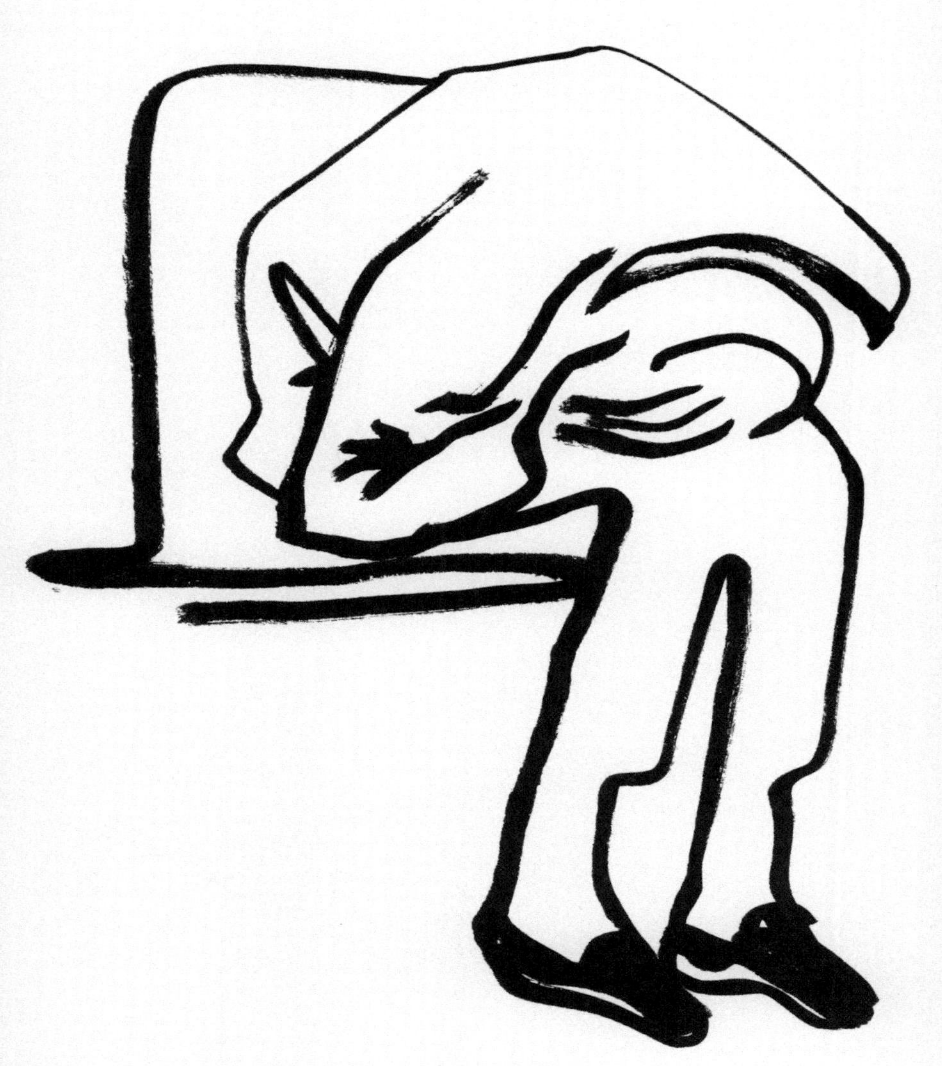

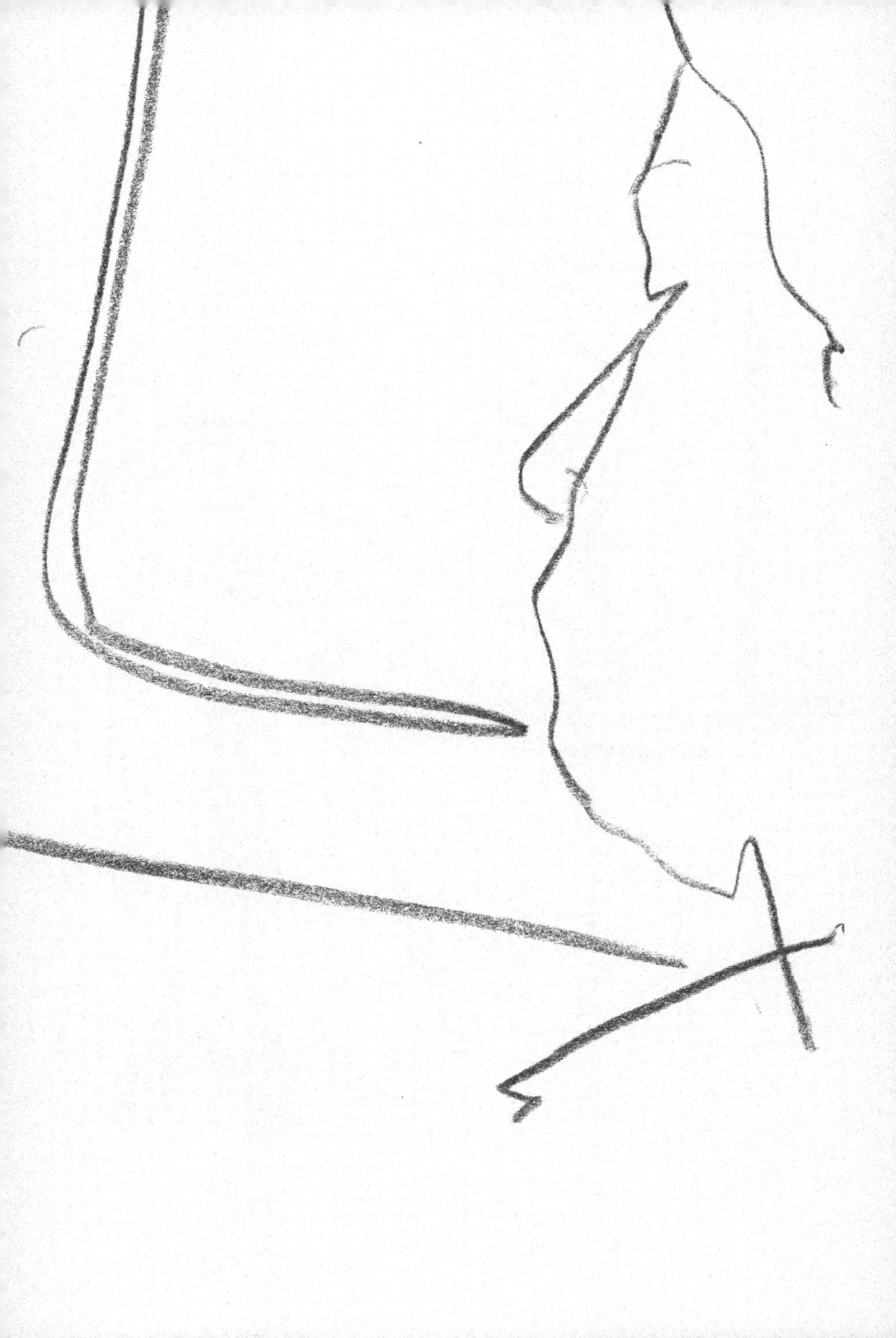

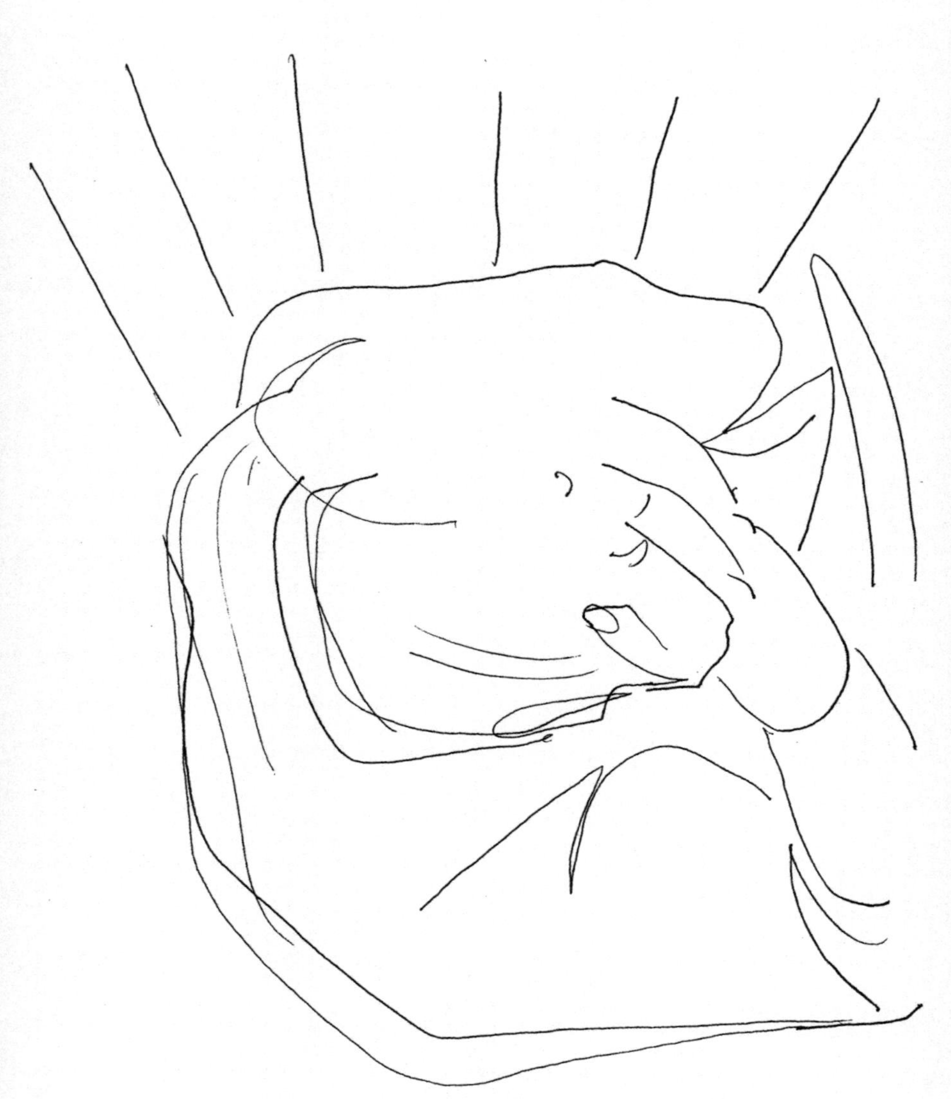

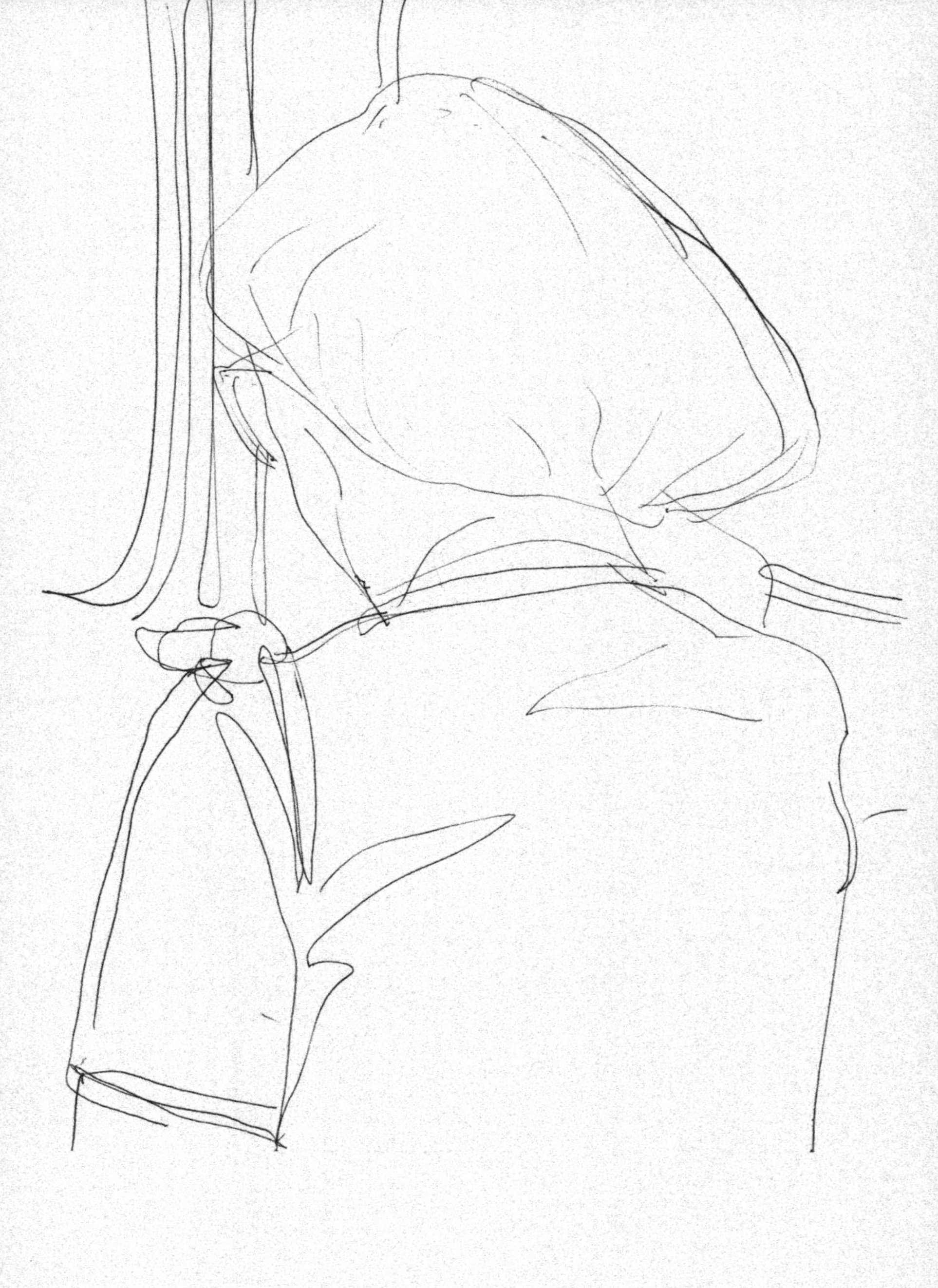

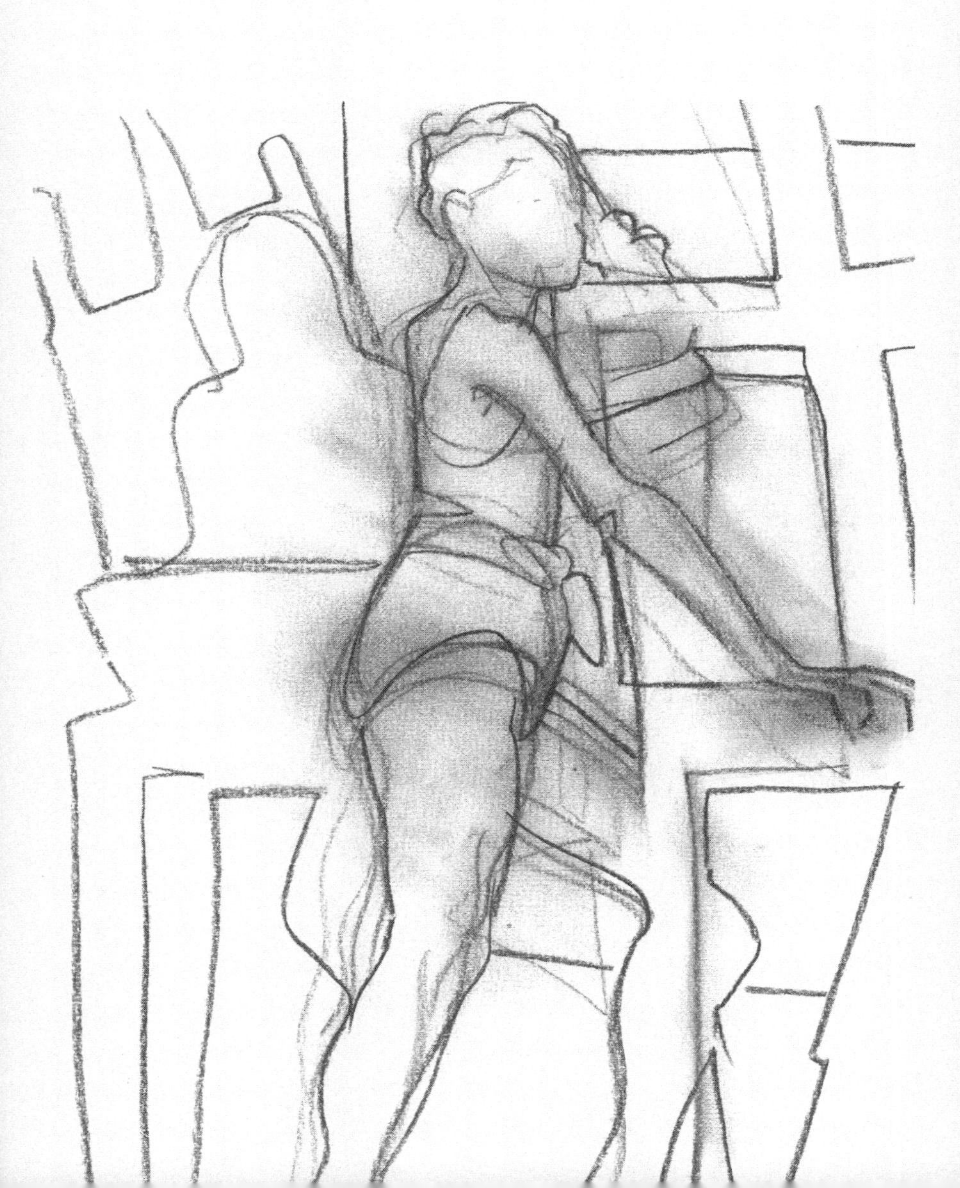

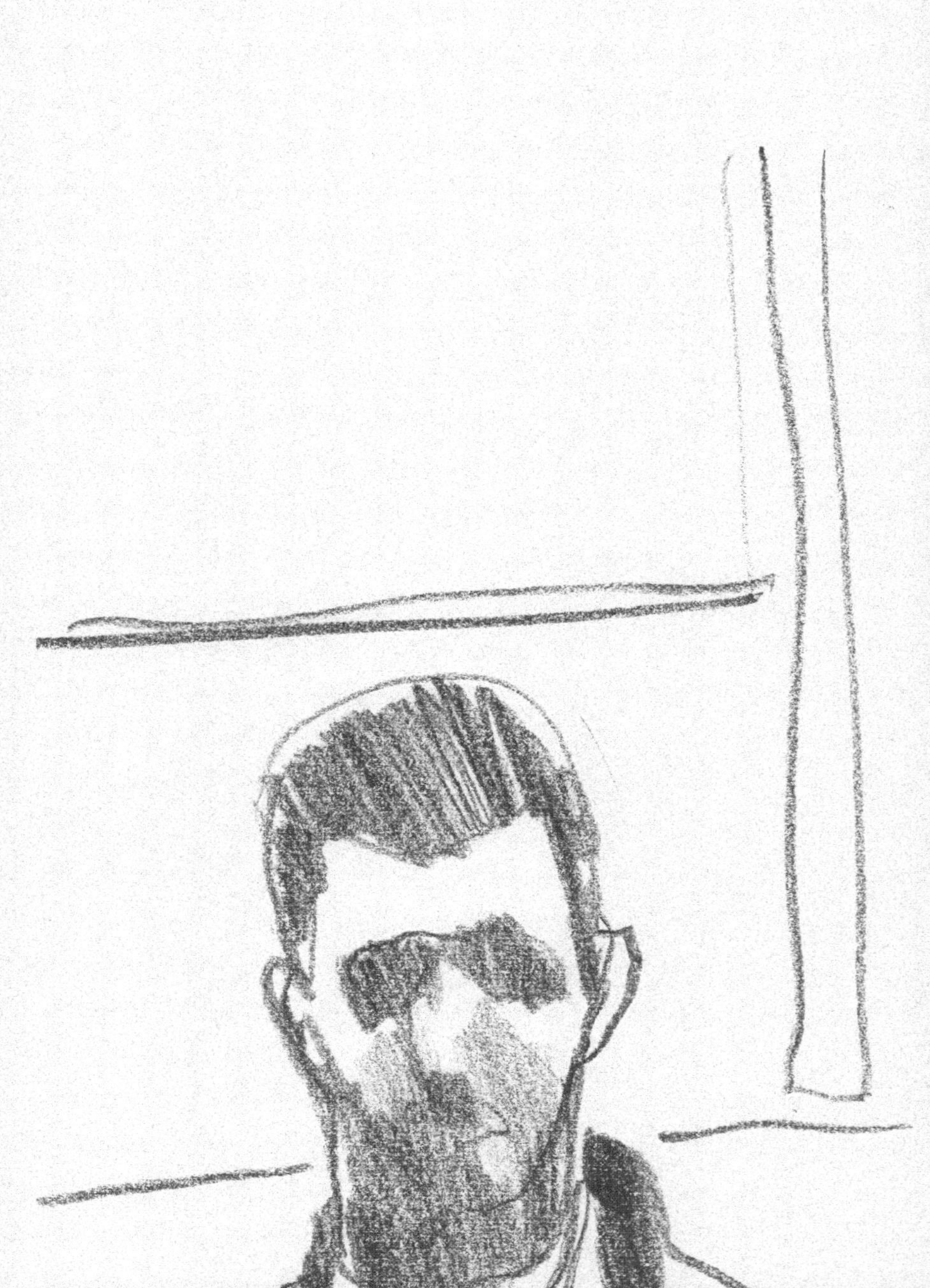

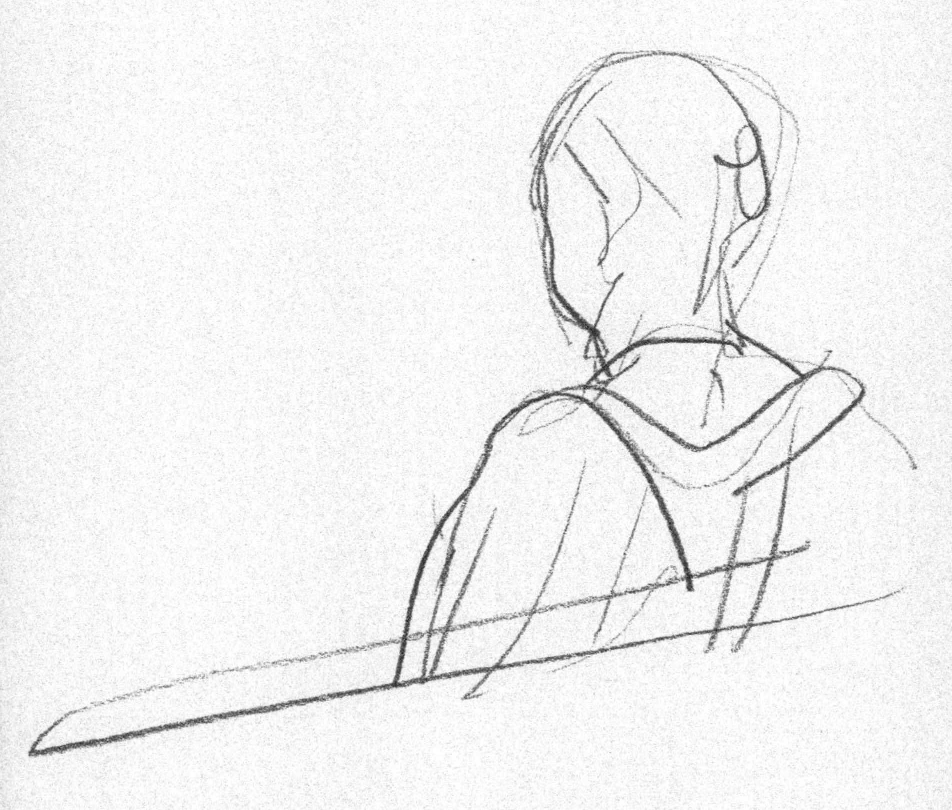

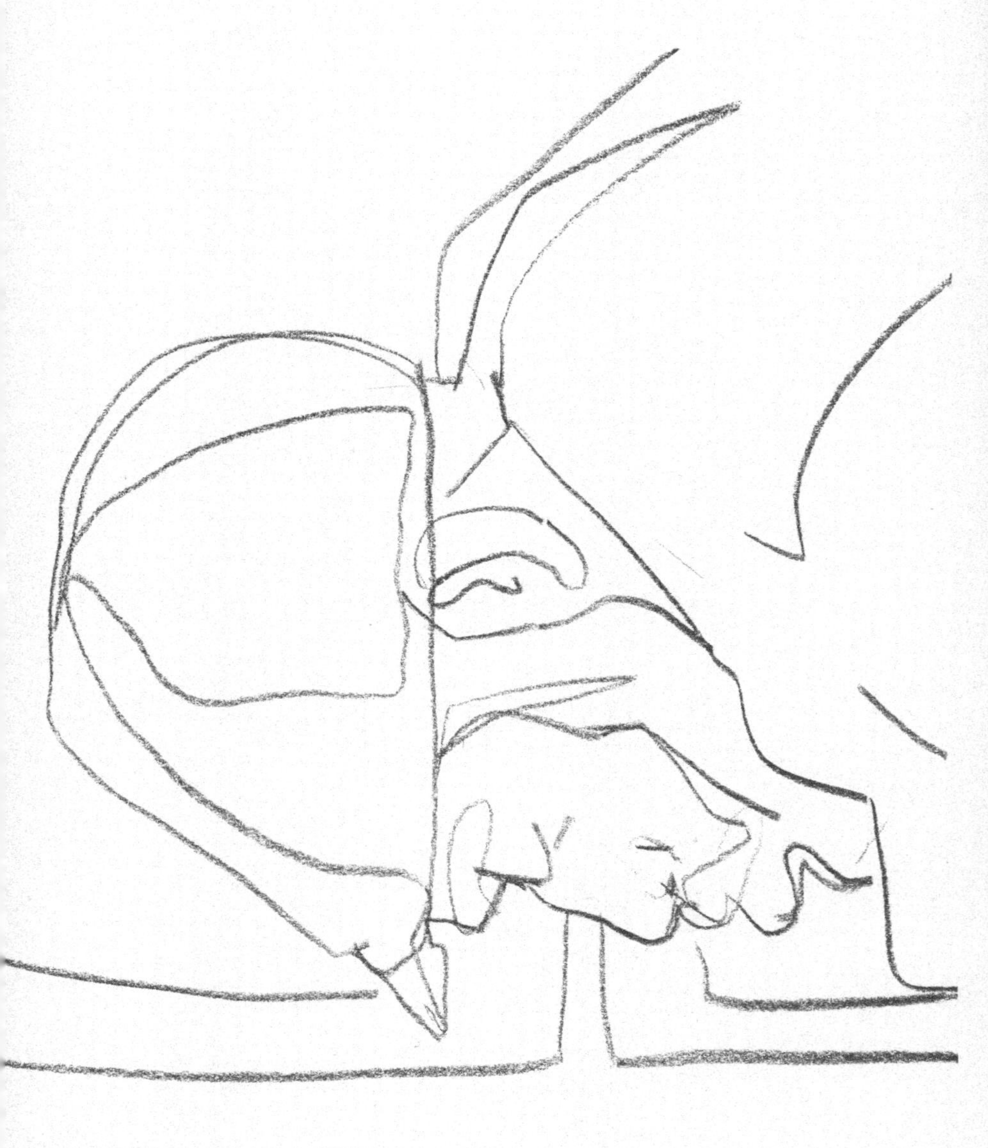

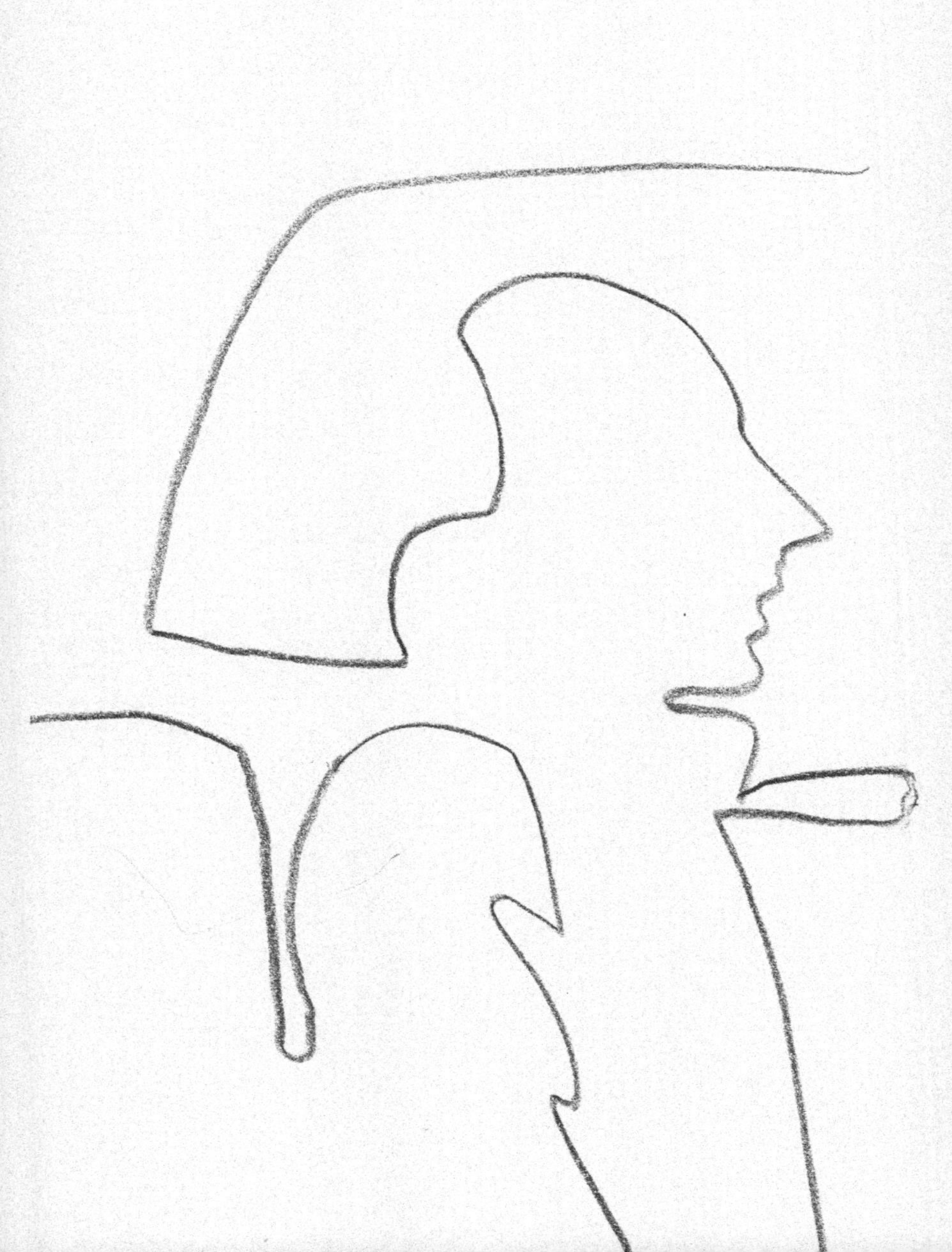

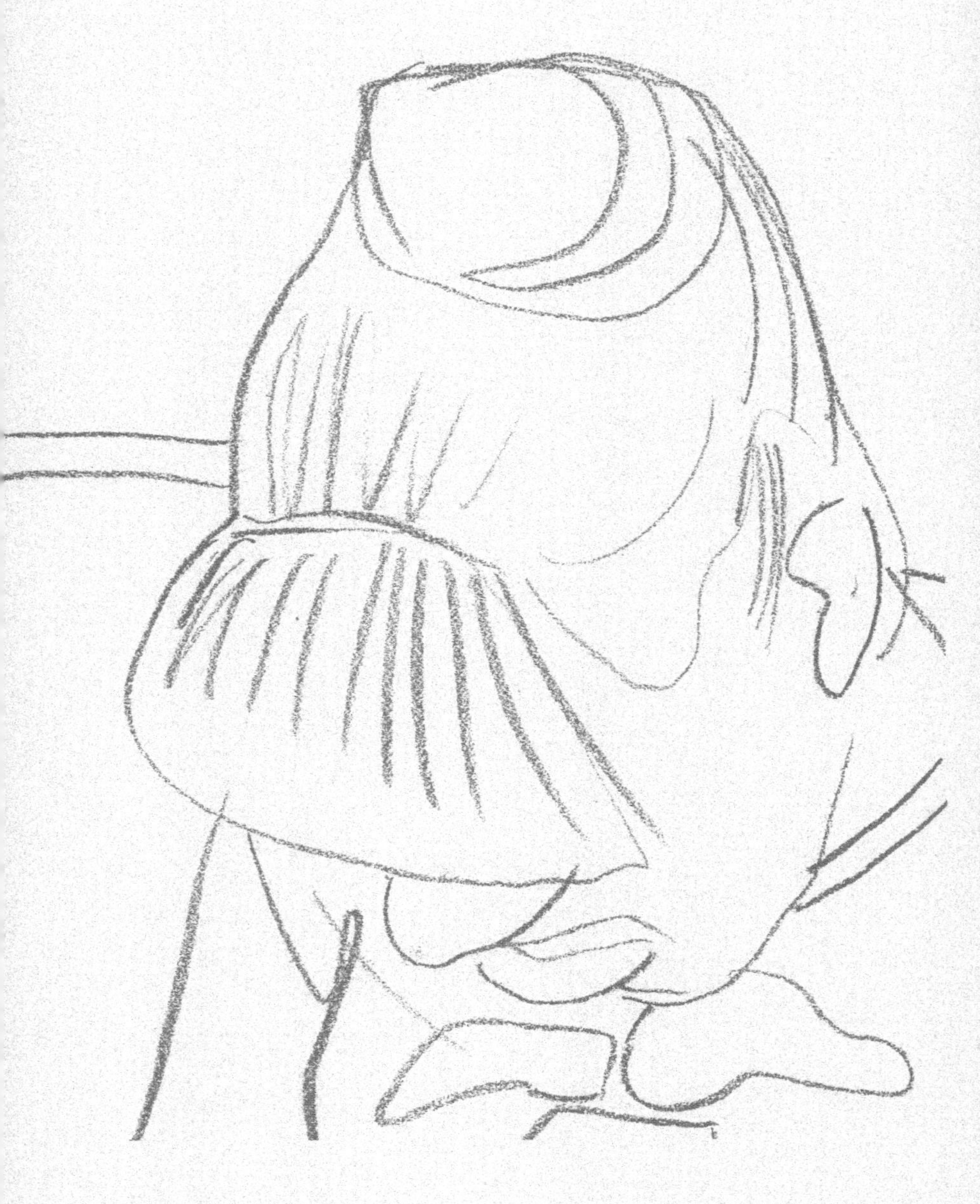

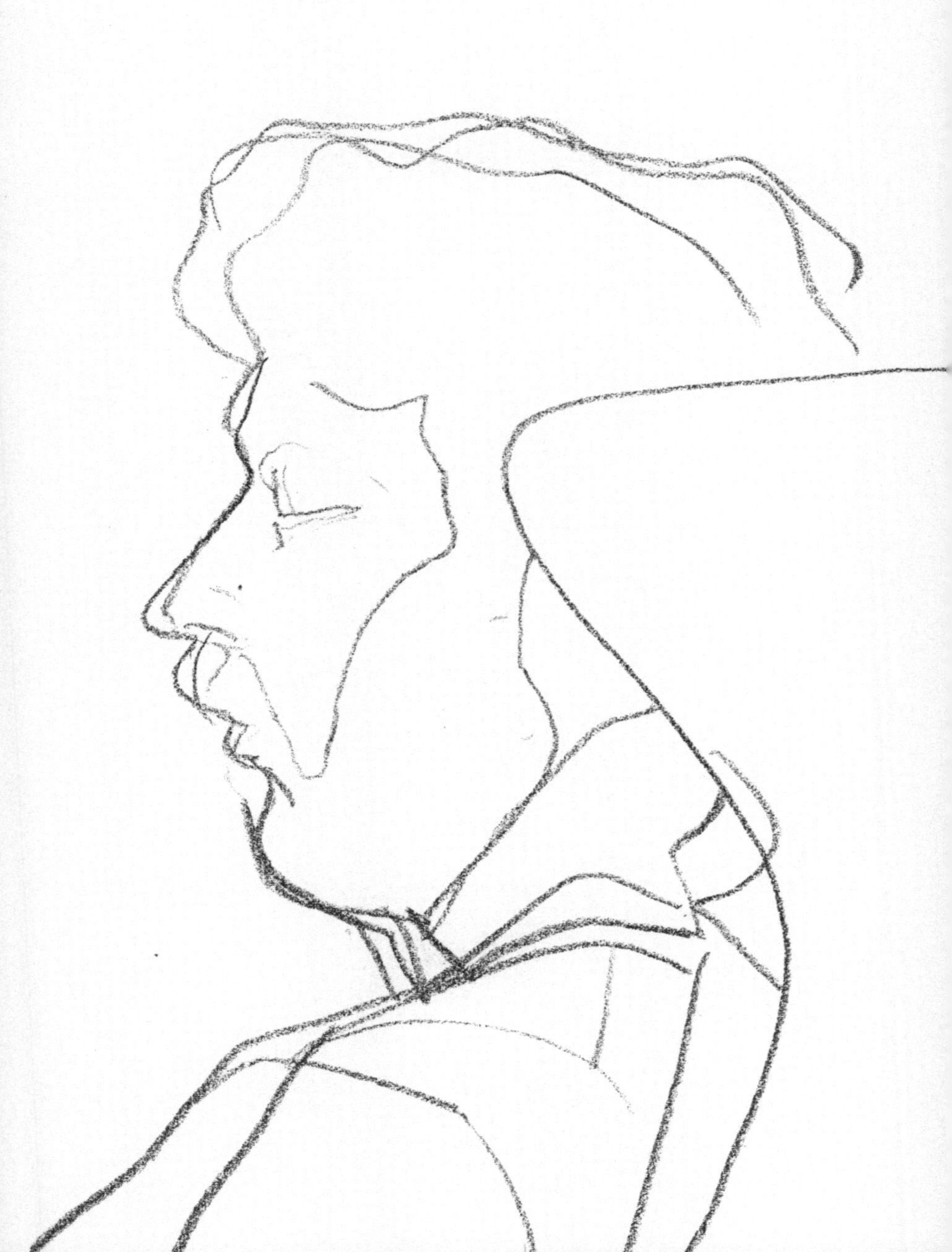

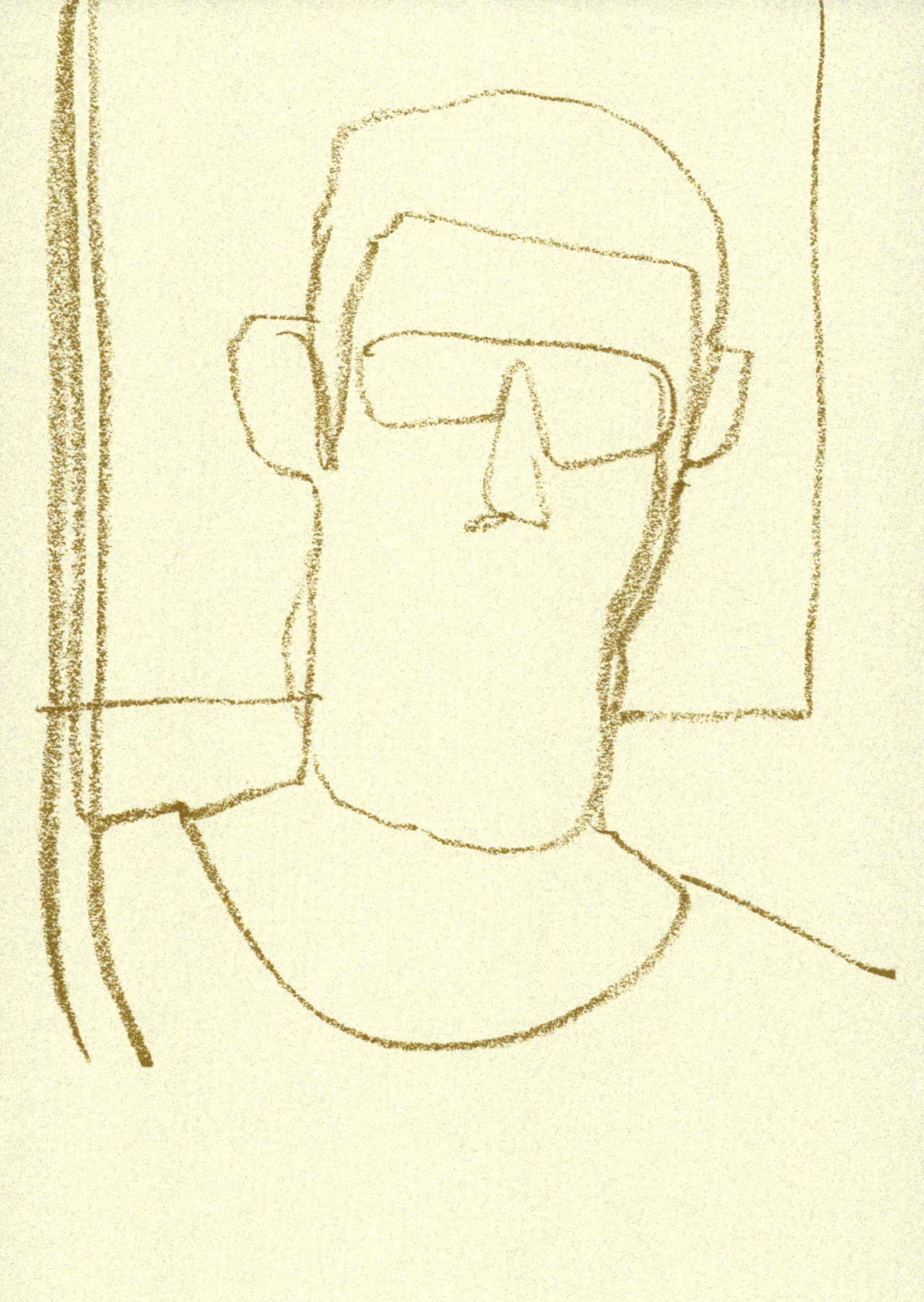

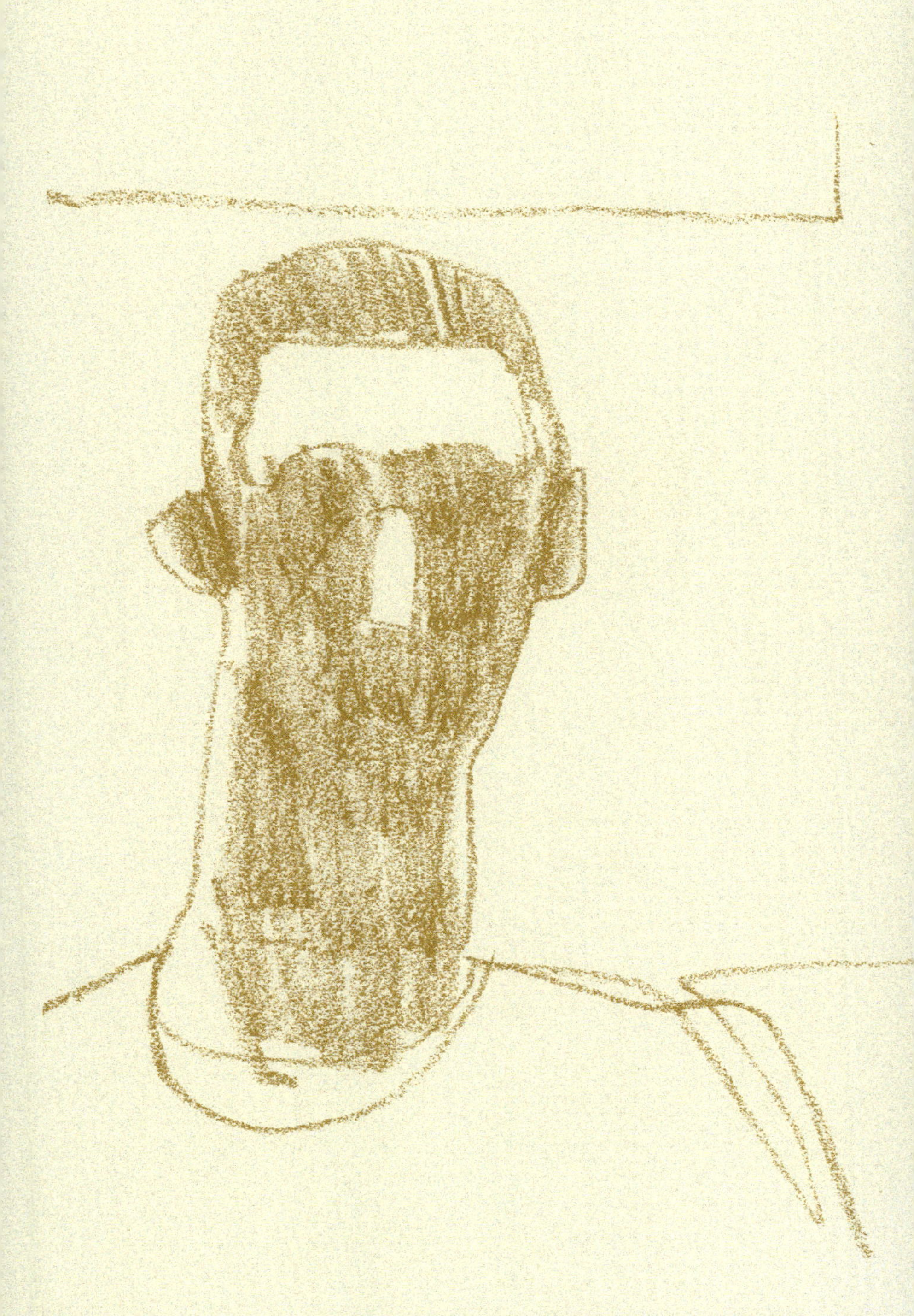

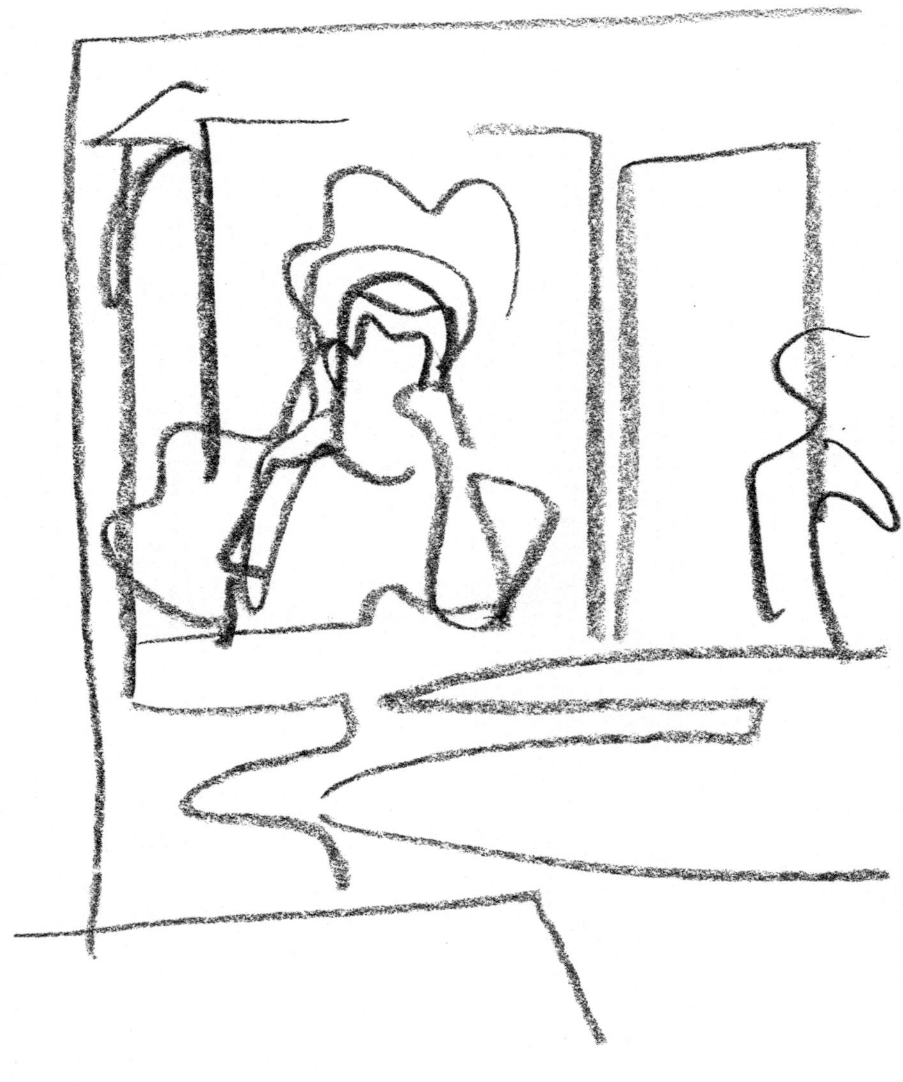

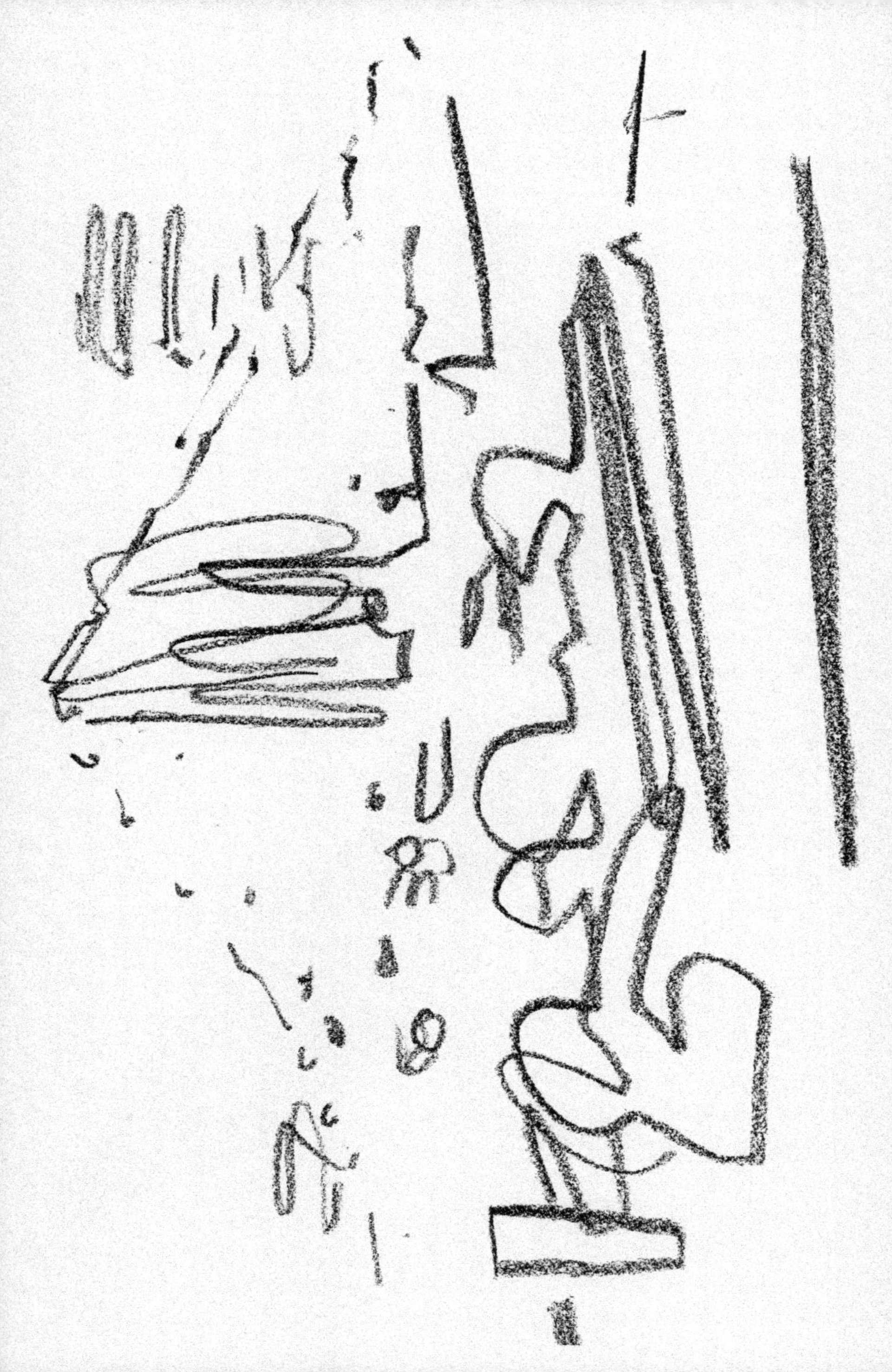

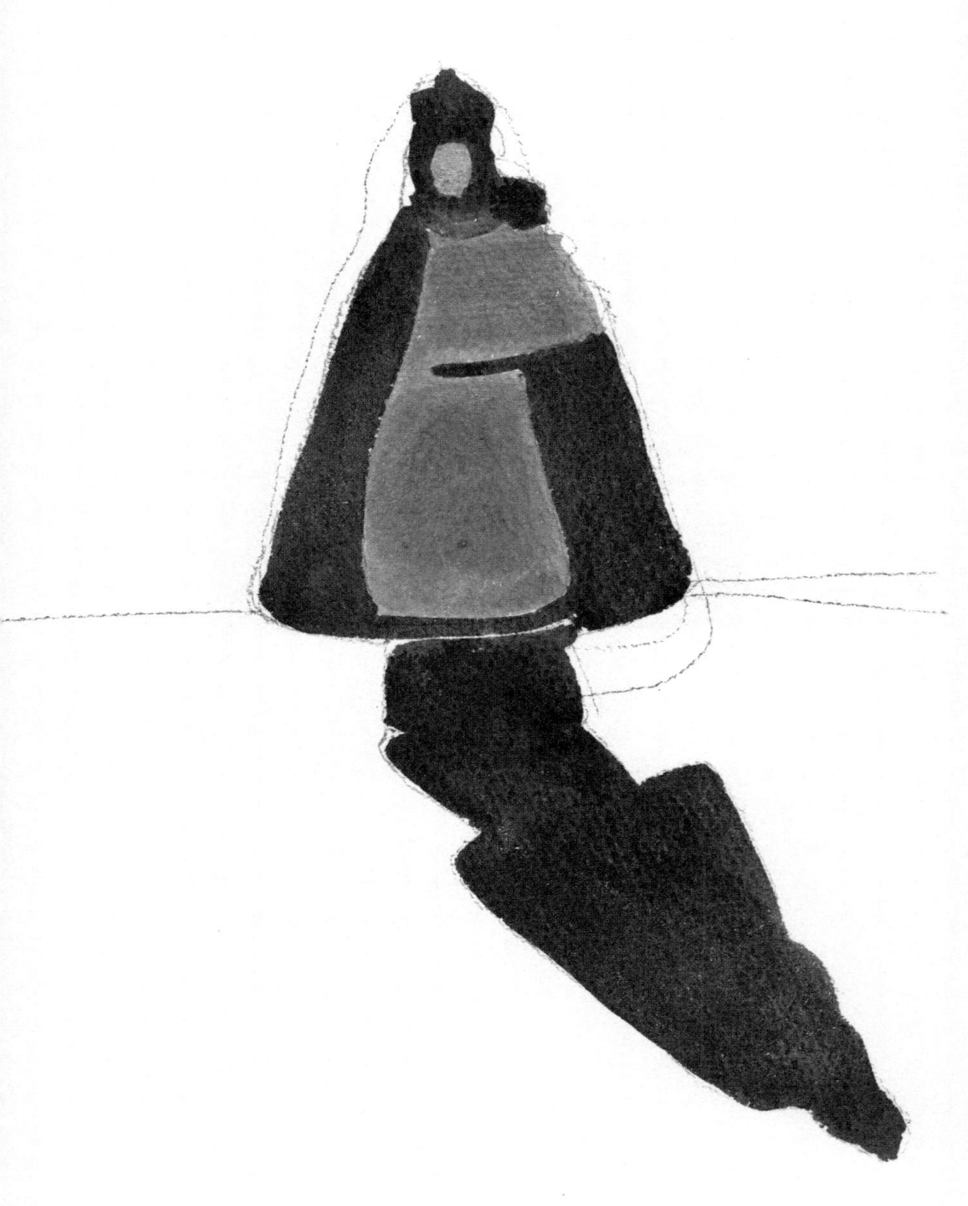

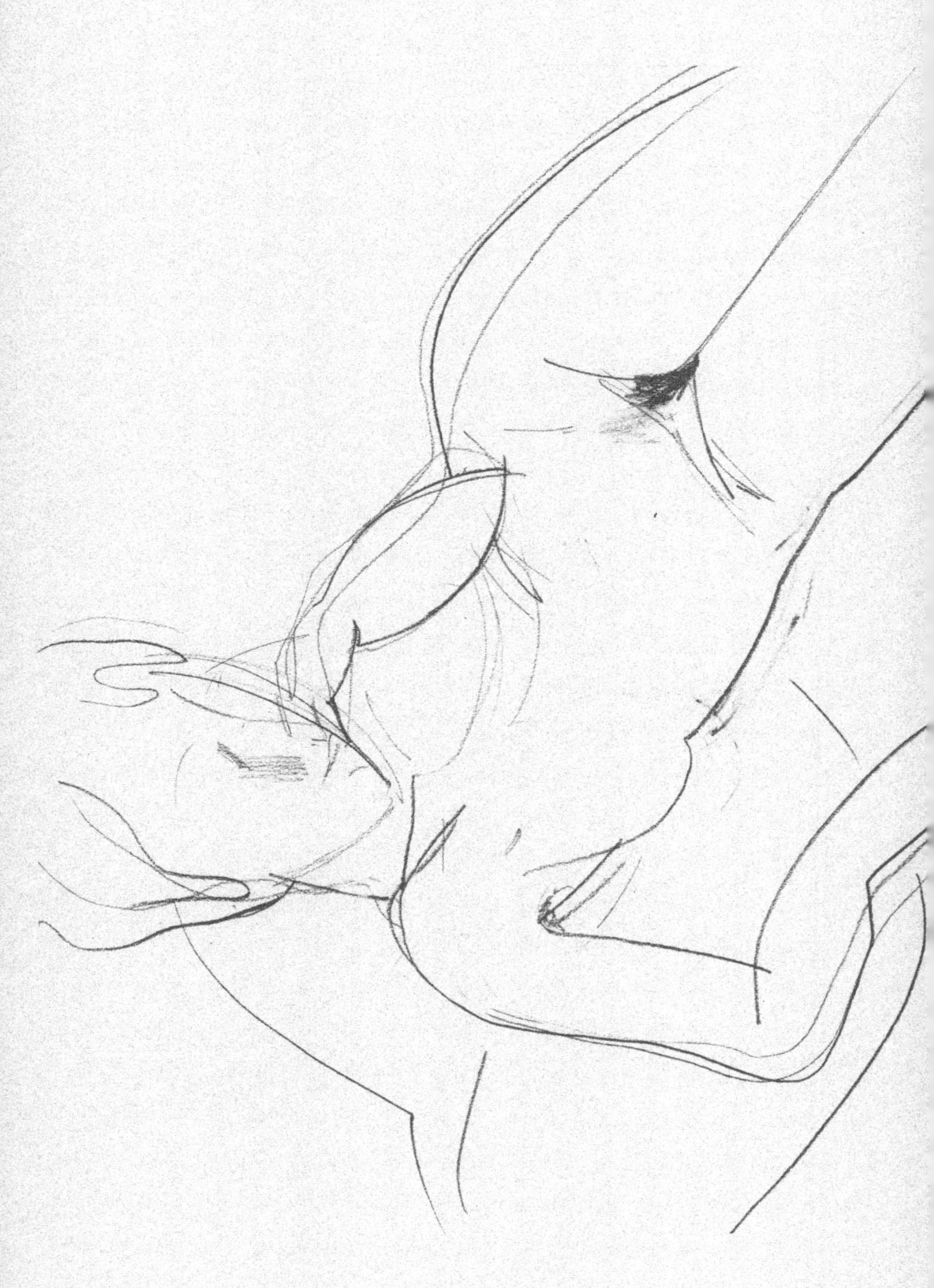

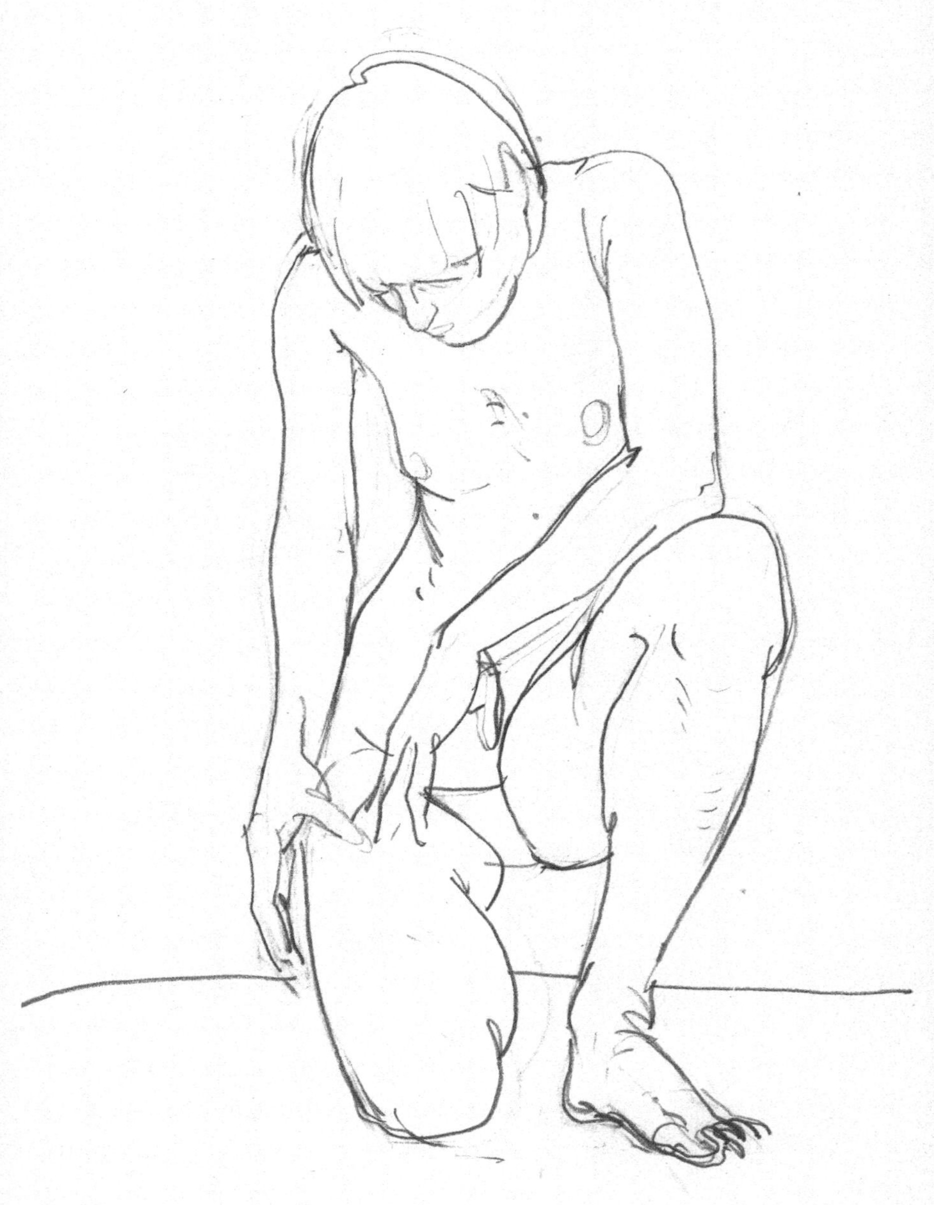

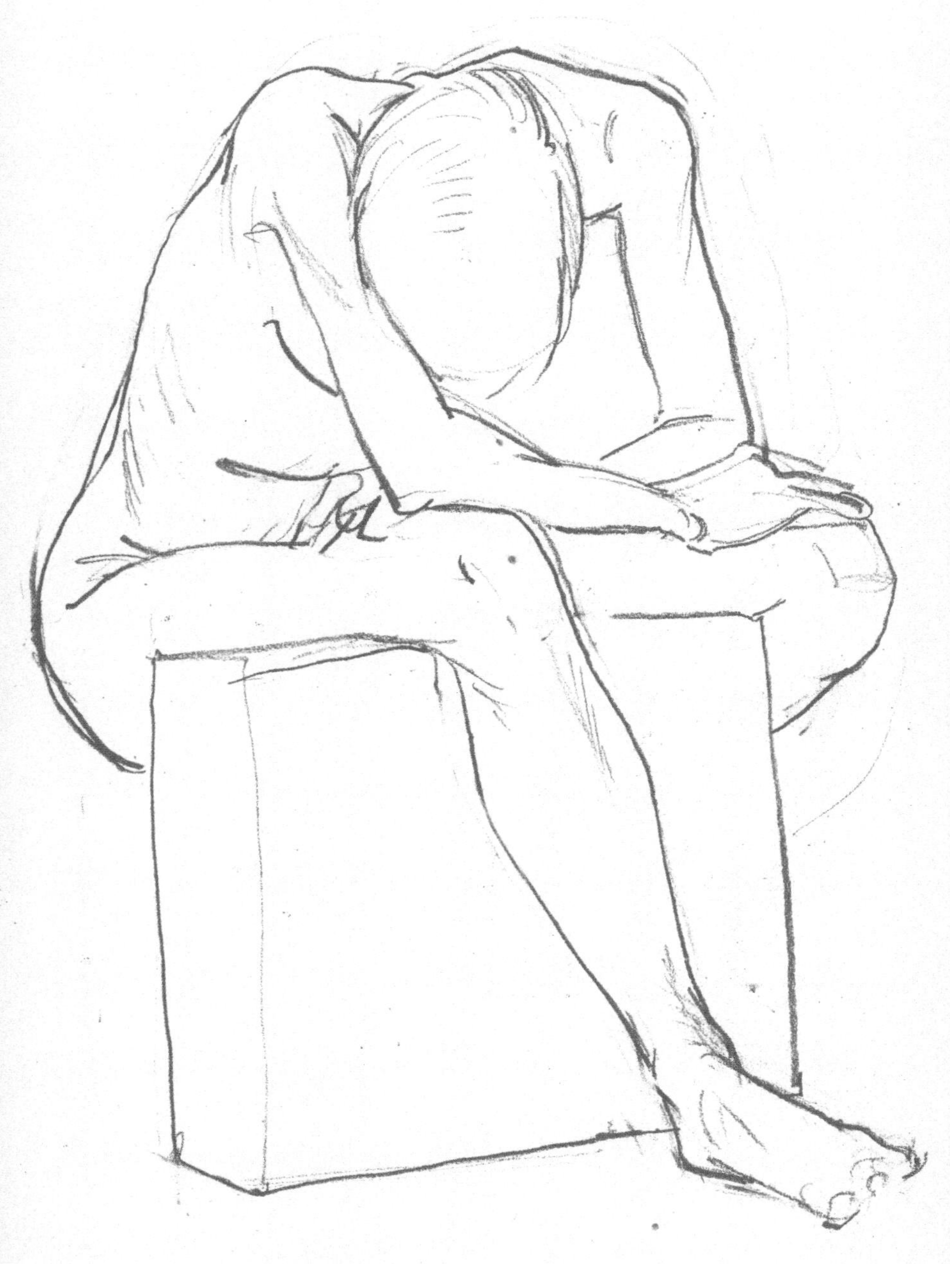

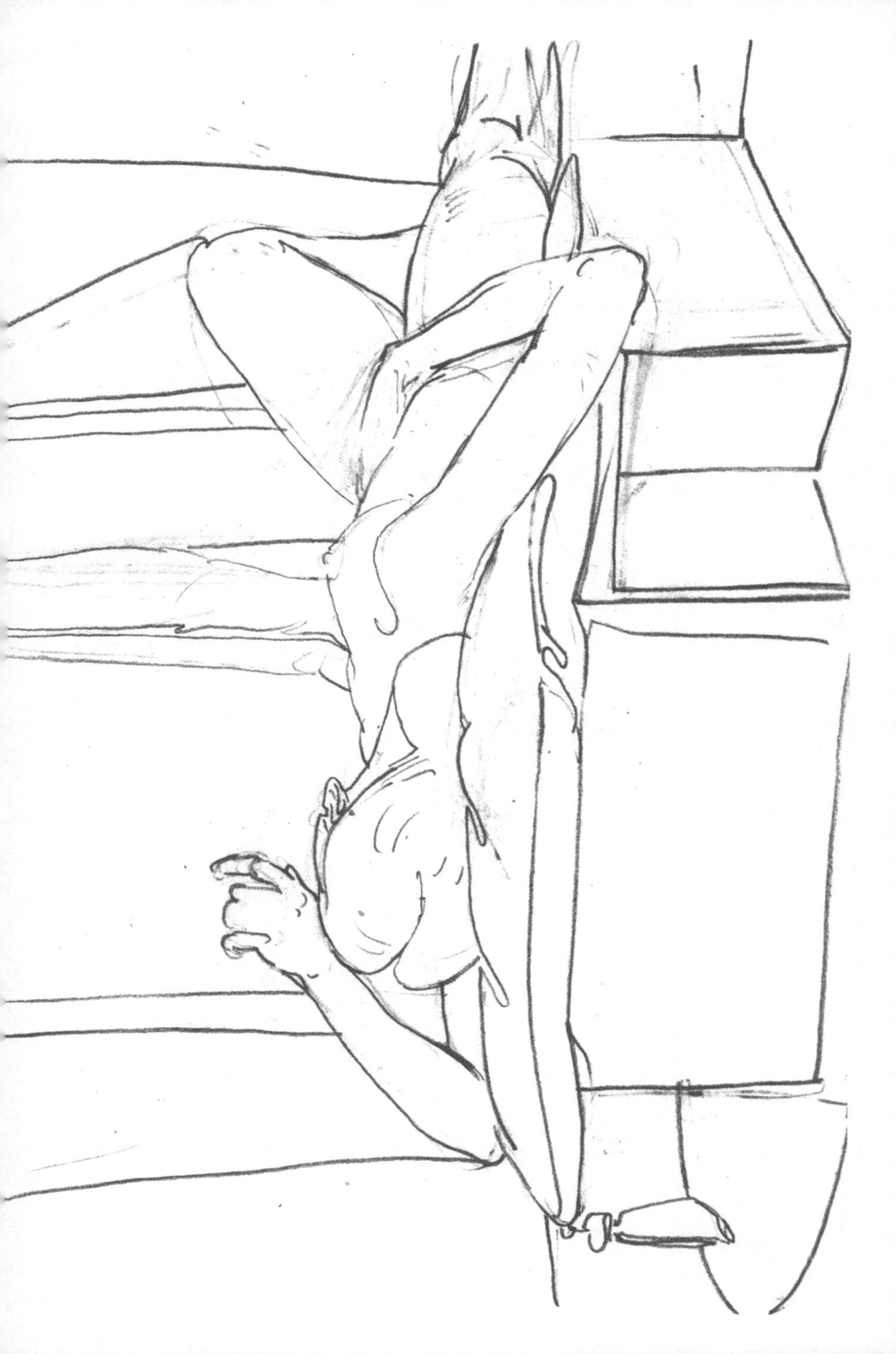

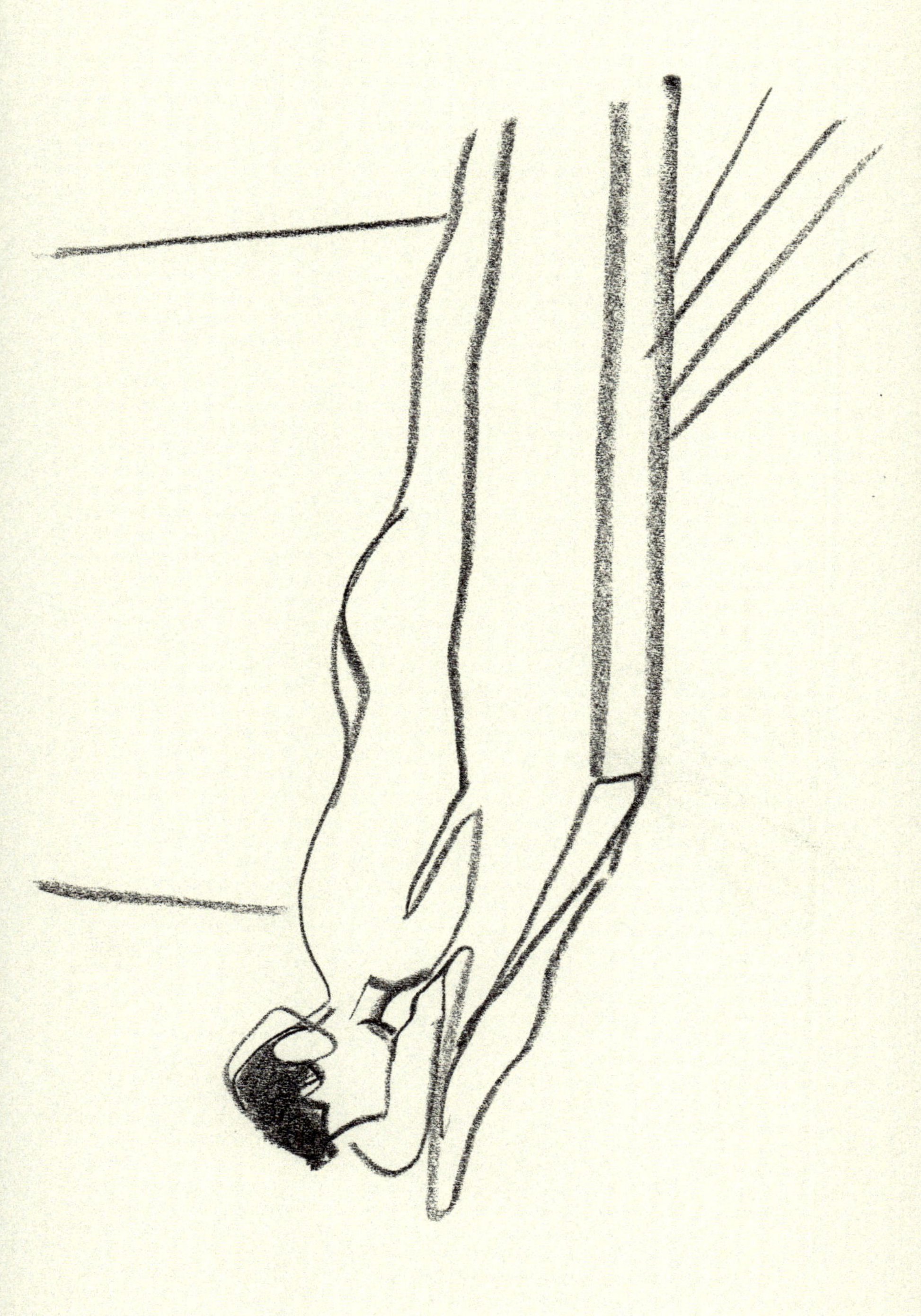

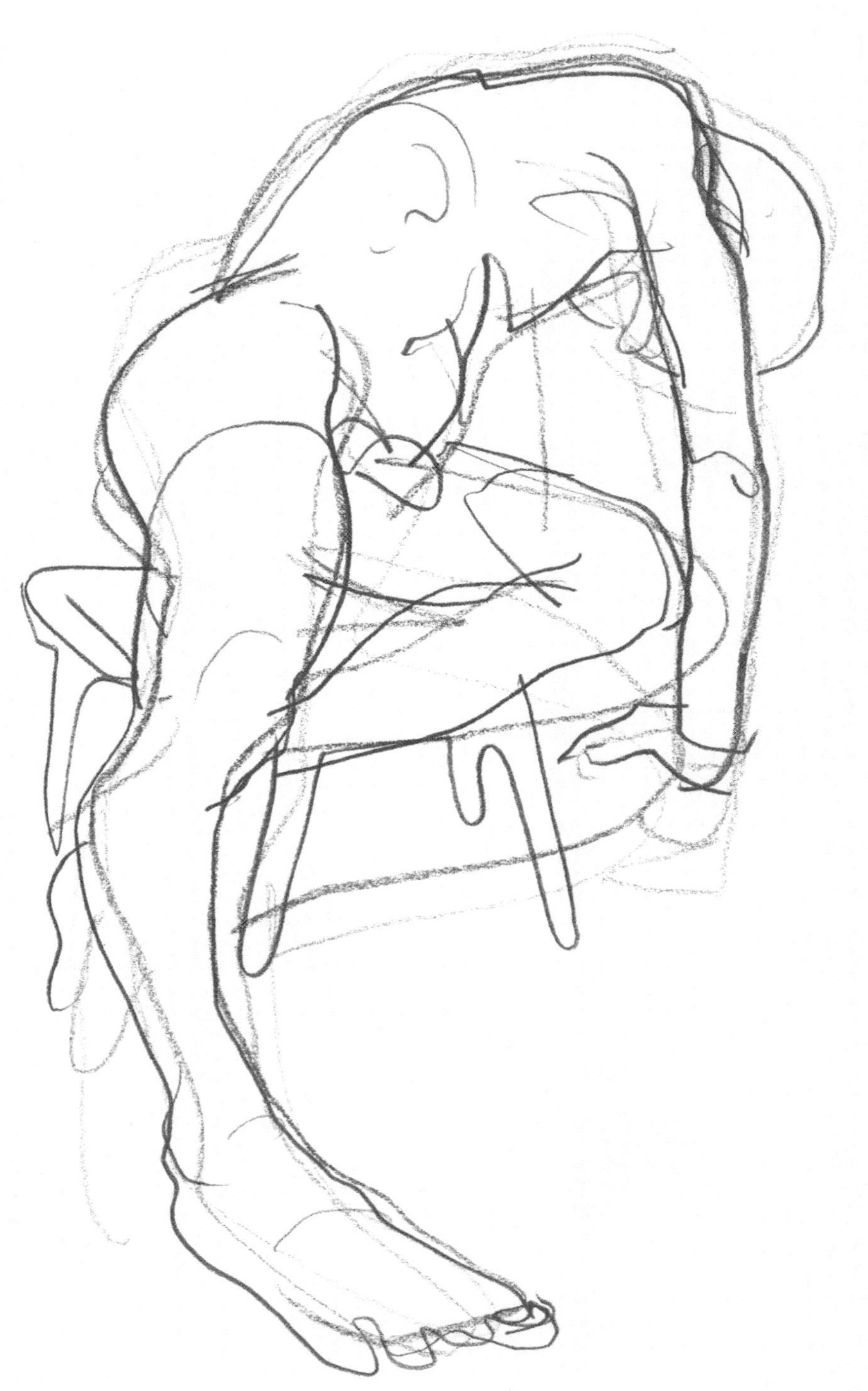

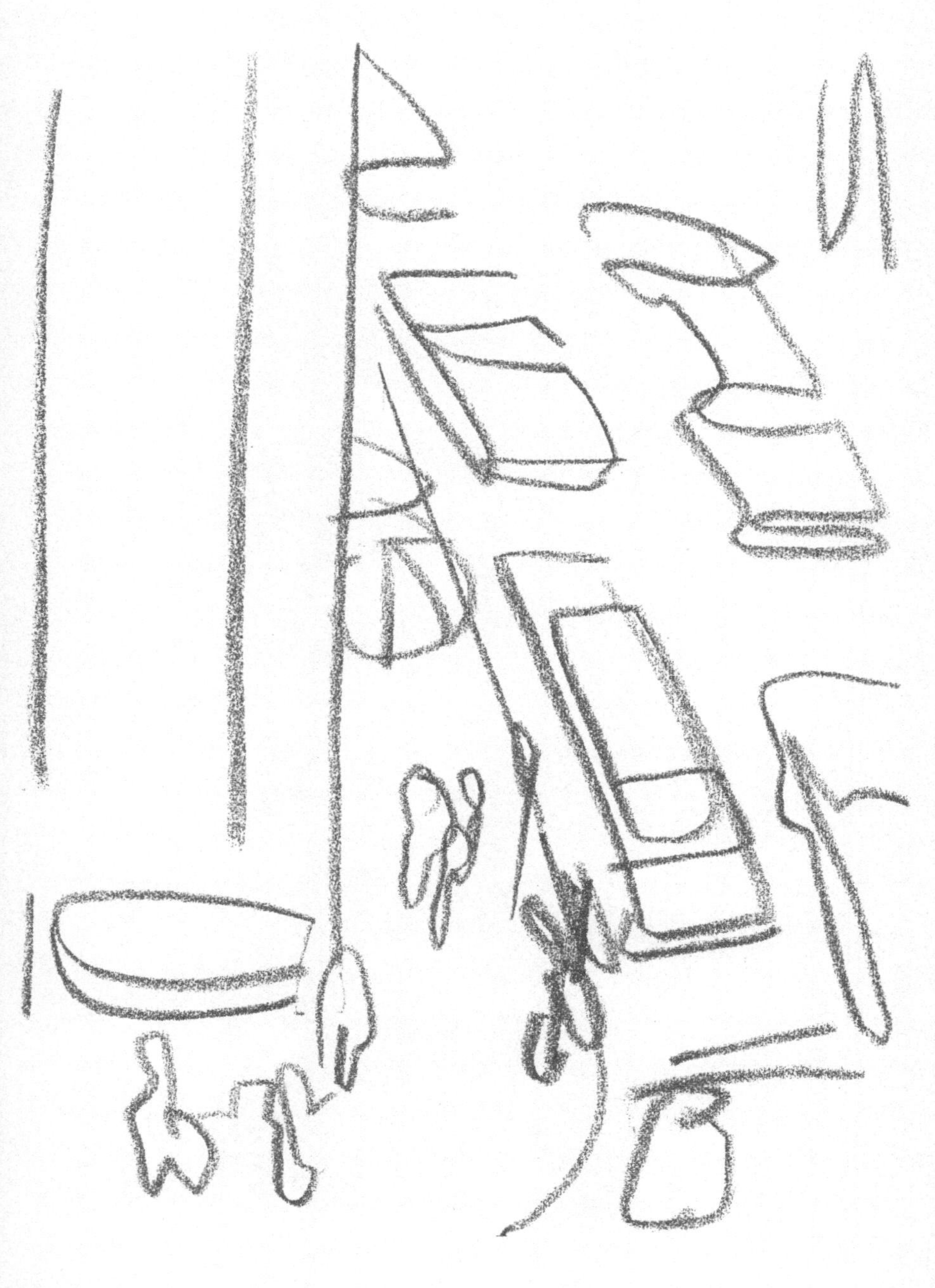

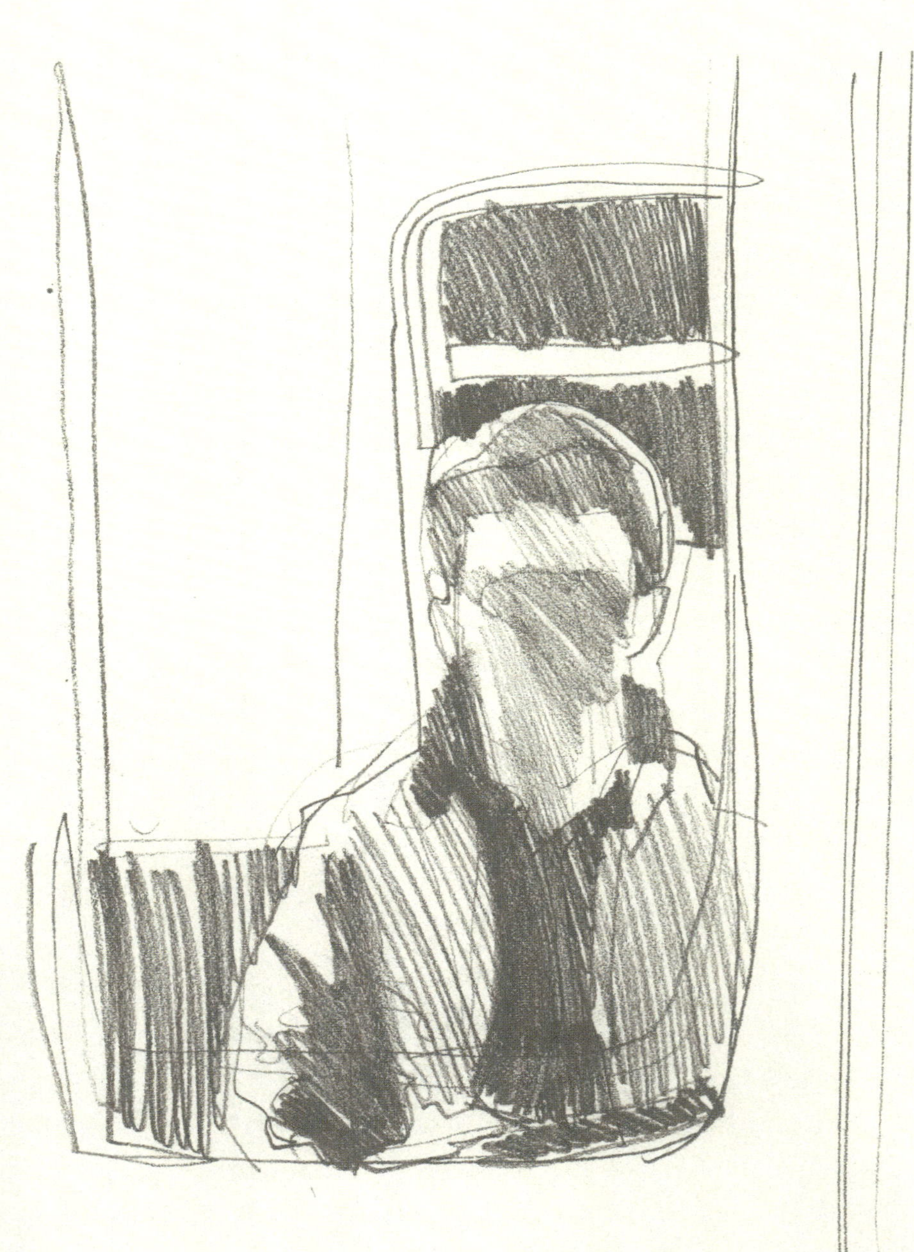

III.

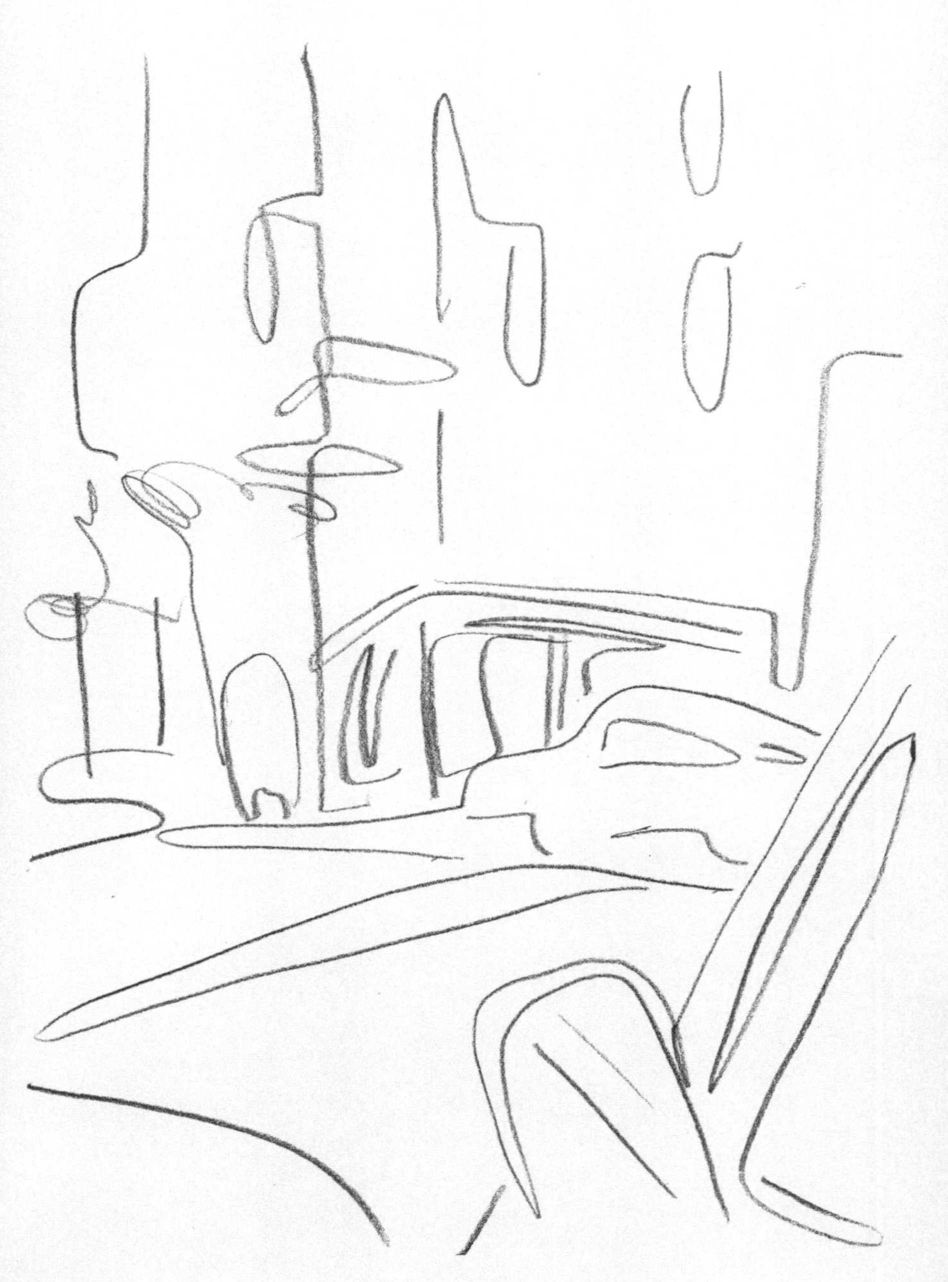

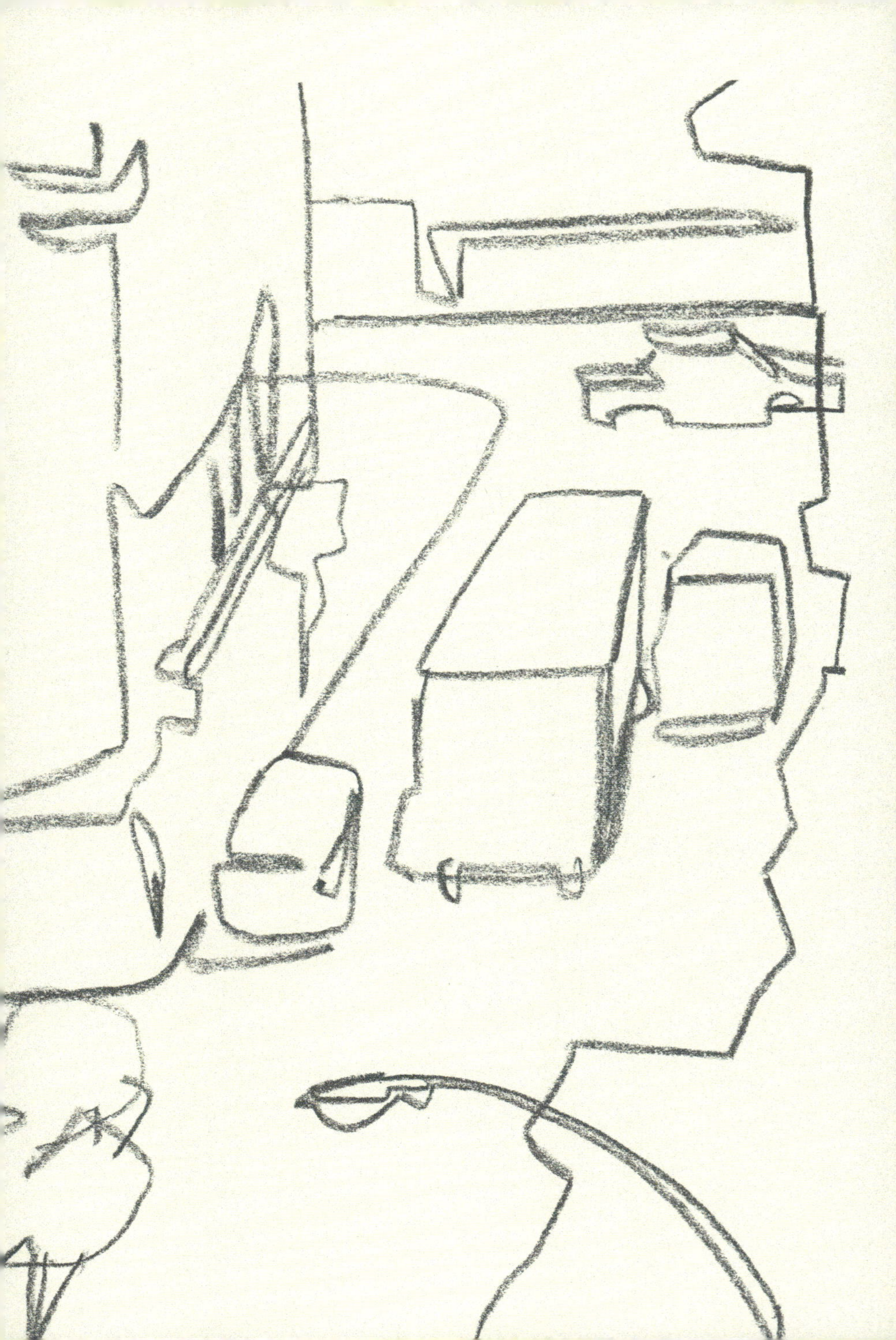

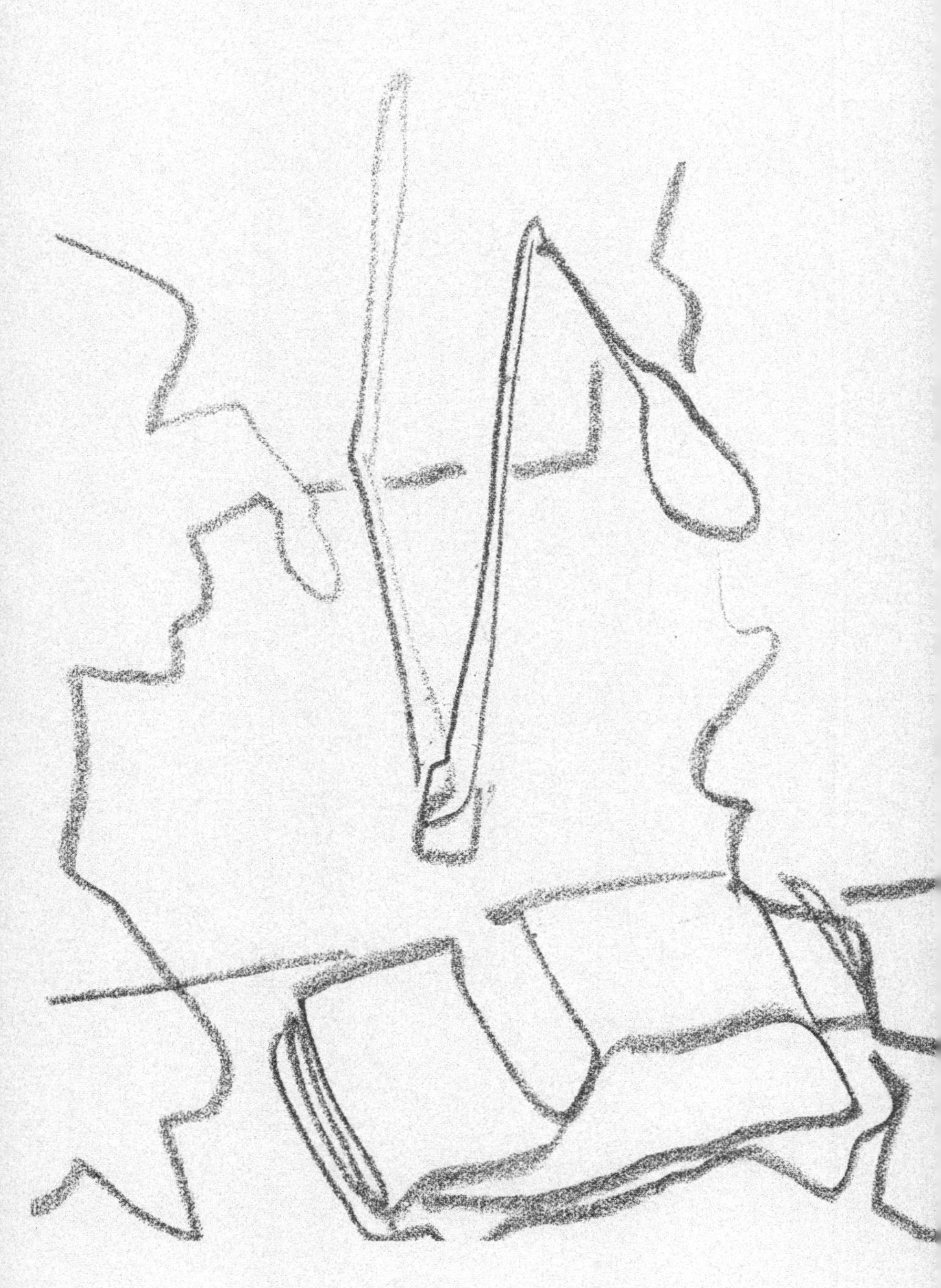

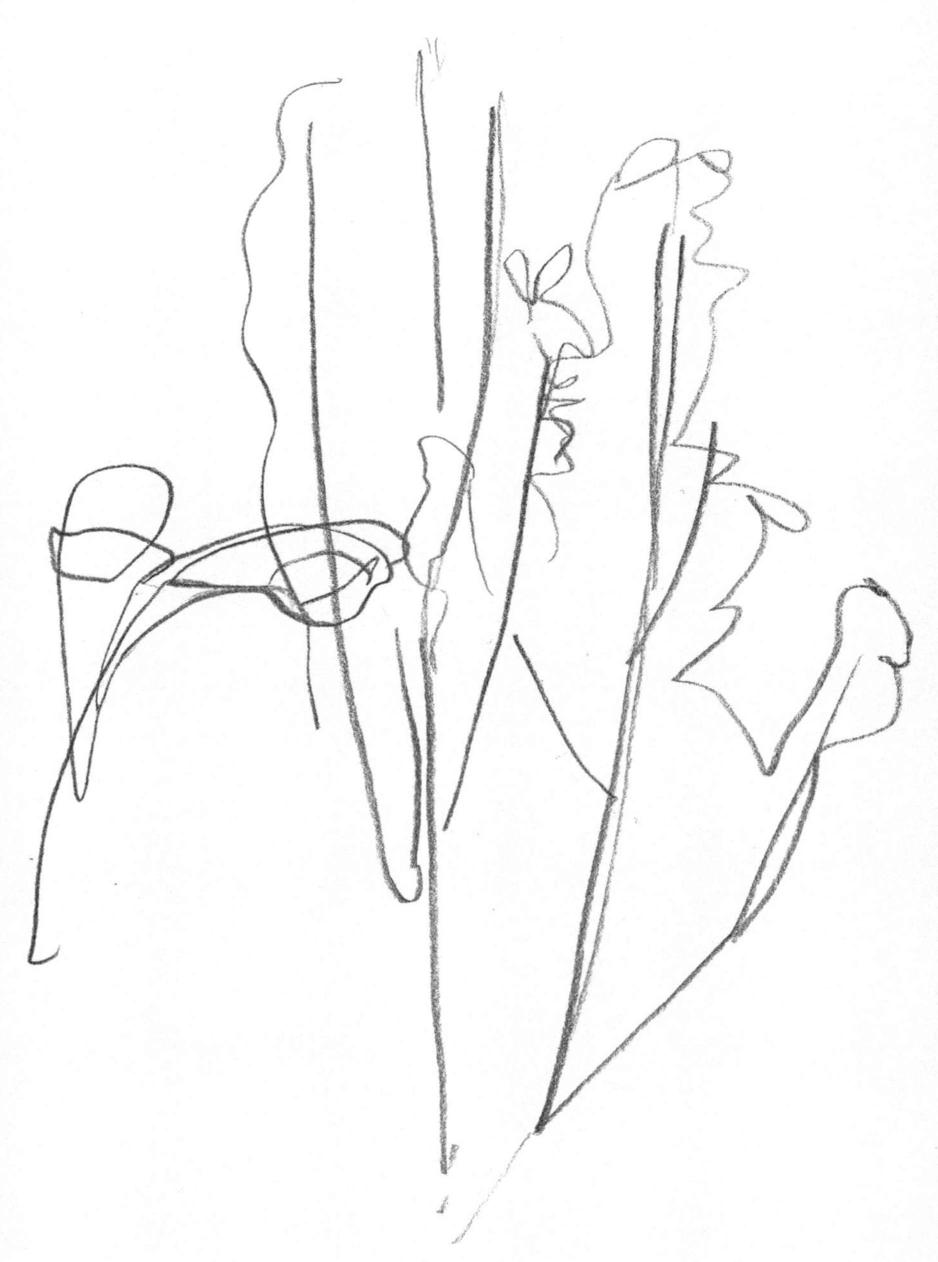

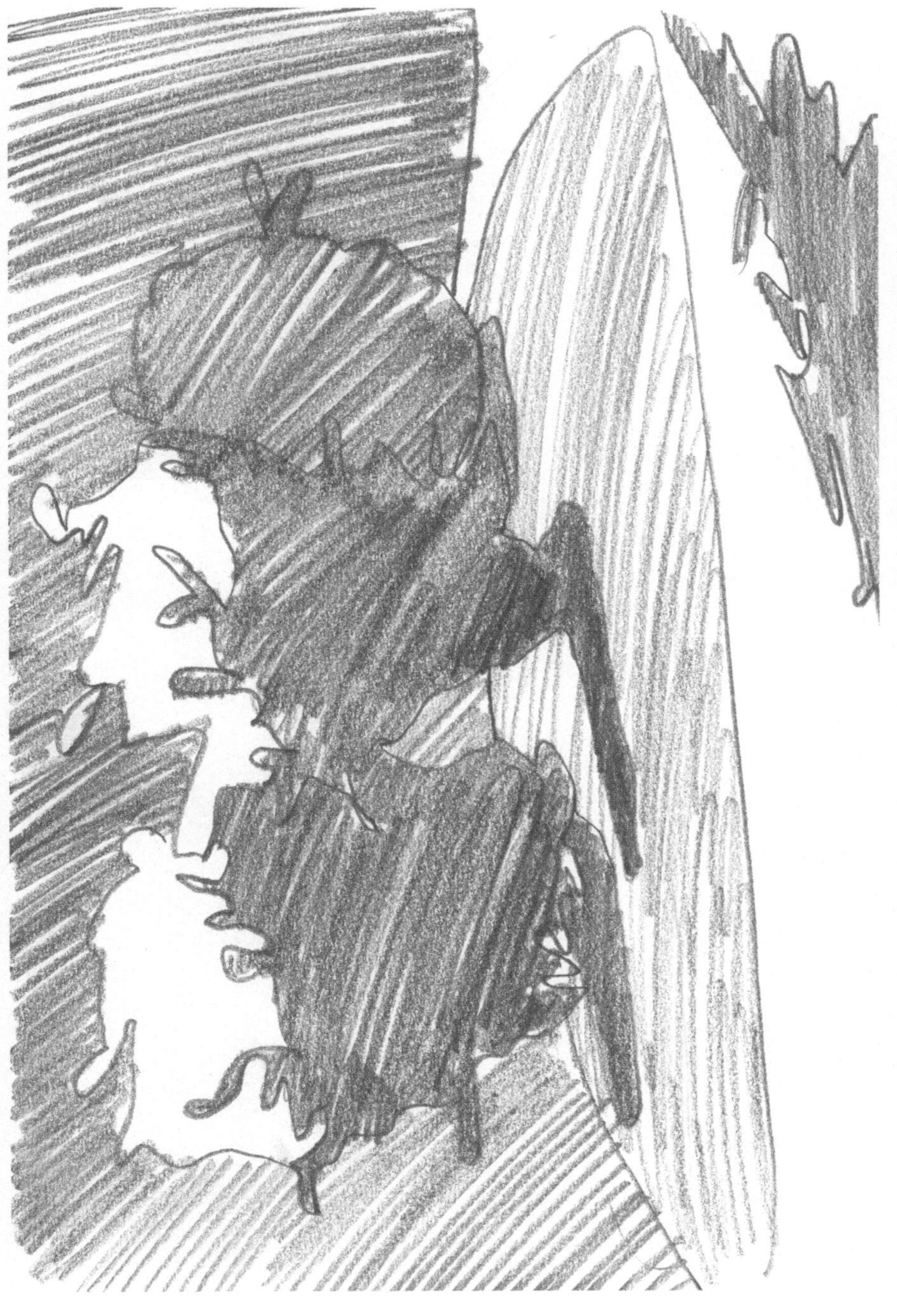

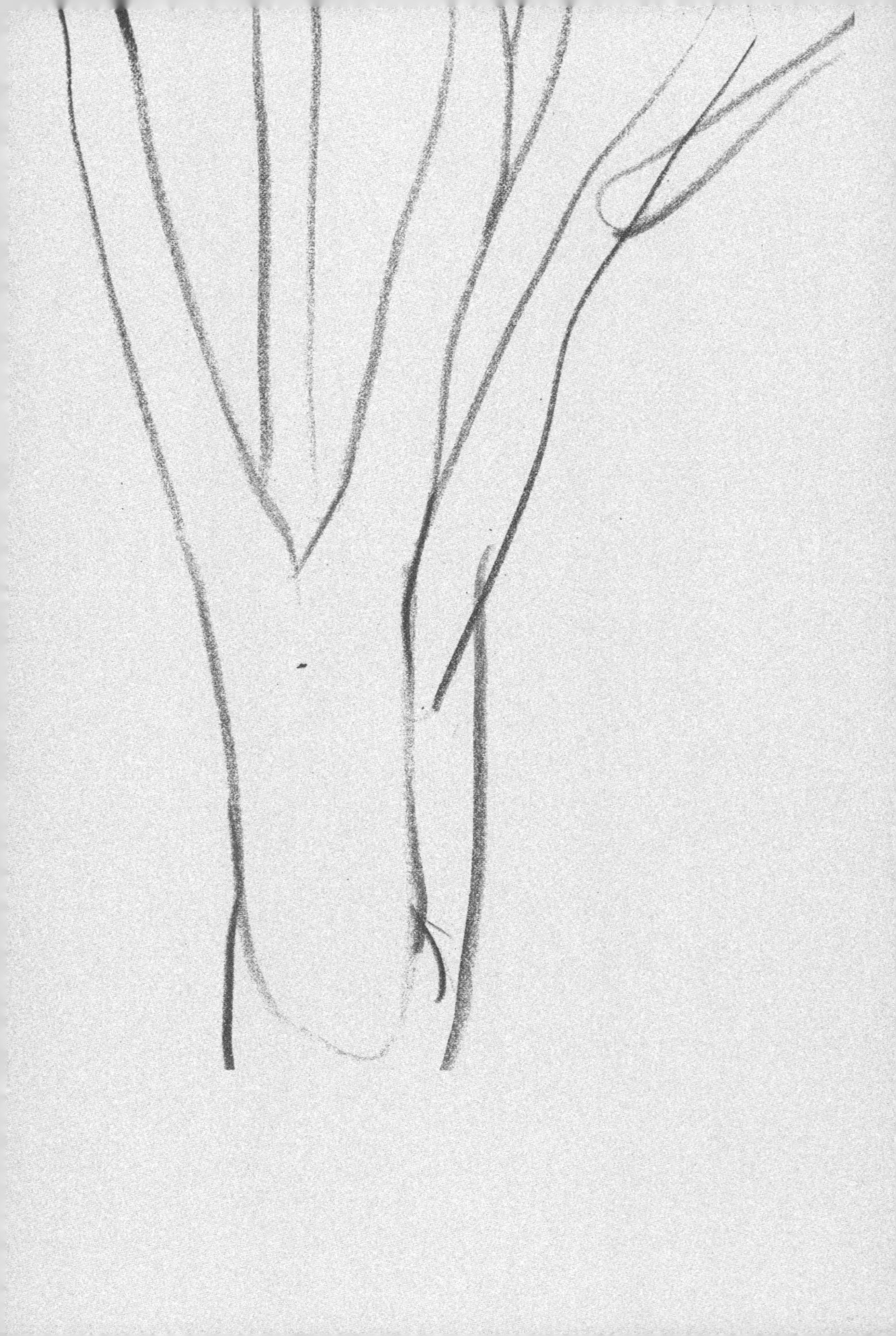

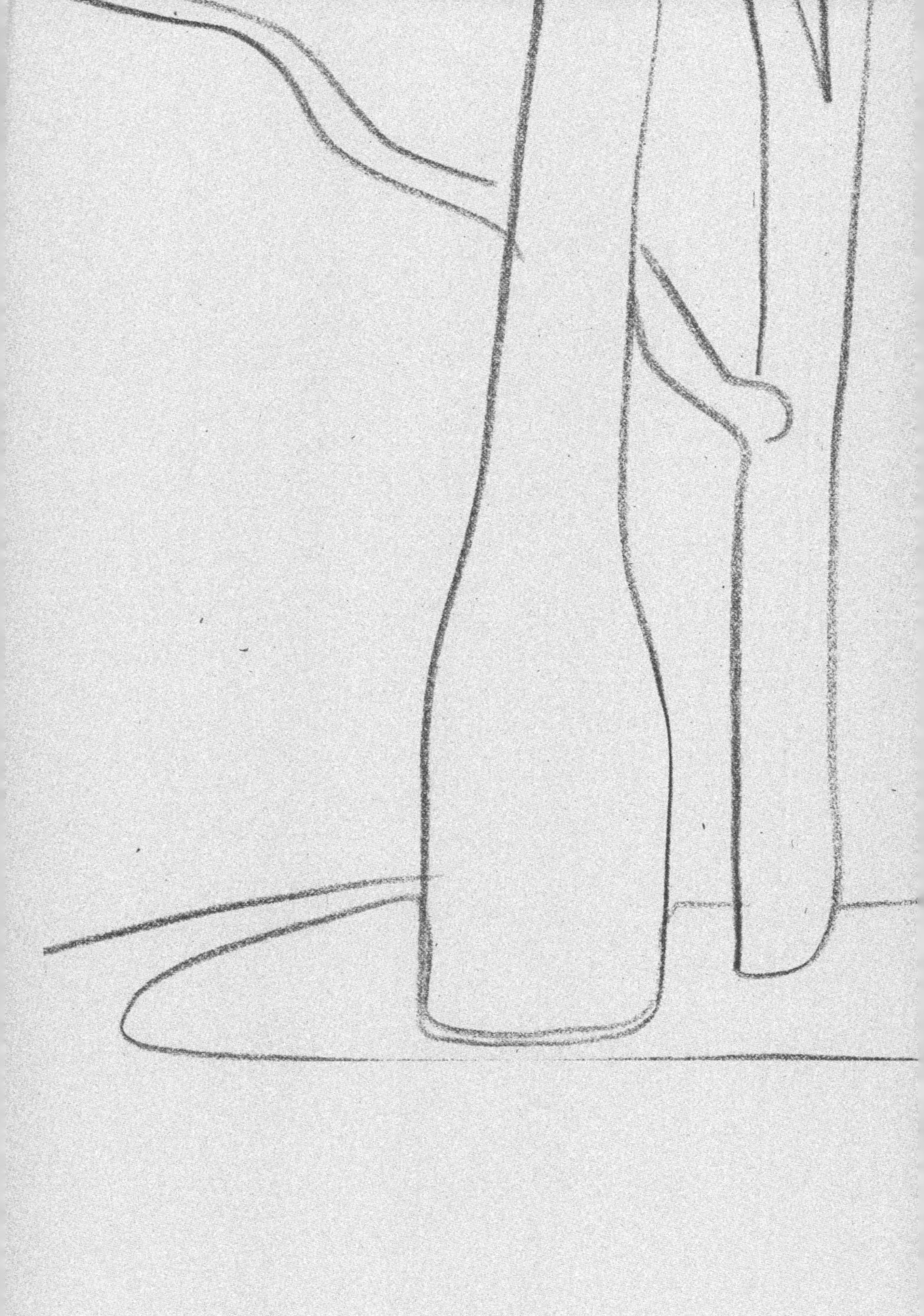

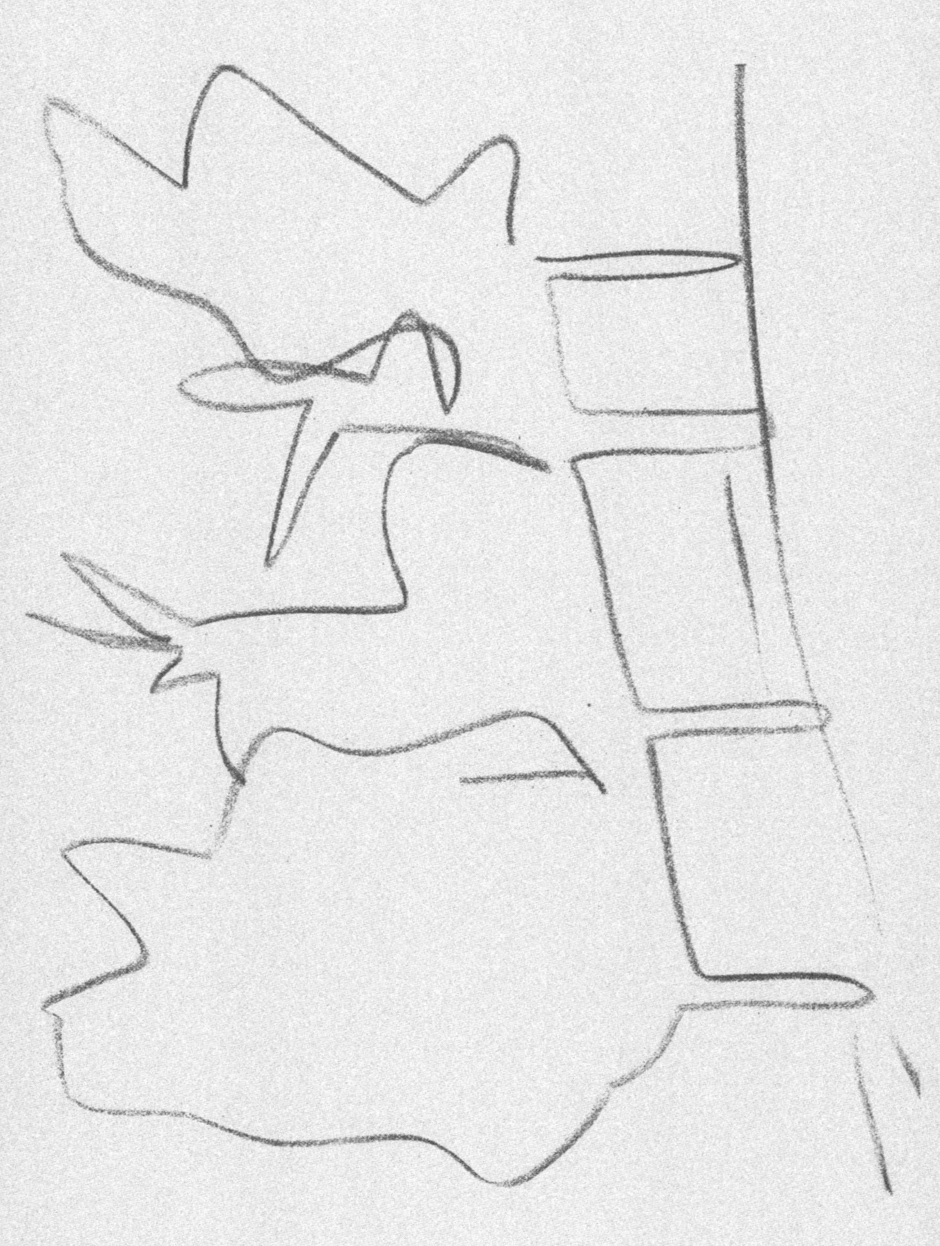

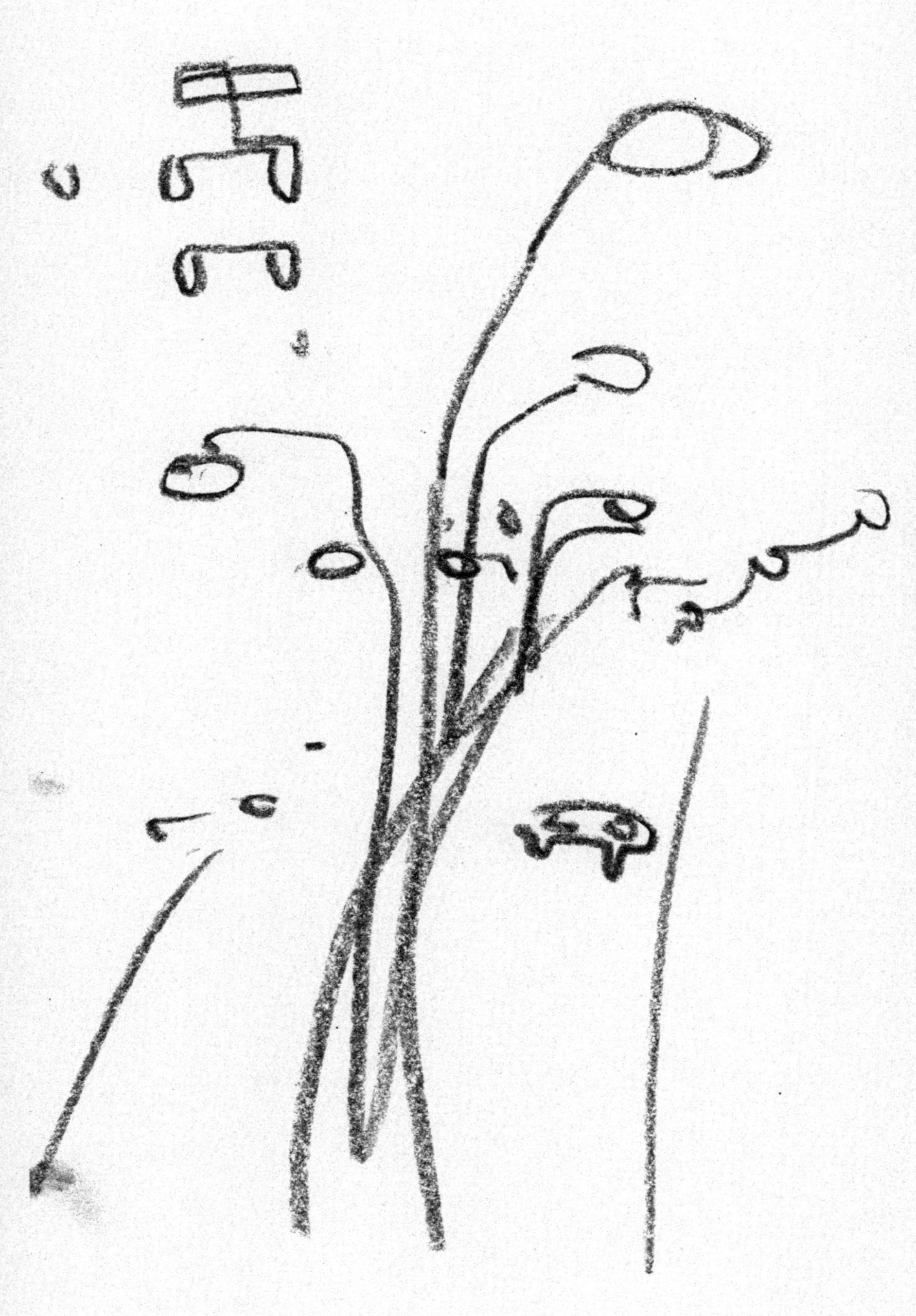

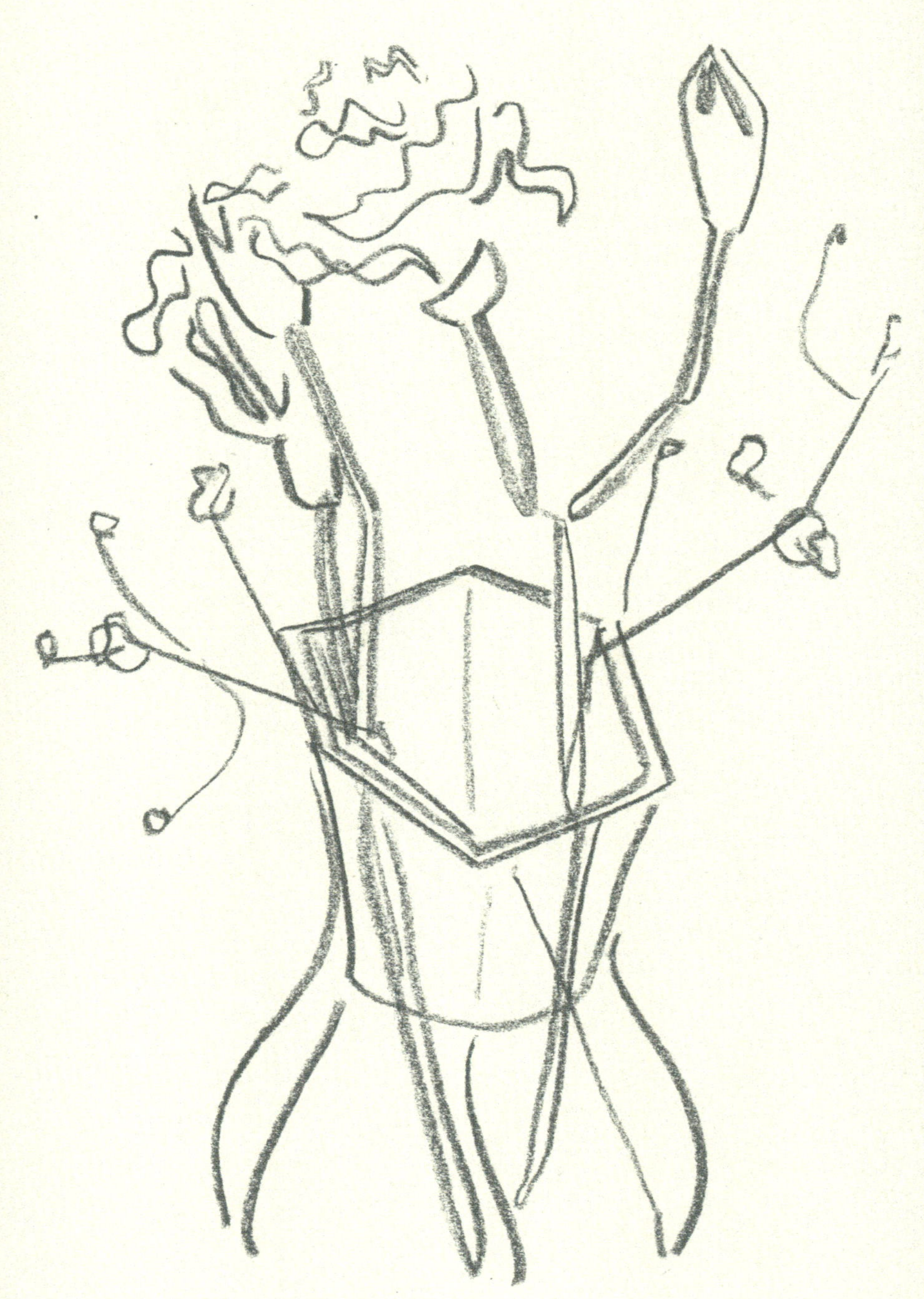

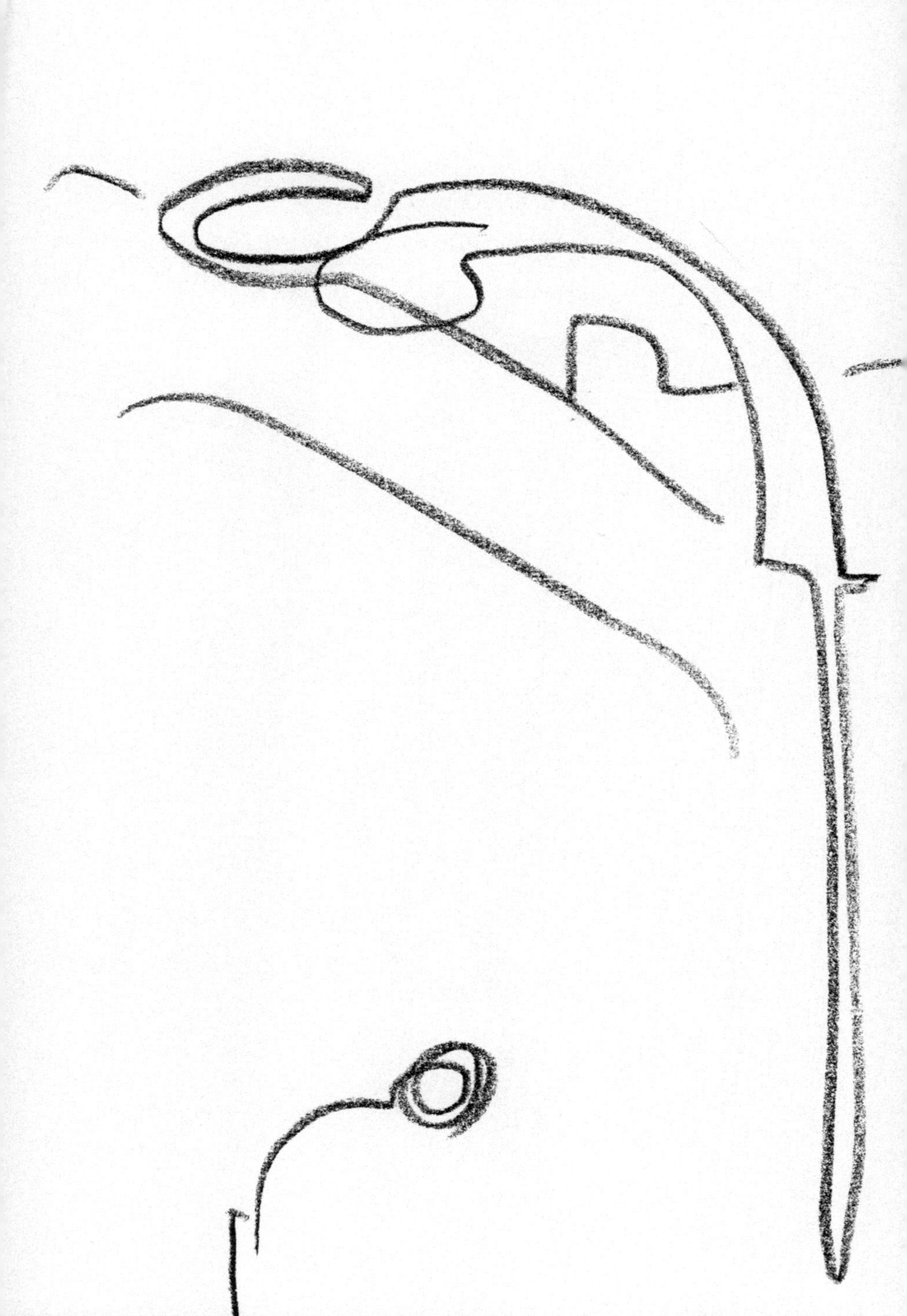

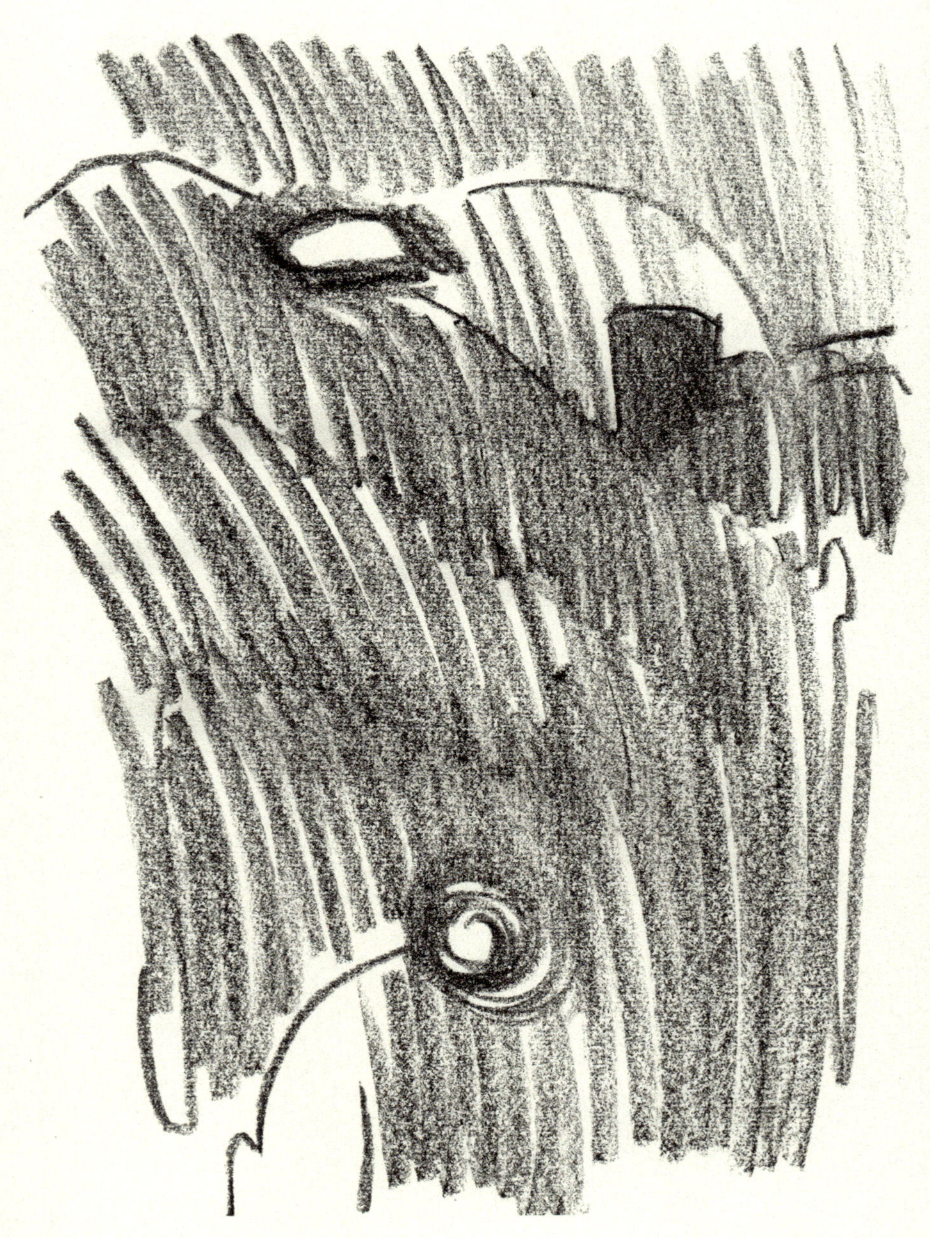

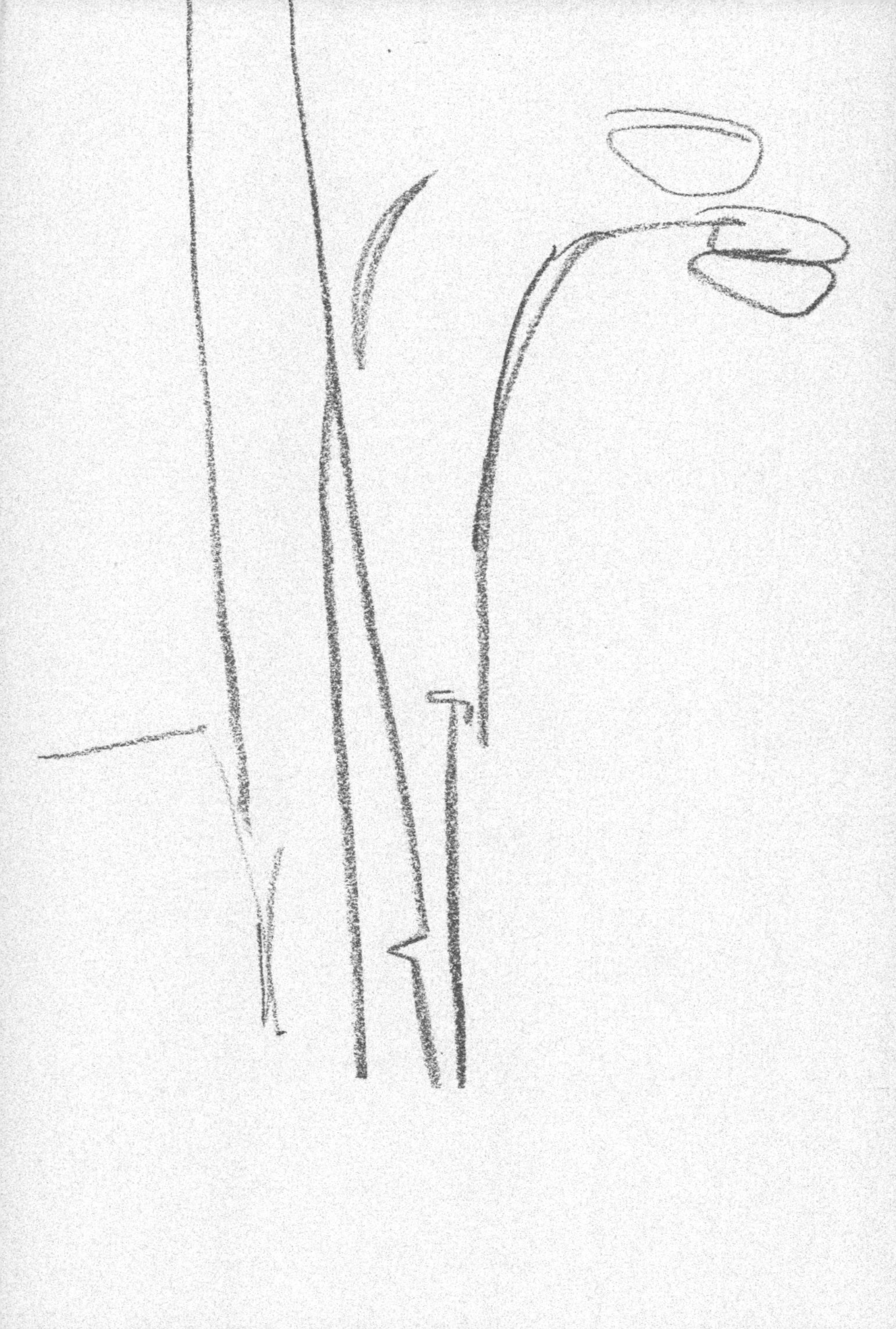

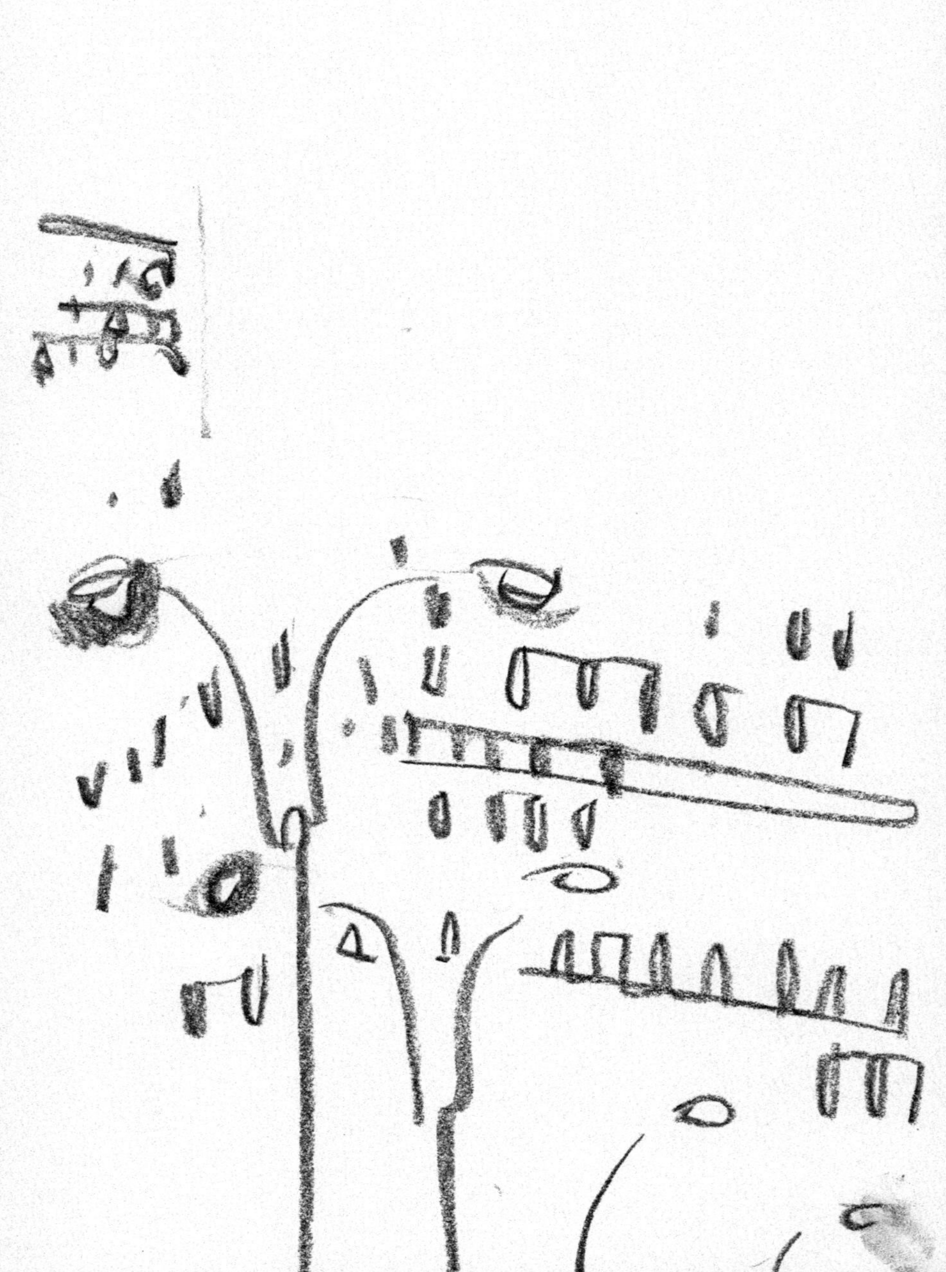

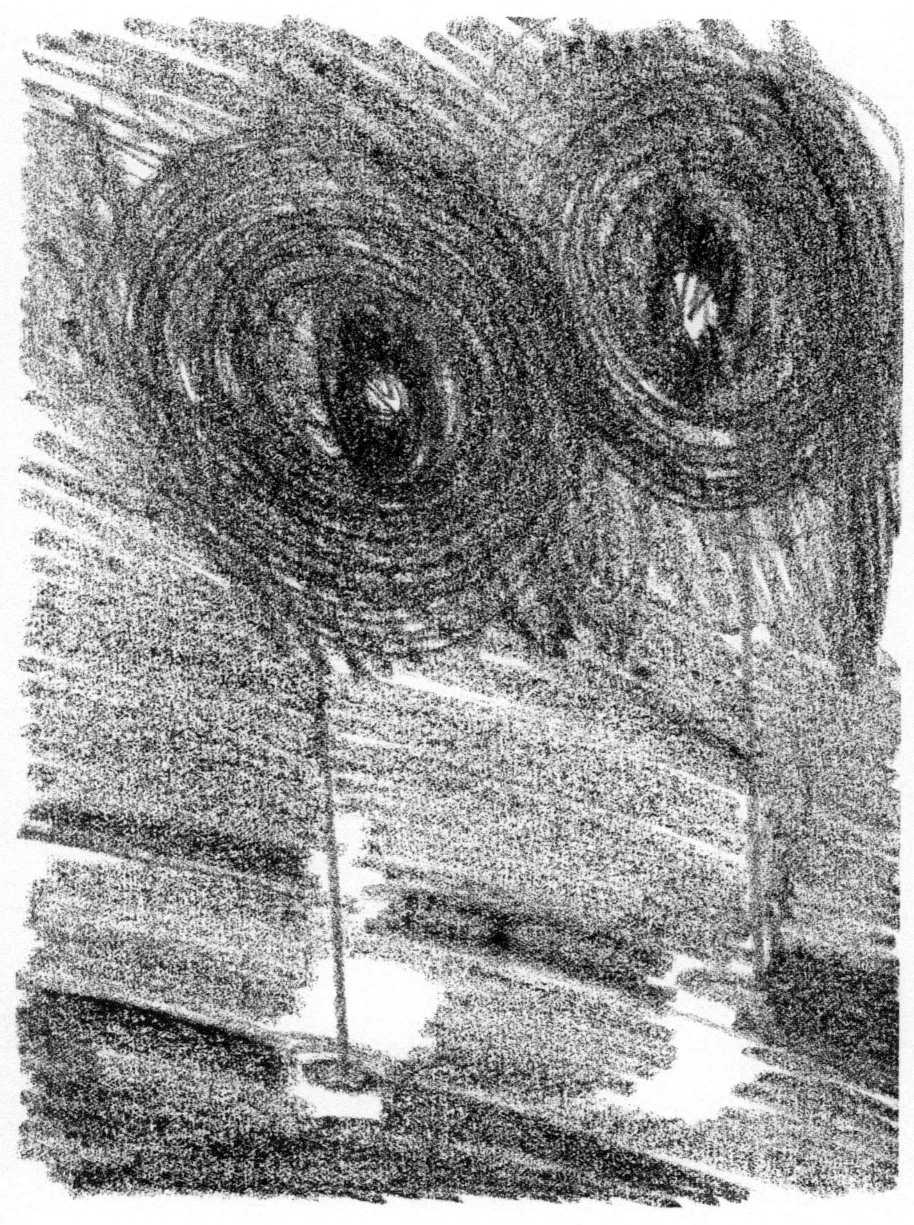

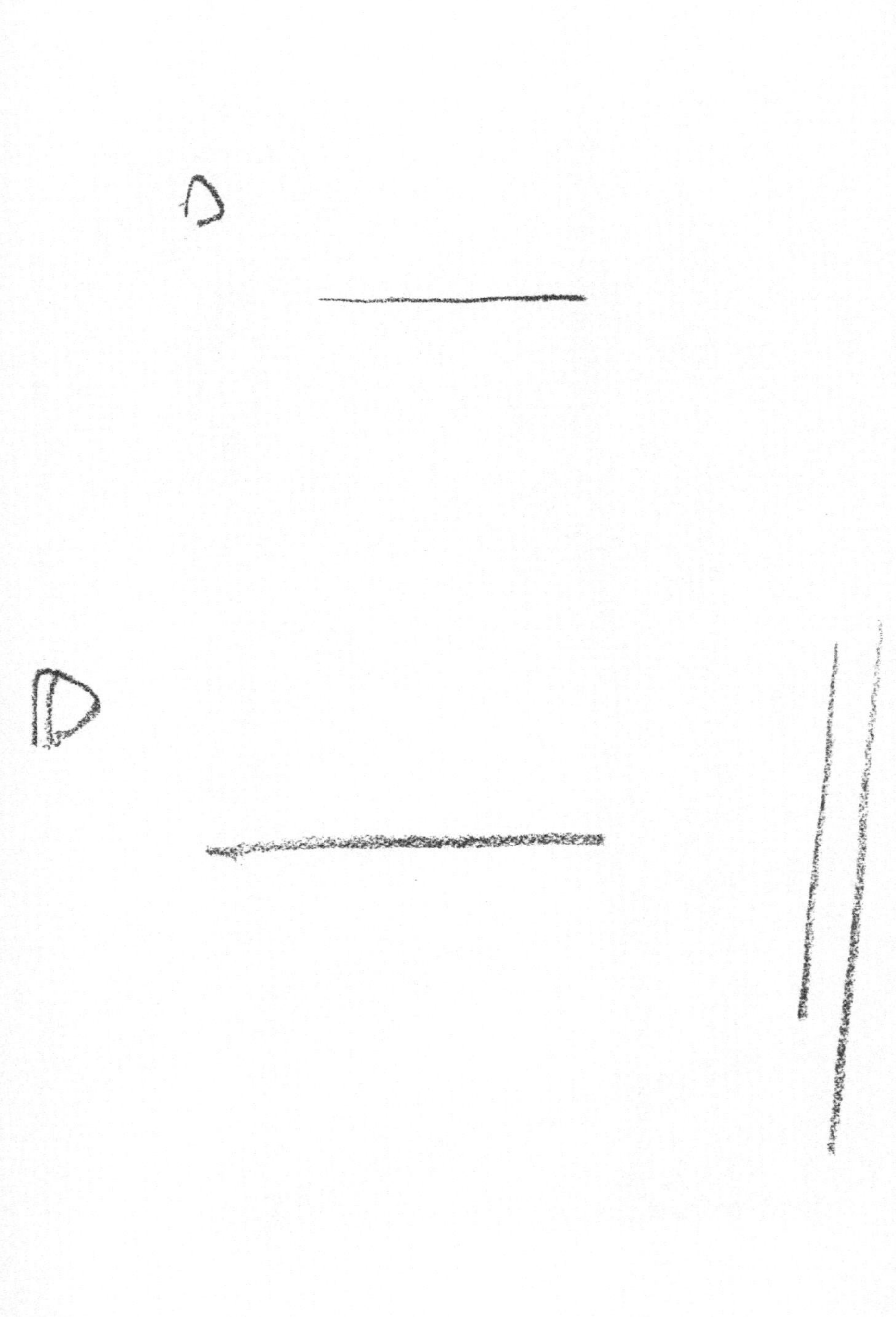

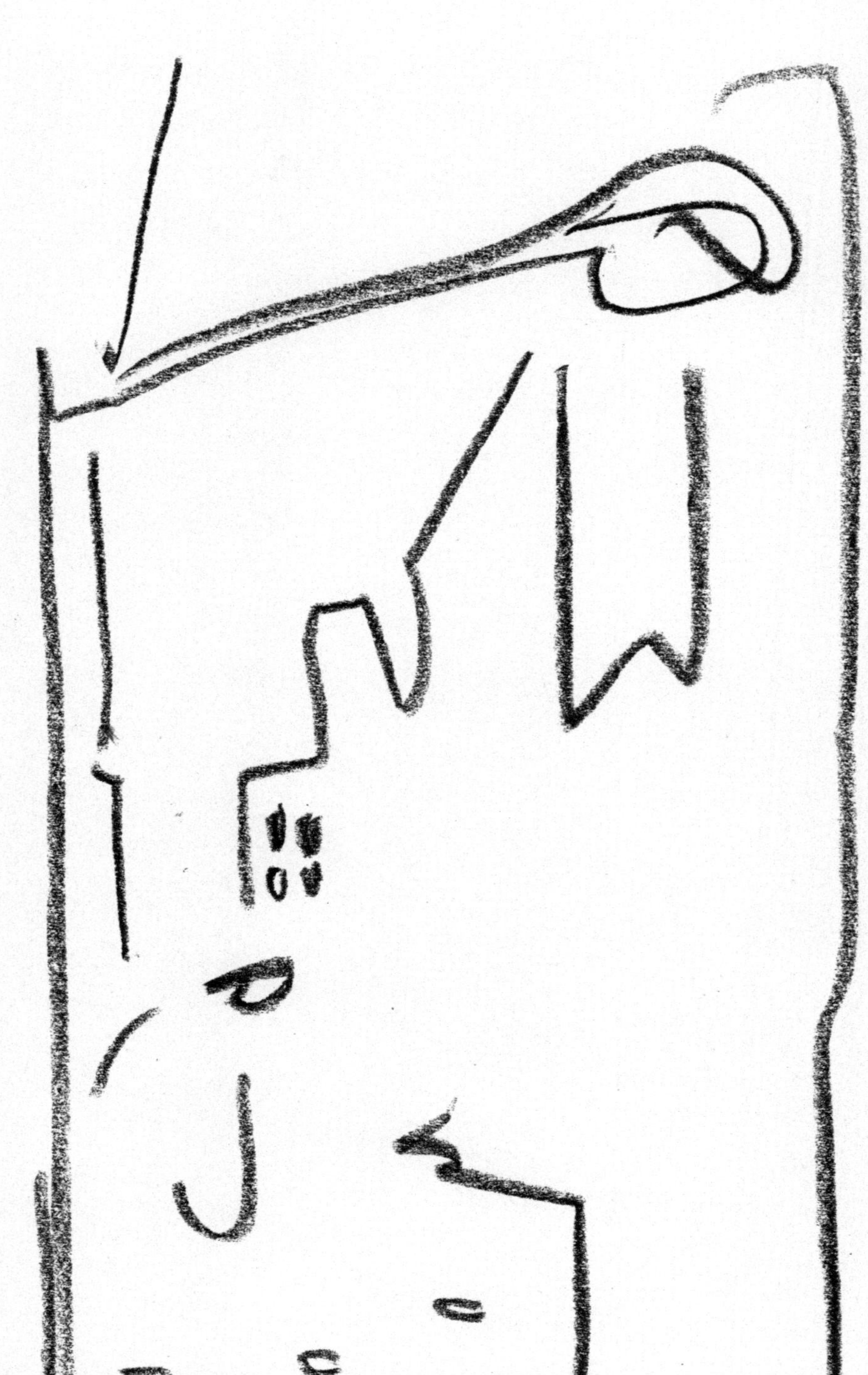

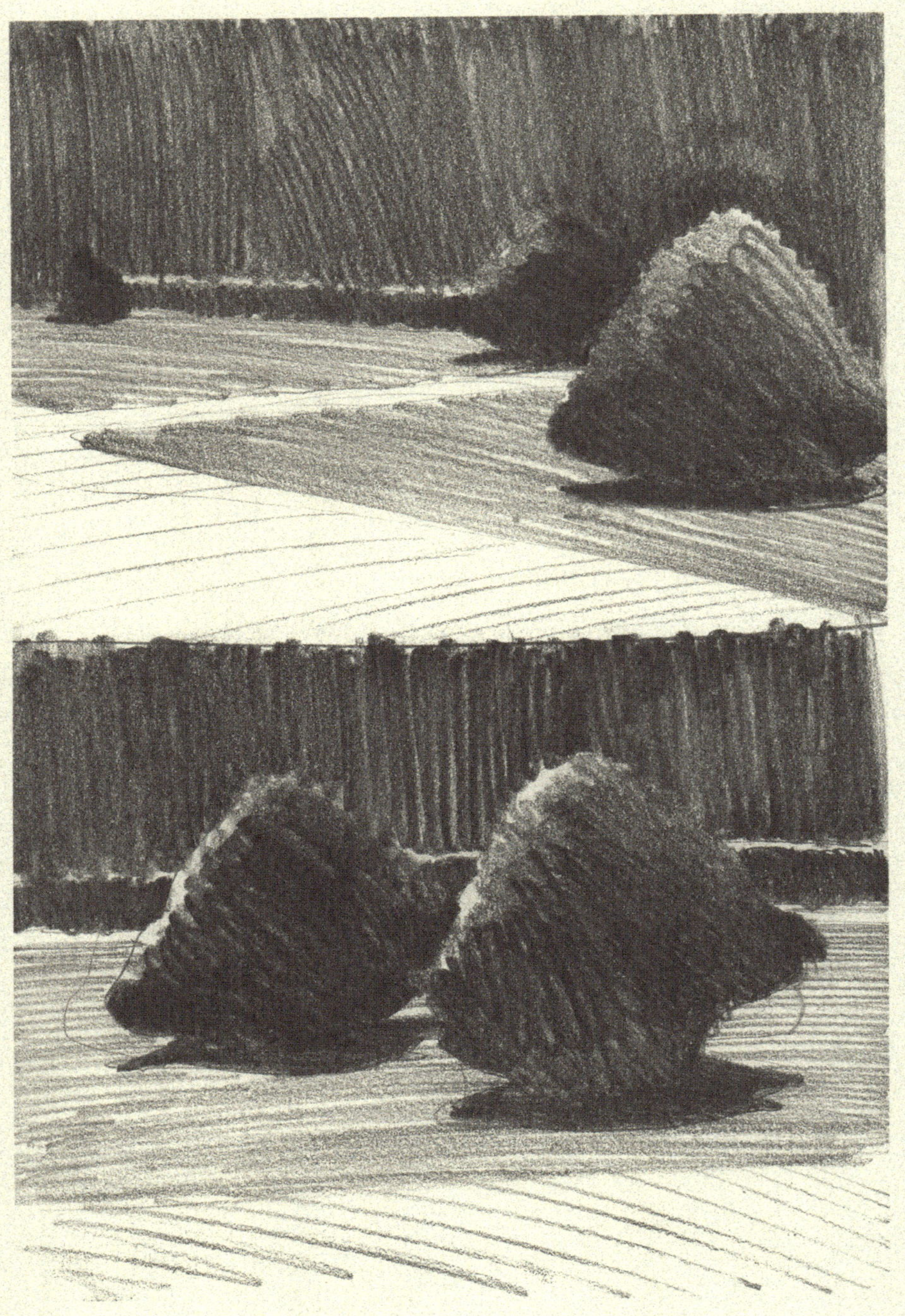

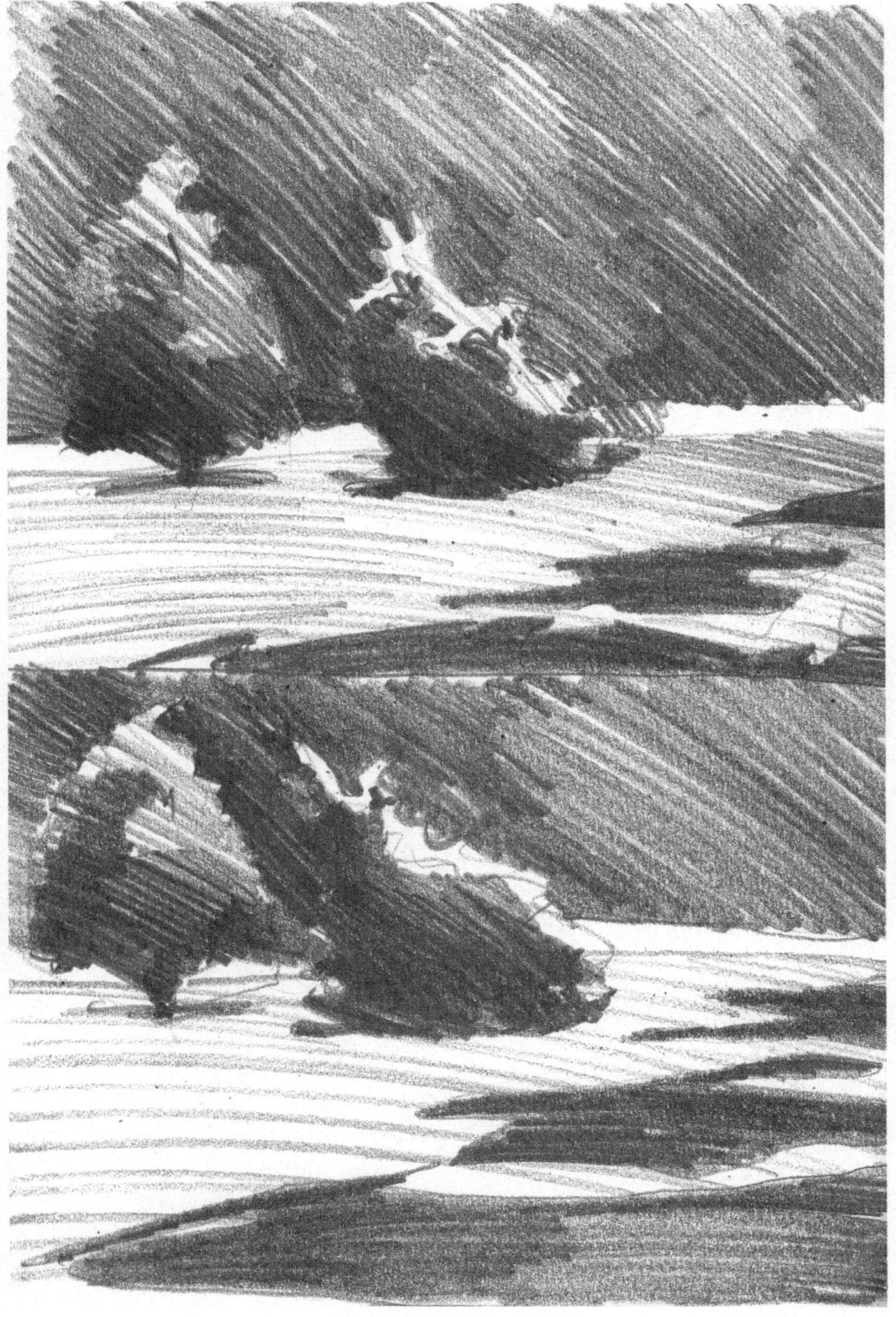

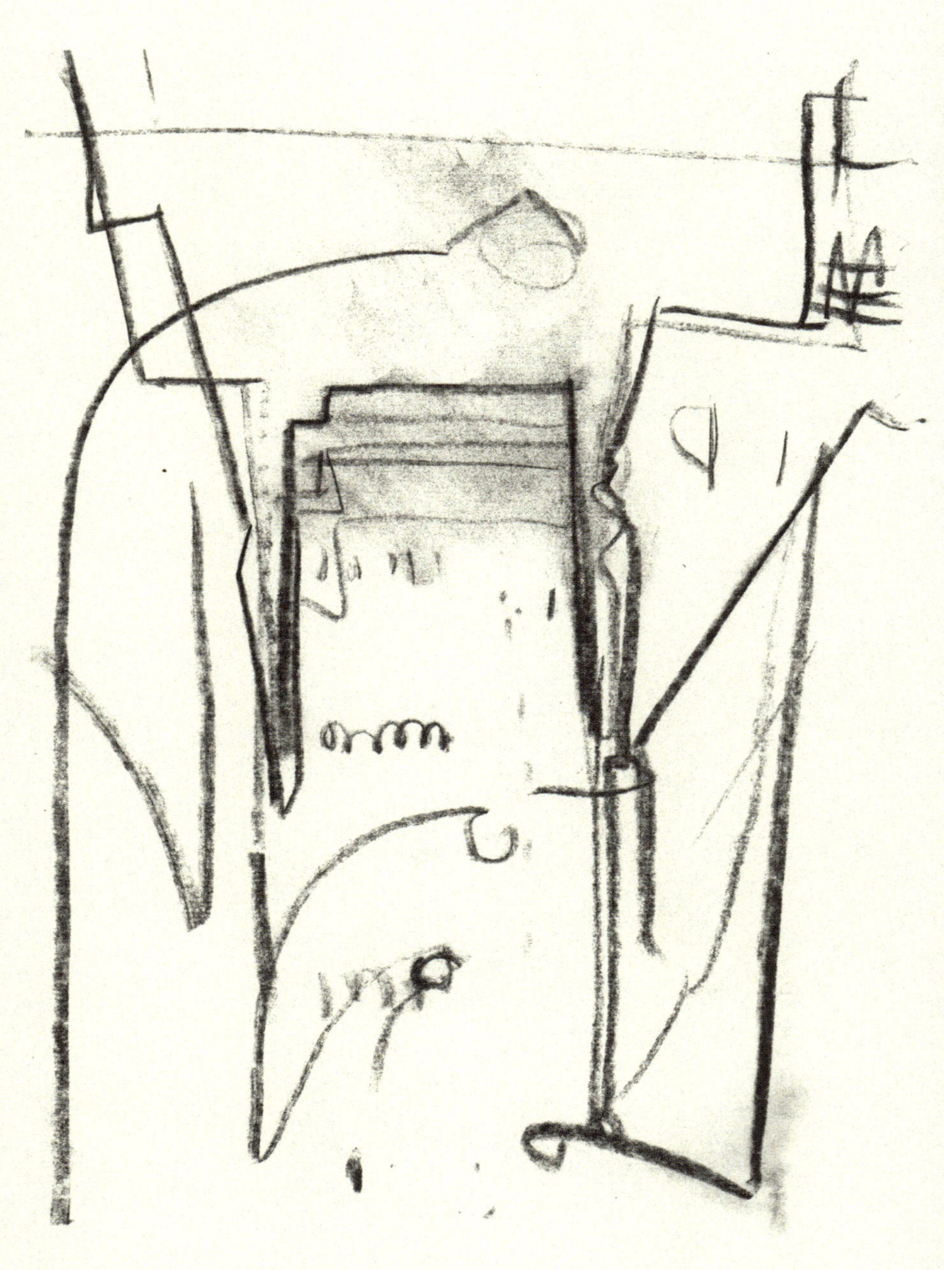

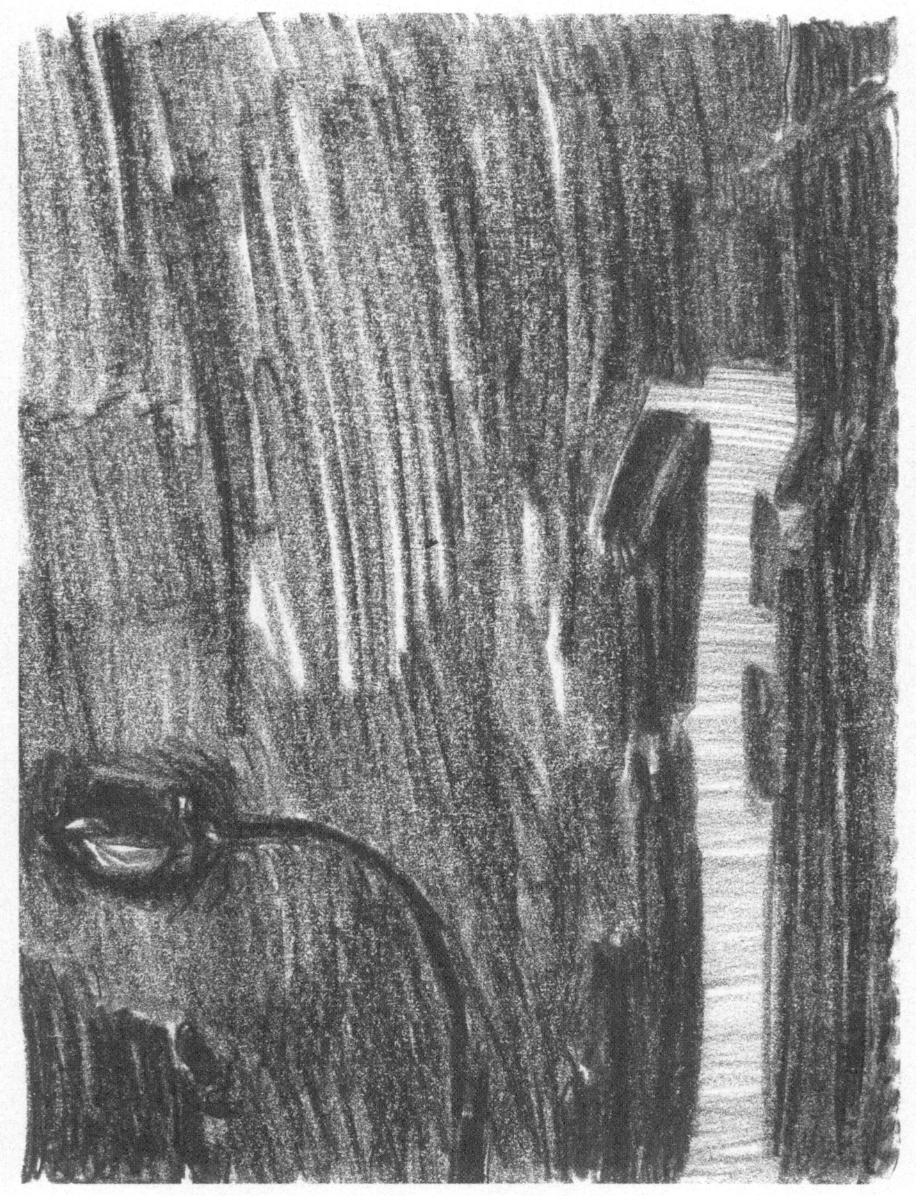

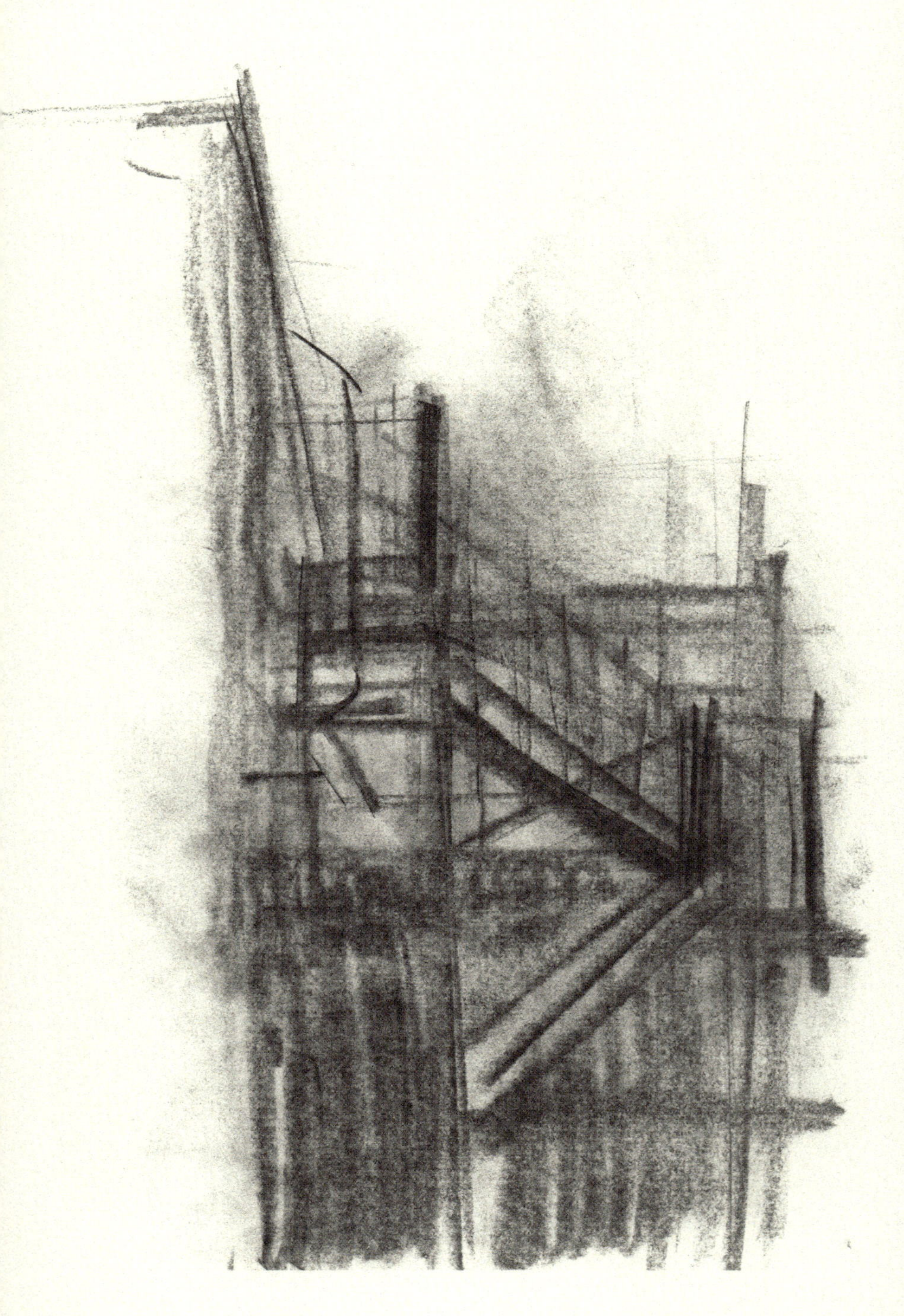

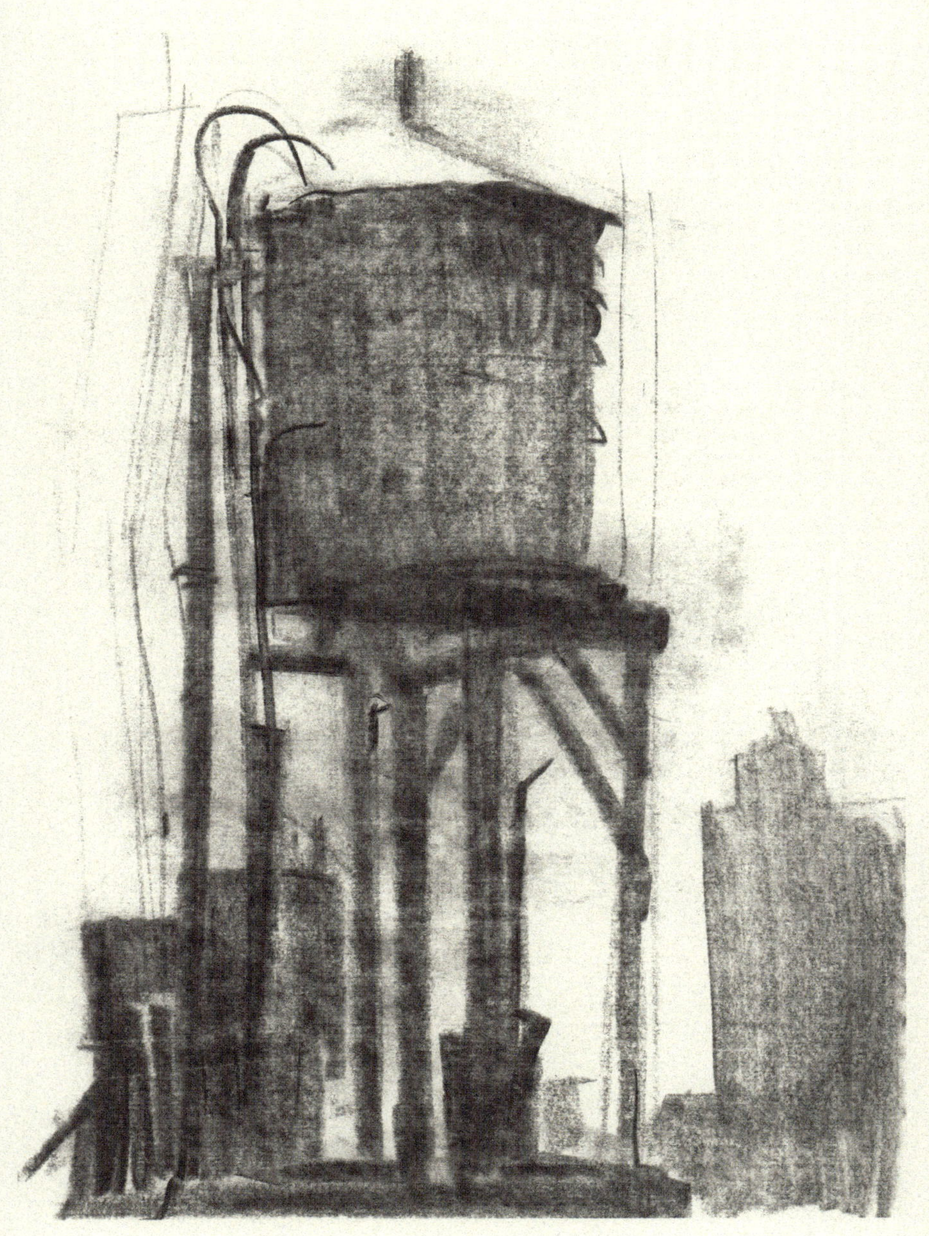

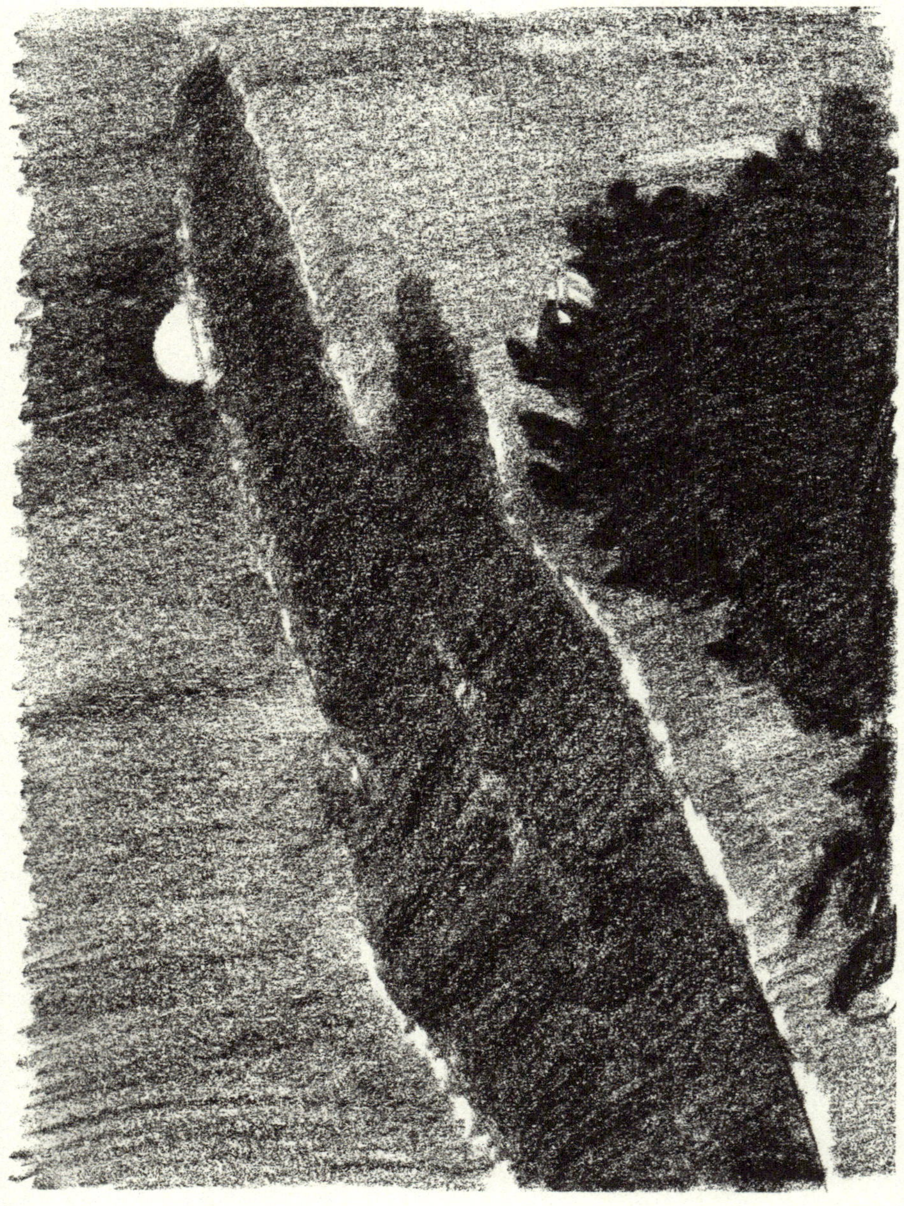

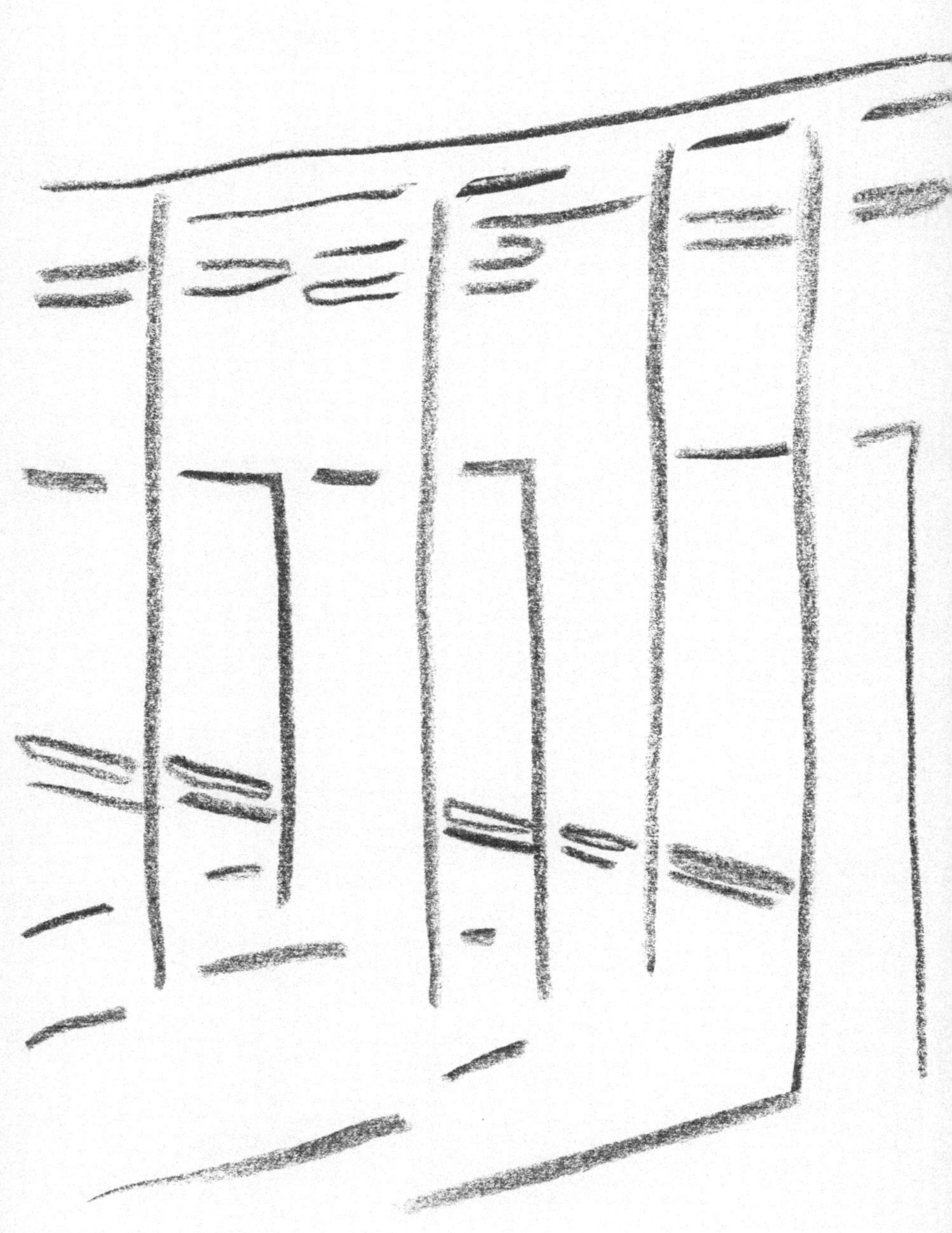

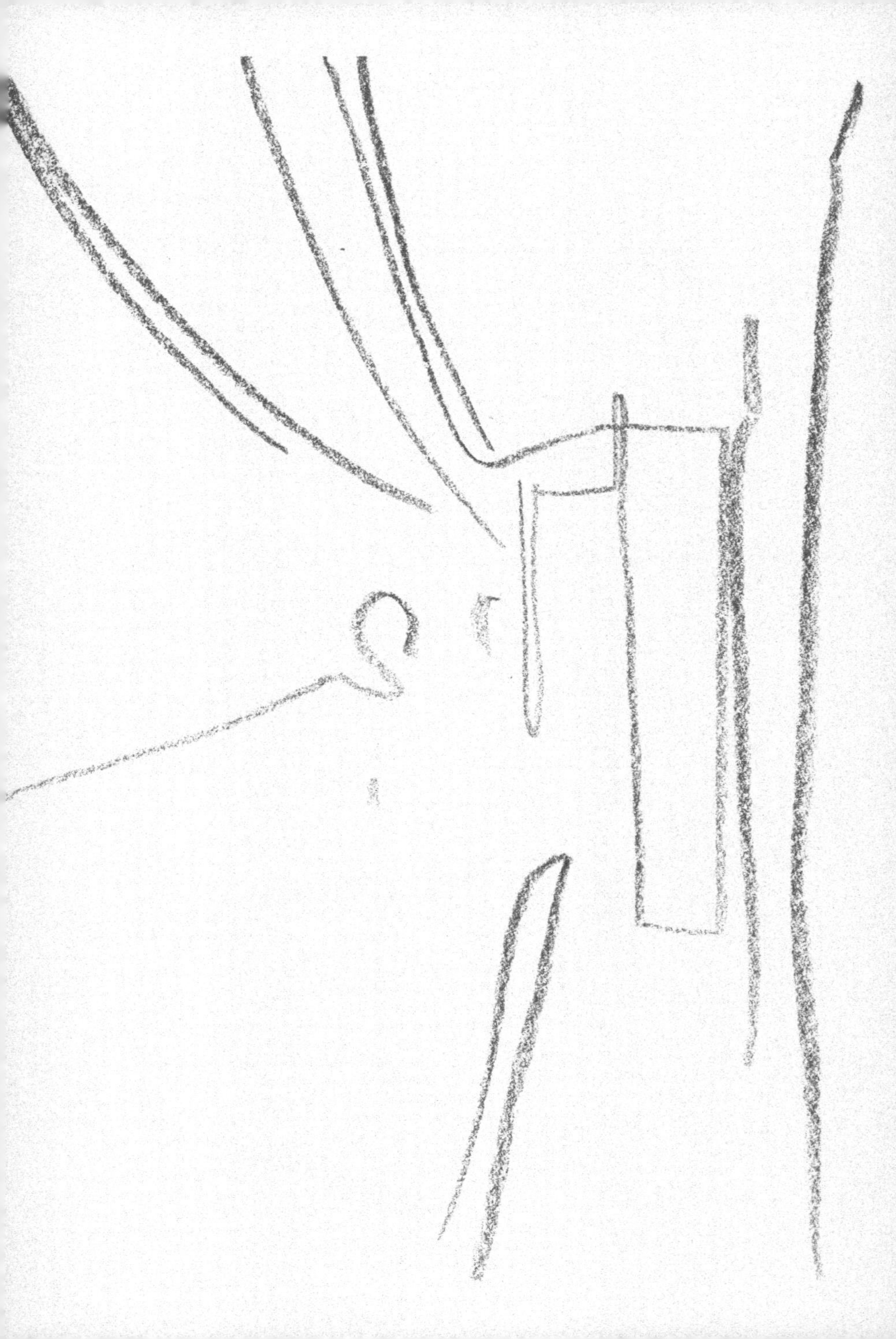

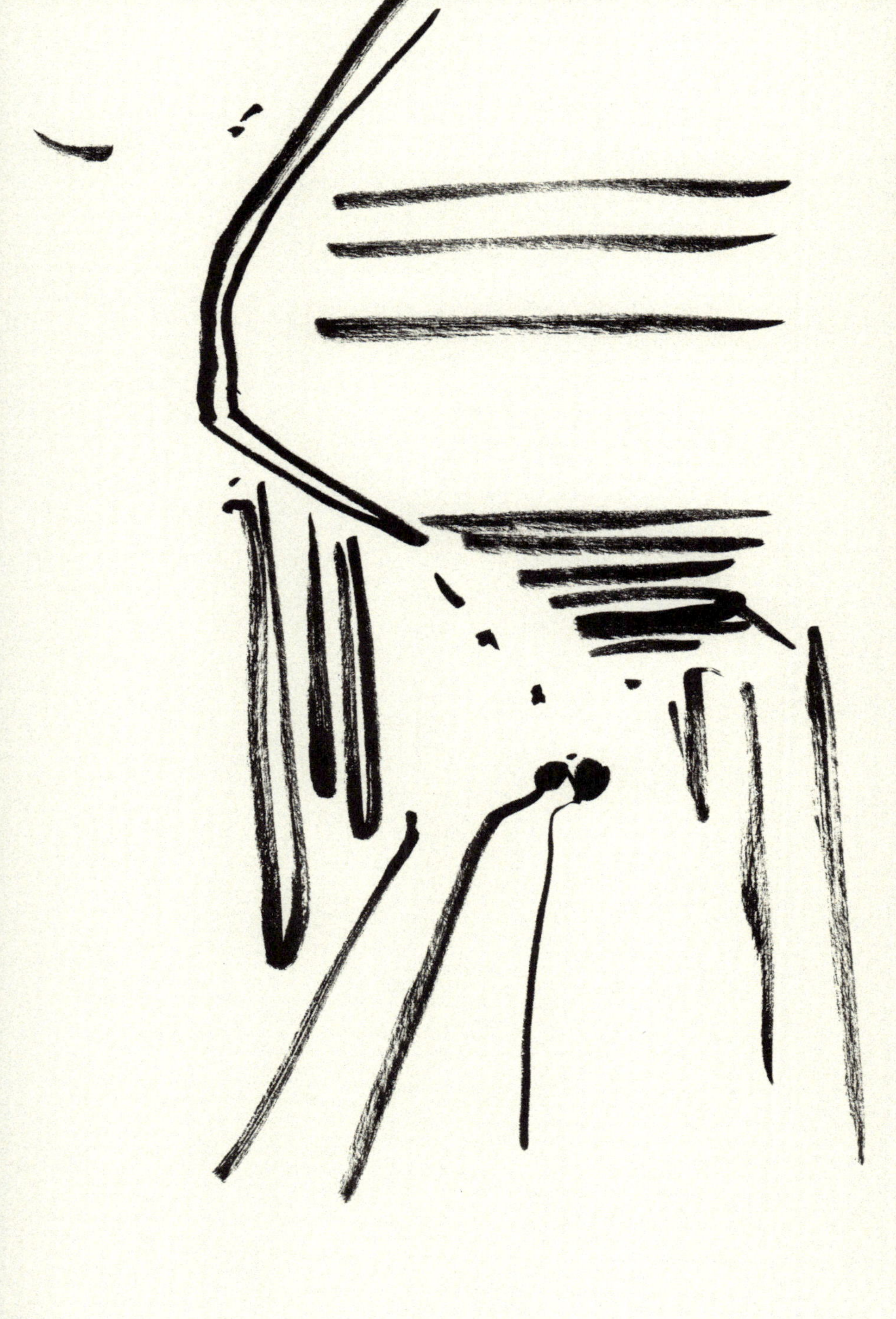

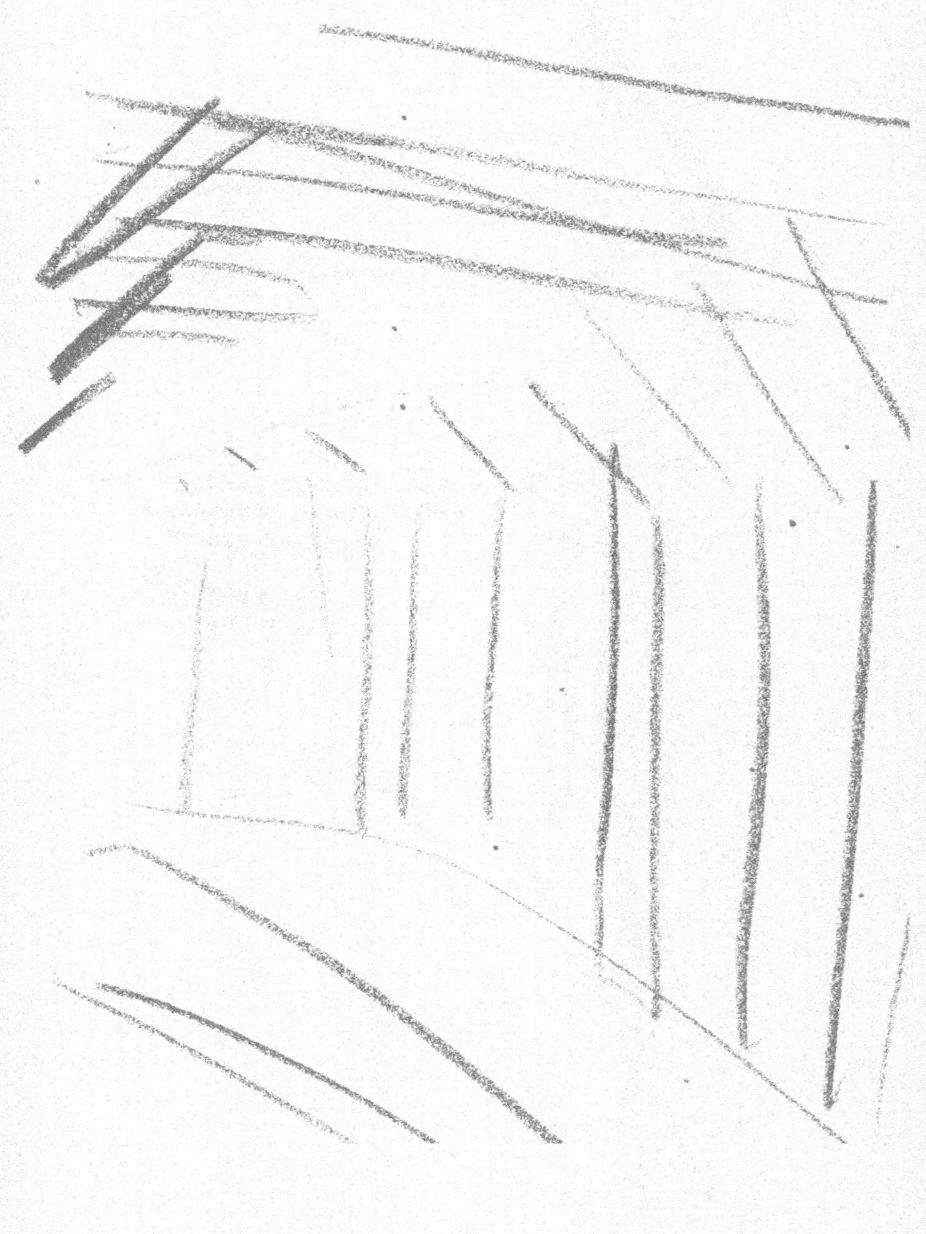

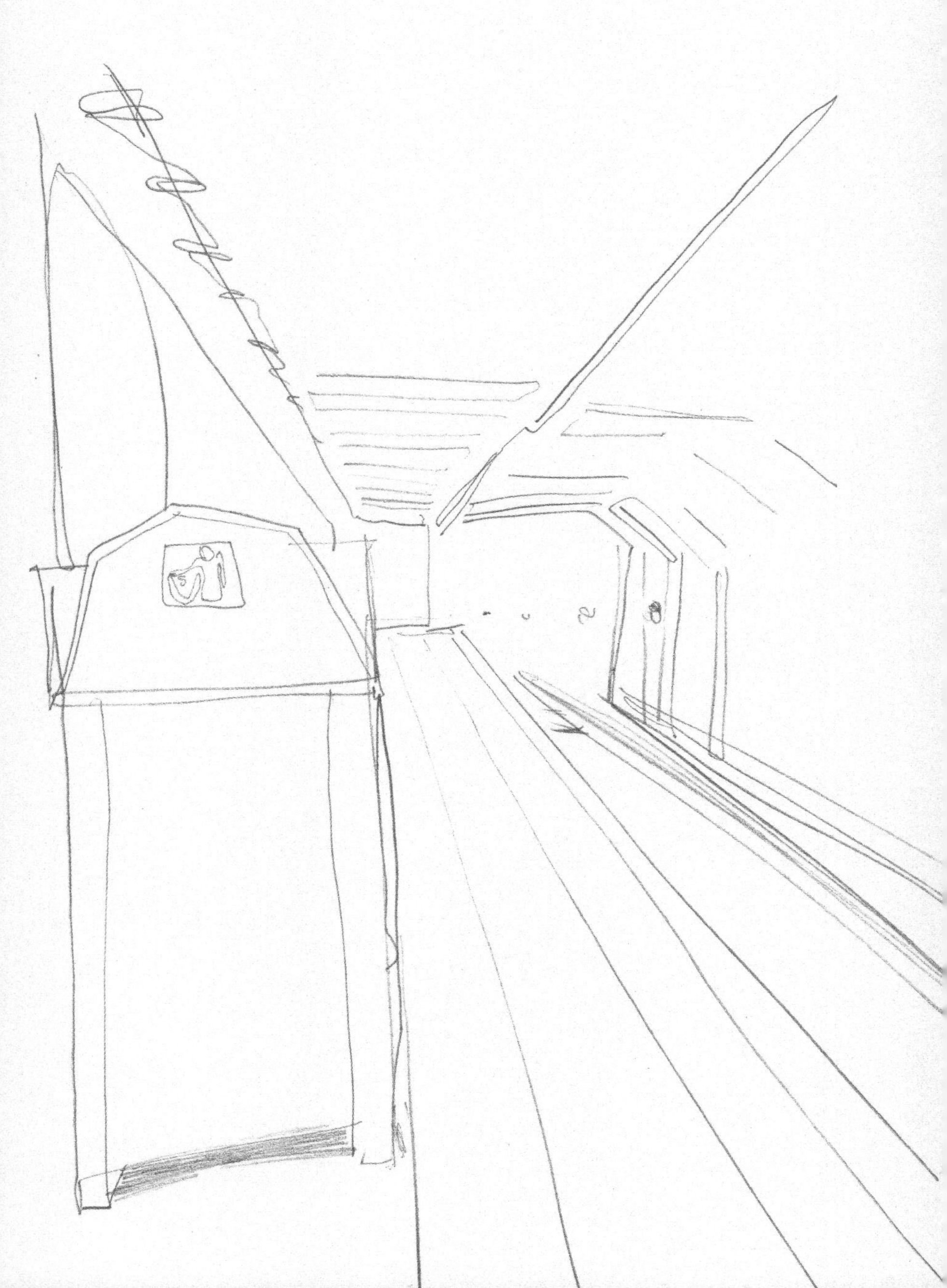

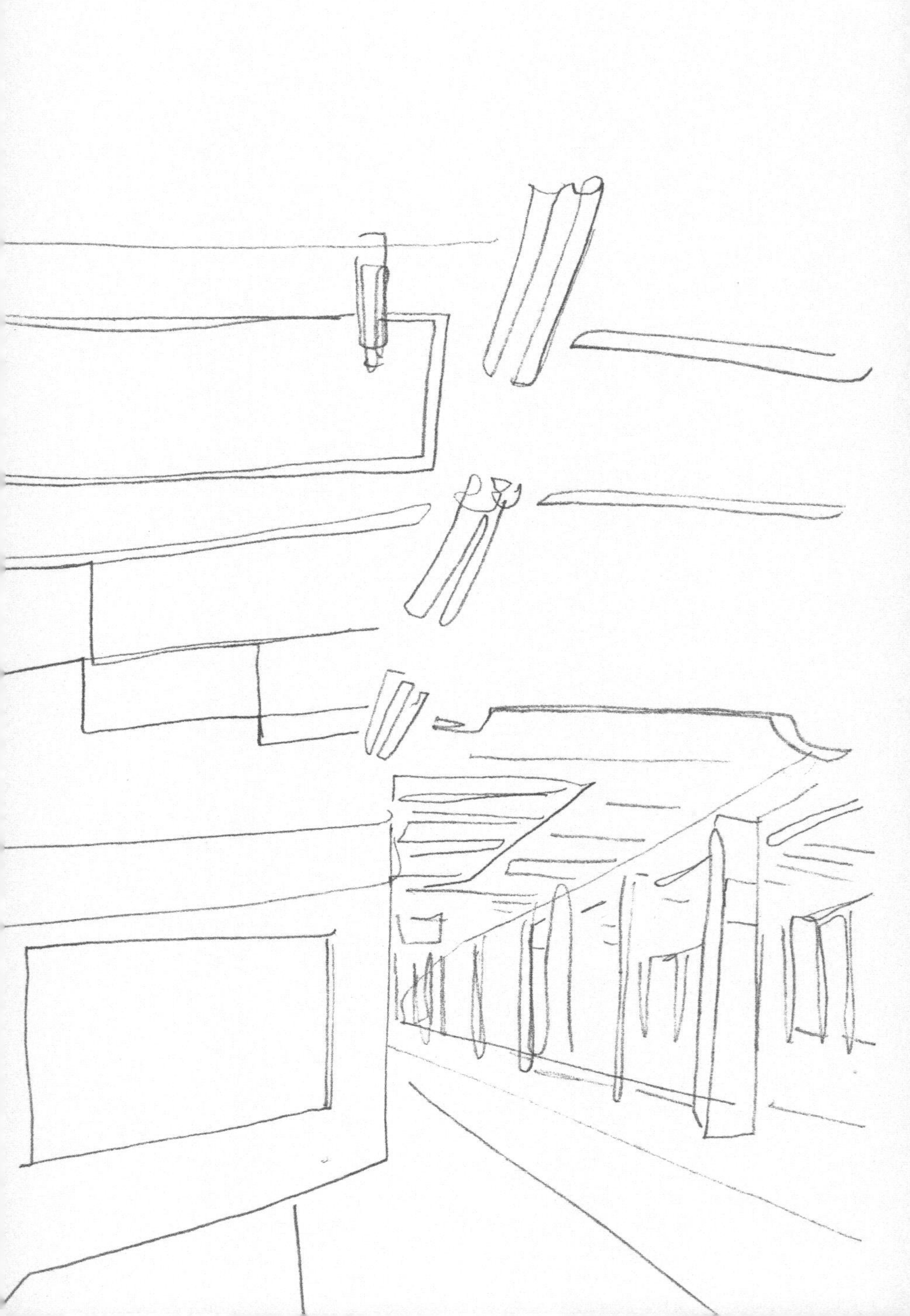

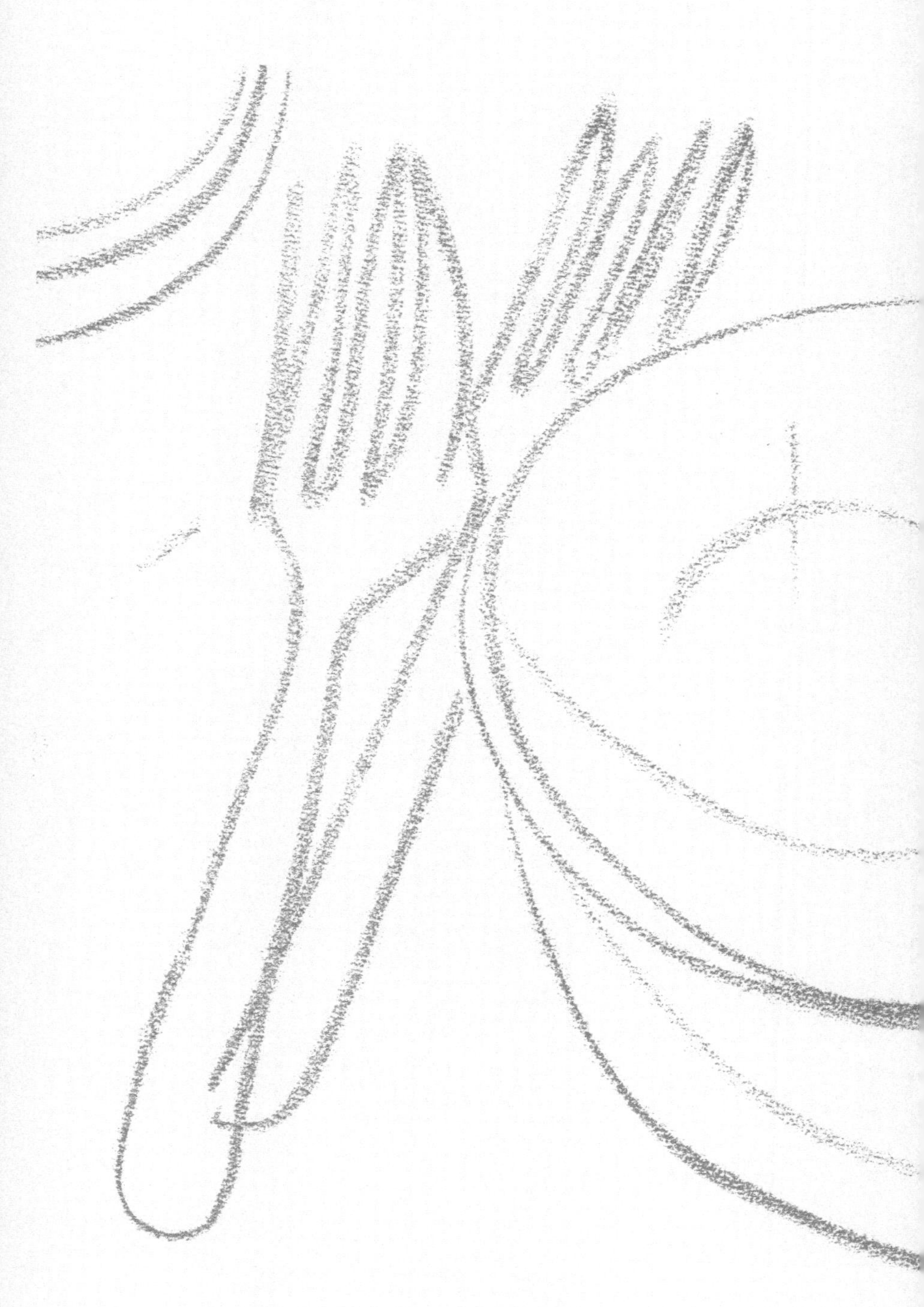

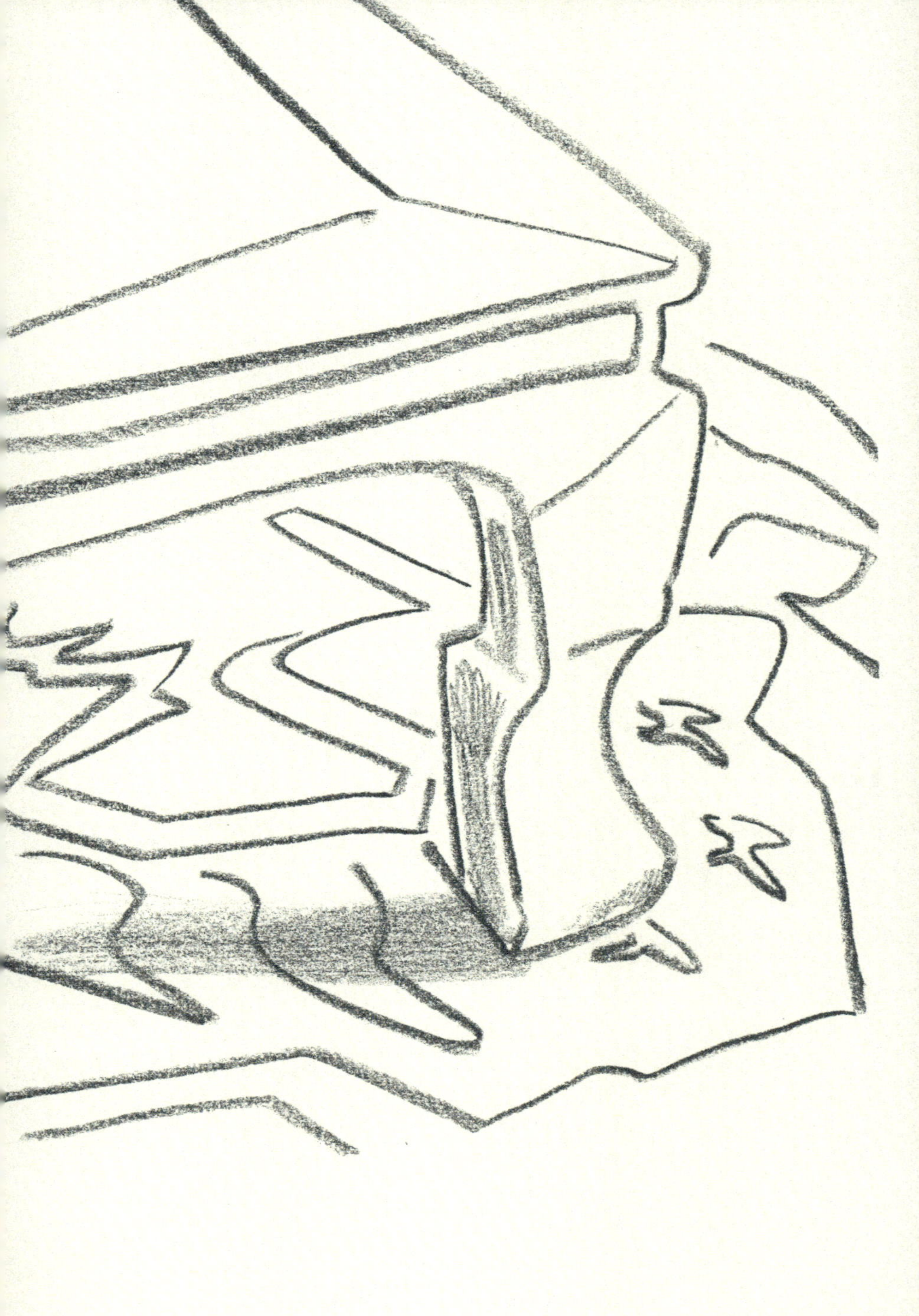

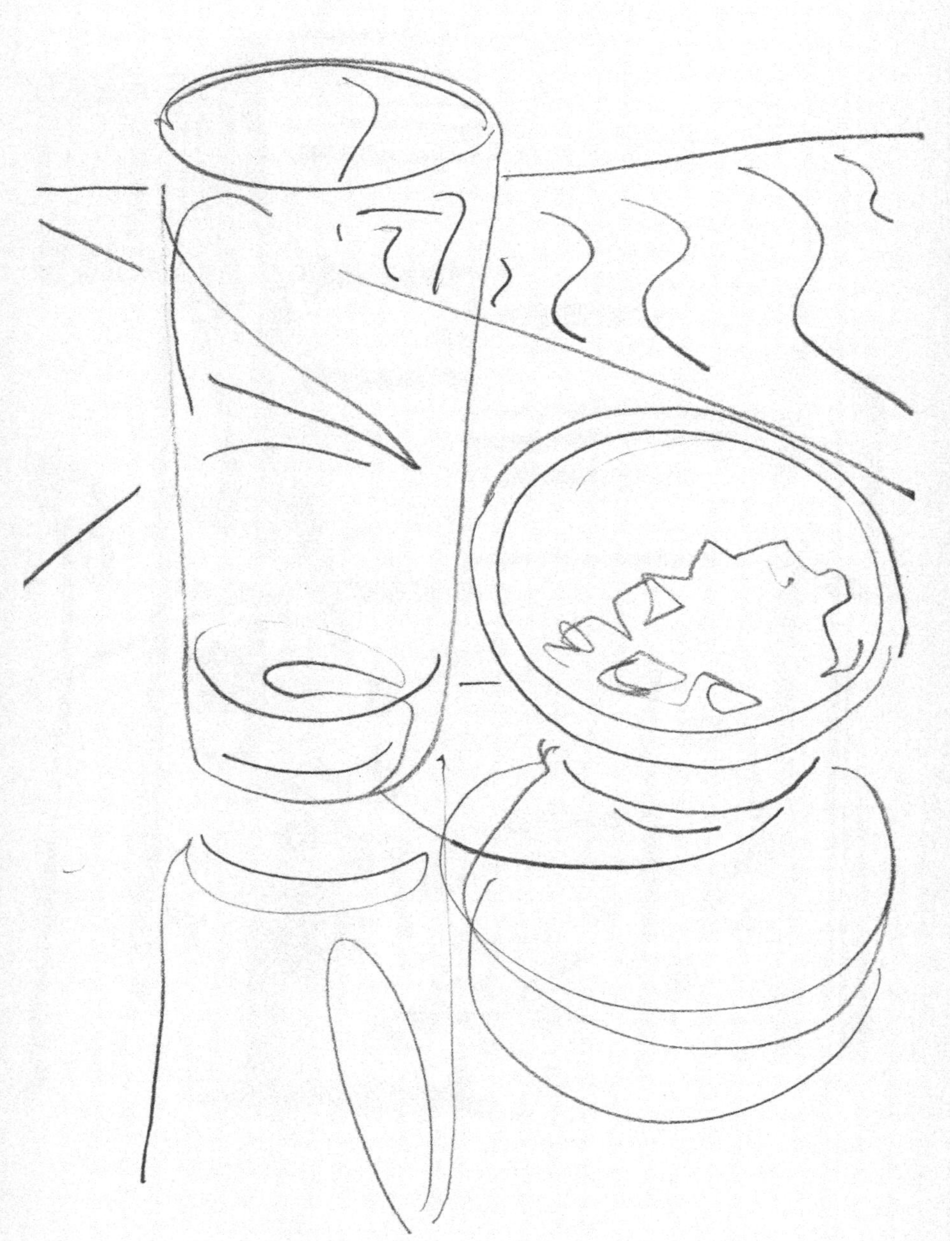

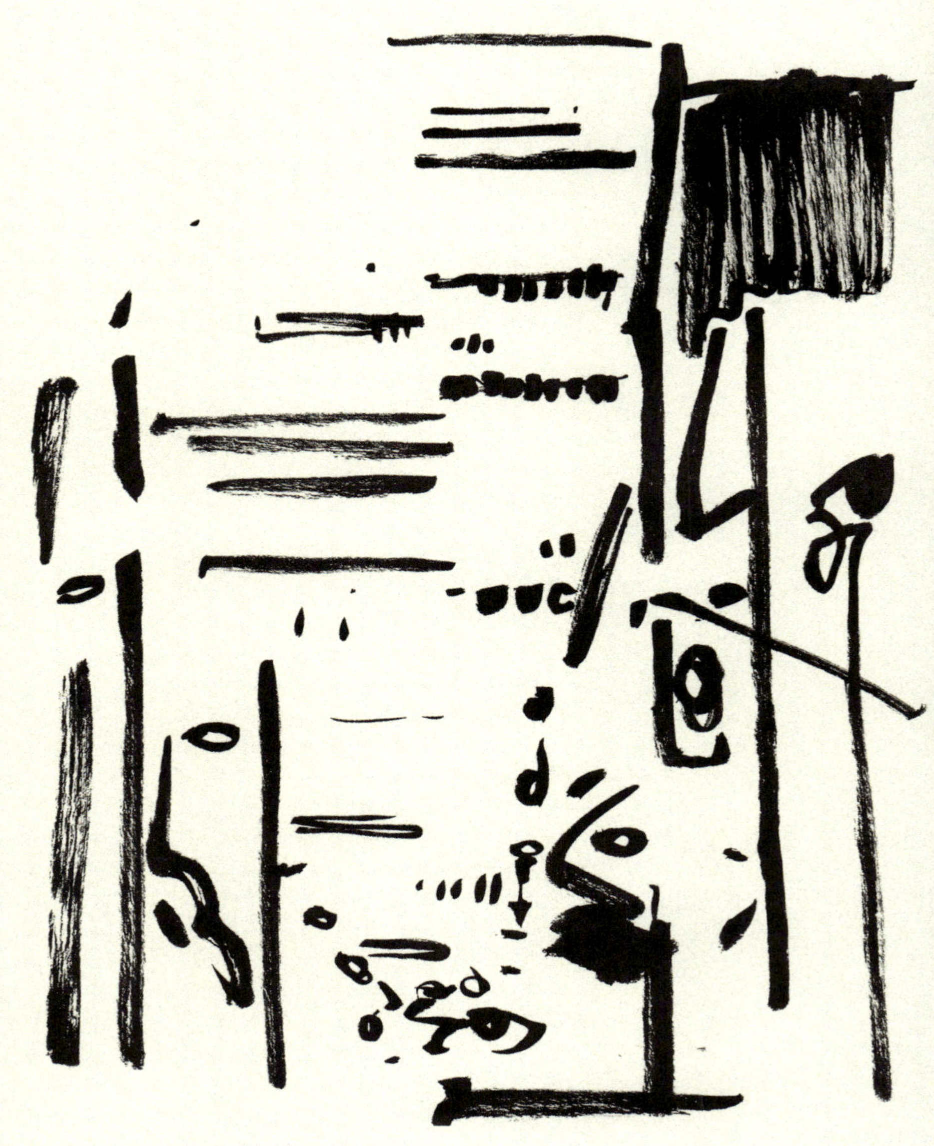

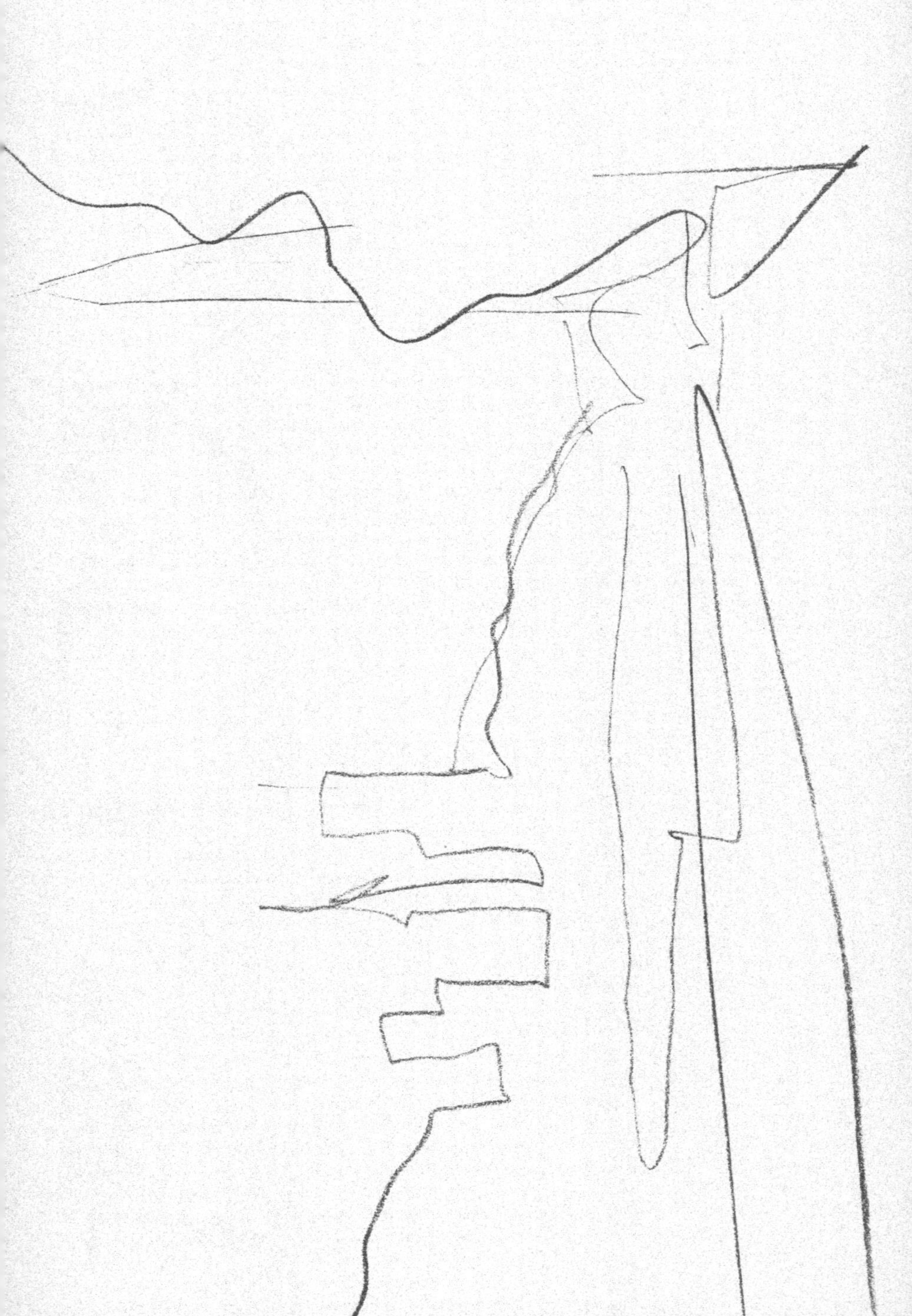

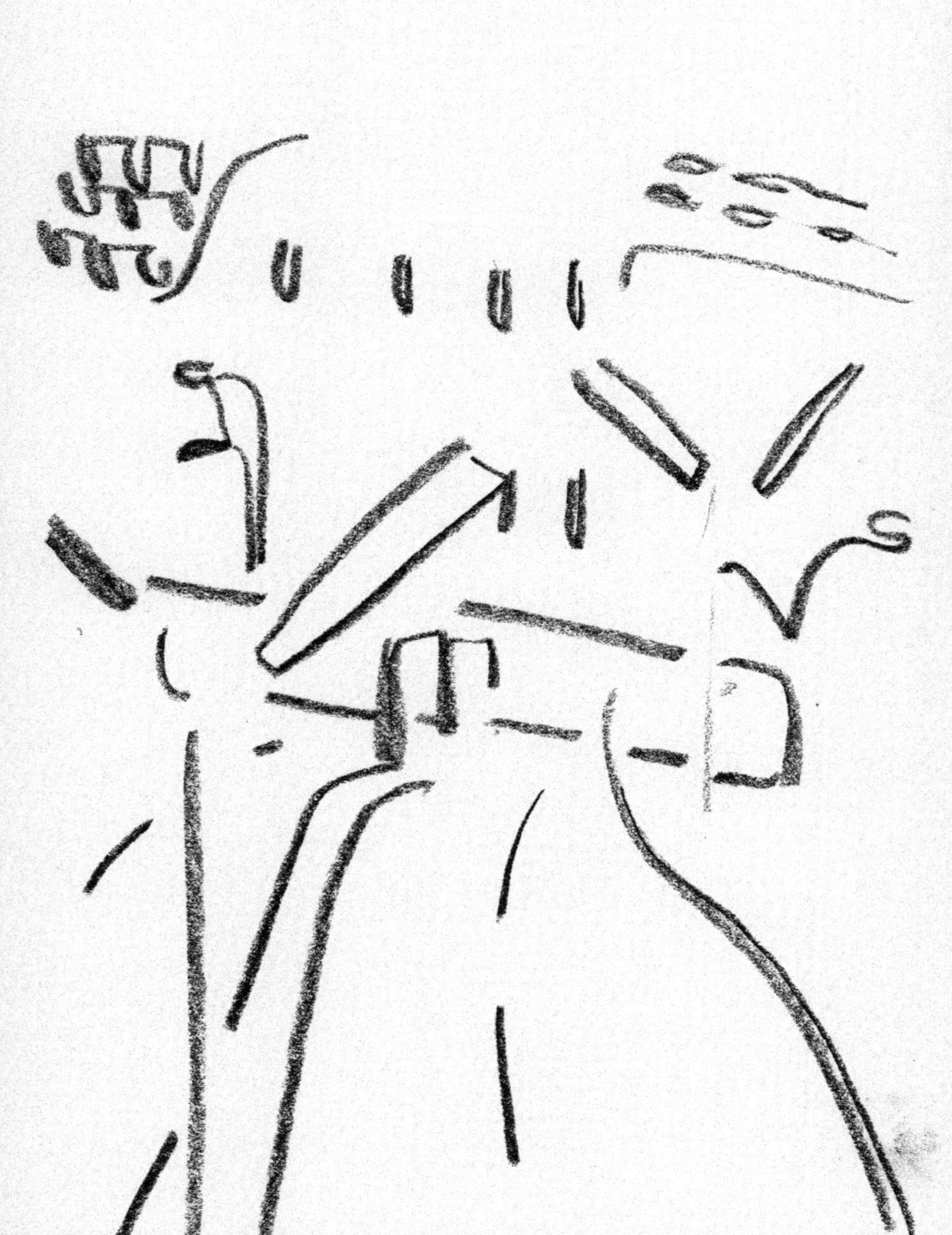

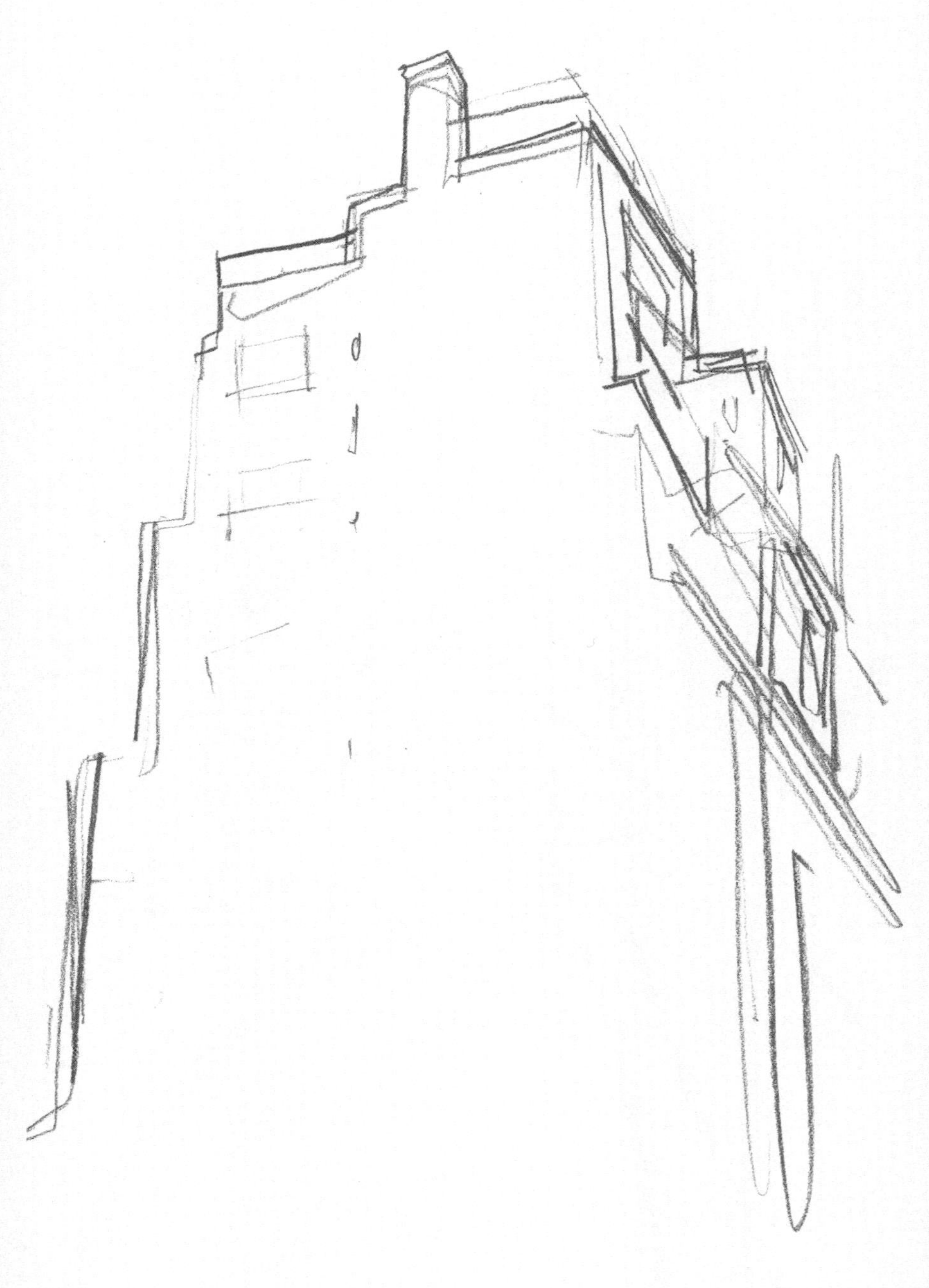

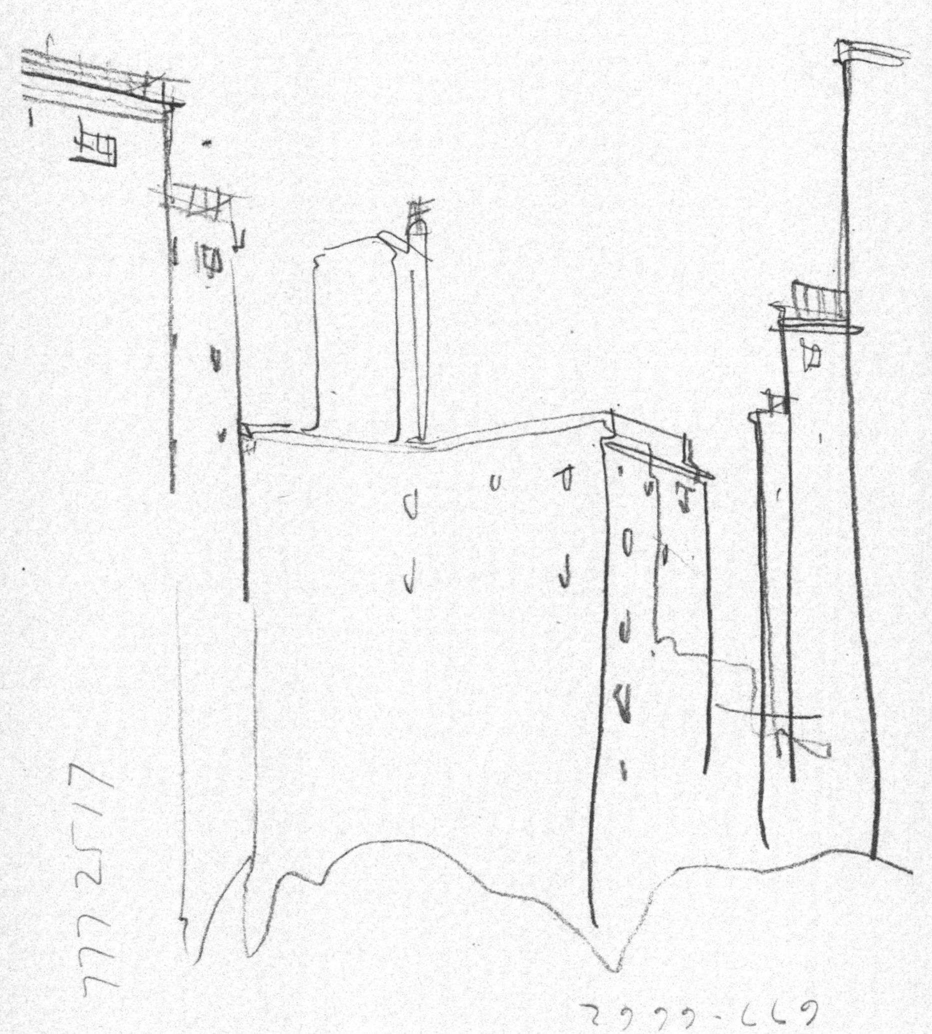

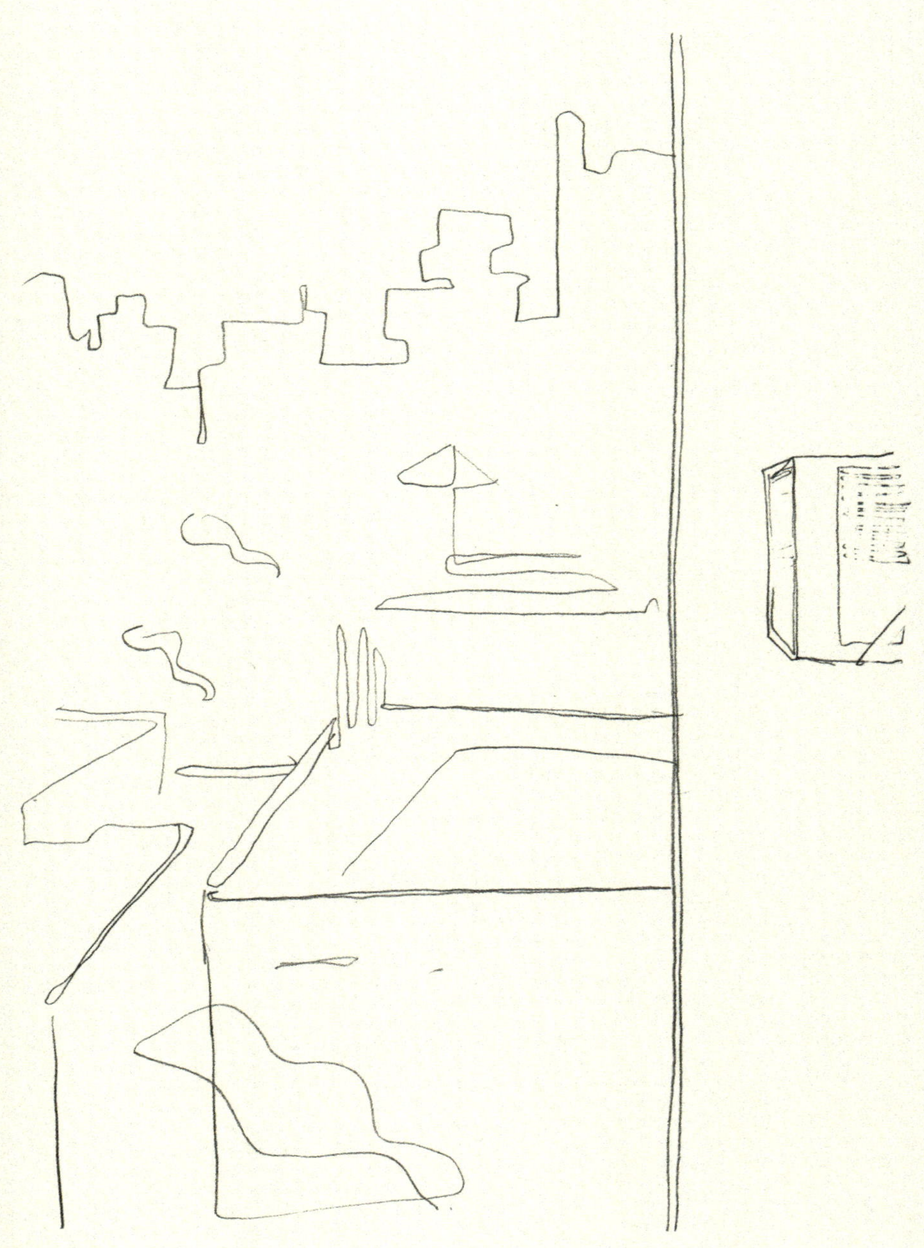

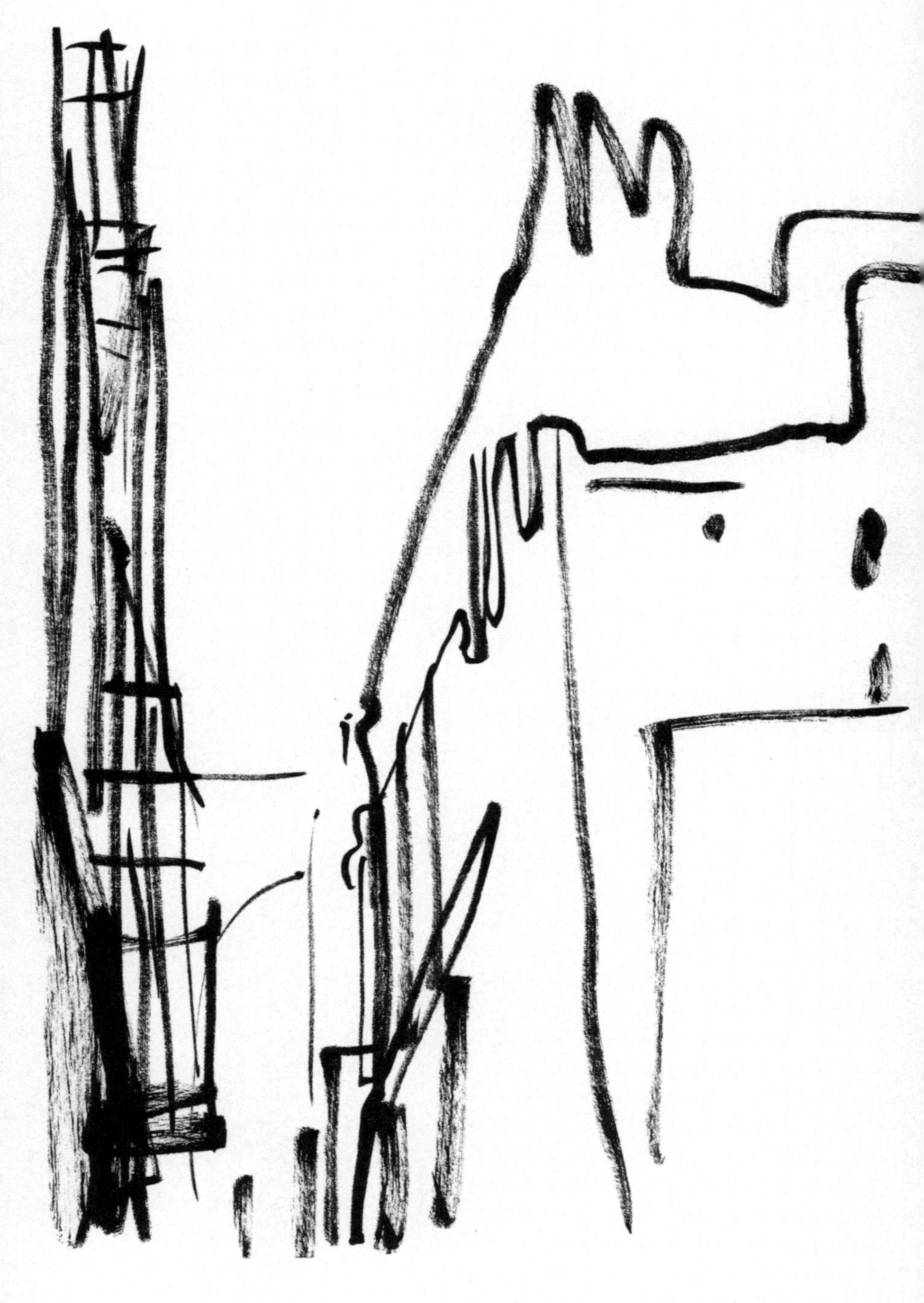

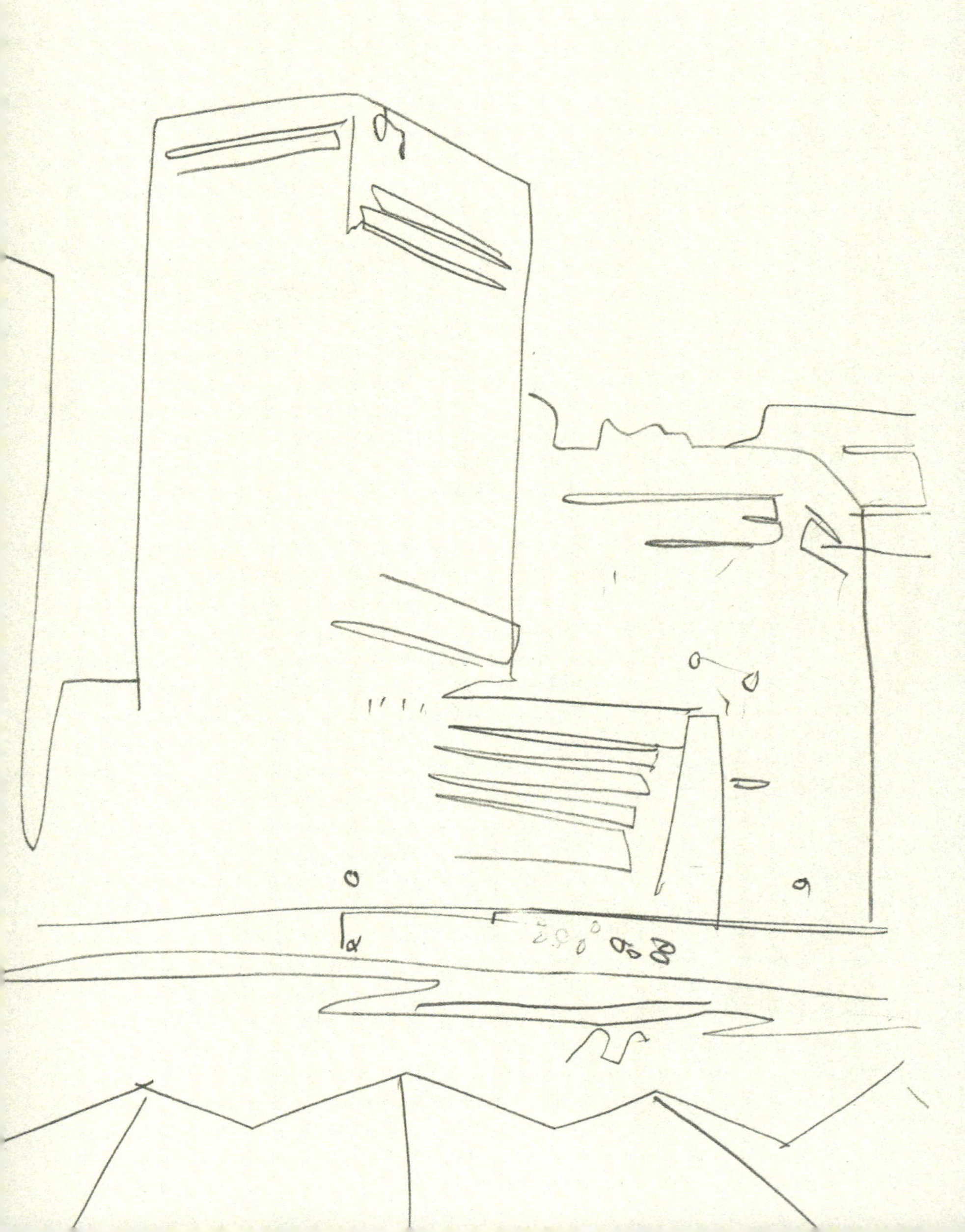

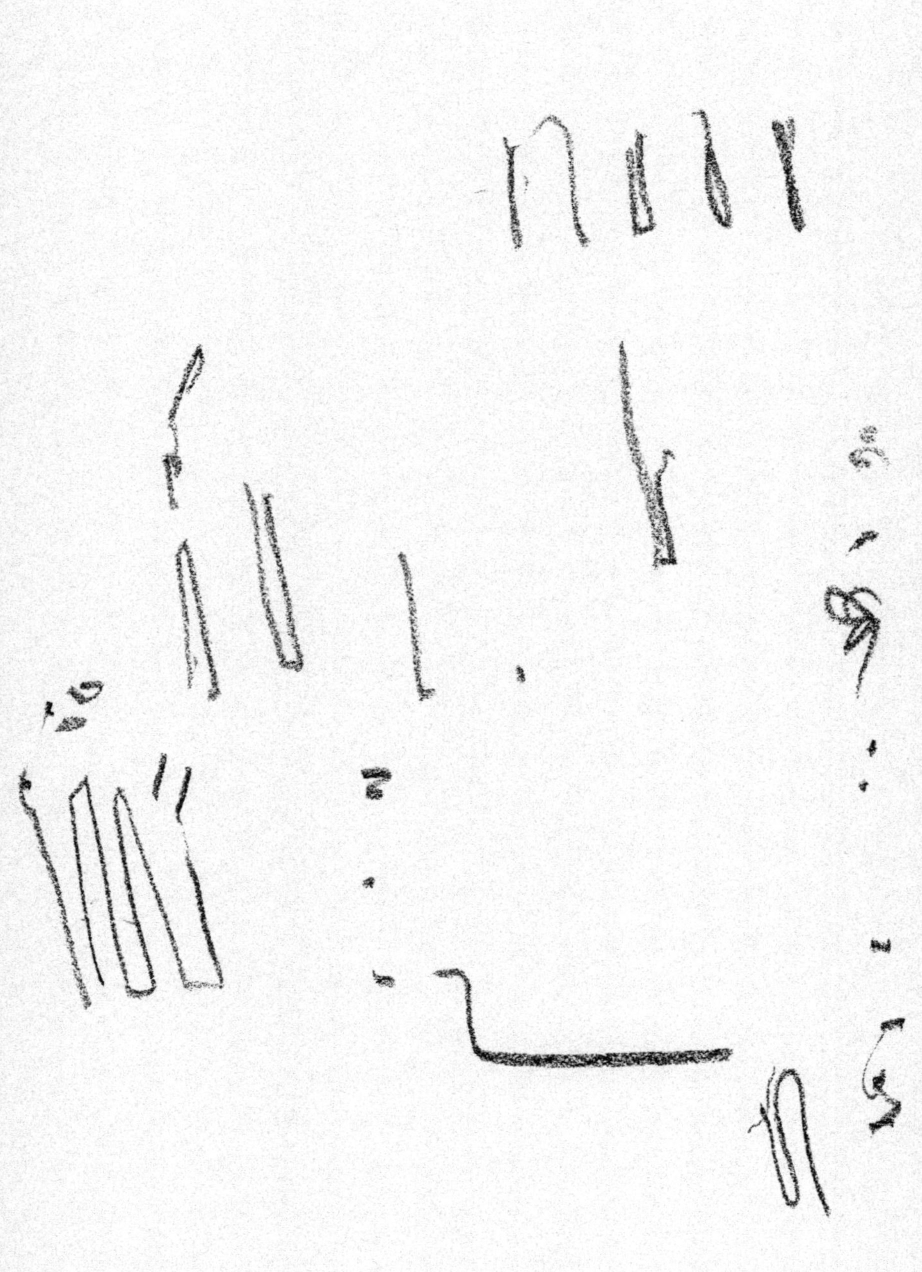

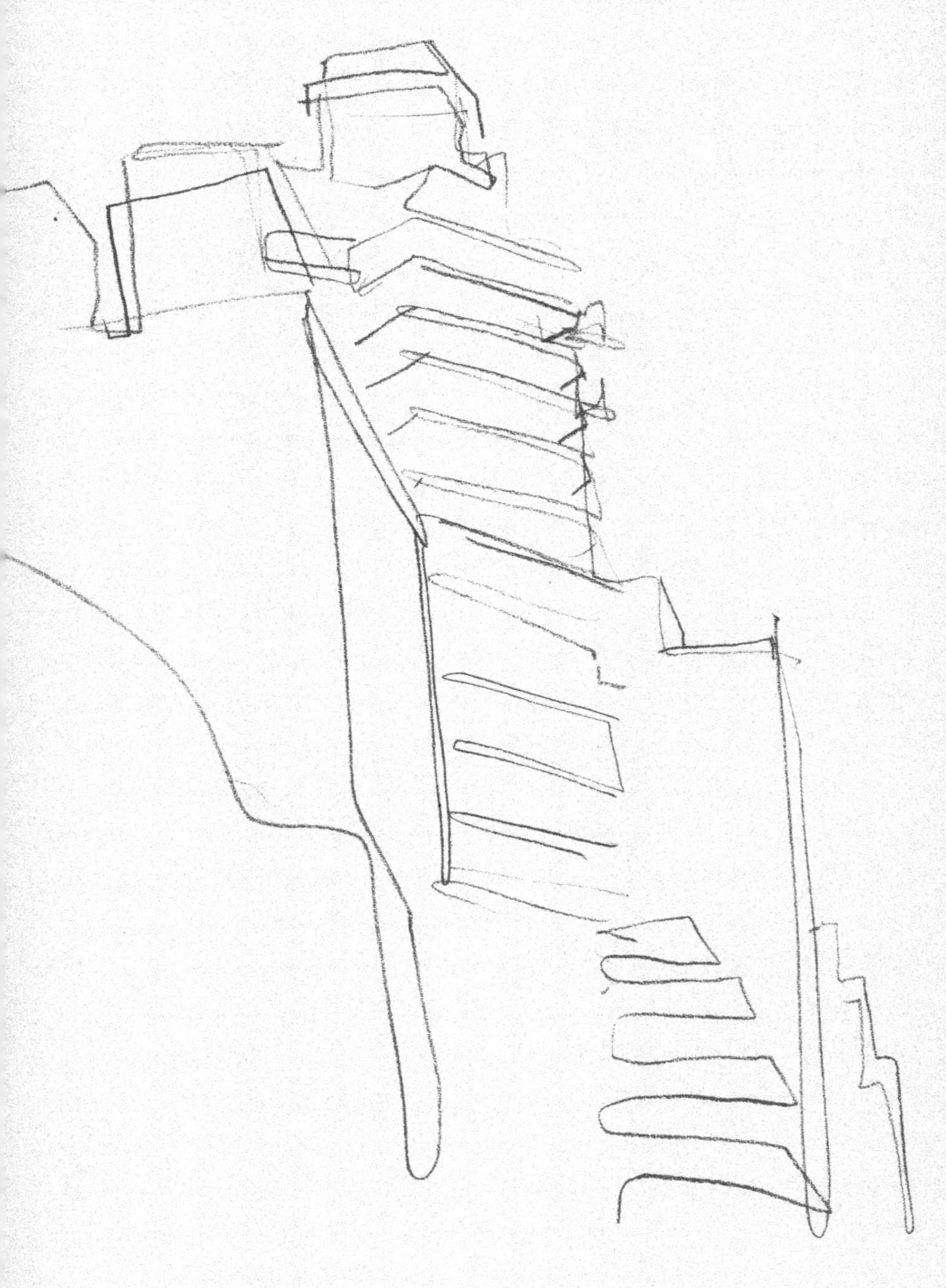

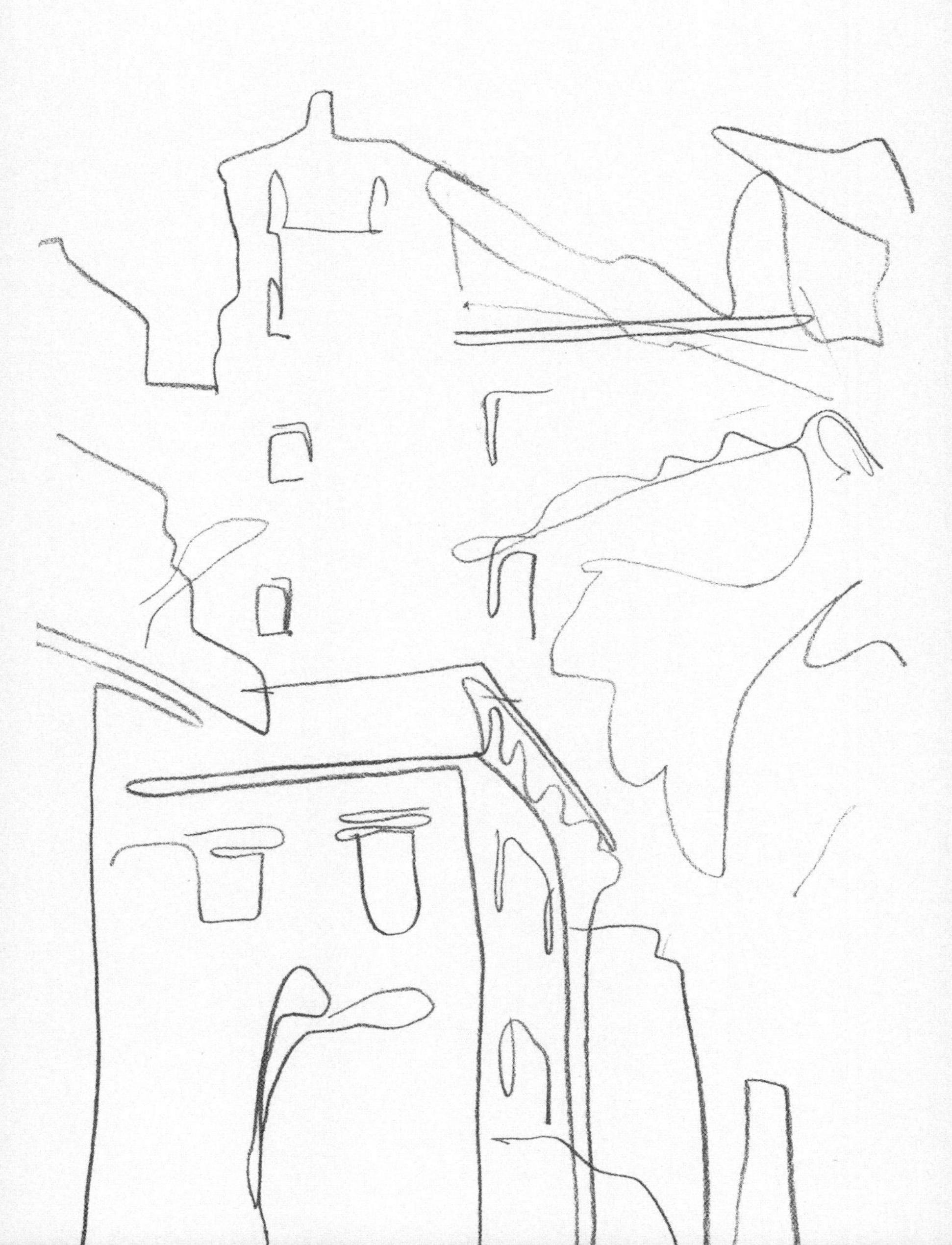

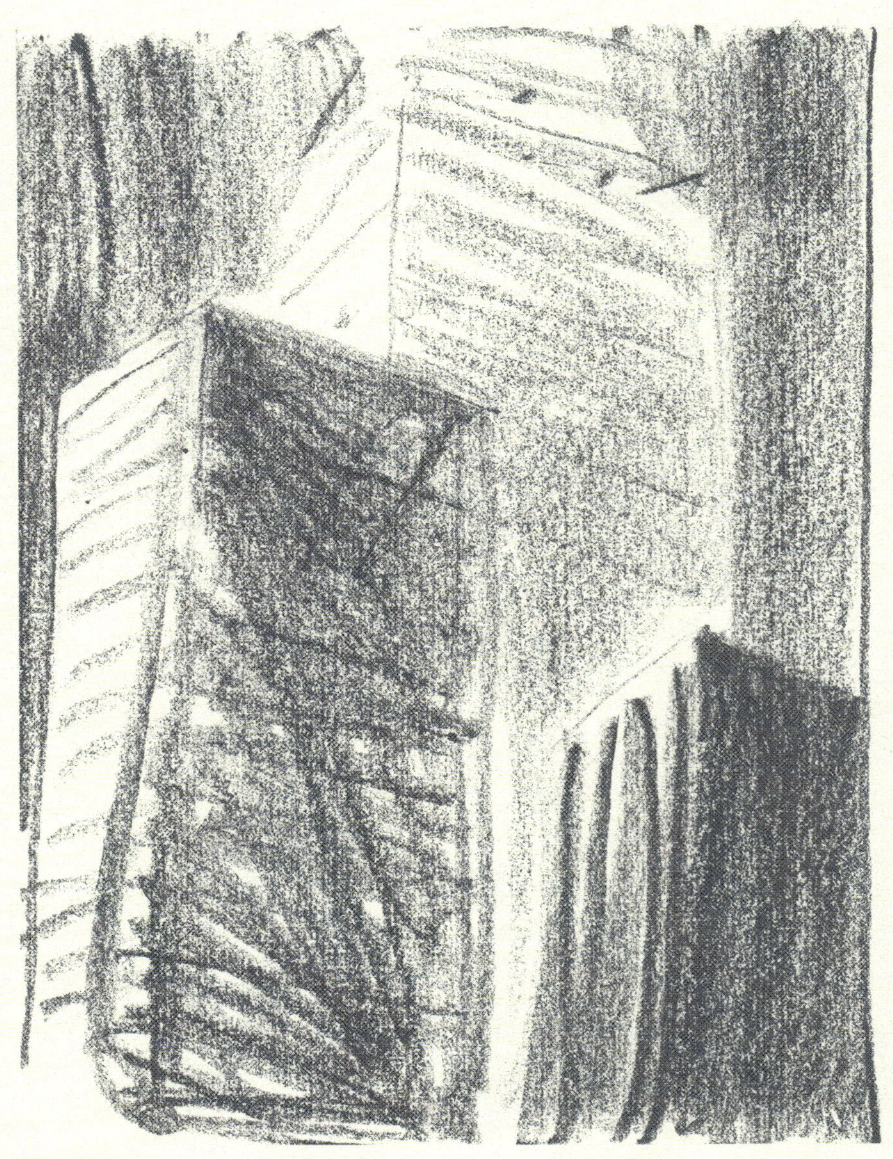

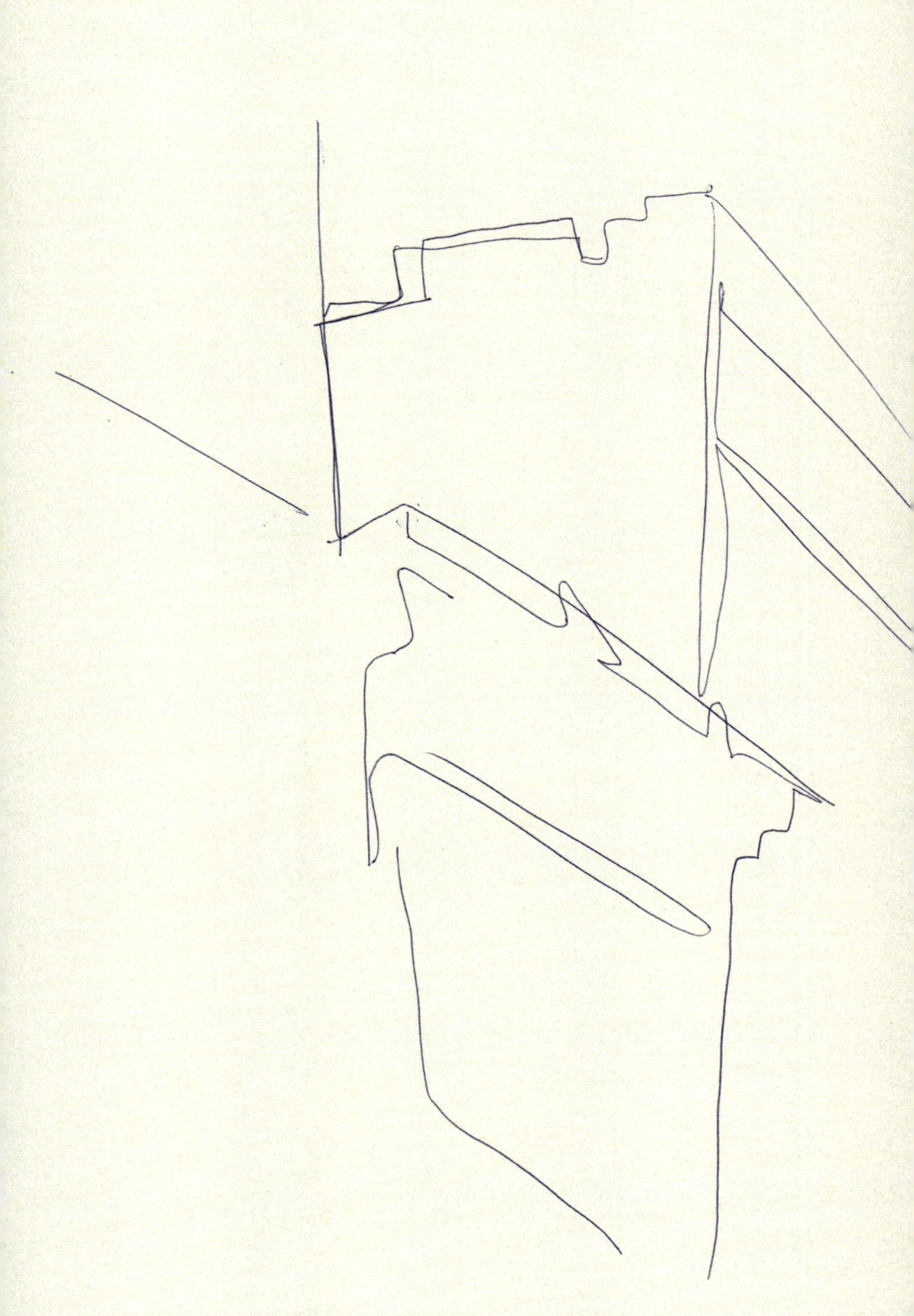

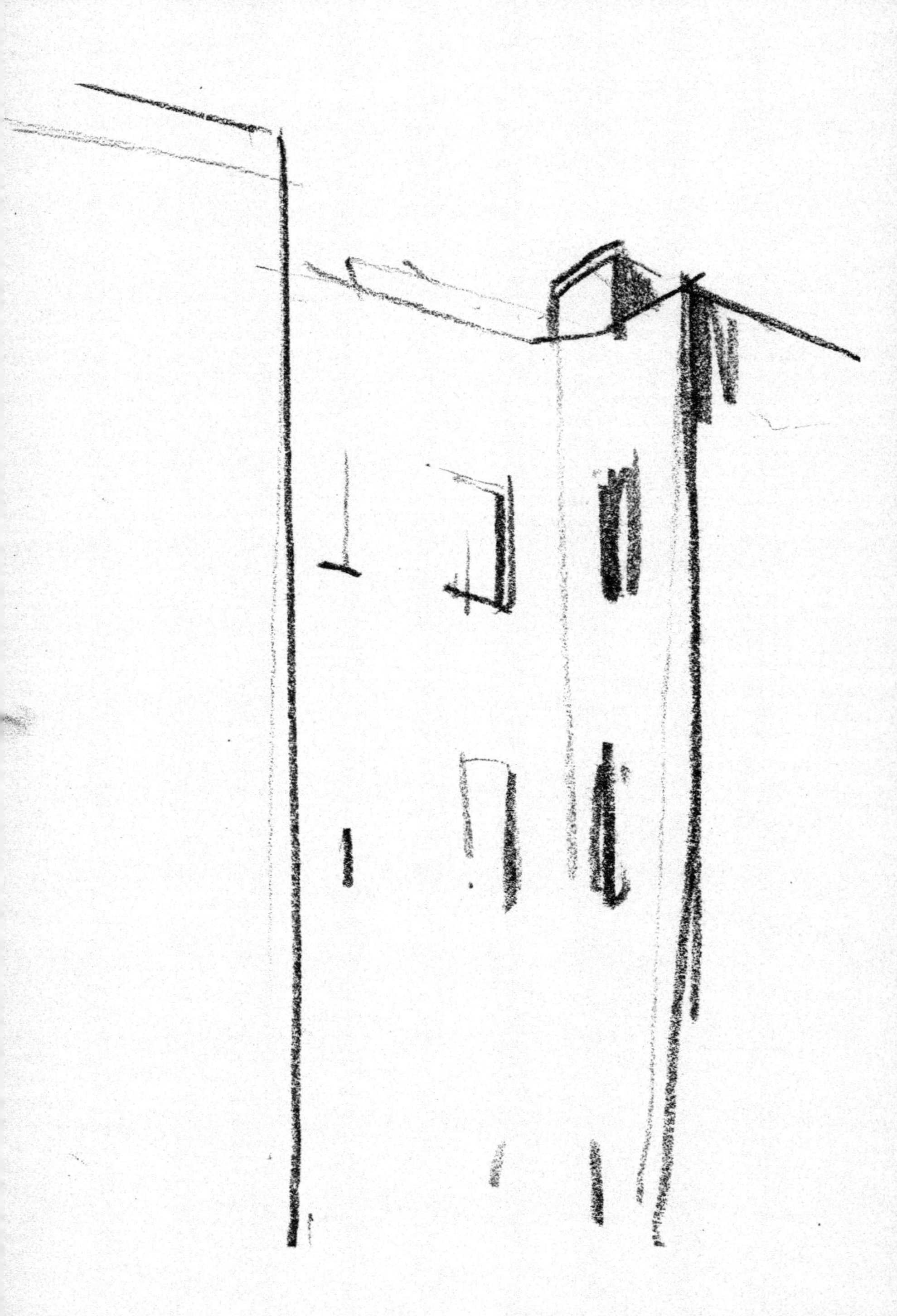

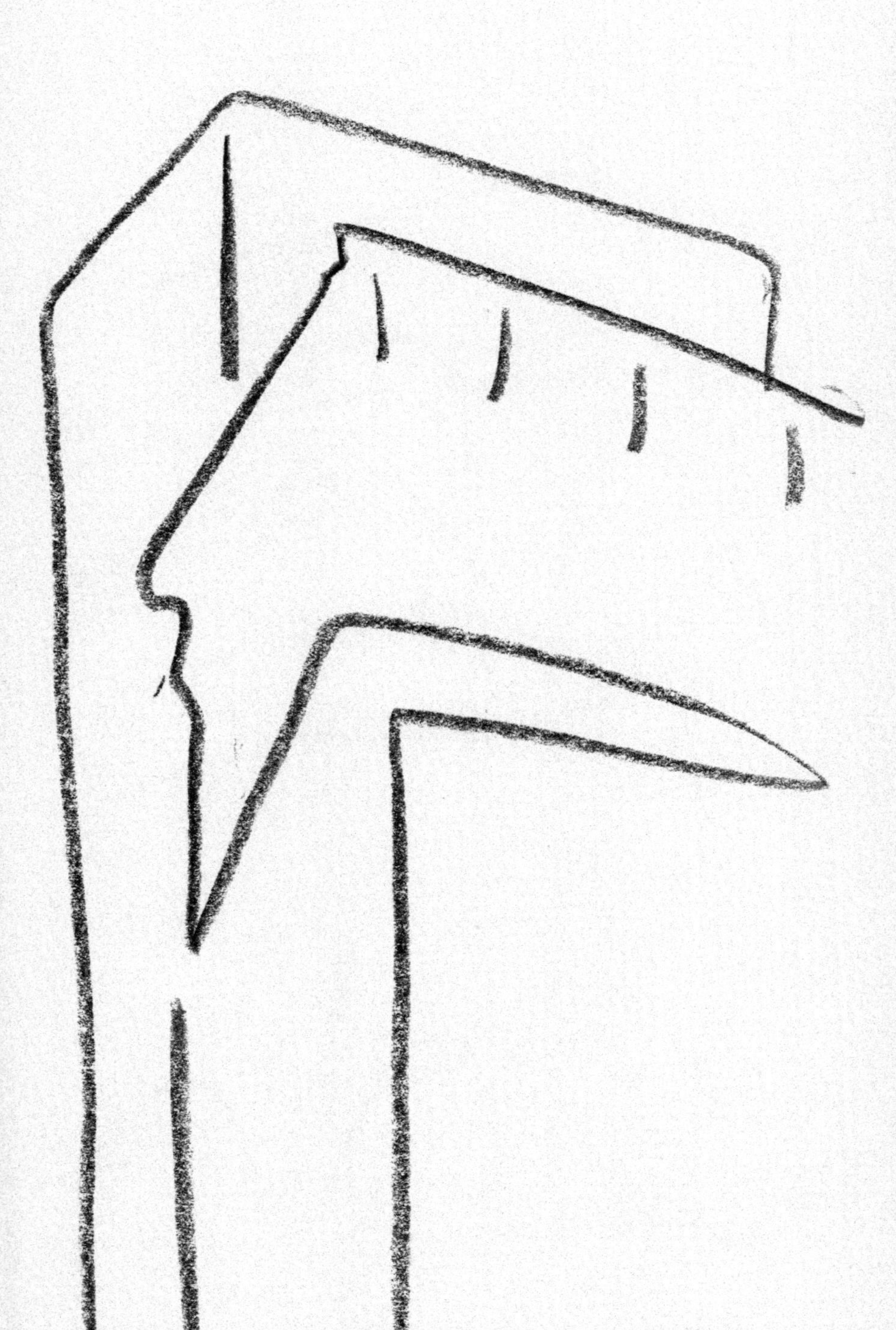

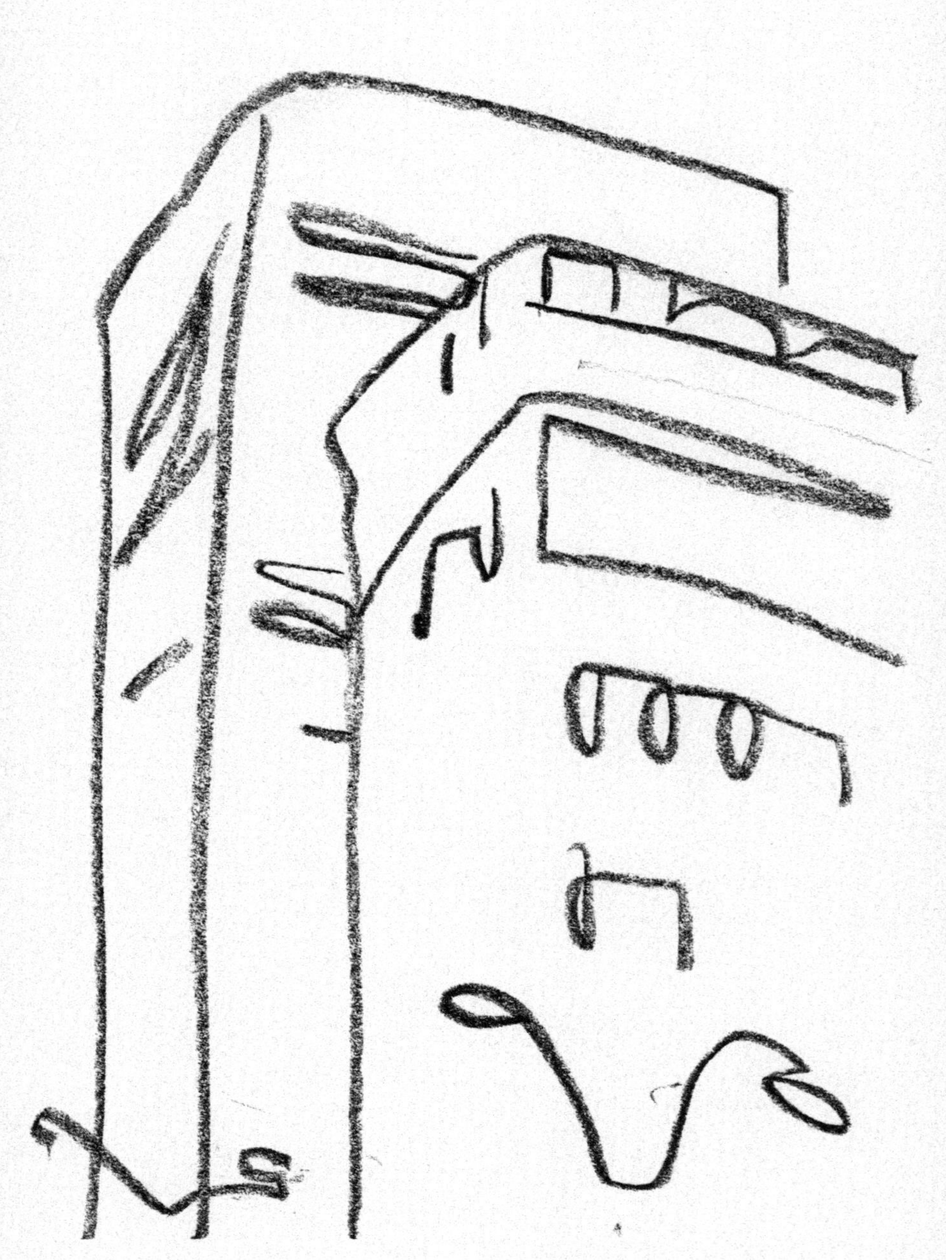

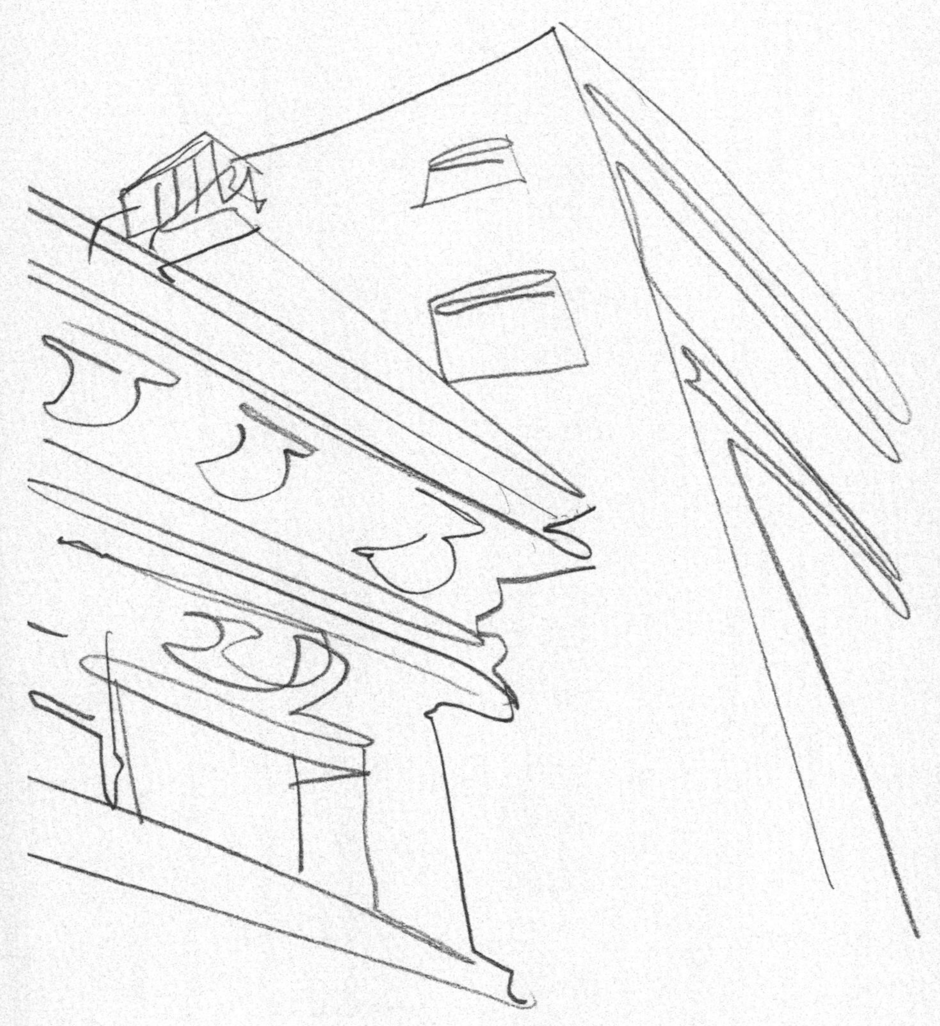

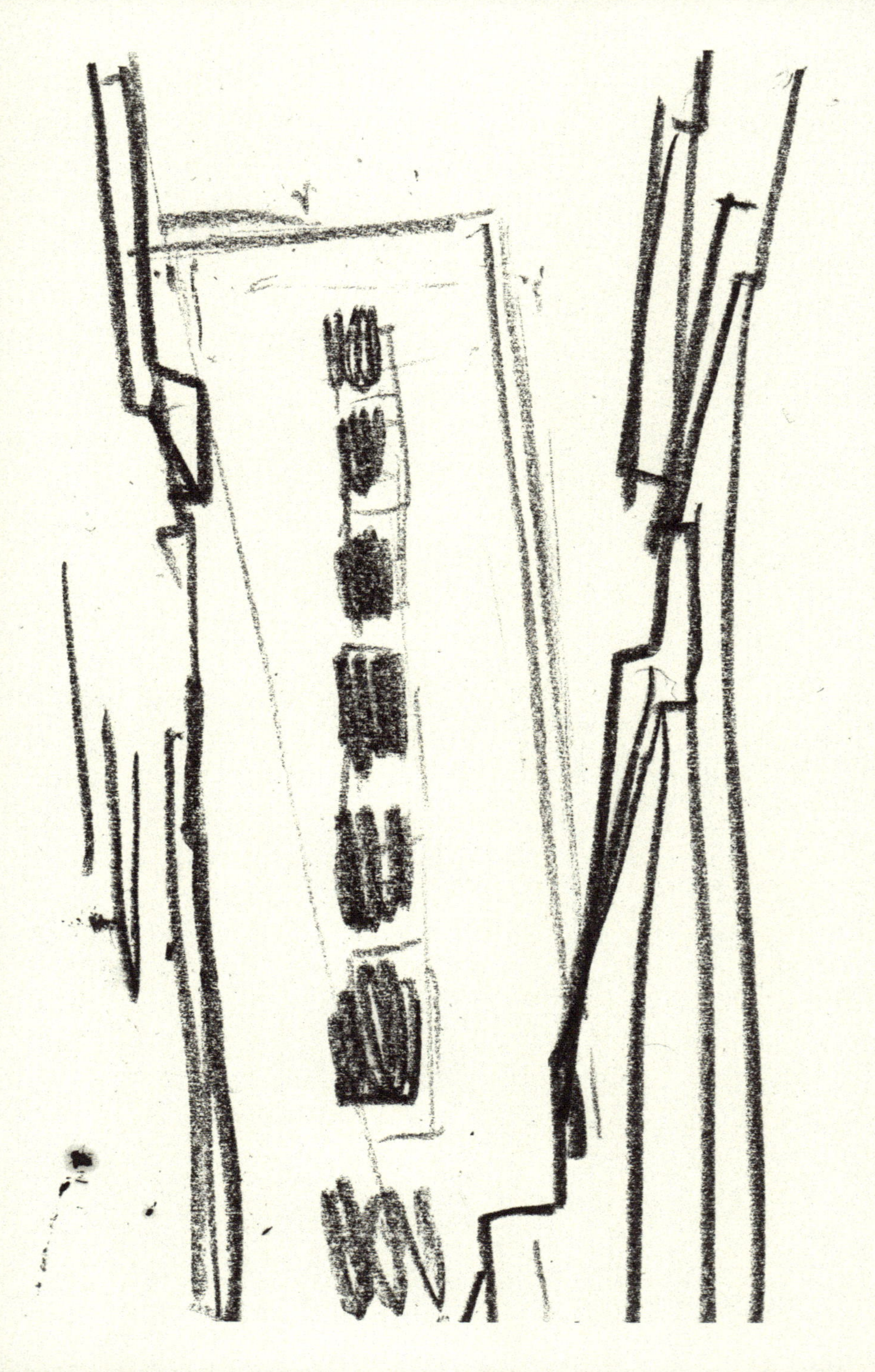

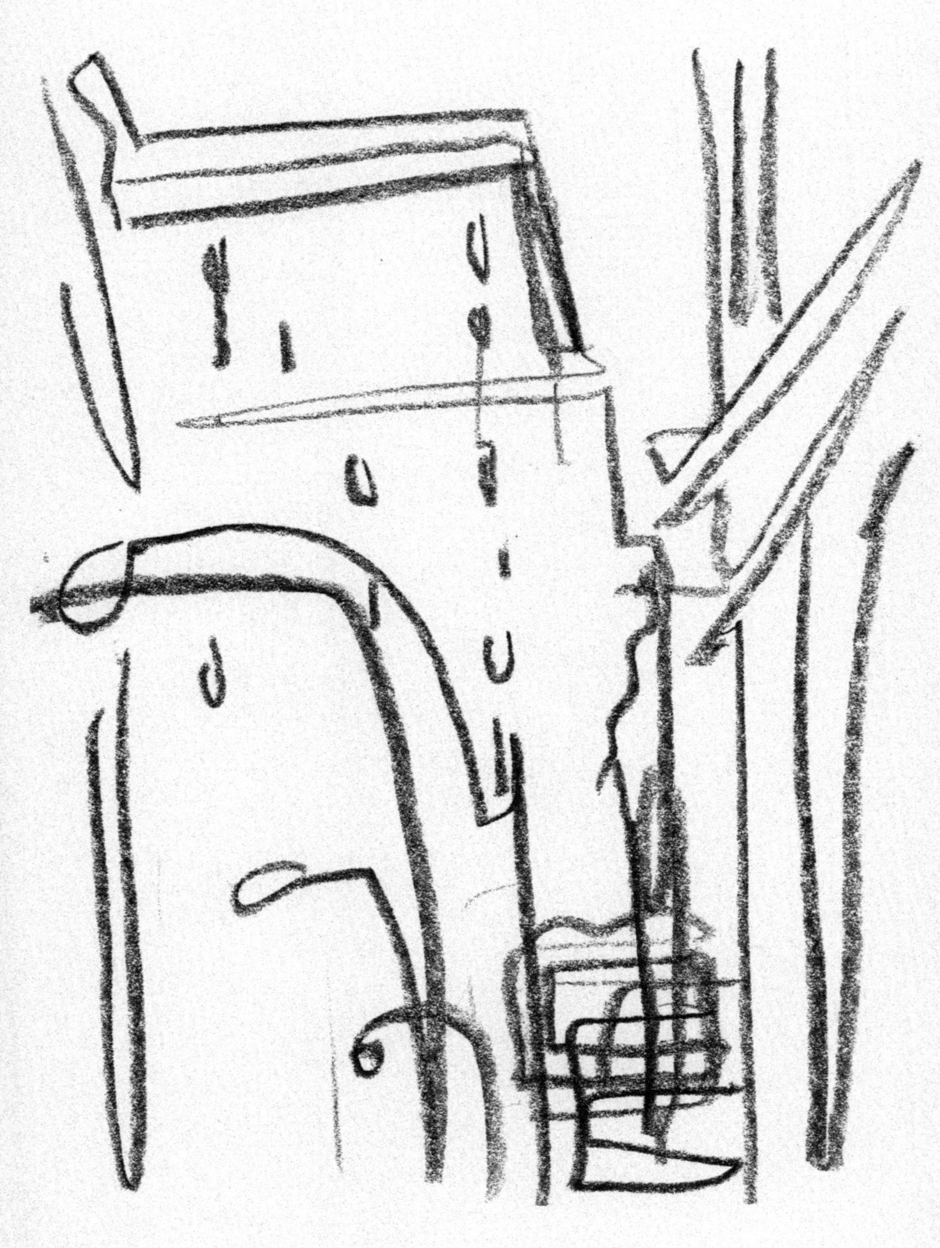

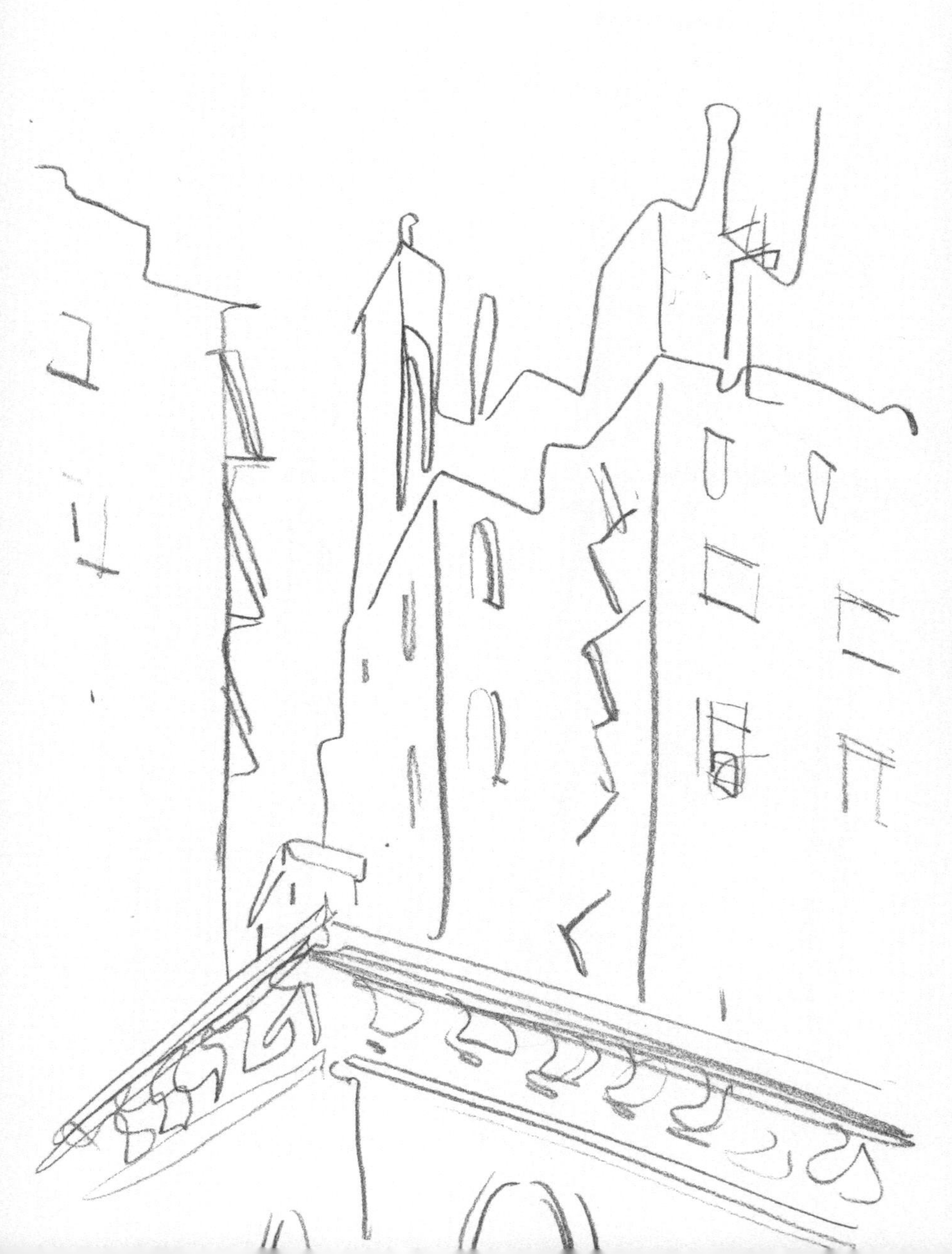

Biography

GUSTAVO OJEDA (September 8, 1958–August 23, 1989) was born in Havana, Cuba, and in 1967, exiled with his family to Spain, and then to Virginia. At seventeen, he moved to New York City to attend Parsons School of Design, where he studied under William Clutz, among others. Upon graduation, he was awarded a CINTAS Fellowship for Cuban artists, which allowed him to travel back to Spain to paint. It was in Madrid that he began to experiment with urban nightscapes, a subject which predominated much of his work, and for which he is best known. After returning to New York, where he would spend the rest of his life, Ojeda became active in the East Village and SoHo art scenes, showing alongside Jean-Michel Basquiat, Bruno Ceccobelli, Tom Bianchi, Luis Frangella, Keith Haring, and David Wojnarowicz. He participated in numerous group exhibitions in New York, including, most notably, *An International Survey of Recent Painting and Sculpture* at the Museum of Modern Art and *East Village Art in Berlin* at Zellermayer Galerie, both in 1984; he also exhibited work at galleries in Chicago, Los Angeles, and Miami. During his decade-long career, Ojeda mounted solo shows at Seventeenth Street Gallery, Garet/Kohn Gallery, P.S.1 Contemporary Art Center (on the heels of a studio fellowship), and David Beitzel Gallery, all in New York, as well as Michael Kohn Gallery in Los Angeles. Ojeda's work received attention in publications such as *Flash Art, Art in America, ARTNews*, and the *Los Angeles Times,* as well as notice from critics Richard Pau-Llosa, Robert L. Pincus, and Michael Laurence, in addition to many others. In 1986, Ojeda was diagnosed with AIDS, and in 1989, he died from AIDS-related complications, just two weeks shy of his thirty-first birthday. Following Ojeda's death, there were several retrospectives of his work, including a memorial exhibition at David Beitzel Gallery in 1990. His paintings are currently held by many collections in the United States, including the Smithsonian American Art Museum and the Jersey City Museum, among others. More information about the artist can be found at gustavoojeda.com.

Acknowledgments

THE EDITORS give their thanks to the Ojeda family, especially Francisco, Acacia, and Paco Ojeda, for their permission and support of this project. Thanks also to Michelle Sagué, Carl Weisbecker, the Estate of Lester Edelstein, Jibreel Powell, Murphy Austin, and other family, friends, and fellow graduate students at Yale and the University of Chicago. All of these people helped with the labor of this book's creation and organization, or supported the editors at various stages of its making.

For their early support of the lifelong project of expanding interest in the artistic legacy of Gustavo Ojeda, deepest gratitude is extended to Heather Holmes, the ICA Philadelphia, Visual AIDS, and the Cintas Foundation. The editors would also like to acknowledge the museums and galleries currently holding art by Gustavo Ojeda.

Additional thanks to Michael Kohn, Ramón Cernuda, William Clutz, Chema Cobo, Robert Yahner, Mark DeMuro, and others, whose friendly correspondence on the life and art of Gustavo Ojeda bolstered the introduction to this publication.

For their work on this publication, warm thanks go to Julia Klein, for her editorial eye and kindness; Rita Lascaro, for her design work; Kristi McGuire, for her copyediting and proofreading; and Jonathan D. Katz and Sianne Ngai, for the kind words that accompany this book. This book is dedicated to the memory of Lester Edelstein.

Soberscove Press Backlist

Andrei Monastyrski: Elementary Poetry | Edited and Translated by Brian Droitcour and Yelena Kalinsky | Preface by Boris Groys *Co-Published with Ugly Duckling Presse

Artists' Sessions at Studio 35 (1950) | Edited by Robert Goodnough

Bullets for Dead Hoods: An Encyclopedia of Chicago Mobsters, c. 1933 | Salvaged by John Corbett

Collective Actions: Audience Recollections from The First Five Years, 1976-1981 | Edited and Translated by Yelena Kalinsky

Deliverance: Writings on Postal Relations | Marc Fischer

Excerpts from the 1971 Journal of Rosemary Mayer | Edited by Marie Warsh

Henry at Home | Nancy Shaver | Interview with Steel Stillman | Text by Lucy Raven

Learning by Doing At The Farm: Craft, Science, and Counterculture in Modern California | Edited by Robert J. Kett and Anna Kryczka

On the Rock: The Acropolis Interviews | Allyson Vieira

Organize Your Own: The Politics and Poetics of Self-Determination Movements | Edited by Anthony Romero | Curated by Daniel Tucker

Refresh | Kristin Lucas

Rosemarie Beck: Letters to a Young Painter and Other Writings | Edited by Eric Sutphin

Scott Burton: Collected Writings on Art and Performance, 1965–1975 | Edited by David J. Getsy

Starting From 'I Don't Know': Interviews on Architecture and Craft | Samuel P. Smith

Subject Matter of the Artist: Writings by Robert Goodnough, 1950–1965 | Edited by Helen A. Harrison | Foreword by Irving Sandler

Temporary Monuments: Work by Rosemary Mayer, 1977–1982 | Edited by Marie Warsh and Max Warsh | Introduction by Gillian Sneed

That Was The Answer: Interviews with Ray Johnson | Edited by Julie J. Thomson

The Cardiff Tapes (1972) | Garth Evans | Commentary by Jon Wood

The Dynamic Library: Organizing Knowledge at the Sitterwerk—Precedents and Possibilities | Edited by Ariane Roth and Marina Schütz | Translated by Alta L. Price

The Elsen Drawings: Every Sculpture Pictured in Albert E. Elsen's Origins of Modern Sculpture: Pioneers and Premises (New York: George Braziller, Inc., 1974) | Laura Davis

The Hysterical Material | Edited by Geof Oppenheimer | Texts by Mieke Bal, Anita Chari, Ankhi Mukherjee, and Geof Oppenheimer

The Place of Sculpture in Daily Life | Edmund Gosse | Edited with an Introduction by Martina Droth | Afterword by David J. Getsy

The Waldorf Panels on Sculpture (1965) | Edited by Natalie Edgar and Phillip Pavia

The World's Worst: A Guide to the Portsmouth Sinfonia | Edited by Christopher M. Reeves and Aaron Walker | Foreword by Gavin Bryars

Where the Future Came From: A Collective Research Project on the Role of Feminism in Chicago's Artist-Run Culture from the Late-Nineteenth Century to the Present | Edited by Meg Duguid